TENURED BOSSES AND DISPOSABLE TEACHERS

Tenured Bosses and Disposable Teachers

WRITING INSTRUCTION IN THE MANAGED UNIVERSITY

Edited by
MARC BOUSQUET
TONY SCOTT
LEO PARASCONDOLA

With a Foreword by
RANDY MARTIN

SOUTHERN ILLINOIS UNIVERSITY PRESS • CARBONDALE

Publication partially funded by a subvention grant from the University
Committee on Academic Publications, University of Louisville.

Library of Congress Cataloging-in-Publication Data

Tenured bosses and disposable teachers : writing instruction in the
managed university / edited by Marc Bousquet, Tony Scott, Leo
Parascondola.
       p. cm.
Includes bibliographical references and index.

    1. English language—Rhetoric—Study and teaching—United States.
2. Report writing—Study and teaching (Higher)—United States.
3. Universities and colleges—United States—Administration.
4. English teachers—United States—Economic conditions.
5. College teachers—United States—Economic conditions.
6. College teachers—Tenure—United States. 7. College teachers' unions—
United States. I. Bousquet, Marc, date. II. Scott, Tony, date.
III. Parascondola, Leo, date.
PE1405.U6T46 2003
808'.042'071173—dc21
ISBN 0-8093-2543-8 (alk. paper)
ISBN 0-8093-2544-6 (pbk. : alk. paper)   2003006724

Printed on recycled paper. ♻

The paper used in this publication meets the minimum requirements of American National
Standard for Information Sciences—Permanence of Paper for Printed Library Materials,
ANSI Z39.48-1992. ⊗

CONTENTS

PART THREE. CRITIQUES OF MANAGERIALISM

PART FOUR. PEDAGOGY AND POSSIBILITY

FOREWORD

I'm writing this foreword from the bowels of middle-management, as an associate dean at New York University. My portfolio includes helping to direct a
composition program for artists and coordinating labor policy for faculty. NYU
has seen its share of initiatives by labor and management, with successful organizing campaigns by graduate students and adjuncts and by a new president who
has designated the school an enterprise university. It is perhaps a sign of the times
that an administrator would have himself walked the picket lines as a graduate
student (as I did at the University of Wisconsin, Madison in 1980) or have edited a volume on academic labor in response to the hot autumn of 1996 (an issue of the journal *Social Text,* which, expanded, became *Chalk Lines: The Politics
of Work in the Managed University,* published by Duke University Press). These
times have also produced the scholar-activists who appear in this important collection, a collection that points to where committed careers can lead. These are
pathways carved within the university that lead to different futures and possibilities for the present—roads very much taken that give different ways of valuing
the work we do together.

It would seem wholly uncontroversial to say that a job is work. Yet the labor
activism occurring on campuses across the United States finds itself repeatedly
having to make the point. Undergraduates, graduate students, adjuncts, staff, and
full-time faculty are organizing, often in intricate coalition with one another, but
they are being met with administrative claims that education is a calling, a service to higher ends than everyday labor. To the administrative mentality, higher
education figures as a world to itself, in which whatever work that occurs is focused on earning a grade, not a dollar. From the administrative point of view,
anyone who would disturb this Victorian chastity by addressing the conditions
under which the work of teaching and learning takes place is dividing the house
of education with alien values by introducing the grime of industry where it does
not belong.

The claim that unions have no place in higher education is factually inaccu-
rate, as public universities are more likely to have organized faculties than most other
occupations. Administrative arguments against unionization appeal to both pre-
industrial values—academics share an intimate community—and postindustrial

ideals—labor has become management (unionization of faculty at private campuses has been hampered by the Yeshiva decision, which treats faculty workers as managerial employees). Both of these arguments disavow the actual industrialization of higher education.

Rather than view education as a "way out" of industrial society, the avant-garde of postindustrial social organization, we have to learn to see higher education as itself undergoing a long, historical process of becoming industrial. Conceptions of the academic workplace as a domain of shared values that elicits participation in the service of a common good may not correspond to many actual campuses, but the idea of a community of interest between management and labor has long been thoroughly assimilated into many other workplaces over the past century— as the practices of scientific management evolved to convert labor militance into productive efficiency.

The fable of the postindustrial society goes something like this: The United States was once dominated by industrial manufacturing, which engendered among workers the rude ways of class conflict. The advent of a service economy freed the population from the hardships of manual labor and the embodied social division of muscle and mind that generated all the distress. The mass worker yielded to the individuated consumer, steeped in the pleasures of what the market had to offer. Like all founding myths, this one rests upon imaginary origins. The work force of the United States was never primarily located in manufacturing. Service workers were always more numerous than those who toiled on the factory floor, and the big shift in what people have done for a living has been from farming to service, a trend already detectable in the early part of the last century. Rather than saying that the rise of services ended industrialization, it is more accurate to say that those occupations concerned with the production of knowledge, information, and affect became industrialized. The dramatic rise in the number of the college educated responded to the need for a certain kind of worker and transformed the university into a center of knowledge-making. The creation of discipline-based departments and professional administrative strata corresponds to the horizontal and vertical dimensions of factory divisions of labor.

The denial that teaching is work is a reaction to the industrialization of the academy on the part of those responsible for managing the business of the university. By concealing the labor component of teaching under the guise of vocationalism or the claim that faculties are self-managing, the managers hope in part to conceal their own rapidly proliferating directive activities. In this, too, the university is not alone, but this displays quite clearly a change in the social compact. If self-management in the academy ranges from peer-reviewed products to votes on permanent employment, the bipartisan dismantling of entitlement programs has meant pay-as-you-go personal finance rather than cradle-to-grave security. The state has positioned itself rhetorically as a guide to personally managed well-being rather than the guarantor of social welfare.

The university as place of employment and space of production lives by and through this new dreamscape. Access to college credit is now properly premised on a lifetime of managed debt and portfolio savings. Intellectual property, patent, and copyright agreements are tightly woven into faculty conditions of employment. Through strategic planning, outcomes assessment, and so forth, university officials apply the logic of the boardroom to the classroom. The management stratum expand the range of their functions. Evidently, the self-management of students and faculty requires constant monitoring and justification.

On the other hand, the losses that faculty have sustained in this juncture—of autonomy, of higher education as a craft of privilege—are, at the same time, recoverable as gains—in an increased capacity for interconnectedness between labor and learning, between value and the grounds for its application, and between critique and commitment. When education becomes a bastion of scientific self-management in both its methods and its ends, the certainties of perspective, purpose, and privilege themselves become unmanageable. The best practice always hints at a better one, even as it winks at the question of "Better for what?" The observable chasm from which activism issues takes the uncertainty of what the university should be as its opportunity. When privilege is no longer taken for granted, it is for all those who labor in the academy to establish what is to be privileged. The industrialization of knowledge, through which the university intersects with myriad professions of law, medicine, business, accounting, arts, media, engineering, sciences, and sport, forces an ongoing calibration of pedagogical methods with educational ends. For now, the university figures in the training, credentialing, regulation of services, and evaluation of products that tie it ever closer to the industrial world of which it is part.

In all of this specialized training, the only universal is the technical composition of self. Composition emerges as the generalized requirement of this educational enterprise and the principal means for the enunciation of self as something assembled through curricular intervention. The work of literacy that acknowledges the politics of its own labors and the possibilities for managing its different ways of being is best positioned as a portal to all this world has become. For that promise the present volume will prove a central document.

Randy Martin
New York University

TENURED BOSSES AND DISPOSABLE TEACHERS

Introduction: Does a "Good Job Market in Composition" Help Composition Labor?

Marc Bousquet

As a new assistant professor in late 1998, I was asked to give a talk on job-hunting to advanced graduate students at the University of Louisville, which offers a Ph.D. in rhetoric and composition (and not in literature). In my experience of other English departments, little is expected of these talks on the job search besides a few cautionary remarks about "how tough it is out there" and shopworn advice (wear conservative outfits, don't send creative-writing samples to a critical job, etc.) Even so, most of the junior faculty I know have been made uncomfortable by these performances, in part because we know that what job candidates in most fields face is the likelihood of years of disappointment, even for the fortunate ones who eventually find tenure-track jobs. Taking all academic fields together, doctoral degrees are awarded around age thirty-three, but the average age of those winning tenure-stream jobs is thirty-nine. This means that even those who *do* manage to find tenure-stream work must find a way to endure an average of nearly six years of rejection, term lectureships, and crushing debt; "beginning" a career so late means subjecting yourself to tenure review at age forty-five or later, a time when persons in many other lines of public-service work (schoolteachers, police officers, military personnel, civil servants) are able to consider retirement. In many fields, the majority of persons entering graduate school leave without taking a doctorate: Most are compelled to ask themselves the rational question, "Am I willing to gamble my future and the happiness of my partner and/or children on a labor system arranged on such exploitative terms?" Even more startling is the realization that those who get to the position of tenure review in their forties are at the fortunate pinnacle of the academic labor system. Since the late 1960s, as a means of cutting costs and consolidating control, campus management has continuously substituted the labor of students and other casually employed persons for professorial faculty. At the present time, tenure-stream faculty perform as little as 25 percent of all campus teaching, with the rest performed by a vast corps of flex-time and nontenurable teachers, most of them under direct administrative control, generally without the pay, support, research commitments, classroom autonomy, and academic freedoms enjoyed by traditional faculty.

The talk that I prepared covered some of this ground. I also observed that the pervasive substitution of student and other flex labor for faculty labor has a meaning that the profession has yet to fully absorb: *For many graduate students, the receipt of the Ph.D. is the end and not the beginning of a long teaching career.* Contrary to the Fordist analysis predominating in academic professional associations, which imagine that the holder of the Ph.D. is the "product" of a graduate school, we now have to recognize that in many circumstances the degree holder is really the "waste product" of a labor system that primarily makes use of graduate schools to maintain a pool of cheap workers. The product of graduate education is the cheap and traditionally docile graduate-student worker, not the holder of the Ph.D.—hence the passion for developing "alternate careers" for Ph.D.s, which dispose of the degree-holding by-product while making room for new cheap graduate employee workers (Bousquet, "Waste Product").

A few minutes into the talk, one of my colleagues interrupted. "But you know, don't you, that all of *our* graduate students expect to get jobs?"

There was a chorus of assent from the graduate students. It turned out that persons awarded doctorates from the English department at the University of Louisville enjoyed what was effectively a 100 percent success rate in finding tenure-stream academic jobs, many of them at doctorate-granting institutions.

Reacting to my obvious astonishment, another member of the faculty said, "I think the employment prospects are different for rhetoric and composition than for other fields in English."

If anything, this was an understatement. Graduate students in the department commonly receive a dozen (or even two dozen) invitations to interview for rhetcomp jobs at MLA; several students here have turned down more interviews than many grad students in literature or cultural studies will ever receive. While of course I had been informed of the programmatic separation in English graduate study between the two largest public universities in the state, so that the University of Kentucky was constrained to award only the Ph.D. in literature, and—by the same act of the legislature—U of L's graduate English faculty permitted to award only the Ph.D. in rhetoric and composition, I had otherwise thought little about it.

So much for my talk. For the rest of the session, I listened, and it became clear to me what my colleagues and these students already knew—there was something different about the field of rhetoric and composition.

Over the next several months, some of the critically oriented graduate students (including coeditor Tony Scott, now employed at University of North Carolina–Charlotte) drew me into an investigation of this difference. Was rhet-comp simply becoming popular? Could the popularity of the field be understood as a "market fluctuation," in the same sense that perhaps next year Anglo-Saxon would be "in demand"? Or was there a structural and historical relationship between the employability of rhet-comp Ph.D.s and the labor system? The answers are numerous, intertwined, and contradictory. There does appear to be a renewal of interest in writing instruction, for example, accompanied by a lessened credibility for literature as the primary work of an English department (perhaps in connection with the waning need for the nation-state to legitimate itself through literary studies, observed by Bill Readings and others). Furthermore, there is a great deal of variety in the kind of opportunities available to persons with rhet-comp degrees, corresponding in part to the nature of their graduate study and other factors. Much of the renewed interest in writing instruction as a matter of curricular focus can be attributed to a more general turn in the academic-industrial complex toward vocationalism, job training, and skills-based outcomes; nonetheless, other aspects, such as the increased efforts devoted to critical literacies, owe a great deal to the continuation of social-movement commitment to the expansion of civil democracy.

However, the element of the larger pattern that interested us most was the question of structure: Is there any systematic relationship between the relative ease with which rhet-comp Ph.D.s earn tenure-stream jobs and the way in which the same labor system uses graduate students in other fields in English as disposable workers—persons whose teaching careers are commonly finished with the award of the doctorate?

A great deal of research remains to be done in this area. For ourselves, together with many other critical scholars observing the field such as Eileen E. Schell, Bruce Horner, Donna Strickland, and David Downing, the difference between rhet-comp and the other fields of English has much to do with its specific positioning in the disciplinary division of labor. Perhaps the key point is that persons holding the rhet-comp Ph.D. will frequently expect to serve the managed university *as management.* There is enormous variety in the way that rhet-comp scholars are employed, but as one of the field's leading young thinkers on the question of administering the university writes, "most" rhet-comp Ph.D.s will be "required" during some portion of their career to manage a writing program, "oversee the labor of others" and perform "other such managerial tasks" (Richard E. Miller, "Let's" 98–99). In this context, the others whose labor is overseen by the holder of the rhet-comp Ph.D. are commonly persons who have experience of graduate study in the other fields of English—current or former graduate students working as flexible labor, rather than as colleagues.

This is hardly a circumstance in which holders of rhet-comp doctorates are alone. The managerial functions of the full-time faculty have grown so pervasive as to present substantial legal obstacles to organizing the professoriate, especially on private campuses. And as Clyde Barrow, Harry Braverman, and Evan Watkins have been at pains to demonstrate, the conventional academic disciplines as a group, including English, have demonstrated a pronounced tendency over the past century to show compatibility with management theory and practice or even at times to serve as a branch of management science altogether. Nonetheless, the administrative character is indeed more pronounced in rhet-comp, so that professional compositionists as a group tend to be interpellated as lower management: That is, even those holders of rhet-comp doctorates who evade the "requirement" to serve directly as lower managers can be viewed as theorizing and/or providing legitimation (through the production of scholarship, inventing classroom praxis, etc.) in connection with what Marx called "the work of supervision."

Rhetoric and composition appears to exemplify the sad ideal of labor relations in the managed university. As little as 7 percent of the teaching is done by tenure-stream faculty. In rhet-comp, traditional faculty working conditions are enjoyed primarily by managers, not by teachers. This is a discipline in which administrators can consistently expect academic freedom, a professional wage, pleasant working conditions, job security, and participation in campus governance. By contrast, writing *teachers* are commonly paid less than seventeen thousand dollars a year for a 4-4 load, frequently denied such basic classroom autonomies as choosing their texts, assignments, and pedagogies (hence the good food served up by publishers to rhet-comp managers at CCCC), often fired without cause, rarely enjoy health insurance, and are "generously" relieved of service obligations by managers who acknowledge that their workers are "paid too poorly to spend the time on campus participating in governance." Although rhet-comp's official discourse acknowledges that these professorial freedoms and protections are desirable for writing teachers (or at least that many writing teachers desire them, which isn't quite the same thing), the "professionalization" of the field has gained them only for management.

As I note in my contribution to this book, nearly every participant in the composition conversation would like to see writing instructors become more like faculty—to have the chance to govern, participate more fully in the intellectual community, develop as an instructor, enjoy better pay, benefits, protections, and security. However, this hasn't translated into a consensus among professional and managerial compositionists that writing instructors should actually *be* faculty. Why not? Isn't composition work faculty work? Or is composition's faculty work essentially managerial work, or the supervision of parafaculty?

If rhet-comp is the canary in the mine for the academy more generally, what it tells us is that the professorial jobs of the future are jobs for an increasingly managerial faculty. Getting tenure will more and more nakedly mean: being a manager. From the perspective of the already vast majority of university teachers ineligible for tenure, it is obvious that the security and benefits of the "fortunate" managerial minority are predicated on the insecurity and exploitation of the teaching majority. However, anyone who has read the discourse of writing program administrators is unlikely to be persuaded that this fortunate group of people has found in their managerial positions the kind of satisfactions they hoped from academic work. Indeed, one of the more widespread structures of feeling among WPAs is the desire to be released from their managerial service into the general population of tenure-stream faculty.

What all this suggests is that *academic managerialism is a relation between the managed and the managers that ensures the unhappiness of both groups.* Although the discontent of the managed and the managers takes different forms, many of the contributors to this volume will argue that *both forms of unhappiness can be measured by their distance from the same benchmark: traditional faculty work.* That is to say, both managers and the managed would be happier as members of the professoriate, colleagues rather than "bosses" and subordinates. This doesn't mean that all persons teaching as adjunct lecturers want or need to change their job descriptions (and for example start to do research): far from it. As in the two-year colleges and most liberal arts institutions, teaching without an extensive research profile is a traditional function of the tenured professoriate in nearly all academic fields. Nor do we have to suggest that all adjuncts have to work full time to join the professoriate as colleagues: There is precedent for pro rata pay (and even tenure) for those genuinely preferring to work on a part-time basis. Similarly, writing programs founded on collegial structures will generally require administration, but as Bill Hendricks points out in his contribution to this volume, at his unionized campus the writing program administrator is the executor of policies created by her colleagues, all of whom are tenurable faculty.

The WPA as the convenor of a group of colleagues who teach writing is a very different experience for all concerned than the gross managerial relation now taken for granted in thinking about writing programs. The disciplinarization of composition, marked by a great blossoming and new vitality in rhet-comp scholarship, has been accompanied by the near-total conversion of composition work to a system of flexible managed labor—so that, *despite a great increase in rhet-comp Ph.D.s, a college writing student is increasingly likely to be taught by someone who does not hold a doctorate and whose working conditions are radically different from those of traditional faculty.* Though composition has commonly professed a politically committed orientation, many of the people who do composition scholarship find that they are being asked to supervise, theorize, and legitimate the steady degradation of the scene of college writing.

This collection explores the nature, extent, and economics of the managed-labor problem in composition, where as much as 93 percent of all sections are taught by graduate students and other "disposable" teachers. Bringing together a diversity of perspectives in the academic labor and left-composition conversations, ranging from pragmatism to historical materialism, the contributors ask tough questions regarding the relationship of workplace practices in higher education to the service economy more generally, the consequences of managerialism for the politics of rhet-comp scholarship, and the effect of corporatization on the nature of the literacy disseminated in composition classrooms.

In the first section, "Disciplinarity and Capitalist Ideology," Richard Ohmann explores the degree to which increased managerialism in composition leads to sharpening inequalities of education, opportunity, wealth, and power between groups of students and citizens. Seeking a transformative role for the composition intellectual, Donna Strickland in "The Managerial Unconscious of Composition Studies" observes that the composition discourse has elided distinctions in the material situations of composition professionals and writing teachers, with the consequence of obscuring the intrinsic historical relation between the "rise of composition" and the rise of the managed-labor paradigm in the corporate university. David Downing provides a trenchant critique of the origins in Taylorist industrial management of what he describes as a "managed disciplinarity" in English studies, subjecting teachers and writers to the imperatives of global capitalism. Paul Lauter, in "From Adelphi to Enron—and Back," studies the relationship between market ideology and managerial domination of the workplace in a variety of institutional contexts, often with drastic consequences for the public served. My own effort, "Composition as Management Science," questions the advisability of the "pragmatist turn" in rhet-comp scholarship, observing that corporate rhetoric and practices are less likely to lead to democratic outcomes than democratic procedures, workplace solidarity, and a rhetoric of transformation.

The second section, "Putting Labor First," explores the consequences and possibilities of putting the intellect, commitments, and interests of those who labor at the teaching of composition ahead of those who manage the teaching of composition. In the lead contribution, Bill Hendricks's important discussion of composition and academic unions observes that although more than 40 percent of all full-time faculty (nearly two-thirds at public institutions) are unionized, unionism has appeared tangentially, if at all, in many of the most prominent discussions of composition work; the essay goes on to enumerate several important ways that unions have empirically improved the circumstances of teaching and learning in the composition classroom. In "Toward a New Labor Movement in Higher Education," Eileen Schell analyzes the way in which campus, municipal, statewide, and national organizing campaigns have worked in coalitions with revitalized academic unions to develop political and legislative initiatives in support of improved working conditions. Eric Marshall's "Teaching Writing in a Managed Environment" provides a compelling first-person narrative of the making of an academic unionist—from graduate student and adjunct writing instructor to professional organizer in some of the most significant university organizing campaigns of the moment. Steven Parks examines the ways that writing programs can bring students to greater consciousness of themselves as workers in solidarity with other workers, in the university and beyond. Writing through the lens of one composition instructor who works as a supermarket cashier to supplement her teaching income, William H. Thelin and Leann Bertoncini explore the challenges that adjunct faculty face when trying to implement critical pedagogy. Completing the section, Ruth Kiefson explains the processes of adjunct exploitation under academic capitalism within the larger framework of market society and an unfolding general crisis for working people in all walks of life.

Coeditor Tony Scott leads off the next section, devoted to the critique of managerialism, with a study of the way that the managerial reality and liberatory ambitions of professional compositionists can lead to contradictory literacies and a fractured disciplinarity identity, one that advocates reflexive practice everywhere but in the basement offices of its own practitioners. Bill Vaughn's "I Was an Adjunct Administrator" pursues the material ironies consequent upon the degree to which downsizing, outsourcing, and perma-temping pervades composition—to the point where even managers are becoming part-timers. Amanda Godley and Jennifer Seibel Trainor provide a fascinating sequel to the authors' "After Wyoming" study of the rhetorics of labor and student need used by well-meaning managerial faculty in their efforts to affect the labor relations in basic-writing programs at two California campuses, ultimately expressing reservations about the usefulness of corporate rhetoric in improving working conditions. With his piece on "bureaucratic essentialism," Chris Carter suggests that the corporate-bureaucratic structure of composition programs increasingly leads teachers and writers to find the university as a space to practice rather than critique capitalism. Katherine Wills explores the causes and consequences of a labor system in which many workers are expected to accept non-wage compensation (such as "psychic income") for their effort. Walter Jacobsohn examines the contingent status of most composition workers in the context of recent critiques of liberatory pedagogy, focusing on the contradictory ambitions of liberation and the inability of the academy to practice justice for its own workforce.

In the final section, "Pedagogy and Possibilities," contributors explore a range of alternative practices and rhetorics based in everyday circumstances of teaching, program design, and professional or disciplinary self-understanding, many of which are intended to be deployed in alliance with the unionism and ensemble activism discussed in section two. Coeditor Leo Parascondola opens the section with "'Write-to-Earn': College Writing and Management Discourse," questioning the intersection of managerial logic with the rhetoric of "writing to learn" in critical and progressive pedagogies, with the consequence of converting liberatory goals to the reduced horizon of job-readiness or "writing to earn." Ray Watkins studies the ways in which the faculty associated with literary and business English can collaborate in writing programs, serving students more effectively while improving the solidarity and self-organization of the academic workforce. Examining some of the values often taken for granted in writing instruction, Robin Truth Goodman studies how some superficially transparent ambitions such as individuality and self-expression can be harnessed to consumerism, anti-solidarity, and the continuing marginalization of the oppressed. Christopher Ferry cautions against the abandonment of liberatory pedagogy, especially in light of the special risk that composition runs of having its aims appropriated by the corporate forces ascendant at many institutions. Donald Lazere discusses the ways in which the political semantics of critical theory and culture studies affect the possibility (and wisdom) of writing teachers appearing neutral about labor issues in their classrooms.

The author of *Managed Professionals: Unionized Faculty and Restructuring Academic Labor,* Gary Rhoades provides an afterword that observes the multiple frames in which the "managed professionals" who do teaching work see themselves and must correspondingly organize themselves: as educators, workers, professionals, critics, and scholars.

Particular thanks are due to coeditor Tony Scott for suggesting that *Workplace: A Journal for Academic Labor* (www.workplace-gsc.com) prepare a special topic cluster devoted to labor issues in writing programs and to Tony Baker and Leo Parascondola, as well as the entire *Workplace* collective, for collaborating in the realization of that vision. Early versions of five essays appearing in this revised and much-expanded volume appeared in that topic cluster. Also available at the *Workplace* Web site (go to the main page and click on *back issues*) are interviews and colloquies on writing programs and academic labor featuring Ira Shor, Patty Harkin, James J. Sosnoski, Michael Murphy, Cary Nelson, Sharon Crowley, and many others.

PART ONE

DISCIPLINARITY AND CAPITALIST IDEOLOGY

1
Composition as Management Science

Marc Bousquet

Our basic claim is this: Though institutions are certainly powerful, they are not monoliths; they are rhetorically constructed human designs (whose power is reinforced by buildings, laws, traditions and knowledge-making practices) and so are changeable. In other words, we made 'em, we can fix 'em. Institutions R Us. Further, for those of you who think such optimism is politically naïve and hopelessly liberal and romantic, we believe that we (and you, too) have to commit to this hypothesis anyway, the alternative—political despair—being worse.
　　　　—James Porter, Patricia A. Sullivan, et al., "Institutional Critique"

Time was, the only place a guy could expound the mumbo jumbo of the free market was in the country club locker room or the pages of *Reader's Digest.* Spout off about it anywhere else and you'd be taken for a Bircher or some new strain of Jehovah's Witness. After all, in the America of 1968, when the great backlash began, the average citizen, whether housewife or hardhat or salary-man, still had an all-too-vivid recollection of the Depression. Not to mention a fairly clear understanding of what social class was all about. Pushing laissez-faire ideology back then had all the prestige and credibility of hosting a Tupperware party.
　　　　—Thomas Frank, "The God That Sucked"

The first epigraph is drawn from the winner of the 2001 Braddock award for best essay published in a leading journal in rhetoric and composition. Most people working in the field will agree with the general supposition of Porter, Sullivan, et al., that the "institutions" of rhet-comp and higher education more generally are very much in need of "change," as well as with their basic and most urgent claim—that change is possible. Later on, I quarrel with the essayists' ramification of their argument, especially that change presupposes a managerial insider prepared to make the sort of arguments by which universities are "likely to be swayed," "ask for" resources using "effective rhetorical strategies," and work to build "disciplinary status" that can be "parlayed into institutional capital" (615–16).[1] This follows a general train of thinking in rhet-comp scholarship emphasizing how to "make arguments" that will be "convincing" to those "with the power" inside the institution (Joseph Harris, Richard E. Miller, Michael Murphy, Nancy Grimm, among many others).

Despite the evident sincerity of this line of inquiry, on the whole I'm profoundly unconvinced that a management theory of agency and what I call the rhetoric of "pleasing the prince" is particularly useful—much less necessary—to the project of transforming institutions. I prefer instead a *labor* theory of agency and a rhetoric of solidarity, aimed at constituting, nurturing, and empowering collective action by persons in groups. I think most of the historical evidence shows that education management and its rhetoric of the past thirty years—"the mumbo jumbo of the free market"—has created the institutions we need to change. Similarly, I think the historical evidence shows that the primary agents of resistance and ultimately transformation are the organized efforts of those whose labor is composed by the university, including students. The purpose of this essay is to survey the degree to which the managerial subjectivity predominates in composition, distorting the field's understanding of materialism and critique to the point that it consistently attempts to offer solutions to its "labor problem" without accounting for the historical reality of organized academic labor.

To that end, my ultimate claim will be that change in composition depends primarily upon the organized voice and collective action of composition labor. However, insofar as "Institutional Critique" insists upon the availability of alternatives to grotesque current realities, I'm prepared to make common cause with its authors. After all, Marx was among the first to insist that managers were workers, too.

The Heroic WPA

> [Now capital] hands over the work of direct and constant supervision of the individual workers and groups of workers to a special kind of wage-laborer. An industrial army of workers under the command of a capitalist requires, like a real army, officers (managers) and N.C.O.s (foremen, overseers), who command during the labor process in the name of capital. The work of supervision becomes their established and exclusive function.
>
> —Karl Marx, *Capital*

The Porter, Sullivan, et al. essay makes several important points. Following a number of philosophers working in the Marxist tradition (David Harvey, Diana Haraway, and Iris Marion Young), their effort is at least partially an attempt to hold onto critical theory, to a commitment to justice, and a materialist frame of analysis, and they make a point of reaching out to rhet-comp scholars engaging in cultural-studies practices, especially James J. Sosnoski and James A. Berlin. In particular, the piece emphasizes the necessity of critical theorizing to social change and furthermore that critical theorizing implies a materialist analytical frame and "an action plan" for transformation. Of special importance is the authors' suggestion, in allusion to leading criticism of exploitative labor practices (Gary Nelson, Michael Bérubé), that transforming the practices of rhet-comp depends upon transforming individual campuses and the material situation of those campuses. The authors are right to emphasize that the "disciplinary practices" of composition are not those that composition has imagined for itself in a vacuum; they are practices that have emerged in specific historical and material realities that themselves need to be changed in order to enable new disciplinary practices.

However, for purposes of getting started in our own inquiry, the most compelling question raised by the Porter essay is metadiscursive. Exactly what has gone on in the rhet-comp discourse that the essay's dramatic rhetoric frames the otherwise banal observation that "institutions can be changed" as a revelation to its readership? What hopeless structure of feeling so dramatically composes the audience for this piece that such an uncontroversial claim needs to be advanced at all, much less receive the disciplinary equivalent of a standing ovation (the Braddock award)?

A big part of the answer has to do with current trends in the discourse, away from critical theory toward institutionally focused pragmatism, toward acceptance of market logic, and toward increasing collaboration with a vocational and technical model of education. This movement in rhet-comp follows the larger movement traced by Thomas Frank and others, the historical re-emergence beginning about 1970 of substantial political support for the "market god," together with an accompanying revival of intellectual credibility for those "pushing laissez-faire ideology."

Perhaps the core understanding for our purposes is that the implied audience of the piece is lower-level management in the managed university. As Porter, Sullivan, and their coauthors eventually make clear, the "we" that they are addressing in their research encompasses primarily "academics" with specific "professional class status," such as writing program administrators (634, n. 3). Although they mention the possibility of groups being involved in "effective strategies for institutional change," their real interest is in generating "rhetorical strategies" and "institutional capital" for individual writer/rhetors: "This method insists that sometimes individuals . . . can rewrite institutions through rhetorical action" (613). Insisting that critique should lead to action, the one example that the authors offer of a critique actually leading to change is the establishment by Porter and Sullivan of a business-writing lab. This example falls well within the article's orientation toward the subjectivity of lower administration: "Those of us who are WPAs contend (if not outright *fight*) on a daily basis with our academic institutions for material resources, control over processes, and disciplinary validity" (614; italics in original).

This is not to say that the authors don't mention other subjects, only that the administrative subjectivity is privileged. Ringing a variant on the teacher-hero narratives of exploited pedagogical labor, we might call the familiar figure of Porter and Sullivan's narrative the "heroic WPA." Porter and Sullivan credit individual WPAs with two forms of "institutional action," the formation of graduate programs in rhetoric and composition and the formation of undergraduate writing majors. Together with the establishment of the business-writing lab at Purdue University, these two forms of "action" are meant to serve as inspirational exemplars: "When we start to get discouraged about the possibility of rewriting institutions, we should remember our own history." Throughout the article, meaningful change primarily refers to actions taken by individuals rather than groups, administrators rather than labor, and persons envisioning themselves belonging to a professional or managerial class, but just barely, in connection with a "struggle for respectability" and "validity" (615).

It is in the context of this specific positioning that the otherwise unremarkable claim that institutions can be changed requires the kind of urgency and repetition that it receives in the Porter and Sullivan article. In the modern era, social transformation has transpired with many groups serving as the agent of change: students, political parties, trade unions, agrarian revolutionaries, and social movements animated by the experience of racial, ethnic, and gendered oppression. Counterrevolutions have been led by military, industrial, and paramilitary interests, by the propertied classes, by superpower and colonial political surrogates, by fascist organizations, and by the intelligentsia. Professionals and managers, like most people, have been sometimes on one side and sometimes on the other of most transformative events. The professional-managerial group as a whole is conditioned by contradictory class status. On the one hand, they are persons who work to live (for most of their working lives, even the more highly paid physicians, lawyers, and managers cannot afford to stop working, tending to "cash in" toward the end of an arduous career). Nonetheless, the higher level of earnings associated with their positions, as well as the status economy, tends to foster identification with the class that enjoys real wealth. This affective connection to real wealth leads professionals and managers to the purchase of consumer items intended to display their identification with bourgeois enjoyments: For most of her working life, the average member of the professional-managerial class is far more likely to own boat shoes than a boat.

It is not clear that lower management as a group has ever figured in any substantial transformation of society or its institutions or that lower management represents a particularly strong standpoint for individuals advocating change to upper management. Indeed, despite the occasional exception, the opposite would seem to be the case. Lower management is particularly vulnerable, highly individuated, and easily replaced. Managers at the lowest level are not usually even on the corporate ladder but are commonly tracked separately from upper-management echelons. In this way, persons managing a Taco Bell franchise are sometimes, but not often, the same persons who do management work at the parent TriCon Corporation. The strong individuation runs up from the labor pool as well. Spending its days on the shop floor, lower management is nonetheless distinguished by its near-complete ideological identification with upper management, so the isolation of lower management is really a double movement. Isolated ideologically from the workers with whom they live face-to-face, the mental and ideological engagement with upper management affected by lower management does not typically lift what amounts to a kind of social and workplace quarantine from those on the ladder of promotional possibility. Whereas both workers and upper management typically spend most of their face-to-face time with those who share their interests, lower management's loyalties generally tend to be continuously at odds with its embodied intimacies.

Within academic capitalism, the heroic WPA might be seen as playing what Marx identified as the very working-class role of "a special kind of wage-laborer," the noncommissioned officer, or foreman, the members of the working class whose particular labor is to directly administer the labor of other members of their class at the front line of the extraction of surplus value. (In Marx's view, which I share, the commissioned officers or upper managers are likewise workers whose special task is to creatively theorize and enact procedures to the disadvantage of other workers.)[2] As Richard E. Miller has observed, many professional compositionists will directly serve as lower management: He writes that most rhet-comp Ph.D.s will be required to manage a writing program, "oversee the labor of others," and perform "other such managerial tasks" ("Let's" 98–99). Consistent with the general orientation of the Porter and Sullivan article, Miller's observation suggests that professional compositionists more generally are interpellated as lower management: That is, that even those holders of rhet-comp doctorates who evade the requirement to serve directly as lower managers will need to be viewed as theorizing and/or providing legitimation (through the production of scholarship, inventing classroom praxis, etc.) in connection with this front-line relationship between composition labor and the work of supervision performed by professional-managerial compositionists.

Although the experience of promotion can be experienced subjectively as a change of class ("The working class can kiss me arse/I've got the foreman's job at last") and is usually accomplished by material privileges, it is probably better to view the differences between lower-level management and labor as indicating a change of class loyalties, not an objective change of "class status."[3] Despite the quotidian embodied intimacy that the WPA and composition scholars more generally share with the rank and file of composition labor (from which they sometimes have emerged; a significant number of rhet-comp doctorates appear to be awarded to persons who have served as adjunct comp labor), the lower-managerial lifeway of fighting for personal "control" over instructional "resources" and disciplinary status recognition is very different from the ethos of struggle usually associated with social and workplace transformation: the raising of consciousness, the formation of solidarities, coalition building, and so forth. If the analogy to the foreman or noncommissioned officer holds true, we would expect to find not only acquiescence to the necessities framed by the ruling class represented by upper management and commissioned officers but even an enlarged loyalty to those imperatives. (As in the trope of the grizzled master sergeant who understands the "necessity" of sending troops under fire while the new second lieutenant sentimentally condones desertion and "cowardice," the noncommissioned officer–WPA is still embodied enlisted labor but as lower management is required to be more loyal to the "necessities" maintaining the class structure than those who genuinely benefit from it.) In this context, the "heroism" of the heroic WPA consists precisely in her capacity to represent the interests of the ruling class as the interests of the workers (teachers and students) in their charge. Gunner is particularly trenchant in this connection, noting that the "tyrannical positions" held by many WPAs in relation to their writing staff are commonly justified by sincerely held convictions of "benevolence" (158–59).

Certainly the heroism of the heroic WPA trades on the intimacy of the professional or managerial compositionist with the composition labor force. This intimacy is reflected by a certain ambiguity in the first-person plural in composition scholarship: Who is the *we* indexed by composition scholars? Who is meant by the term *compositionist*? Sometimes it means those of us who teach composition; sometimes it means those of us who theorize and supervise the teaching of composition. The movement between these meanings always has a pronounced tendency to obscure the interests and voice of those who teach composition in subfaculty conditions, ultimately to the advantage of university management. At the same time, it imbues the ambition of the professional or managerial compositionist for respect and validity with the same urgency as the struggle of composition labor for wages, health care, and office space. Commonly, this confusion of the professional and lower-managerial interests with the labor struggle takes the form of suggesting that the set of demands overlap or that the labor struggle depends upon the prior satisfaction of the professional and managerial agenda. From a materialist standpoint, the intimacy enabling the multiple meanings of *we* becomes a vector for continuing exploitation. Understanding this intimacy as a structural relationship requires careful examination of the possibility that the heroic narrative of disciplinary success for professional and managerial compositionists has depended in part on the continuing *failure* of the labor struggle.

A materialist view of the disciplinarization of rhetoric and composition would situate this ascendance not (only) in the heroic struggle of writing-program intellectuals for recognition and status but in the objective conditions of labor casualization created by upper management—the steady substitution of student and other non-, para-, and subfaculty labor for teacher labor, the establishment of multiple tiers of work, and the consolidation of control over the campus by upper administration, legislatures, and trustees. For instance, if we are to locate rhet-comp's ascendance in the years 1975–1995, then we must also acknowledge that this is a period of time in which undergraduate admissions substantially expanded while the full-time faculty was reduced by 10 percent, and the number of graduate-student employees was increased by 40 percent (Lafer 2). How can composition's "success" be separated from this story of failure for academic labor more generally? Clearly, the emergence of rhetoric and composition into some form of (marginal) respectability and (institutional-bureaucratic) validity has a great deal to do with its usefulness to upper management, by legitimating the practice of writing instruction with a revolving labor force of graduate employees and other contingent teachers. The discipline's enormous usefulness to academic capitalism—in delivering cheap teaching, training a supervisory stratum, and producing a group of intellectuals theorizing and legitimating this scene of managed labor—has to be given at least as much credit in this expansion as the heroic efforts that Porter and Sullivan call the WPA's "strong track record for enacting change" (614). There is therefore a certain honesty in the tendency of some compositionists urging the rest of the discipline to "admit" and embrace their "complicity" in a "corporate system" (Harris, "Meet the New Boss" 51–52; Richard E. Miller, "Arts"). Indeed, in at least some cases, the advocacy of certain changes in composition seems to follow well behind the curve of academic capitalism's accomplished facts.

The Intricate Evasions of As

> The professional life of an adjunct comes with its own set of challenges.
> At Houghton Mifflin, we understand the valuable role that adjuncts play
> in higher education, and we hope the information on this web site helps
> you to negotiate those challenges.
>
> —Adjuncts.com

Houghton Mifflin's college division registered the domain name www.adjuncts.com and created the Web site primarily to introduce nontenurable faculty to its textbooks. The site additionally invites visitors to use a variety of resources organized by field (under a menu headed "Go to Your Discipline") and tailored to what it describes as the unique needs of the nontenurable faculty (their "own" challenges). Houghton Mifflin's language of "understand[ing]" the "valuable role" of adjunct labor is redolent of composition's professional-managerial discourse on "the labor problem," which likewise features itself as offering help to composition labor in "negotiating" their "challenges" (Houghton Mifflin). Most of the material on the site adopts the tone of a *Chronicle of Higher Education* advice column, such as Jill Carroll's "How to Be One of the Gang When You're Not," which urges adjunct labor to overcome the social "prejudice" of research faculty by "acting like" someone with a professorial job. This acting like includes: showing up at guest lectures, eating at the faculty club, organizing conferences, volunteering for committee work, doing scholarship, writing items for the faculty newsletter, and attending department and campus meetings. Acknowledging that most of these actions constitute unwaged labor, Carroll represents that at least for those who have "made peace" with the "dominant facts of adjunct life" ("the low pay, the lack of respect, the lack of job stability"), all of this unpaid "acting like" a member of the professoriate might enable more "social interaction" with better-paid colleagues, ultimately paying off in the coin of emotion: "relationships with other faculty members can be intellectually rich and one of the most satisfying aspects of the job."

A reading of Carroll's text could press in a number of directions—a reading that looked to the feminization of teaching, in the vein of Eileen Schell's work, for example, would comment on the concomitant feminization of reward in passages like this one, perhaps proceeding to critically explore the advocacy of a "service ethos" for composition labor by Richard Miller: How much of the uniqueness of adjunct life's special "challenges" and rewards, such as "service" and "relationships" are coded as opportunities for women? Another line of critique would drive at the fairness issues raised by a discourse urging professionalization of work ("Go to Your Discipline") in the absence of a concomitant professionalization of reward (But Look for Your Paycheck Elsewhere). These issues can be gotten at most vigorously by the growing literature on super- or hyper-exploitation, such as Andrew Ross's "The Mental Labor Problem," which names a radical erosion of the wage in many sectors of knowledge work, sometimes by substituting nonmaterial rewards such as the chance to work at an exciting/creative/professional manner: "being creative" or "being professional" in this respect substitutes for a substantial portion of the wage itself.

Perhaps the most interesting reading, to which I'll return in closing, would relate this problem of adjunct labor to the obsession among professional compositionists with their disciplinary status, a structure of feeling that can easily be represented as "how to be one of the gang" of disciplines.[4] In my view, the problem of composition labor's felt exteriority to the gang of professors cannot be separated from the problem of composition management's felt exteriority to the gang of disciplines: The two structures of feeling are inseparably related along the "degree zero" of the material specificity of composition work, which is to say, work conducted in the scene of managed parafaculty labor. (I borrow the term *degree zero* from Paolo Virno, who uses it describe the "neutral kernel" of material determination that unites related but apparently contradictory structures of feeling. He asks, "What are the modes of being and feeling that characterize the emotional situations both of those who bow obsequiously to the status quo and those who dream of revolt?" (28). That is, How is it that the same determining circumstances support those who go along and those who resist?) This problem is not composition's problem alone—foreign-language acquisition and health sciences are also particularly visible in this respect—but nowhere is the scene so prevalent and institutionalized as in composition, where the terminal degree does not presently signify certification of professional labor but, as Richard Miller observes, testifies instead to the likely requirement of serving in lower management. This is not to say, of course, that the circumstance is composition's fault—far from it—only that it is a place of managed paraprofessional teaching where the conversion of the university to an "education management organization" (EMO) is visible, just as health sciences reveals the movement to managed care (the HMO). Professional composition, in my view, will never feel like one of the gang of disciplines until its labor patterns are more like those in other fields. (Of course, this equivalence could easily come about by the frightening but very real possibility—evidenced by clear statistical trends—that labor patterns in other disciplines will become more like those in composition rather than the other way around.) To put it in blunt terms, so long as composition's discourse remains a management science—or, alternatively, until history, engineering, and philosophy are management science to the same extent—it is likely to fail to enjoy the status it seeks of a discipline among peers. Insofar as we observe the continuing realization of the logic of the EMO, however, composition's "peerlessness"—its nonequivalence with the other disciplines—is likely to become increasingly visible as its "excellence," in Bill Readings's sense, *with composition exemplifying the ideal labor relation of the managed university* to which all other disciplines must conform.

One interesting variant on this last reading would push the identity crisis of composition management yet further and critically examine the ways that composition management either tries to be one with the gang of composition labor or demonstrate its understanding and appreciation ("I feel your pain" or "I hear your song"), co-opting the voice of labor in the process. Yet another variant would reverse the observation that managers are workers, too, and investigate the degree to which the working subject is also a managerial subject, as well as rhet-comp's role in what Randy Martin, following a long line of cultural-studies critique of "the managed self" (Brantlinger, Watkins), describes as a campus-based "national pedagogy" promoting a "calculus of the self that eclipses labor's actual opportunities" (26).

The urgency and interest of other readings notwithstanding, at this juncture my primary concern with Carroll's column is the overall strategy represented by the line of thought it exemplifies ("advice for adjuncts"). What characterizes this field of knowledge, much of it generated by adjuncts themselves (such as Carroll), is the dissemination of tactics for "getting ahead in the system as it is." The keynote of this genre is that there are facts of life in the corporate university and most possible versions of agency revolve around learning the ropes of the corporation rather than imagining alternatives to corporatism. Most professional compositionists will recognize the emergence of this note in their own conversation in a twin sense. First, insofar as this kind of advice frequently comes from adjunct labor, this kind of discourse frequently is permitted to pass as the voice of composition labor—commonly to the exclusion or marginalization of the very different voice represented, for example, by the fifty-campus movement of organized graduate employees. This other voice is committed not to the recognition of the inevitability of the corporate university but to struggling toward a different reality. Second, composition management deploys the value "getting ahead" together with a set of assertions about "the system as it is" in order to adopt a paternalist standpoint of care within a general strategy of lowered expectations: that is, given current "realities," the best "we can do" for the teachers and students in our care is to help them to get ahead.

In terms of theorizing agency and change, therefore, a large sector of the composition discourse appears to be moving toward an extremely limited notion of both, characterized by a sense of belatedness, in exactly the sense of Francis Fukuyama's claim regarding the "end of history" or Daniel Bell's earlier claim of an "end to ideology." As noted above, the implications of an end of history for the discourse of managerial compositionists is that any changes that may be wrought in future will be wrought within the frame of recognizing the inevitability of the corporate university or, as Richard Miller puts it, "conceding the reality of academic working conditions" ("As If" 22).

The recent calls in the rhet-comp mainstream for non-tenure-track instructorships (Murphy and Harris among many others) as a solution to the super-exploitation of composition labor is a good example of what is most disturbing about this line of thought. Although the subtitle of Murphy's piece "New Faculty" suggests that he is writing, in September 2000, prospectively "toward a full-time teaching-intensive faculty track in composition" (as if such a thing required inventing), he confesses in his article that he is really seeking only to "acknowledge what has *actually already taken place*" (23). What Murphy means by this is that part-time teachers are in most cases "really" full-time teachers, even if they have to teach at multiple institutions in order to do so. He cites his own case, teaching five courses per semester on two separate campuses, essentially, he writes, "splitting my appointment as a full-time teacher" (24). He goes on to propose that universities "formally recognize" this circumstance by "creating full-time [nontenurable] positions those teachers could grow into over the course of a career." The ultimate aim is that teaching-intensive faculty would participate in governance and administration and enjoy recognition as "legitimate full-time academic citizens," albeit with "salaries running parallel to, although always somewhat behind, those of traditional faculty" (25).

One may agree or disagree with this proposal; I for one would feel constrained to point out that there have, historically, been plenty of teaching-intensive assistant professorships requiring little research and plenty of teaching, as in the community colleges and most liberal arts colleges—why not advocate for the (re)creation of professorships rather than nontenurable instructorships? Insofar as many if not most teaching-intensive positions have traditionally been professorial—what exactly is the appeal of making them nontenurable, if not, as the American Association of University Professors and the major academic unions have long observed, to consolidate managerial control? Further, the invention of nontenurable instructorships, frequently paying less than $30,000 for teaching a 5-5 load, coincides with a radically gendered segmentation of the academic workforce: The persons being offered these jobs (involving more than full-time work but yielding less than full-time pay and rewards) are overwhelmingly women, whereas in higher education at large the tenured faculty and upper administration continue to be primarily men. Is the work nontenurable because it is done by women? Or is it "women's work" because it is nontenurable? (Minority faculty likewise are overrepresented in the ranks of the nontenurable full-time positions.) The leading studies of non-tenure-track faculty indicate that about half are dissatisfied with their job security, salaries, and ability to keep up with knowledge in their field. Furthermore, contrary to Murphy's projection of a stable non-tenure-track workforce, the full-time non-tenure-track population is characterized by high turnover. At any given moment, slightly more than half of non-tenure-track faculty expect to leave their current position "within three years," many of them for jobs outside of academe altogether (NEA redaction of NSOPF-93, 1–4). Even *U.S. News and World Report*—never known for a bias in favor of labor—reports on the trend toward non-tenure-track instructorship under the headline of "The New Insecurity" and feels constrained to observe, in a featured box, that 57 percent of these jobs are held by women (as compared to 26 percent of tenured positions). All of which is to say that rhet-comp's enthusiasm for this kind of appointment is, at the very least, up for debate.

The important point for considering Murphy's article here is that what he proposes "has actually already taken place" in a much more straightforward sense than he seems to be aware. Although Murphy acknowledges in a footnote that full-time non-tenure-track appointments "have already been experimented with" at a "surprising" number of schools (37, n. 2), the reality was that all major data sources in the early- and mid-1990s (most of them drawing from the NSOPF-93 data set) already showed that as of fall 1992 *more than 20 percent* of the full-time faculty served in non-tenure-track positions—for a total of more than 100,000 persons employed in this "experimental" way. Furthermore, by April, 1999, the *Chronicle of Higher Education* and other major education journals circulated the results of the Chronister-Baldwin study showing that by 1995, the proportion of full-time faculty working off the tenure track had climbed to *28 percent* from 19 percent in 1975, while the proportion of those on the tenure track (but not yet tenured) dropped correspondingly, from 29 percent to 20 percent (Leatherman). To be fair to Murphy, his overall intention might still be grasped as attempting to affect the proportions within the mixed employment pattern that presently obtains in composition by increasing the percentage of the full-time lectureships relative to the number of part-time lectureships. Nonetheless, a kind of position held by between one-quarter and one-third of all full-time faculty and trending steadily upward really can't be framed as an "experiment" in "new" kinds of faculty work.[5] Even the somewhat less rigorous Coalition on Academic Workforce voluntary survey—which probably undercounts nontraditional faculty work—showed that full-time non-tenure-track instructors accounted for close to one-fifth of the instruction in all English and freestanding composition departments ("Summary," tables 2, 2a, 2b).[6] Indeed, the U.S. Department of Education's National Center for Education Studies' "New Entrants" white paper, commenting that persons beginning full-time academic employment in 1985 or later were more than twice as likely overall (33 percent) to serve off the tenure track than persons hired before 1985 (17 percent), postulated that the eye-opening statistical change toward nontenurable work for the whole cohort of younger scholars had a lot to do with the "considerable number of non-tenure-track appointments for foreign-language and writing specialists" (29).

In this instance, then, what passed for a reasonable proposal for rhet-comp—even, portentously, as a "new faculty for a new university"—was in fact a practice well-established in the management-dominated university by the mid-1980s. In this light, Murphy's proposal stands revealed not as the prospective and imaginary excursion into a better world but to a certain disappointing extent thoroughly reactive and even apologist, functioning to *idealize after the fact,* legitimating an already existing reality that few people are pleased with. Furthermore, insofar as the major source of data on the higher-education workforce had identified fifteen years earlier the creation of nontenurable full-time positions as a noteworthy trend *particular to writing instruction*—a disciplinary trend in new writing faculty so pronounced that it affected the statistical profile of the pool of *all* entering faculty—that Murphy's article has so far been eagerly taken up elsewhere in the rhet-comp literature as a genuinely innovative proposal for "new faculty" suggests a pervasive self-ignorance in the rhet-comp discourse. How does it come about that one of the discipline's two or three leading journals is prepared to publish a "practical proposal" regarding composition labor that is to this degree out of touch with the statistical reality of the composition workplace? This is ultimately not a question of Murphy's individual research but of the warm reception that this proposal-which-is-not-one received by professional compositionists (e.g., Harris who goes so far as to congratulate Murphy for "doing the numbers" when at least in this respect Murphy hasn't done the numbers at all).

So it is perhaps unsurprising that the readership of the Porter and Sullivan article would need to be encouraged to believe in their own agency as regards institutional transformation. After more than three decades of casualization, corporatization, and not incidentally disciplinary advances for professional and managerial compositionists, most readers will have understood by now that their track record has everything to do with the *kinds* of change being enacted.[7] A lab for business writing? Sure. Salary, tenure, and research budget for writing program administrators? No problem. A graduate program or certificate in rhet-comp? Go for it. But when it comes to employing the "institutional capital" that comes from overseeing a large cheap labor force for purposes that run counter to institutional capitalism, such as addressing the scandalous working conditions of the labor force itself, the lower-management "track record of enacting change" is pretty poor. Although there is very substantial evidence that even in this early stage of the movement, organized adjunct faculty and graduate employees have the power to transform their working conditions—get health insurance, job security, the protections of due process, and raises of 40 percent, often by acting collectively to change local and national law or struggling successfully with the frequently illegal actions of university management—there is little evidence that lower management has the same power for these kinds of "change."[8]

There is an earnest materialism to the pessimistic structure of feeling addressed by the Porter and Sullivan essay. Most professional and managerial compositionists want to do something about the exploitative system of academic labor. However, whether they do so logically, intuitively, or from the experience of essaying numerous "rhetorical strategies" with disappointing results, most also understand that there is little they can do about the labor system either as individuals or as administrators. Indeed, perhaps the most important realization of the administrative subjectivity is that "having" administrative power is to be subject to administrative imperatives—that is, to be individually powerless before a version of necessity originating from some other source. This is—in part—the lesson of Annette Kolodny's compelling recent memoir of her deanship at the University of Arizona, a position she correctly dubs "academic middle management." She accepted the job in the belief that one committed administrator, "a feminist committed to both equity and educational excellence," could make the kind of difference that Porter and Sullivan hope for the WPA, serving as "an instrument for progressive evolution." In doing so, Kolodny ultimately felt compelled, with many reservations, to employ many of the wiles of the canny bureaucrat: "If logic and hard data failed me and I thought it would help, I teased, I cajoled, I flirted, I pouted. I bought small gifts for one provost and always remembered the birthday of another" (21). And despite some modest successes, many of them the result of committed overexertions with consequences for her health, ideals, and friendships, she ultimately concludes she'd attempted something that could not be done by administrative agency, and she devotes the last section of the book to rediscovering such agents of historical change as unionism and mass political movements—demanding, for example, a more just distribution of material wealth and opportunity.

As Kolodny's experience suggests, university administrators are doubly implicated in the set of transformations dubbed academic capitalism, being required both to make the university responsive to "exterior market forces" as well as to actively cultivate market behavior in the faculty. In this context, it seems clear that administrators, especially lower administrators, are more—not less—subject to the dictates of academic capitalism than the faculty. The faculty are at least free to resist marketization, albeit with varying degrees of success; whereas it seems that the work of academic managers at the present time fully overlaps with the project of marketization; there is literally no way to be a manager without feeling the necessity of adopting and promoting market values. The installation of managerialism as the core subjectivity of the discipline of rhetoric and composition is therefore not so much an indicator of the field's success as evidence of its particular susceptibility, the very terms of its intellectual evolution intertwined with the university's accelerated move toward corporate partnership, executive control, and acceptance of profitability and accumulation as values in decision making.

The Hidden Idealism of Managerial Materialism

> Management theory has become so variegated in recent years that, for
> some, it now constitutes a perfectly viable replacement for old-fashioned
> intellectual life. There's so much to choose from! So many deep thinkers,
> so many flashy popularizers, so many schools of thought, so many bold
> predictions, so many controversies!
>
> For all this vast and sparkling intellectual production, though, we hear
> surprisingly little about what it's like to *be managed.*
> —Thomas Frank, "The God That Sucked"

One consequence of the materialist self-understanding of the compositionist as a
managerial intellectual has been a turn toward pragmatic philosophies in the rhet-
comp discourse. These urge the rhet-comp intellectual to acknowledge this "complicity" and adopt the posture of a "canny bureaucrat" (Richard Miller, "Arts").
Collapsing critical theory and cultural studies into classroom manifestations, this
standpoint tends to characterize critical theory in crude terms (i.e., as the dosing
of students with outmoded lefty truisms). Its primary tactic is to attempt to turn
the critique of enlightenment theories of knowledge against its authors in critical
theory, cultural studies, and radical pedagogy. For instance, Freirean pedagogues
elaborating a critique of the banking theory of knowledge are (mis)represented
by the pragmatist movement as themselves attempting to deposit "out of date"
anticapitalisms in the helpless student brain. For these pragmatists, the ideals of
critical pedagogy are part of the problem, insofar as these idealisms are inevitably
out of touch with fundamental "realities" of the corporate university. Ultimately,
this attempted debunking of critical theory and cultural studies has acquired no
traction outside the field of rhetoric and composition and probably offers little
of enduring interest even within the field beyond the useful but unremarkable
observations that classroom activities are an insufficient lever for social change and
that it is possible for teachers to deploy radical pedagogy in dominative ways. This
last observation is indeed useful—far too many teachers, just as Richard Miller
suggests, adopt radical pedagogy because it can be made to "cover over" our complicity with domination, but in my view, this usefulness hardly adds up to a convincing argument that the only remaining option is for teachers to adopt a pedagogy overtly complicit with domination, or in Miller's words, "strategically deploy
the thoughts and ideas of the corporate world" ("Let's" 98).

What is most interesting about this pragmatic movement is that it has managed to conceal its own hidden idealism—its less than critical adherence to what
Thomas Frank dubs the "market god" and its concomitant elevation of corporate management to a priestly class. By concealing its own market idealism underneath a rhetoric of exclusive purchase on reality, pragmatist ideologues have
had a fair amount of success at discouraging the effort to realize any *other* ideals
than those of the market. (This is the imposition of what Fredric Jameson calls
"the Reagan-Kemp and Thatcher utopias," and what David Harvey calls a "political correctness of the market.") Among the many useful observations of the

critical tradition is that despite the fantasies of those Marx loved to call the "vulgar political economists," markets don't exist transhistorically; they have reality to the extent that they are installed and maintained by human agents devoted to achieving particular market ideals. Pragmatist idealizations of the market conceal the human agency in the creation and maintenance of markets—what Sheila Slaughter and Larry L. Leslie describe as the conscious and deliberate "marketizing" of higher education in the United States and globally since the Nixon administration. Brought about not by necessity but by the planned and intentional defunding of public institutions together with a corresponding diversion of public funds to private ventures (corporate welfare), market ideals were energetically wrestled into reality by embodied agents with political and economic force, in the process rolling back alternative ideals that themselves had been realized in law and policy by collective social action throughout the twentieth century (hence "neo"liberalism, referring to the reinstallation of nineteenth-century laissez-faire or liberal economic policies).

Changing the managed university (and the politics of work therein) requires understanding that the market fundamentalism current among university managers has no more purchase on what is and what should be than any other system of foundational belief. Understood as a humanly engineered historical emergence of the past three decades, the managed university names a global phenomenon: the forced privatization of public higher education; the erosion of faculty, student, and citizen participation in higher-education policy except through academic-capitalist and consumerist practices; the steady conversion of socially beneficial activities (cultivation of a knowledge commons, development of a democratic citizenry fit to govern itself) to the commodity form—the sale of information goods, such as patents and corporate-sponsored research, and the production of a job-ready workforce (Rhoades and Slaughter; Slaughter and Leslie; Martin). As Martin makes clear, these circumstances are not brought about in the North American and European context because the state has "withdrawn" from higher education, but because it "invests itself" ever more aggressively "in promoting an alignment of human initiative with business interest" (7). Globally, the International Monetary Fund and the World Bank have actively promoted a similar "reform agenda" with respect to higher education and used their power to impose involuntary privatization on national higher-education systems, especially in Africa, requiring tuition fees, and effectively "recolonizing" cultural and intellectual life throughout the global South, as direct policy intervention combined with neoliberal "constraints" caused universities to "substitute new staff, standardize pedagogical materials, and marginalize local knowledges" (Levidow para. 24–36).[9]

In all of these and most responsible materialist accounts, human agency drives history, but in the pragmatist-managerial version of materialism, collective human agencies are conspicuously absent. Even the agency of individuals is radically evacuated: for pragmatists, markets are real agents, and persons generally are not, except in their acquiescence to market dicta. Richard Miller, for example, writes, "the truth is that the question of who's qualified to teach first-year writing was settled long ago by the market" ("Let's" 99). In a world of systems "governed" by the "arbitrary," the "only possible" human agency becomes something like flexible self-specialization, the continuous retooling of self in response to market "demands," a subjectivity that Richard Sennett observes is just as unsatisfying a "corrosion of character" for those who "win" the market game as for those who "lose." In this view, persons can only be agents by adopting the arts of corporate domination and by fitting themselves to the demands of the market, "working within a system governed by shifting and arbitrary requirements" (Richard Miller, "Arts" 26). Representing corporate domination as a fact of life, this brand of pragmatism ultimately conceals a historically specific ideological orientation (neoliberalism) behind an aggressive (re)description of reality, in which left-wing bogeymen are sometimes raised as the threats to human agency—see Kurt Spellmeyer's redbaiting review of *Left Margins*—when the real threat to human agency is the corporate-bureaucratic limits to human possibility established by the pragmatists themselves. The pragmatist turn has left its trace nearly everywhere in the composition discourse. Even while attempting to resuscitate the commitment to social transformation, following the lead of Marxist geographer Harvey, Porter and Sullivan, for example, hold up as the straw man of "ineffectual" critique the figure of "academics railing at monopoly capitalism." Rather ironically for adherents of Harvey, they thereby reinscribe capitalist exploitation as the outer limit of "change" (and leaving one wondering exactly how one can read Harvey and not see a member of the academy "railing" at capitalist exploitation and attempting to map its exterior?)

What most troubles me about the pragmatist movement is the way it seeks to curb the ambitions of our speech and rhetoric. In the pragmatist account, contemporary realities dictate that all nonmarket idealisms will be "dismissed as the plaintive bleating of sheep" but corporate-friendly speech "can be heard as reasoned arguments" ("Arts" 27). I find this language intrinsically offensive, associating movement idealism and social-project identities and activist collectivity generally with the subhuman, rather than (as I see it) the fundamentally human capacity to think and act cooperatively. More important than the adjectives and analogies, however, is the substructure of assumptions about *what rhetoric is for.* The implicit scene of speech suggested here is of "pleasing the prince," featuring an all-powerful auditor with values beyond challenge and a speaker only able to share power by association with the dominating logic of the scene—a speaker whose very humanity depends upon speaking a complicity with domination. As a cultural-studies scholar, I respect the lived realities of subjectivity under domination and thoroughly understand the need for frequent speech acts of complicity. However, this does not suggest for me that this scene offers the central *topos* constitutive of human agency nor that the prince—however powerful—should be the object of our rhetoric.

Most astonishing about the recent success of claims that the logic and rhetoric of solidarity or justice cannot be heard is that these claims are so patently false, both as a matter of history and of contemporary reality. What do claims like these make of the achieved historical transformation associated with groups united by the idealism and critical imagination of rhetors such as Emma Goldman, W. E. B. DuBois, Eugene Debs, and Nelson Mandela? What of the gains of democratic revolutions after 1750? Or the nineteenth-century gains of abolition, decolonization, feminism, communism, and trades-unionism? Were any of these gains, together with the gains of the social movements after 1960, achieved by the sort of recognition of institutional constraints advocated by the pragmatists? In the contemporary frame, despite the great success of corporate management at disorganizing labor, are the still- (and newly) organized voices of labor really dismissed as the plaintive bleating of sheep by management at Ford Motor Company or at the California state universities? Hardly. The millions of dollars and dozens of managerial careers openly devoted to the perpetual struggle to contain and divide labor at both places suggests the magnitude of the power they are attempting to defuse. (The graduate-employee union at the University of Michigan calculated the annual salaries of the university's full-time bargaining team—$630,000—amounted to only slightly less than the cost of the contract improvements that the union was seeking ($700,000 per year). Likewise, are the nonprofit values of social entitlement, dignity, and equality advocated by the organized voices of AARP, NAACP, and NOW similarly dismissed by Washington bureaucrats? Not really.

So what should we make of a discourse that pretends that the organized voice of persons seeking social justice is impractical and sheep-like and that agency is primarily possible in adopting a bureaucratic persona? In my view, we should call it a management discourse, of the sort that Frank barely exaggerates in suggesting that it threatens to take the place of intellectual life altogether. In holding our gaze on the managerialism of the composition discourse, we ultimately need to ask, *cui bono?* Who benefits? Despite its rhetoric of student need and customer service, is the university of job-readiness really good for students? If it is really designed to serve student needs, then why do so many students drop out in the first year and fail to graduate? If it is more efficient to reduce education to vocation, then why does it cost more and more money to go to college (certainly the salary costs for instruction aren't the reason)—exactly who receives the economic benefits (if any) of lowered salaries, reduced services, and lowered expectations? Why are so many young people underemployed if they are being increasingly well trained for corporate life? Or, as in David Brodsky's scathing account, does the managed university primarily serve the interests of "the nomadic managerial hordes" that have "torn up the social contract" to govern in their own interest? It is not only adjunct faculty like Brodsky who suggest that the liberated self-interest of university management may not fully coincide with the interests of society. In an opinion piece excoriating the "dumbing down" of university leadership as a result of the ascent of managerialism and the market ethos, one university president observes that the "peripatetic" class of candidates for top administration "are more interested in landing better jobs than contributing to higher education" (Lovett).

In seeking to transform institutions, then, the discourse of rhetoric and composition might share the skepticism of adjuncts like Brodsky for the claims of management discourse to deliver democratic outcomes through corporate processes and to deliver "change" for the many by liberating the self-interest of a few. At its best, the managerial discourse in composition has an earnest commitment to bettering the circumstances of embodied composition labor and a real enthusiasm for a better world. Nonetheless, it has yet to acknowledge the limits presented by its failure to confront, in Frank's words, "what it's like to *be managed.*"

Toward a New Class Consciousness in Composition

> The only worker who is productive is one who is productive *for capital.* [A] schoolmaster is productive when, in addition to belaboring the heads of his pupils, he works himself into the ground in order to enrich the owner of the school. That the latter has laid out his capital in a teaching factory, instead of a sausage factory, makes no difference to the relation.
>
> To be a productive worker is therefore not a piece of luck, but a misfortune.
>
> —Karl Marx, *Capital*

At the beginning of this essay, I suggested a willingness to make common cause with the administrative subject targeted by Porter and Sullivan (because managers are workers, too). In closing, I'd like to ramify that willingness briefly, in connection with Joseph Harris's call for a "new class consciousness" in composition.

What Harris means by a "new" class consciousness is "one that joins the interests of bosses and workers around the issue of good teaching for fair pay" ("Meet the Boss" 45). Living in a right-to-work state, I have to say that my first reading of this evidently sincere rubric literally gave me a chill. At its most disturbing, this is Toyotist rhetoric clothed in academic Marxism, grafting the total-quality "team" of management and labor onto disciplinary identity, borrowing the term *class consciousness* to add an aura of legitimacy to the plan. As in all Toyotist versions of an "identity of interest" between management and labor, this plan simply consolidates managerial control. "What the director of a writing program wants," Harris continues,

> is to be able to interview, hire, and train a teaching staff, to fire teachers who don't work out, to establish curriculum, to set policies and to represent the program as he or she sees best. What teachers want are reasonable salaries, benefits, working conditions, and job security; autonomy over their work; and to be treated with respect as colleagues. (57)

Leaving aside the question of whether this managerial portrait genuinely represents either class consciousness or what teachers want, I have to wonder by what mechanism would we adjudicate the conflicts that inhere even in this rosy representation? That is, how does the WPA's right to establish curriculum and set policies square with the teachers' right to autonomy over their work? Who defines teaching that doesn't work out? Why should it be the WPA and not other teachers, as in other disciplines?

Moreover, to anyone familiar with labor history, this rhetoric isn't new at all but sounds exactly like the old partnership between labor and capital rhetoric of nineteenth-century anti-unionism, inked most famously by the dean of American political cartoonists, Thomas Nast. In his most famous images on the theme, Nast opposed both organized (or monopoly) capital and organized labor and insisted on a community of interest between the two. For instance, in a *Harper's Weekly* cartoon of 23 November 1878, he shows a smith using a hammer labeled "Labor" to forge another hammerhead labeled "Capital" under the didactic headline: "One and Inseparable: Capital Makes Labor and Labor Makes Capital." In "The American Twins," reproduced here, Nash shows a worker and a top-hatted capitalist boss as Siamese twins, joined at the chest. Under the rubric "The *Real*

THE AMERICAN TWINS.
" United we stand, Divided we fall."

"The American Twins" (cartoon) by Thomas Nast. Audio-Visual Archives, Special Collections and Archives, University of Kentucky Libraries.

Union," the reader is invited to see labor's interests as harmonizing with the boss on exactly the sort of principle that Harris suggests ("good [work] for fair pay") rather than in collective bargaining.

Fortunately for the rest of us, the nineteenth-century labor movement rejected this rhetoric and worked in solidarity to establish the eight-hour day, reductions in the exploitation of youth and student labor, a more-just wage, health benefits, released time for education and recreation, a safer workplace, and so forth. The contemporary labor movement in the academy will reject Harris's rhetoric as well, in part because so many of these nineteenth-century demands are once again relevant but also because it is in their power (and not lower management's) to accomplish these things. Furthermore, what a large sector of composition labor (graduate employees and former graduate employees working off the tenure track) "really wants" is not to be *treated as* colleagues but instead to *be* colleagues. Nearly every participant in the composition conversation would like to see writing instructors become more like faculty—to have the chance to govern, enjoy an intellectual life, and develop as an instructor as well as enjoy better pay, benefits, protections, and security. This has not translated into a consensus among professional and managerial compositionists that writing instructors should actually *be* faculty. Why not? Isn't composition work faculty work? Or is composition's faculty work the supervision of parafaculty? Harris's vision for "our joined interests as composition workers and bosses" appears really to mean accomplishing the disciplinary and managerial agenda of "more direct control over our [*sic*] curricula and staffing—within departments of English, or, if need be, outside them" (57–58). It is hard to see how composition *labor* can have more direct control over "our" staffing without transcending the evasions of *as* and actually becoming colleagues who participate in a hiring and tenuring process, just as the faculty do. So, unsurprisingly, nowhere in the actually existing academic labor movement over the past century has anyone discovered that what academic labor really needs is for lower-level management to have more direct control of curricula and staffing (or to have the chance to set up new departments for disciplines that do not envision tenure for their workforce!). Somewhat predictably, this managerial plan for labor dignity is accompanied by digs at the CCCC statement's "uncritical embrace of the tenure system as a guarantor of good teaching" (55).

So, on what basis might a real class consciousness in composition unfold? One clear way a genuine community of interest might unfold is in the mold of social-movement unionism, currently being practiced in a number of places in the academy, widespread in public-employee unionism more generally, and very significant in organizing efforts targeting the service economy. Advocated by Bruce Horner among others (*Terms of Work* 207–8), movement unionism relates the public interest to the interest of the organized public employee, whose work is the "production of society itself" (a position that Horner redacts from Paul Johnston and that can be found more theoretically elaborated in the tradition of Italian autonomist Marxism, such as Virno, but perhaps even more relevantly for the feminized labor of composition also importantly theorized in the feminist political economy of Selma James and Maria Dalla Costa). The movement union becomes a nexus for multiple struggles to converge and articulate an identity of interest in the project of transformation—a nexus of real-world agency through which organized humanity can once again see itself as the engine of history. The consciousness of class would invoke an identity of interests based not on workplace disciplines ("Oncologists unite!") but on the common experience of selling one's labor in order to live and on the desire widespread in the academy but also common in many sectors of service work, to be productive for society rather than capital.

How could professional and managerial compositionists participate in this class consciousness or project identity? Certainly not as managers seeking more direct control of staff and curricula. Nevertheless—just as it is sometimes possible for deans and presidents to shed the administrative subjectivity and return to the labor of the professoriate, perhaps the professional and managerial compositionist can likewise shed the desire for control and embrace the reality of collective agency. Are we so sure after all that what the professional compositionist really wants is more control over people she must creatively treat *as* colleagues? Perhaps what the professional compositionist really wants is to lay down the requirement to serve as WPA and become a colleague among colleagues. Harris himself repeatedly identifies himself as a worker in a "collective educational project" and (unlike most contributors to the managerialist discourse) makes a point of endorsing collective bargaining, and underlines the structural and economic nature of the problems we face. If we remove the taint of the pragmatist—the limits to the possible imposed by the intellectual-bureaucrat—we find in Harris's boss a worker struggling to make himself available to the rhetoric and social project of solidarity.

What is ultimately most important about the efforts of Harris or Porter and Sullivan are not their various complicities but their genuine attempt to explore "a level of institutional critique . . . that we are not used to enacting in rhetoric and composition," including changing law and public policy. Nonetheless, because these are areas in which organized academic labor has been struggling, often effectively, for decades, Porter and Sullivan's statement that we are unused to acting in those arenas is false to an important extent. Indeed, any version of *us* that includes graduate-employee and contingent labor organizations would have to acknowledge that we are very much used to struggling at law with the university employer and in the arena of policy with legislatures, labor policy boards, community groups, and the media. *This means that if institutional critique is the answer to the pessimistic structure of feeling that presently characterizes professional and managerial compositionists, it is a kind of critique that the professionals and managers will have to learn from the workers in their charge.* In order to realize the scene of lower management learning to practice institutional critique and the arts of solidarity from labor, we will eventually have to reconsider the limits to thought imposed by pragmatism and learn once again to question the inevitability of the scene of managed labor to composition. In my view, composition's best chance to contribute to a better world and to achieve disciplinary status depends on learning to write as colleagues among colleagues—a condition predicated on working toward a university without a WPA.

Notes

An excerpt from this chapter, revised and expanded, has appeared in *Minnesota Review*, and a version at the full length has appeared in *JAC: Journal of Advanced Composition*. It could not have been written without the inspiration and thoughtful engagement of my co-editors, Tony Scott and Leo Parascondola. I have benefited enormously from the intellectual partnership of Heather Julien, Christopher Carter, and Laura Bartlett Snyder, as well as from the generous contributions of the collective of *Workplace: A Journal for Academic Labor* (http://www.workplace-gsc.com), James Seitz, Jeff Williams, Lynn Worsham, and the readers for Southern Illinois University Press. With respect to the Nast cartoon, I am very grateful for the gifts of time and knowledge donated by Granville Ganter, Delinda Buie, Mildred Franks, and Harry Rubenstein, curator for labor history at the Smithsonian Institute.

1. They write:

> In effect, we are assuming that individuals and groups/communities can indeed change institutions. But we are also assuming an agent of fairly powerful status already working within an institution: probably a member of the managerial or professional class who has entered an institution (e.g., the corporation) in some employee status that allows him or her to begin to make changes at least at a local level. (613, n. 3)

2. For more on the labor of the professional-managerial class, which differs from real wealth despite its elite status in that each generation has to renew its knowledge capital through hard work (whereas the capital of real wealth seems to renew itself without effort), see Barbara Ehrenreich. The fear of falling out of the professional-managerial fraction of the working class is a prospect that professionals and managers worry about not just for their children but for themselves. The accelerated industrialization of knowledge work in the knowledge economy has meant that professionals and managers must continuously rehabilitate their knowledge just to maintain their own career prospects and status. The privations of severe discipline and continuous self-fashioning associated with training and apprenticeship (in undergraduate, professional-school, and early-career pressures) have become lifetime requirements for professionals and managers.

3. My purpose in this section is not to critique the work of actually existing WPAs but to discuss the figure of the WPA as it interpellates rhet-comp scholarship more generally, as part of a historical turn toward practical and theoretical accommodation of the "realities" of the managed university. This would be a discussion of the WPA as canny bureaucrat–pragmatist boss, as constructed by Miller and Harris, among others, insofar as that constructed figure threatens to become the field's dominant subject position and not the vexed and contradictory intentions and experiences of individuals. The real experiences of WPAs are simply too diverse to be addressed here. Not all WPAs, for example, are administrators—some serve as a kind of peer adviser in departments in which most of the writing instruction is done by full-time faculty. Some WPAs are adjuncts themselves; many are graduate students. Neither is it my goal for this essay to be part of an effort to reform the practices of actually existing WPAs (as if the "bad policy" of lower administration caused the labor system), nor would such suggestions be consistent with this project's larger commitments. In the big picture, my goal would be not to reform but rather to *abolish* the WPA as part of a more general abolition of the scene of managed labor in the academy. In disci-

plinary terms, this would form part of a process of founding rhet-comp teaching and scholarship on the basis of collegiality and self-governance that obtains elsewhere in the academy rather than in the managed relation so firmly crystallized in the bodies and figure of the actually existing WPA.

Nonetheless, it may be helpful for some readers to trace the real experience behind the rhetorical figure. For instance, tracing the risk of schizophrenia involved in moving from academic labor to academic lower management, Roxanne Mountford observes that "having once been one of the instructor-laborers," the WPA genuinely wants to consider herself a labor "insider" and even an advocate but discovers herself willy-nilly "a representative of institutional interests" who suffers a radical "change in values" in connection with upper management, becoming in effect, "'one of them'" (41–43). Diana George's collection of narratives by WPAs is particularly evocative for those interested in the complex movement of the class allegiances of the actual persons in the job. Nancy Conroy Grimm's "The Way the Rich People Does It" explores the strong equivalence between the diminished notion of what counts as critical for the members of her family who did maid service and the pragmatism of administration in a writing program: "For the Conroy women, a 'critical' approach to the habits of the rich people meant [correcting their relatives] whose habits fell short," a kind of pragmatic approach to the idea of the critical that Grimm calls "useful" in learning to "pay attention" to "things that matter" to the "rich people" of the academy (i.e., "the people in funding positions in the university") (15–16). In the same collection, Johanna Atwood explores the problem ("the peer who isn't a peer") of graduate students who serve as administrators of other graduate employees in a way that can be extended analytically to the structure of feeling animating the whole field of composition. Doug Hesse explores the consequences in his own life of living the role of "WPA-as-father," in a set of paternalist iterations ranging from the mass-mediated images of paternal caretaking represented by Anthony Hopkins in *Remains of the Day,* David Bartholomae's image of the WPA as Michael Keaton's Batman "protecting and responsible, yet also brooding" and the images drawn from Hesse's own adolescence "climbing on and off a garbage truck" (47, 50). For a critique of the many ways that actually existing WPAs become subject to the various ideologies of paternalism and benevolence and of the way in which even a shared sense of speaking from the outside can be mobilized by the administrative subject "in defense of tyranny," see Jeanne Gunner, "Among the Composition People." For a discussion of the WPA as a worker with little control over the disposition of her own labor, see Laura Micciche.

4. David Downing in "Beyond Disciplinary English" systematically relates the operation of disciplinarity in English to the exploitative division of labor in the field, a formation he calls "managed disciplinarity" (28).

5. An opinion piece by Michael Murphy, "Adjuncts Should Not Just Be Visitors in the Academic Promised Land," appeared in the *Chronicle of Higher Education* while I was revising this chapter. Overall, his opinion piece retains the rhetoric of his "New Faculty" article ("We should formalize the . . . heterogeneity that actually exists in higher education") but substantially modifies his proposal in two respects. First, in the new piece, he now proposes creating *tenure-track* positions for full-timers who concentrate on teaching, and second, he limits the proposal to "institutions where other faculty members now get significant load reductions for research and where large numbers of part-timers are now used" (B15). Insofar as these kinds of institutions already have a full-time faculty comprised of between 17 percent to 28 percent non-tenure-track faculty, many of whom concentrate on teaching (some are non-tenure-track researchers), one has to ask *even if* the new full-time positions were created by combining the part-time faculty positions into new tenure-track teaching positions, how would these new tenure-track teaching positions relate

to the huge number of already existing non-tenure-track teaching positions? Or is Murphy now just arguing for the tenure eligibility of persons who concentrate on teaching, consistent with past academic practice at many institutions and the policies of all academic unions (as well as with my own views)? If so, kudos, but one still has to ask why does he now exclude non-research-oriented schools from his new recommendations, where the tenuring of faculty on the basis of teaching is common practice?

6. The survey breaks down teaching by department into introductory, all other, and all undergraduate courses. In English and freestanding composition courses, this schematic does not quite capture the role of writing instruction, which comprises a significant percentage of introductory courses, but is far from the total percentage. Similarly, a great deal of writing instruction takes place in upper-division classes, such as business and professional writing, and writing about literature or culture. The survey represents that 17–18 percent of introductory courses in the English and freestanding composition departments that were surveyed are taught by full-time non-tenure-track faculty.

7. See Jeanne Gunner for a skeptical account of what happens to proposals for change that threaten the "structural base" of disciplinary power as well as the measure of improvements in "professional conditions" ("basically, the tenure rate for WPAs") ("Among the Composition People" 154, 160).

8. For instance, the UAW-affiliated New York University graduate-employee union won raises of $5,000 per year in its first contract (2002) for more than a third of its membership, with stipends increasing as much as 38 percent over the life of the contract, plus 100 percent health coverage. By 2004, the minimum graduate-employee stipend at NYU will be $18,000 for a twenty-hour week (Parascondola). Similar gains are expected by the newly organized bargaining unit for non-tenure-track faculty on the same campus, the largest unit of its kind in the country. At the University of Michigan, the Graduate Employees Organization negotiated almost half a million dollars in additional child care subsidy from its employer, to $1,700/semester for the first child plus $850/semester per child thereafter. Similarly, at the largest public university system in the country, California State, the union's 2002 contract compelled the university to hire 20 percent more tenure-track faculty in each year of the contract as well as expanded benefits and security for existing non-tenure-track faculty, including three-year contracts for those with six years of service (Phillips). For more details, see Gordon Lafer on graduate-employee unionism, Susan Griffin on contingent-faculty unionism in composition, the Coalition of Graduate Employee Unions Web site (http://www.cgeu.org) and Workplace: A Journal for Academic Labor (http://www.workplace-gsc.com).

9. In an article entitled "The Worldwide Rise of Private Colleges" in the *Chronicle of Higher Education,* David Cohen portrays privatization as a kind of corporate "white knight" that emerges in aftermath of the "failure" of the public sector:

> As the world's hunger for higher education has outstripped the ability of many governments to pay for it, a type of institution has come to the rescue that is well established in the United States . . . private colleges.

Associating the public with failure, scarcity, and famine (world hunger), the piece assigns heroic agency to market institutions and the U.S. On this wildly rhetorical foundation, the piece proceeds to a stunningly propagandistic reversal of cause and effect in describing the privatization process:

> In Mexico, a nine-month strike last year over the introduction of tuition at the country's largest public institution, the National Autonomous University, drove some

middle-class students who were impatient with the strike's socialist ideals onto the campuses of private colleges. (A47–48)

It is of course the forced introduction of tuition in a public institution that leads to the nine-month strike, so if there is a cause for middle-class flight from public institutions, it is not the strike or socialist ideals but the prior act of de-funding. One must ask, why does the article install impatient middle-class students as the normative subjectivity rather than the subject *actually the norm on the scene, that is, a striking student subject* engaged in a heroically protracted resistance to privatization?

The "Worldwide" piece heads a cluster in *CHE* on global privatizations: The piece on South Africa is typical in using its lead paragraph to introduce the reader to a student who visited a public university in Johannesburg only to be "put off by the dirty campus and by the common sight of demonstrating students doing the *toyi-toyi,* a rhythmic dance of protest" (A51). It is easy enough to pick out the faults of journalistic writing in the *Chronicle,* a journal aimed in large part at an administrative readership, but it seems less clear why rhet-comp should adopt the same aversion to the striking and demonstrating subject.

2
Citizenship and Literacy Work: Thoughts Without a Conclusion
Richard Ohmann

Democracy cannot work unless citizens are literate and informed: That's the starting point of one familiar justification for universal schooling. College faculties and administrations may articulate it in ideological moments or see it as too obvious to need articulation. Naturally, compositionists have taken encouragement from and sought support by affiliating with this amiably righteous principle. A closely allied rationale is that by building, preserving, and transmitting the national culture, university education fortifies the nation itself. Bill Readings elaborated this idea in *The University in Ruins.*[1] Compositionists do not press this claim for their work so often as perhaps they did when usage and correctness were coin of their professional realm.[2] However, it is implicit in our offer to help immigrants and children of the working class enter a national conversation by first mastering conventions of academic discourse.

In my view, these ideas are better than some old ones we might recall (the university's task is to perfect the gentleman) and especially to others we hear now (education's task is to foster economic growth and American competitiveness). Still, the telos of democratic citizenship and that of national culture are themselves laced with contradiction and ideological trouble. In particular, for my purpose here—which is to wonder about the prospects for democratic literacy work in this time of privatized knowledge and education as a business—both rationales allow inequality to flourish and to seem natural and inevitable.

Cultural studies after Raymond Williams has probably made it impossible, any longer, to think of culture as a realm cleansed of power or as homogeneous throughout a nation. If universities fostered nationhood, they did so by valuing the culture of some over that of others, by recovering or creating selective traditions, by giving people unequal access to respectable culture, by helping some turn culture into cultural capital, by letting their children draw on that capital to extend privilege generationally, and so on. This is not to say that culture is another name for snobbery or national culture just a ruling class trick, only that the university cannot stand apart from the class system of its society. The point is perhaps even more obvious for literacy, which, in spite of many compositionists' egalitarian hopes, is a birthright to some, a meritocratic attainment for others, a low-grade marketable skill for many, and a remedial insult to still others.

The trouble with citizenship is perhaps deeper—and more vexing, because citizenship is theoretically a relation of basic equality: You and I, however unlike in birth or circumstance, are supposed to have the same rights and obligations before the law and the same weight in governance. Of course, this has a hollow ring in the era of hundred-million-dollar campaign warchests, bought pardons, and Supreme Court sleight-of-hand. However, there is reason to doubt that the ideal of equal citizenship could ever be realized in a society like ours, even if (unthinkably) Congress were bold enough to have a serious go at taking big money out of electoral politics.

T. H. Marshall posed the fundamental question fifty years ago: Is citizenship—a relation of basic equality—compatible with capitalist class structure? Or, to point up the contradiction: Because capitalism was the condition of possibility for both citizenship and class inequality, "How is it that these two opposing principles could grow and flourish side by side in the same soil?" (84).[3] Marshall answered by showing that in fact capitalist inequality was consequent upon the principle of equal civil rights, which in turn was necessary to the free play of capitalist economic activities. Each person (earlier, man) had to have the right to enter contracts, pursue gain, seek advancement, and in general act as a free individual in the market. Free labor and free capital needed a relation like citizenship as their legal basis. So, in effect, citizenship was the "soil" in which capitalist inequality flourished. Marshall particularly emphasized a universal right to education as critical for full citizenship: "The status acquired by education is carried out into the world bearing the stamp of legitimacy, because it has been conferred by an institution designed to give the citizen his just rights," and in this way, "citizenship operates as an instrument of social stratification" (110). In other words, equal opportunity and universal access to education are compatible with great inequality, and, because they make it seem the result of unequal merit and effort, they also make it seem both inevitable and just. There is no way for egalitarian movements in composition or for education generally to escape this logic, though the reforms they promote may make teaching practices kinder and more effective.

To explicate the point, consider primary and secondary schooling, which, unlike attendance at college, is in the U.S. not only a universal right but a legal requirement. Access is universal. Yet, even across the public schools, inequality is in Jonathan Kozol's word "savage." Attempts to level it out have always failed, and the currently popular strategies will surely also fail. About vouchers, and the privatization that would accompany them, I need not comment to likely readers of this essay. Charter schools financed in the most common way take funds from the budgets of the regular schools that feed them, almost certainly making those schools worse, so that however bright and free the charter schools may be, the system as a whole remains as unequal as before, or more so. A third strategy—mandated statewide curricula with high-stakes testing—is spreading across the country, with its advocates stating always their intention of offering tough love to the weakest schools—that is, state help with professional development for teachers, tutorial work for failing students but no diplomas for students who nonetheless fail the tests, and various penalties for teachers and schools that don't make the grade. In Massachusetts, where I live, the first cohort of students to take the tests for real did so in spring of 2001, and, as was predictable, a majority of poor kids, kids in underfunded schools, kids with special needs, those for whom English is not the first language, and those in vocational schools scored below the level they must eventually reach in order to graduate. The sorting by class, race, and (dis)ability that went on more subtly before will now proceed with stark clarity as every student is measured on the same scale and either given or denied a diploma. This will amount to an ideological simplification, too, in that each eighteen-year-old's trajectory into college, career, dead-end job, or prison will now be explainable by reference to his or her numerically expressed merit. Unless, of course, as seems possible, the parents, students, and teachers of Massachusetts rise up to defeat this unpleasant outcome.

The fourth strategy, just now gaining momentum, is to legislate or sue for much more equality[4] in public school funding, which has from the beginning depended on local property taxes and thus been a fluid transmitter of social class across generations. This kind of redistribution will disrupt privilege far more in most states than it has so far done in Vermont (under Law 60 passed a few years ago, which shifts money from richer to poorer towns), so it seems unlikely to take place nationwide unless driven by a twenty-first-century equivalent of Brown v. Board of Education. Even if it did—and I certainly favor it wherever possible— I suppose that Scarsdale and Oak Park and Beverly Hills would have little difficulty finding ways to preserve the advantage their children have over kids from Harlem and the Chicago projects and South Central L. A. Universal and equal schooling will be a central policy of any truly democratic society, but the sad truth is that there can be no equal schooling in an unequal society, nor, I think, can such schooling be the vanguard of egalitarian change. Aside from the unfairness of sending children to fight their elders' battles, as in Little Rock and South Boston years ago, democratic reform of the educational system does not make the rest of the society democratic. Almost fifty years after Brown, public schools remain at least as segregated as back then.

If this holds for K–12, it holds more evidently for higher education, where universal access has never been a reality, and where, should we somehow achieve it, access would be to Princeton and then Wall Street for some and to the current array of less favored colleges and life trajectories for the rest, with perhaps an additional tier at the bottom for new arrivals. After thirty-five years of relatively open admissions, the university system remains highly stratified and carries out its work of social reproduction quite efficiently. Good will and heroic efforts there by administrators, literary workers, activist students, and the faculty can make the institution more open and decent but cannot in a stratified university system nourish citizenship in the basic sense, as a relation of equality. That will—to repeat—require a broader egalitarian movement.

What a good college education can and does achieve in the arena of citizenship is nearly the opposite: It helps some students refine and develop their literacy into a vehicle of self-advancement and perhaps in that advancement achieve control over others. I do not refer to the economic advantage differential literacies will give some students over others, though it does that; I have in mind the direct leverage it provides in public affairs. Some people exercise their citizenship more vigorously than others. All have obligations, but the obligations are pretty slim in this country—paying taxes, obeying laws, providing census information, and the like. No law requires them to vote, and most do not. Beyond the minimal and (for each individual person) inconsequential act of voting, the body of citizens as a whole must serve in elective office, take turns on the PTO or zoning board, and so on. The tasks are required, but only a relative few volunteer to do them. A small number of activist citizens organize civic projects not mandated by any law. For instance, they agitate to close down the nuclear power plant, set up clinics for old people, try to get obscene books out of the library, establish favorable terms for businesses considering a move into the area, fight to keep some businesses out (e.g., Wal-Mart), found ballet companies or right-wing think tanks, and organize TA unions and NRA chapters. Such work gives the society its texture and shapes its future. Well before the days of bowling alone, most people declined to join in. Those who do expand their citizenship in such ways help set the terms of social life for the rest. It is obvious that advanced literacy gives activists an edge in assuming such leadership, and also, more tautologically, that those destined by birthright to be leaders will be offered advanced literacy along the way.

Now, that is no reason to deplore expanded citizenship (we could not do without it) or to give up on the project of offering it to working-class students. It is a reason, however, to dismiss claims that university education in general and composition in particular inevitably improve citizenship, especially if improvement means putting all citizens on a more-equal footing and helping them work well together. What American universities have done for a hundred years is prepare some youth to take up places in the professional-managerial class and, if they wish, exercise robust citizenship, too—while preparing other youth for more technical work and narrower citizenship. Liberal and progressive composition instructors have worked within these limits of possibility, with more or less effectiveness depending on who their students were and what political winds were blowing in and outside of the university.

Why am I saying these abstract and gloomy things? I have meant to ground the question of citizenship and composition in terms and ideas that applied to the university system at least until recently. Today, as the title of this project indicates and as is suggested by much analysis and speculation, our system of higher education is modulating from its midcentury form into something very different. The *managed university* names it well, and similar epithets such as the *corporate university* and *Campus Inc.* (Geoffrey White's title) identify something that most observers from left to right and from *The Chronicle of Higher Education* to *Business Week* agree is happening. How does it change the conditions of post-secondary work in literacy? How does it bear on the question of citizenship?

Readings's much-discussed book has pointed some toward a direct-enough answer: that the new university has detached itself from service to the national culture. In *College English* for January, 2001, I come across this, by Daniel Green: "The role established for the modern university over the past 200 years, to mold educated citizens who will take productive places in the nation-state, is no longer tenable," because—and he goes on to quote Readings—the university "is becoming a different kind of institution, one that is no longer linked to the destiny of the nation-state by virtue of its role as producer, protector, and inculcator of an idea of national culture" (280). The university is becoming a transnational corporation, Green says, and although I suppose you could argue that it now prepares the young for global citizenship, this does not help much and does not at all capture Readings's point. In my view, the concept of privatization gives us more analytic leverage than that of globalization in trying to grasp what is happening in postsecondary education.

To be sure, U.S. universities are selling their degrees and their knowledge "products" on a world market—attracting many thousands of international students, starting up branches abroad, and using the Internet to carry learning across global distances. Also, corporations shop worldwide for educated labor and hence indirectly for education itself: If one of them sets up a facility in India to take advantage of engineers who earn a small fraction of what their American counterparts do, that company is also in effect buying specialized education that is cheap by comparison to engineering degrees in the U.S. But then, capital has always sought cheap (and docile) labor in poor countries or colonies, just as it has sought or created markets abroad for its products. The international mobility of capital in recent decades is real and important, but to repeat, the idea of privatization works better to underline the gradual subsumption of higher education within markets and market-like processes and thus to explain many recent changes in our lives.

Those involving academic labor are all too familiar. Part-timers doubling as a percentage of the workforce from 1970 to the 1990s; full-time, tenure-track hires through the last decade amounting to only about one-third of all hires; the consolidation of a two-tier labor market with the upper tier shrinking; the oversupply of credentialed workers and the disappearance of many from university work: Such painful changes are the givens of this symposium and need not be enumerated further. I want simply to mention two contexts for them. First, similar changes have taken place throughout the economy since 1970, in the era of agile competition and flexible accumulation. The old, Fordist, core labor force of unionized, job-secure, well-paid, benefited workers has everywhere fallen on hard times, and a host of new and old arrangements now becomes dominant: outsourcing, subcontracting, job-sharing, temp work, part-time work, sweat-shops, maquiladoras, prison labor, and so on. Second, the conditions of academic (and other mental) labor increasingly approximate those of industrial labor, es-pecially for professionals in the lower tier. That has happened precisely because the academic profession is no longer functioning in the way successful profes-sions do. It has failed to limit entry, regulate careers, restrict the practice of teach-ing to fully credentialed members and selected apprentices, control the defini-tion and assessment of its work, and secure the high pay and prestige that people in strong professions enjoy.

Are there any strong professions these days, as medicine and law were strong a few decades ago? I cannot argue the point here but believe there is a good case that the forces of agile capitalism are undermining most of the professions. As capital seeks to bring all areas of human activity into the market, it has increas-ingly commodified information, including the kinds that we proudly but per-haps quaintly call knowledge and that professions have amassed as cultural capital in order to ground their practices and justify their exclusiveness. This point may seem remote from what has happened to English studies and literacy work, com-pared, say, to the commodification of medical services by HMOs. However, think about the various learning companies offering literary culture for sale; about provision of literacy skills on the Internet; about the fights over who owns and can profit from courseware; or about Rudolph Giuliani's threat, a few years back, to eliminate "remedial" work from the City University and subcontract it to private companies: It will be evident that nothing intrinsic to the subject matter of our own profession will protect it from commercial exploitation, any more than the knowledge and skills of weavers protected their trade against the capi-talists of Manchester.

Whether the emergent profession of rhetoric and composition is turned back by commodification remains to be seen, but there is no doubt that the corpo-rate university is a less and less friendly home for it, as well as for the older professionalized disciplines. To be a little more precise: By "corporate university," I mean an institution that acts like a profit-making business rather than a pub-lic or philanthropic trust. Thus, we hear of universities applying productivity and performance measures to teaching (Illinois); of plans to put departments in com-petition with one another for resources (Florida); of cutting faculty costs not only by replacing full-timers with part-timers and temps and by subcontracting for everything from food services to the total management of physical plant but also by substituting various schemes of computerized instruction; and so on.

Marketing the educational product becomes a far more self-conscious activ-ity than it used to be: Universities try to identify their niches, turn their names into brands, develop signatures and slogans. (The college where I used to teach paid consultants to invent a killer slogan for us; they came up with "the alternative ivy," which students soon laughed out of court.) Universities have always prepared students in a general way for different job markets. Now, all but the fancier colleges tout specific training and credentials for specific kinds of work. Many now do what community colleges have long done: tailor course offerings to the just-in-time needs of students entering or returning to the job market. They frankly imagine students as customers, not as citizens or as future leaders or as novices in a common culture. Universities also look around for other customers, in some cases selling their students to those customers, through large, long-term, exclusive contracts with such as Coke and Pepsi. Administrators scan the university for whatever resources they can take to market: research, patents, courseware, faculty reputations. They seek to partner with corporations in developing these products, or they seek venture capital to help launch businesses that the university will partly own. They use their own venture capital to set up incubators for small, often local businesses, some of which will hit it big and bring fame or fortune to the university along the way (van der Werf and Blumenstyk A28).

In the old days, administrators made pitches to trustees, regents, or legislators, seeking a mix of income sources (tax moneys, tuition, yield from the endowment), and staged their mainly traditional activities within the limits so established. In boom times such as the two postwar decades, they added new programs and expanded campuses. In lean times, they trimmed costs. Now, like agile corporations, universities look to develop new products, enter new markets, preserve flexibility in labor and plant, and in general direct their efforts where they can generate income in excess of costs. They are not profit-making institutions as a whole, but they seek profit-like gains in whatever part of the operation such gains may be generated.

The causes of this shift are complex and not really to the point of this essay. They include a decisive reduction in direct state funding of public universities— from roughly half of their total budgets in the early 1970s to less than a third now and quite a bit less than that (20–25 percent) at major research campuses like the University of California, Berkeley and the University of California, Los Angeles. That reduction followed in part on the "fiscal crisis of the State" around 1970, the accountability movement that sprang up at the same moment, and the conservative reaction to social rebellions and educational reforms of the 1960s. As government support declined, competition from nontraditional universities and programs greatly increased. Proprietary institutions grew apace. Most famous is the University of Phoenix, with its hundred-plus "campuses," nearly 100,000 students, no library, and no full-time faculty. However, many others are making money in the same way, by providing skills, learning, and credentials for people looking to advance in their jobs or find better ones. Finally, corporate universities abound. General Electric started the first one in 1955, and there are now eighteen hundred of them providing just-in-time training to their own employees.

These and other incursions by for-profit companies have forced universities to think of themselves as players in the same market for postsecondary education.

Along with this refiguring of education as a commodity, an ideology of education valued for the economic benefits it brings has become salient. When the senior George Bush took office in 1988, staking out his claim to be the education president, he gave exactly four reasons in support of his showcase proposal, the Educational Excellence Act of 1989: "I believe that greater educational achievement promotes sustained economic growth, enhances the nation's competitive position in world markets, increases productivity, and leads to higher incomes for everyone" (Bush). Most of the provisions in that act bore on K–12 education, but government increasingly demands that higher education as well repay expenditures on it within the same economic calculus. Critical intelligence? Historical consciousness? Appreciation of beauty? Spiritual growth? Ethical refinement? However loudly the Right may cheer when a Lynne Cheney or William Bennett or E. D. Hirsch or Allan Bloom condemns the politically correct as barbarians and calls for reestablishment of the Great Books, when it comes to federal support for education, a market rationale takes precedence. Students seem to have got the message: 75 percent now cite being "well-off financially" as an essential goal in their educations, compared to 41 percent thirty years ago; back then, 82 percent listed development of a sound "philosophy of life" among their main goals, twice as many as do today.

Needless to say, although citizenship, too, gets a nod in pious moments, it has a smaller place now than before in official rationales for higher education and no place at all in the play of economic forces that are remaking the university. For students, citizenship is a recreational choice, an individual taste. For capital it is nearly irrelevant—of even less interest than other leisure activities because it cannot easily be commodified. In fact, robust citizenship is a downer for capital, a threat to its freedom of movement and its ability to mold the future society that best suits its needs. Those needs include quiet citizens and social calm, maintained by the police when necessary, not a vibrant public sphere where needs other than capital's can be asserted and dominance contested.

To return to the main question: How does literacy work fit into the configuration I have been describing? Into the corporate university and the commodification of knowledge? One might answer, only a bit sardonically, that it does not have to—that higher education as a whole has reconfigured itself on the model of literacy work, having learned from English 101 how to give the customer decent service while keeping costs down and the labor force contingent. The professionalization of comp, while installing the usual apparatus (journals, conferences, a professional society, and graduate programs and degrees), bringing a great advance in theoretical sophistication, and winning job security and good compensation for advanced practitioners, has made little if any improvement in who does the front-line work, under what regimen, for what pay, and so on. Indeed, front-line practitioners may actually work in worse conditions now than they did before professionalization of the field. Meanwhile, English, the old professional home of literacy work, has itself fallen on hard times, along with most academic professions, losing much of its ability to maintain a market haven for its members. So the adjuncts and graduate students who teach composition instantiate well the floating, peripheral labor force of contemporary capitalism.

Additionally, the service that adjuncts and graduate students provide is not the kind that can easily be packaged and sold as a job credential or career boost. It remains socially defined as basic if not remedial, a foundation on which to build other marketable skills and capabilities. With this justification, it seems likely that composition will go on being taught chiefly as a kind of sweatshop operation. Within the average literacy classroom, a dispossessed intellectual works at survival wages transmitting skills to people hoping they can trade these for more-than-survival wages. The instructor may be a graduate student TA, a part-time adjunct, a moonlighting high school teacher at a proprietary university such as Phoenix, or a full-time teacher off the tenure track. Low pay, low status, and job insecurity erase differences across these groups and make it nearly irrelevant that some have Ph.D.s, some are A.B.D., some have M.A.s, and some have no advanced degrees. In short, the academic profession as a whole is losing much of the ground it won a hundred years ago. Literacy workers within or outside of English departments have long been exploited and marginalized, and the professionalization of composition as a discipline has not created professional pay or working conditions for front-line literacy workers.

The idea that universal education underwrites a polity of free and equal citizens was contradictory to begin with. However, an illusion can serve well as a common goal, and the dream of a mutually responsible, educated citizenry probably did help open the gates to higher education in the U.S., through at least the first twenty postwar years. In the present time of privatization and agile capital, the illusion shatters: Education becomes a commodity among other commodities, with claims made for its contribution to the common good only on the basis of economic advantage. Meanwhile, the same forces of capitalist transformation and market imperialism have pressed the university to act like a business in many ways, including the casualization of its labor force and commodification of the knowledge it creates through research. All that is solid melts into air, yet again.

If this picture is even roughly accurate, what directions does it point for the progressives who, I think, make up a majority among literacy workers? Let me put out two ideas for discussion. First, given the fading chances for strong professionalization among literacy workers, the present move to unionize and to ally with other groups of university workers is right and necessary. Further, adjuncts and grad students should continue to lean on professional and scholarly organizations to support unions and act more like unions, though they cannot become effective unions. The labor-related resolutions passed by the Delegate Assembly at the Modern Language Association meetings in 2000 show many members to be in agreement with the Graduate Student and Radical Caucuses—that struggle for better working conditions is now in the interest of both contingent and core academic labor forces and in the interest of those professional values that are worth defending. We need solidarity, in short, pointing *out* toward a late capitalist extension of embattled citizenship, one that clarifies and builds upon class antagonisms. Of course, a further extension—logical but famously difficult— would make common cause with workers everywhere and thus complete the ruin of national citizenship that capital has begun.

Second, if privatization is driving higher education into the market, to the point where even education presidents forget to include citizenship in official proclamations, deferring instead to gross domestic product and international competitiveness, could this be a time for literacy workers to take whatever high ground is available in public relations and in fights over budget and curriculum? If the Ph.D.-holding and tenured directors of writing programs work with those in the trenches to refuse the economic justification for comp, stressing instead historical, social, and critical thinking . . . well, what? Not the revolution. Maybe the beginning of a fight to retake the university for education and to broaden citizenship within and outside it. This fight and the one for decent working conditions might enforce one another. One can hope.

Notes

1. A powerful recent reminder that some would like the university to underwrite national culture was the November, 2001 report of the American Council of Trustees and Alumni, "Defending Civilization." It cited over a hundred post–September-11 statements by university people for weak or absent patriotism and blamed this *trahison des clercs* on the university's abandonment of a core curriculum explaining the values of our founding fathers and of Western civilization. Such a curriculum, the report said, was America's "first line of defense."

2. A professor of rhetoric at Minnesota wrote in 1895 that, where students who were otherwise promising could not speak without Scandinavian accents or write without foreign idioms, "the fundamental work of the University must be a struggle for correctness" (Payne, 96; Ohmann, *English in America* 249).

3. I am paraphrasing in this paragraph from my "Thick Citizenship and Textual Relations."

4. The suits may also be for a higher level of "adequacy," regardless of equity. Suits demanding that states provide resources to bring poor schools up to a level that will "equip students for their roles as citizens and enable them to succeed economically and personally" have succeeded in a number of states (Schrag 18). A decision in New York in 2002 used similar language, mandating education for "productive citizenship" and "civic engagement" and holding that the state's system of financing schools denied such education to many children in New York City (Schrag 19). The principle, more and more widely accepted, that states have such responsibilities in small part explains their recent intrusiveness in curriculum and assessment.

3

The Managerial Unconscious
of Composition Studies

Donna Strickland

To profess composition is to occupy a position in the contemporary college or university unlike almost any other—certainly unlike any other in departments of English, where most composition specialists find their homes. While junior faculty in literature are hired primarily to teach and—depending on the institution—to conduct research, composition specialists are hired to do those things *and* to direct and develop programs, either immediately or in the near future. Department chairs also perform administrative work, of course, which might suggest that composition specialists are not so unique, after all. As Charles I. Schuster has pointed out, however, "No department I know of would hire a beginning assistant professor of literature to chair the department . . . Yet these same departments choose freshly minted PhDs to direct writing centers and composition programs" (94).

Despite the centrality of the administrative function in the professional lives of most composition specialists, these specialists have tended to avoid defining their field through an association with management. Rather, composition studies is popularly understood among its specialists to be a "teaching subject," one which, in the words of Joseph Harris, "defines itself through an interest in the work students and teachers do together" (*Teaching* ix). Without a doubt, composition specialists have done much to expand the possibilities of what it might mean to teach writing and to make visible the intellectual richness and political complexities involved in the teaching and learning of writing. My own entry into the field, certainly, was prompted by an interest in pedagogy—not by an interest in administration—and I would venture to guess that the same is true of many of my peers. Nonetheless, the *material* conditions that have made the field of composition studies, as we know it, possible and the material conditions that shape the professional lives of most composition professionals involve the administration of writing programs.[1]

These material conditions have been largely absent from historical studies and critical interpretations within the field, even from those that purport to be materialist. James A. Berlin, for instance, in his study of writing instruction since 1900, focuses on the pedagogies and attendant epistemologies that have circulated among composition professionals, giving only six pages to the development of "organized freshman writing programs" (*Rhetoric and Reality* 65–71). More recently, Bruce Horner has written a "materialist critique" of work in composition. While his book offers many useful insights into the material constraints within which composition professionals work, Horner privileges teaching in defining the work of compositionists.[2] This persistent tendency to align composition primarily with teaching, resulting in an obscuring of the administrative function, suggests that the official story of composition is built on what I will call a *managerial unconscious*.

By naming it a managerial unconscious, I am, of course, alluding to Fredric Jameson's theory of the political unconscious. For Jameson, in a famous phrase, "everything is 'in the last analysis' political"; everything, in short, plays out class conflict (*Political Unconscious* 20). By describing the unconscious of composition studies as managerial, I would seem to be missing the point—management is not what Antonio Gramsci calls a "fundamental social group," not, in other words, a traditionally Marxist politico-economic class. What is crucial to see, however, is that management, too, is a site of struggle; indeed, attitudes toward management and theories of management are themselves narratives of the political unconscious. Composition scholarship has tended to either obscure or take as a given the administrative function, a tendency with material economic and political consequences for the huge numbers of contingent faculty who teach most first-year writing classes.

My point in arguing that the field's understanding of itself belies traces of a managerial unconscious is not to imply that composition professionals never speak of themselves as administrators or write from the point of view of administrators. A significant body of scholarship on administrative work exists in the field, and the Council of Writing Program Administrators provides a number of forums—including an annual convention, a biannual journal, and an e-mail discussion group—in which administrators regularly discuss their work.[3] It is not the case, by any means, that composition professionals never think of themselves as administrators. It is the case, however, that composition professionals who have sought to tell the story of composition have for the most part avoided framing the story as a tale of the rise of management. As a result, the administrative function, if it appears at all in scholarship, tends to be presented simply as fact rather than as a particular material condition with a history and with material consequences. The stories composition professionals tell about the field, along with the unwritten narratives that serve as warrants for composition theory, can thus be read symptomatically as narratives of the managerial unconscious, narratives that leave unsaid the material struggles that speak them. The field needs new stories, ones that will look more carefully and critically at the material conditions that have made the administration of writing a central feature of the composition profession. Although I cannot, in the space of this essay, offer these new narratives, I can point to one particularly symptomatic kind of narrative—a narrative that elides the distinction between composition professionals and composition teachers—in order to illustrate the rhetorical work of the managerial unconscious and suggest the political possibilities of exposing and strategically deploying the managerial function.

The Conflation of Teaching with Management

A particularly telling symptom of the managerial unconscious is the propagation of a teaching–research dichotomy and the alignment of composition studies with teaching in this dichotomy, an alignment that tends to obscure the managerial function of composition professionals. Horner, for example, alludes to "the by now familiar debates between . . . teaching and research" and expresses some concern that too much emphasis on knowledge production threatens the field's alignment with teaching. Maintaining that some compositionists have attempted to . . . seek academic disciplinary status for Composition by directing their efforts at producing knowledge about writing in general on which composition 'scholars' (or 'researchers') can claim professional expertise," he further contends that "these efforts threaten to distance Composition from its material ties to and identification with teaching (*Terms* 15). Horner does not privilege teaching at the expense of research: He is not, in other words, arguing against knowledge production but is arguing rather against the material and conceptual separation of teaching and research. Still, he clearly identifies teaching as the fundamental material circumstance that has constructed the field's identity.

Lynn Worsham observes that the "will to pedagogy" is one of the dominant "needs and desires governing the field," an imperative that requires "every theory of writing to translate into a pedagogical practice or at least some specific advice for teachers" (98, 96). This alignment with teaching, Worsham argues, leads composition professionals to put theory to use only as a classroom strategy rather than as a tool for critically examining the field's ideological investments—including, I contend, the field's dependence upon its administrative function. In other words, the pedagogical imperative is made possible by a managerial imperative: The production of knowledge about teaching—the will to pedagogy—is made necessary because composition professionals are responsible for *what gets taught:* They preside over the teaching of writing and so produce knowledge to see that it is done in a professionally approved way.

The tendency to dichotomize the duties of a professor—a tendency that is pronounced in but by no means unique to composition studies—overlooks and thus renders invisible a third term with which academics are usually evaluated: service. This third term is generally the catch-all for work that falls outside of teaching classes and publishing scholarship, and it generally counts the least in tenure and promotion decisions. Administrative duties, duties which distinguish the work of composition professionals, traditionally have counted as service. Yet, there seems to be a collective repression of this distinction among composition professionals—and for understandable, self-protective (if perhaps not always conscious) reasons. If a significant part of one's duties involves service, and yet service is the least valued of the three criteria for evaluation, it would make little sense to actively align oneself with that term. Teaching may not be valued as highly as publishing, particularly at research universities, but it is surely valued more than service.[4]

Although an alignment with teaching might thus be understandable, this alignment has tended to conflate teaching with the *management* of teaching. It has made it possible for composition specialists to speak, for example, of the feminization and proletarianization of *composition,* as if the entire field were marginalized because those who teach it—as opposed to those who specialize in it—are economically and ideologically marginalized. Indeed, the teaching of composition *is* feminized—as is evident in the low pay and low status accorded to most teachers of composition (see Holbrook; Susan Miller; Schell, *Gypsy Academics*). However, composition teachers and composition specialists are not always the same people. While scholars holding Ph.D.s in rhetoric and composition studies can usually look forward to reasonably well-paid, tenure-track positions (often, positions managing but not always teaching composition), scholars without this degree (whether holding only a master's degree or a Ph.D. outside of composition) are more likely to teach sections of first-year writing for low pay and little job security.

The conflation of the teaching of composition with the management of composition has led, further, to an odd, politically diversionary debate within the field concerning the necessity of professionalizing composition. Some have argued that fully professionalizing composition will release the field from its marginal status and will thus ensure better working conditions for teachers of composition. In response, others have argued that composition's professional status is less important than ensuring that undergraduates are taught well in their writing classes (see, for example, Harris, *Teaching;* and Horner, *Terms*). The debate, however, is premised again on the conflation of teaching and management, so that what is obscured is that composition studies is already professionalized: The field has its own professional organization, its own journals, its own conferences, and its own terminal degrees. However, this professionalization has benefited the vast majority of those who teach composition far less than it has benefited those who manage the teaching of writing. To suggest that one is unconcerned about professionalism, then, is to speak from a position of privilege, a position that can afford to forget its own professional privilege.

It is this sort of forgetting that makes the managerial unconscious so problematic and insidious. This forgetting means that the managerial unconscious, in that it underlies a privileging of teaching, can continue to operate even in work that would confront the division between the teaching and managing of writing. For example, Harris has recently argued that composition bosses—he takes up James Sledd's terminology—and composition teachers need to forge a class alliance, an argument that is admirable and distinctive in its willingness to confront the administrative function of composition professionals. However, although Harris recognizes that the interests of bosses and teachers are not identical, he nonetheless argues for an area of shared desire:

> Here is where the interests of composition workers and bosses might come together. What the director of a writing program wants, it seems to me, is to be able to interview, hire, and train a teaching staff, to fire teachers who don't work out, to establish curriculum, to set policies, and to represent the program as he or she sees best. What teachers want are reasonable salaries, benefits, working conditions, and job security, autonomy over their work; and to be treated as respect as colleagues. All of us want to provide the best teaching possible for undergraduates. But the treatment of writing teachers in English departments has been a scandal for years, while the authority of composition directors has been consistently compromised to suit the needs of English graduate programs and faculty. It thus seems in our joined interests as composition workers and bosses to press for more direct control over our curricula and staffing—within departments of English or, if need be, outside them. ("Meet the New Boss" 57–58)

While I respect anyone who argues for a new hegemony based on the solidarity of diverse groups, I am wary of this call for collective action "to press for more direct control over *our* curricula and staffing." It seems politically problematic for a self-proclaimed composition boss to set the terms for solidarity and to begin to use the term *our*. Political struggles in the past have shown that *our* too easily means the dominant group, and in this case composition bosses clearly have the upper hand. While it is true that composition specialists do not regularly have adequate power to control the programs that they must direct, a situation that certainly also needs the field's attention, they nonetheless typically have more control—and, quite often, make more money—than teachers.

The managerial unconscious, then, remains at work, and it becomes perhaps more clear when Harris imagines a future workplace: "In return for better working conditions, we need to insist that teachers in our programs keep up with new work in composition and that they revise their practices in light of their reading" ("Meet the New Boss" 57). I by no means wish to suggest that it is somehow a bad idea to ask teachers to read composition scholarship and to use that scholarship to rethink their pedagogical strategies; however, it is clear that the first-person pronoun here no longer refers to bosses and teachers in solidarity.

Rather, "we" (administrators/composition professionals) must make sure that "they" (teachers) keep up with the current scholarship. This argument seems particularly odd given that Harris earlier claims, "I am less worried . . . about the status of composition as a discipline than about whether composition programs treat instructors fairly and teach undergraduates to write well" ("Meet the New Boss" 56). To insist that teachers "keep up with new work in composition" is to enforce a disciplinary imperative; it is to enact one's managerial prerogative. The field of composition studies *is* disciplined, *is* professionalized; otherwise, a growing body of scholarship would not exist. To suggest that it is not, that one's concern is only with the teaching of undergraduates, is to ignore the managerial privilege that the discipline confers on its professionals. I do not intend to put Harris's sincerity into question nor to discredit his desire to find common ground. What I *am* putting into question, however, is the privileging of teaching as a value outside of disciplinary concerns, which thereby obscures the power inherent in the functioning of a managerial unconscious. To demand that teachers keep up with scholarship in the field in exchange for better working conditions is a demand made possible by disciplinary power and the administrative function that underwrites the discipline.

Composition Professionals in the Managed University

Confronting the managerial unconscious seems an especially crucial task for composition specialists at this historical moment, as academics outside of composition are bringing attention to the encroachment of corporate managerial structures into the academy, which has led among other things to the hiring of increasing numbers of administrators and flexible workers and decreasing numbers of tenure-line faculty (see, for example, Martin). Gary Rhoades and Sheila Slaughter have argued that university faculty "are increasingly 'managed professionals,'" whose work lives are subject to managerial "restructuring" (43). At the same time, universities and colleges are hiring increasing numbers of "managerial professionals," who at times displace the more traditional faculty:

> These employees do not fit squarely into the category of *faculty* or *administrator* but constitute an occupational type that bridges conventional categories. They share many characteristics of traditional liberal professions—a technical body of knowledge, advanced education (and in some cases certification), professional associations and journals, and codes of ethics. Yet they also mark a break with the liberal profession of faculty, being more closely linked and subordinate to managers and indeed being very much managers themselves. (49–50)

Based upon this description, composition professionals clearly could be considered managerial professionals. Like the group Rhoades and Slaughter describe, composition professionals fail to fit neatly into traditional categories; they too, when hired to take on administrative duties, are more closely linked to management than are traditional faculty. Moreover, like managerial professionals, composition specialists often find their days "marked by more contact with superiors and subordinates than with peers or clients" (50). At the same time, however, composition specialists rarely are hired to take on a nine-to-five day and only occasionally have an eleven-month contract, two characteristics of managerial professionals' "workday existence" (50). Rather, because composition professionals usually also are required to teach and, depending on the institution, to publish, they officially have schedules like traditional faculty. (Whether or not their days are, in fact, like traditional faculty's is another question.) Composition specialists, then, occupy the border between traditional academic faculty and this new group of managerial professionals. The rather good job prospects that composition specialists face, compared to others in English studies, is no doubt due to the rise of managerial structures in the university rather than to a renewed interest in pedagogical or rhetorical scholarship in colleges and universities. On the flip side, because they must also perform as traditional faculty, they may face difficulties in gaining tenure if their administrative duties have prevented them from actively publishing (see Schuster 87).

In suggesting that composition specialists enjoy relatively good job prospects and in arguing that management looms large in their professional lives, I may seem to be aligning myself with those critics outside of composition studies who characterize members of the field as opportunists (Bové, *Wake* 163), who function as mere "technobureaucrats," imposing what Richard Ohmann has called "administered thought" on students in composition classes (Ohmann, *English in America* 133–71; see also Guillory 79). As a composition specialist myself, I am, rather, working to meet those accusations with something other than silence or outright rejection.

At the same time, my attitude toward the managerial function of composition professionals is not as sanguine as the one Richard E. Miller advocates in *As If Learning Mattered.* Miller, himself a composition professional, has argued that condemnations of composition specialists as "technobureaucrats" are based on a failure to understand the bureaucratic function of *all* university faculty; Miller, it might be said, detects a bureaucratic unconscious functioning broadly in colleges and universities. This unconscious, for Miller, is made possible by "the fanciful notion that learning occurs only under conditions of absolute freedom" (7). These "utopian visions" privilege "the production of critique" over "the administrator's pragmatic decisions," thus rendering any potentially transformative action in the academy impossible (7). Miller argues that all faculty should spend less time "denying, bemoaning, or critiquing" their constraints and should instead embrace their bureaucratic functions, because it is only through this kind of work that anything gets done that would actually benefit students (9).

While I respect Miller's commitment to improving higher education and agree that education has been made to function as a mechanism for "sifting, sorting, and credentialing the otherwise undifferentiated masses"—a function that Michel

Foucault masterfully describes in *Discipline and Punish*—I consider it politically and ethically necessary to maintain a distinction between the managerial function of composition specialists and the broader bureaucratic function of universities that implicates all college and university faculty (Miller, *As If Learning Mattered* 22). To conflate the two seems to me to be a further conflation of teaching and management. Miller seems eager to conflate the two, arguing for example that the anxieties that new teachers experience are based on a kind of "bureaucratic unconscious":

> [T]he absolutely predictable anxiety that emerges around the business of grading papers and the consequent desire to escape to a realm of employment where this work is less carefully scrutinized . . . *must* be read as an expression of distress at discovering the essentially bureaucratic nature of teaching in the academy. (210, Miller's emphasis)

As someone who keenly remembers her own anxiety as a new teacher and who encounters this anxiety with a new group of teaching assistants each fall, I wonder—why *must* this anxiety be read as a response to bureaucracy? Could such anxiety not be read, for example, as a crisis of knowledge, a crisis brought on by lacking the metalanguage to discuss writing? And while it could be argued that the necessity to talk about writing with students is a function of the bureaucratic structure of the university—an argument with which I would not, in principle, disagree—it does not follow that the anxiety itself is produced by a latent discomfort with bureaucracy. To suggest that new teachers worry over the bureaucratic nature of their work more than over the intellectual challenge of their work is to again erase the teacher through a conflation of teaching with management.

In terms of function and actual job descriptions, teaching and managing are simply not the same. Certainly, teaching has bureaucratic dimensions and necessarily takes place within bureaucratic structures. However, to paraphrase Gramsci on intellectuals: All teachers are bureaucrats, one could therefore say: but not all teachers in the academy have the function of managers. Unlike most other faculty in colleges and universities, composition professionals are typically hired to carry out administrative work of a kind that is not expected of traditional faculty. Composition professionals have an *overt* bureaucratic function that they cannot overlook in the way that traditional faculty can overlook their own bureaucratic functioning. To suggest that composition professionals are simply like all other faculty because all faculty are also bureaucrats seems to me to be another manifestation of the managerial unconscious.

In conflating teaching and managing, the managerial unconscious tends to obscure the teacher as an intellectual and social being. Such a claim seems paradoxical, given that one important symptom of the managerial unconscious is the alignment of composition studies with teaching. And yet, this is exactly why the managerial unconscious needs to be exposed and understood. Composition specialists, historically, have produced knowledge about the teaching of composition because they have had to manage the teaching of composition. To conflate specialists/managers and teachers is to substitute administrators' needs for teachers' needs, a substitution that can be economically disastrous for the increasing numbers of contingent faculty who teach composition. It is time, then, for the field to confront the administrative function without glossing over it, taking it as a necessity, or blurring its distinctiveness.

The Managerial Made Conscious

Confronting the managerial unconscious of composition studies will mean, for one thing, a revision of histories of the field in order to make visible the managerial function and the material workplaces in which composition teaching has been done. Such histories should offer composition specialists more detailed maps of the material constraints that have made the field possible. These maps, in turn, should provide a sense of both what has been done and what, given these material constraints, can be done. Like Richard Miller, I, too, would like to see bureaucratic power put to work to enable change. Unlike Miller, however, I consider critique to be an important part of the process—critique, followed by praxis, followed by critique. Without the process of critique, there is no standard by which to assess the efficacy of the change. Without critique, there is no possibility of recognizing the limitations of the changes that have been enacted, no space for continuing to question and to press for greater democratic action.

Along with historical critique, then, the field needs to consider what kind of politically engaged praxis is possible, given the administrative function of composition specialists. If, as Rhoades and Slaughter have suggested, "a return to an imagined past . . . of professional self-governance . . . is highly unlikely," then it seems unlikely that this administrative function will diminish (64). Composition professionals committed to equity and social justice must find ways to infuse administrative work with political meaning and action. Rather than simply taking administrative work as a pragmatic given, which often leads to taking business practices as models, composition specialists are in a unique position to expose the political and economic interests of such models as they reach the academy and to look to models outside of business. Situated at the border between traditional faculty and managerial professionals, composition specialists can use their intellectual function as faculty to critique practices and their managerial function to enact new ones.

And yet, even as I am formulating this possibility, it, too, sounds utopian. To explain what I mean and to demonstrate its grounding in a materialist theory, I need to turn to Gramsci's theory of hegemony, a theory that might be said to contain within it a theory of management. One of the key and yet potentially contradictory terms in Gramsci's *Prison Notebooks* is the verb *dirigere*, which can be translated "to direct" but is also used commonly to mean "to manage."[5] As Gramsci's English translators explain, *dirigere*, in its various conjugations and nominalizations, occurs frequently in Gramsci's writing to refer to two distinct concepts: on the one hand, "power based on domination" and on the other, "the exercise of 'direction' or 'hegemony'" (Hoare and Smith xiii). To direct a group of people can suggest either that one dominates them or that one provides guidance, a leading into a new possibility. Intellectuals, according to Gramsci, provide direction: The question is what sort of intellectual one will be.

Traditional intellectuals, according to Gramsci, are indeed functionaries: "The intellectuals are the dominant group's 'deputies' exercising the subaltern functions of social hegemony and political government" (12). Insofar as composition specialists are simultaneously traditional intellectuals—a group that includes lawyers, priests, and teachers—and business-like administrators, there seems to be little hope that they could perform any sort of politically transformative function, that they could manage in the second sense of Gramsci's *dirigere*. However, Gramsci maintains that in the process of hegemonic struggle, traditional intellectuals must be assimilated (10). In other words, traditional intellectuals, while they cannot properly function as organic intellectuals—intellectuals who remain within the class they would lead—can and must nonetheless function as ideological allies in a hegemonic struggle. Moreover, these intellectuals can direct the political action of their peers, providing, as Chantal Mouffe says, vocabulary for the struggle. What is critical is not to mistake oneself as something one is not: specialists who direct writing programs are not economically marginalized laborers. Still, it is possible to reflect critically on one's position and to provide intellectual support and, where appropriate, political leadership (especially to peers, other intellectuals, and the professional-managerial class more generally).

To uncover the managerial unconscious, then, could mean an alliance between composition specialists and composition teachers that creates space for intellectual exchange and action based on that exchange rather than imposing knowledge and action. Above all, it should mean an alliance that privileges teaching *along with teachers,* making visible rather than concealing their labor. For if an alliance is possible, it must be based on teachers' needs and desires, something that can be possible only if composition specialists come to terms with the constraints of their administrative function.

Notes

1. See my "Taking Dictation" for a more detailed analysis of the material conditions that have made possible the workplace of composition, and, by extension, composition studies itself.

2. In saying that Horner privileges teaching, I am simplifying considerably what is really a complex and nuanced argument. Horner distinguishes three meanings of work in composition studies: work as the workplace in which composition teaching is done; work as one's "own" work—that is, one's own scholarship; and work as teaching (*Terms* 1). Horner's concern is that the first two tend to obscure the third.

3. Recent contributions to this body of scholarship include collections edited by Diana George, by Shirley K. Rose and Irwin Weiser, and by Irene Ward and William J. Carpenter.

4. See the Council of Writing Program Administrators' Intellectual Work document, in which various facets of an administrator's work are strategically defined as research or teaching rather than service.

5. My thanks go to Sonia Brighenti, who confirmed this usage of *dirigere*.

4
Global Capitalism, Scientific Management, and Disciplinary English

David B. Downing

In the summer of 1996, I collaborated with a group of seven colleagues at Indiana University of Pennsylvania to investigate a possible new track for our doctoral programs in English.[1] Our intention was to create a more integrated model of graduate study called "Teaching the Writing and Reading of Cultures." We were excited about this possibility precisely because it drew on courses in our department's existing doctoral programs: Literature and Criticism and Rhetoric and Linguistics. It required very little in the way of added funding, faculty, or departmental staff and resources. We anticipated correctly that our proposal would meet administration's cost-effectiveness impulses because it adhered to bureaucratic imperatives to get more from less. We developed a detailed rationale, mission statement, and core curriculum based on a combination of courses drawn from the existing doctoral programs. Our goal was to open a new possibility for students to link reading and writing, literature and composition, poetics and rhetorics, and teaching and research, in ways that the separate programs prohibited.

The existence of two independent, parallel doctoral programs at Indiana University of Pennsylvania, of course, reflects the long-standing divisions in English studies between literature and composition. Our initiative to provide an integrated, alternative track rested largely upon assumptions that perhaps we could negotiate an effective middle ground that, on one hand, allowed for the subdisciplinary integrity of each specialty, and, on the other, opened an integrated possibility for those students interested in a generalist degree. Our group failed even to get this proposal considered by the two program committees. This may reflect what was our inexperience in departmental politics, but it also points to a widely shared fear of blurring disciplinary borders and losing program identities when the institution has organized programs to compete with each other for limited resources. Our experience stands in stark contrast to the extensive curricular changes

Stephen M. North describes at State University of New York–Albany where, for a period of time at least, the English department managed to institutionalize his version of a "fusion-based" curriculum for graduate English studies.

Although not successful, our intense summer collaboration helped our group better understand the obstacles that confront any effort to heal the split between literature and composition, poetics and rhetorics, and reading and writing. The eight of us involved in this abortive curricular experiment drew somewhat different, and sometimes painful, conclusions from the events that transpired, and we also came to share a sense of key issues that transcend local politics. That's what this article is about, at least as told from my perspective.

For one thing, most of us abandoned our hopes that we could reach our goal through an act of disciplinary tinkering. That is, we came to believe that any successful curricular integration of reading and writing would require getting beyond the dominance of the whole disciplinary apparatus of the modern university. As ambitious as that project sounds, it helps to recognize that curricular innovations linking cultural, rhetorical, and composition studies are moving in that direction already. Unfortunately, disciplinary practices still serve to measure success and failure in our profession in ways that often prohibit or defeat the kinds of innovations towards which many of us would like to work. Although the extent of the problem varies considerably from institution to institution, this is a profession-wide story about how all in English studies labor under disciplinary conditions. This essay articulates what such disciplinary reform might call for and how we might go about making such changes.

The Disciplinary Split Between Reading and Writing

The relation of discipline to curricular design is complicated because a kind of endemic instability characterizes the discipline of English.[2] Indeed, making English into a respectable academic discipline that could organize a coherent curriculum has generally been a contentious project.[3] English professors have struggled, at times with success but often with great difficulty, to adapt what they do to disciplinary practices, such as identifying stable bodies of knowledge and methodically verifying truth claims, practices better suited to the needs of scientists.[4]

Historically speaking, it wasn't always the case that disciplines served to structure curricula. Prior to the rise of what Keith W. Hoskin calls the "ecosystem" of disciplinarity in the late-nineteenth century, curricula were determined not by disciplinary but by moral and ethical criteria. Indeed, the origins of disciplinarity in the modern sense involved a significant transformation of the meaning of the term *discipline* as it had been used in colleges prior to the Civil War. As Lawrence R. Veysey explains, prior to the academic transformation of knowledge in the last quarter of the nineteenth century, academic "discipline" referred to moral rules of piety and conduct as in the "mental discipline" necessary to build character:

> Under the banner of "mental discipline," a phrase which referred to the sharpening of young men's faculties through enforced contact with Greek and Latin

grammar and mathematics, the old-time college sought to provide a four-year regime conducive to piety and strength of character. (9)

Belief in such "mental discipline was part of an interlocking set of psychological, theological, and moral convictions" (22). Because in 1870 only about 2 percent of the population in America attended college (Lucas 204), the consequences of such mental discipline served as one possible means to accrue and secure the social status of the ruling classes for those who could afford such luxury as higher education.[5]

With the dramatic increase in scientific investigations, the traditional college curriculum based on the classics and mathematics no longer served to represent the expanding domains of knowledge. Drawing on the models of German universities that had already begun to reshape knowledge, the American universities began a process of academic reform leading up to the departmentalized, hierarchical university structure that virtually all postsecondary institutions had adopted by the early part of the twentieth century. The new curriculum replaced the moral sense of mental discipline with an institutional structure of specific fields of disciplined knowledge, based not on piety but on the "disinterested pursuit of truth" as best exemplified by scientific fields. The research ideal became the dominant model of university work, but, as Richard Ohmann points out, "the central authority behind this concerted transformation was mainly that of the unseen hand that guides a laissez faire economy" (*English in America* 288).

The force of the new curriculum for administering and defining separate fields of departmentalized knowledge as the distinguishing feature of postsecondary education has enabled it to persist in relatively stable form despite the otherwise dramatic shifts in higher education during the past century. As distinguished from its common use as a synonym for the field or profession, the more specialized function of the discipline has fundamentally shaped the divisions between literature and composition. I focus here on just three key characteristics of the institutional mechanisms of disciplinarity: (1) a discipline is constituted by a specific body of knowledge, the *object* of the discipline; (2) the stability of that knowledge is produced, constituted, and warranted by application of specific, identifiable *methods;* and (3) all methods deployed depend on prior protocols for argumentation: refutation, verification, and falsification as rhetorical acts necessary to test and delimit the claims of practitioners. In the case of English, the informal logic of these protocols derives primarily from the more formal logic of the sciences and their ability to produce reliable forms of knowledge (Sosnoski, *Modern*). This means that expository forms of argumentation take precedence over all other imaginative, narrative, figural, or textual innovations.[6]

Although the strict processes of disciplining have become the quintessential measure of academic value, the institutionalized protocols for disciplinary practices often exclude or delimit a significant range of socially valuable intellectual labor.[7] This is especially the case for certain activities many English practitioners perform: research or teaching that focuses on ameliorating the local needs of specific groups of people, process-oriented work, research that does not narrowly define objects of investigation, work that engages rhetorical modes other than expository argumentation, or writing for broad audiences through publication in nonacademic magazines and books (a feather for academic celebrities but a risk for junior faculty seeking tenure credentials). In English departments, disciplinarity both facilitates and justifies the subordination of writing to literature, even though, ironically, writing serves a fundamental role in the practices of examining and grading across all disciplines (Hoskin). The institutional principles of disciplinary knowledge produce what Ellen Messer-Davidow, David R. Shumway, and David J. Sylvan call "economies of value" that will always favor those domains in which the objects of knowledge, such as literary texts (or, as in the disciplining of cultural studies, cultural texts), can be more successfully designated than the "processes" of composing.

The guild nature of the disciplines means that the expository arguments suitable for scholarly publication produce knowledge if those arguments can be measured or "refereed" by an audience of trained professionals (who might be considerably divorced from the local contexts and issues). As Ohmann puts it, disciplinary practices re-enforce "loyalty to the guild rather than to the college or university" (*English in America* 220), or to the students or the local community or the public, for that matter. The disciplinary measure of success, therefore, purposefully displaces any accountability to people immediately affected by a practical innovation, such as the development of an interactive Web site linking local high school, community college, and university English departments in a collaborative network. Although it is no doubt possible to give credit for such work, disciplinary pressure will inevitably tend to give greater significance to the published article about the Web site than reward those who created it and participated in its ongoing success. From the opposite direction, efforts to speak beyond the disciplinary guild to nonacademic audiences also run the risk of being unscholarly, and these risks persist despite an increasing concern within the profession to gain what Michael Bérubé calls "public access." Such instances register forms of disciplinary injustice, although in other contexts such disciplinary distancing of local interests from broader knowledge claims has tremendous value for certain kinds of work. Argument is what the academy does best, and as John Michael contends, becoming "masters of our specific disciplinary technologies" is part of what it means to be a critical intellectual in the contemporary world (3). When claims for knowledge are in dispute, disciplines can serve as critical arbiters for equality, even though race, class, and gender differences as well as corporate interests often compromise claims of disciplinary autonomy. Non- or postdisciplinary activities will be in tension with disciplinary forms of argumentation, so the hard work will always depend on understanding when and for whom the discipline provides a measure of justice.

The picture is especially complicated in English because of the range of professional tasks we regularly perform. However permeable they may sometimes seem, disciplinary conditions establish the parameters for narrowing that range: Academic value accrues to those practices that can more fully specify the primary objects of study, such as literary or cultural texts, as well as the secondary critical methods for producing knowledge about those objects through expository prose. It simultaneously devalues the rhetorical practices of poetic, aesthetic, and imaginative forms of discourse and artistic production. Even though, as James A. Berlin has argued, poetics took precedence over rhetoric, it did so not as the active creation *of* poetic texts but through the secondary activity of publishing expository arguments *about* poetic texts themselves. Consequently, the domination within institutional evaluation practices of disciplinary discourse has often meant the crippling and devaluing of some of our most crucial concrete labor practices.

By the early-twentieth century, the basic disciplinary principles guided the formation of distinct academic departments, defining specialized fields and sub-fields according to their specific objects and methods as the distinguishing feature of the modern university. At the same time, what is perhaps most striking in the three primary characteristics of disciplines is the complete absence of any reference to business, labor, race, class, or gender differences. What has long been considered the key virtue of the disciplinary system is its resistance to market forces or the winds of cultural change. As Menand explains, many academics in the early part of the century argued that protecting the disciplines "against market forces is the only way of elevating excellence over profits in a capitalist economy." In the late-nineteenth-century economy, which was "driven by efficiency and self-interest," the disciplines "set standards for performance that value quality over dollars" ("Demise" 203). To varying degrees, disciplines did and still do provide some measure of resistance to market forces by providing semi-autonomous academic realms where some people who work in English have considerable freedom in terms of concrete labor practices.

It is also true, however, that the disciplines were deeply compromised from the beginning by the material conditions of capitalism, and, as Ohmann first argued, the disciplines were adapted to serve precisely those forces they were supposed to protect against. The disciplinary principles were exactly those that could be appropriated and best serve the principles of scientific management as developed by Frederick Taylor and Henry Ford.[8] One of the most significant consequences of these academic appropriations of corporate models was that teaching became subordinated to research because it was easier to commodify and manage by standardizing and quantifying disciplinary knowledge production than the quality of teaching.

Working under the conditions of managed disciplinarity, English departments grew dramatically in symbiosis with the tremendous growth of the university in the first half of the twentieth century. Despite the statistical successes in rising numbers of faculty and students, English professors competed for disciplinary justifications equal to those of the sciences, even while the intellectual tasks of English professors did not always measure up to disciplinary criteria. The most painful disciplinary squeeze happened to writing practices, even though they were the skills most highly in demand. In order to identify objects and methods as well as literature professors did, composition specialists had little choice but to adapt accordingly. Disciplinary pressure for such specification led to the predominance of what Berlin has called "current-traditional" rhetoric with its dependence on measurable formalist skills (the methods) and quantifiable grammatical errors (the objects). Such formalist adaptations of rhetoric to disciplinary criteria meant a noticeable reduction in the range of writing practices at all levels with, of course, dire consequences for the politics of writing specialists within English departments (Ohmann; Scholes; Winterowd). Because *literature* had become a privileged term in cultural discourse since the Romantic period (1770–1830), it could better meet the requirements for disciplinary discourse. This was particularly the case when the corporate models of management were tied to the political mission of the nation-states, and literature could be seen to inculcate a form of nationalist identity and cultural pride (Readings).

The principles of scientific management had thereby adapted the disciplinary conditions for the production of knowledge. Teaching became so clearly subordinated to research that, for instance, the Modern Language Association of America abandoned teaching in 1916 by revising a clause in the constitution that originally described "the object of the Association as 'the advancement of the *study* of the Modern languages and their literatures'" to read "the advancement of *research* in the Modern languages and their literatures" (Graff, *Professing* 121, Graff's emphasis). With its formation in 1911, the National Council of Teachers of English became the home for teaching and writing in the profession, and the basic splits between composition and literature and between teaching and research became solidified as prestige accrued, naturally enough, to the more disciplinary forms of literary research.

Historical studies such as that of Gerald Graff, David Shumway, Arthur Applebee, Vincent B. Leitch, and others document the intellectual content of the battles to make the unruly field of the literary into a respectable academic discipline with the rise of New Criticism during the period from 1900 to 1945. What is relevant here is that the basic principles of New Criticism gave rise to the greatest period of disciplinary stability for English departments. They authorized English departments to develop curricula that enabled them to define their objects and methods, the primary characteristics of disciplinary discourse, with almost as much confidence as the sciences. Ideological claims for the spiritual richness of the unmediated, unparaphraseable verbal icon of the poetic experience justified study of the intrinsic properties of the text as an object of knowledge, but the ideological claims mattered far less than the powerfully consistent disciplinary practices that became institutionalized in everyday use. Although the New Critics themselves evidenced a much wider range of ideological beliefs about the transcendent values of literary art than many of their critics have acknowledged, their curricular successes depended less on such literary values as upon their working practices with respect to the discipline. In short, with literature as the object, close reading as the method, and expository critical writing about canonized texts as the verifiable procedures for producing knowledge, the program for an English major could now be succinctly mapped by organizing courses on the periods and genres of English and American literature.[9]

However, the categories of difference among the disciplinary objects and the workers in the profession tend to be forgotten. No one needed to pay attention to the circumstance that the profession of literary studies "was for all practical purposes a brotherhood based on race, citizenship, and class, bound together by what might be called, in a play on both its literal and figurative senses, the old school tie" (North, *Refiguring* 22). Indeed, as Messer-Davidow, Shumway, and Sylvan point out, "disciplines produce practitioners," and the orthodox brotherhood that ruled English departments in the first half of this century produced practitioners with a remarkable consistency of race, class, and gender characteristics. Such homogeneity also ensured an underlying disciplinary consistency as well.

With college enrollments nearly quadrupling between 1945 and 1970, the basic inequities of the disciplinary system of English could be tolerated, if not camouflaged, by the postwar economic boom in corporate America. Challenges to the system from new areas of investigation, such as women's studies and African American studies, could be addressed by adding to the existing curriculum without fundamentally changing the orthodox curriculum of literary periods and genres, because there were always enough students to fill whatever classes were offered. Moreover, the corporate structuring of disciplinary hierarchy consolidated itself during the period of New Critical hegemony. North describes how undergraduate and graduate English education took the shape of what he calls "College English Teaching, Inc." In this system, tenured senior professors replicate themselves through apprenticeship programs whereby graduate students teach the composition courses while professors develop literary research in graduate seminars. The ongoing corporate need for writing skills could thus be met in a system calling for increased numbers of Ph.D.s even when graduate training itself had nothing to do with teaching or writing. In short, the discipline set the criteria by which the less-disciplined could be exploited, and in times of relative bounty, few complained vociferously. By the late 1970s, however, College English Teaching, Inc. began to experience deeper signs of crisis.

Flexible Accumulation and Disciplining Class Differences

David Harvey's description of the restructuring of the labor market provides a remarkably precise account of the past thirty years in English departments: A shrinking core of tenured faculty preside over an expanding array of part-time, temporary instructors and graduate students. As Ohmann puts it in his 1996 reissuing of *English in America*, "English has, it would almost seem, served as a small laboratory for innovative uses of flexible labor" (xxxix). These flexible labor practices affect our views about potential curricular reform and the discipline of

English. In times of economic contraction, budget restraint, and the exploitation of part-time labor, one can understand the drive to shore up the discipline, to make English stronger by rigorously defining its subject matter and precisely identifying its subdisciplines. Academics seek, that is, to resist administrative budget cuts and loss of tenure-track faculty by resorting to the traditional mechanism of resisting market forces: disciplinarity. If we could just define our objects more precisely and our methods more specifically, disciplinary integrity should justify our preservation, if not expansion. If we could appear less soft as intellectual dilettantes and more hard as knowledge-producing researchers, then the sharpness of our rhetoric will have more political effect in staying the course against market pressures. At least that's the hope, and sometimes, in strategic places at the right time, it has the desired effect.

Here is the problem. Disciplinarity works better for disciplines, especially the sciences, where specificity and rigor have direct consequences on the securing of grants and endorsements. The "better" the discipline, the better able it is to attract funding agencies. Administrators have not lost sight of this accounting.[10] Disciplinary research in the humanities does not generally produce short-term revenues, and large numbers of full-time English researchers is costly; however, writing, the one marketable skill that everyone needs, gets staffed by less-disciplined, part-time employees. Historically devalued by disciplinary criteria favoring literature, writing is called for by market forces as a skill necessary for any corporate task. Flexible accumulation favors separating writing into smaller, independent units or programs, so that the smaller unit can then be more quickly fine-tuned to shifting market needs, whether towards electronic forms of literacy, professional writing, technical writing, or business writing. We will be hard-pressed to argue that more disciplinary rigor and specialization will heal the wounds that our disciplinary history has produced.

As composition theorists have argued for years, teaching writing and reading at any level calls for all the skills, resources, lore, and knowledge of a wide range of activities and practices, even though some forms of disciplinary criteria may not highly honor such work. These scholars call for specialists to teach, write, and research and to develop links among those activities. As Steven Mailloux has argued:

> A multi-disciplinary coalition of rhetoricians will help consolidate the work in written and spoken rhetoric, histories of literacies and communication technologies, and the cultural study of graphic, audio, visual, and digital media. (23)

In order for such coalitions to happen, however, it will have to go beyond disciplinary specializations, not by negating them, but by recognizing that a broader spectrum of intellectual and rhetorical practices will never be fully accountable under strictly disciplinary criteria of evaluation.

There are also political and intellectual reasons that smaller disciplinary units (or writing, literature, or cultural studies) cut their group members off from the support of their peers. Of course, short-term gains to such compartmentalized subfields can accrue, as evidenced by the history of literary elitism and conde-scension to compositionists. The long-term consequences of this elitism will eventually cast literary separatists into what James J. Sosnoski has called the "un-derworld of the university system" (*Modern* 29). There is little in the long-term economic future to sustain such privileges. The aesthetic and the political, the literary and the rhetorical, the textual and the extratextual are deeply entwined, and their disciplinary separation has been costly. Administrators out to cut bud-gets are the only ones to gain from the internecine warfare among competing subdivisions. In the end, disciplinary isolation makes any small unit or program more vulnerable to administrative surveillance.[11]

Curricular innovations from literary scholars, even when they claim to break down the hierarchies between reading and writing, often disable the institutional force of their worthy innovations by insisting on, as Robert Scholes puts it, "making English studies more rather than less disciplined" (108). Two signifi-cant proposals for curricular reform—Scholes's own curricular model for English studies and Paul Jay's important work on globalizing literary studies—do not sufficiently alter the institutional role of the discipline of English studies. Because neither addresses disciplinarity as the precondition for curricular change, the fine changes that they do recommend will not adequately respond to the increased class differences emerging from the uses and abuses of academic labor.

Scholes's proposal for a reformed English curriculum has many attractive fea-tures, all aimed at linking reading and writing, which he calls consumption and production. He proposes a return to the classic trivium of grammar, dialectic, and rhetoric, and he describes an attractive array of new courses investigating these key terms. Under the new rigors of his disciplinary trivium, he proposes a "re-alignment [of] two types of canonicity . . . between canons of texts and canons of methods" (111). It should be clear from my previous discussion of the rise of disciplinarity that realigning objects and methods will indeed alter the content of the discipline, but it will not significantly alter the conditions for disciplinary discourse because "methods" is one of the central characteristics of disciplinary discourse.[12] Scholes grants that "discipline, like canon, is a word that scarcely conceals its potential for abuses of power. We need disciplines in order to think productively. We also need to challenge them in order to think creatively" (108). This a wise admonition, though disciplines are not a necessary or sufficient pre-requisite to think productively.

Within English departments, the key points of contact for the exercise of disciplinary power take place through evaluation committees and hiring com-mittees and the particular criteria they deploy to make crucial personnel deci-sions. Disciplinary evaluation criteria become measures of competitive individu-alism as colleagues strive to acquire symbolic capital primarily through their publications and other forms of acceptable labor. Without significant alteration, disciplinarity both discourages and devalues the kinds of collaboration necessary for many of the diverse forms of rhetorical, political, and intellectual work that

English professors actually perform. Without considerable study of how to alter our evaluation practices, disciplinary criteria reign in powerful de facto ways. Scholes's analysis focuses on curricular content and method and leaves routine disciplinary evaluation practices in place: As he puts it again, he wants to make English "more rather than less disciplinary."[13]

Although Scholes claims that "the skill of a writer is a happy one because it is based upon play" (102), disciplinarity doesn't often value play unless it produces "serious" forms of knowledge in expository prose that clearly identifies its own objects and methods. Disciplinary criteria will, for example, more highly value an expository article *about* a highly playful and innovative performative literacy event such as a collaborative improvisation by students and faculty at the local writing center but not the event itself. By not revising the basic conditions of disciplinarity, Scholes's curriculum will diminish the value of certain forms of labor that he himself says he values. That is, the power of disciplinarity is such that various kinds of textual and rhetorical innovations, multimedia studies, pedagogical experimentation, collaborative teaching and research projects, and community-literacy endeavors will continue to be subordinated in value even though they may have considerable social and market value for some forms of business. Such hierarchies of value get, as it were, naturalized into the criteria deployed in the evaluation and hiring committees.

With respect to the wider university and public, I find Scholes's use of the "medieval trivium" of "grammar, dialectic, and rhetoric" a troublesome set of terms to "sell," which of course we must do because we need to exercise control over the commodification of our interests. Without more substantial revision of the conditions of disciplinarity accompanying Scholes's reformed curriculum, there is nothing to prevent the new organizational terms from adapting to traditional disciplinary hierarchies. Teachers engaged in various kinds of non-, extra-, or postdisciplinary forms of investigation calling for collaboration with students to improve their learning and their contributions to local communities will find their work diminished by strictly disciplinary criteria. Without a fair assessment of the value of these other activities as determined by nondisciplinary criteria, the disciplinary practices will ensure that a small core of highly trained faculty will have the resources to study the complicated terrain of dialectics and rhetoric, while many of the most valuable practices of most faculty will continue to be devalued or forced to adapt to back-to-the-basics forms of grammar where they can be more easily exploited in a flexible market. Nondisciplinary practices will likely remain subordinated within Scholes's model of English unless disciplinary reform accompanies the curricular remodeling.

In a recent *PMLA* essay, provocatively entitled "Beyond Discipline? Globalization and the Future of English," Paul Jay demonstrates the limits of the older, dominant "nationalist paradigm" for literary study as exemplified by Scholes's articulation of the "story of English." Like Scholes, Jay advocates the need to expand and alter the basic content of the discipline of English to reflect a new, more-proper emphasis on "literature's relation to the historical processes of globalization" (33). He advances the

> need to make a programmatic commitment to the study of English in a newer, global framework, one that recognizes the transnational character of English in the past and the global context in which it will be produced in the future. (46)

In themselves, these are superb goals designed to stretch the borders of the discipline, because, as Jay comments, without "such a commitment, we may see the discipline of English become ever more marginal, in the university of the future" (46). However important such expanding borders must inevitably be, Jay's title is ironic to the extent that it should really read: "Beyond the Current Content of the Discipline of English Literary Studies." The changes he recommends do not get "beyond" disciplinary English at all in the sense in which I am arguing that we must. That is, although Jay mentions that writing and composition are equally important and that he only excludes them for purposes of space in his article, Jay does not envision any particular change in the disciplinary practices as I have outlined them in this essay. He advocates remapping the literary terrain, in order to "develop new terms and paradigms to describe what we do" (44). However, as I have argued elsewhere, paradigms themselves inevitably call for a reassertion of the hierarchy of disciplinary forms (Downing, "Mop-up"). Moreover, whether one teaches Hawthorne or Achebe will likely not matter so much in terms of public accountability if the pressing need is for literacy and rhetorical skills. As Evan Watkins puts it:

> Just as a political praxis of change is not only a matter of inventing new concrete work practices, it is not a matter either of changing the texts we teach, reforming the "canon." Such reform can of course be made part of a "war of position," but the point is that it must be *made* so against the working organization of English. (*Work Time* 27)

Bracketing off the literary skills from the literacy component strikes at the core of the disciplinary problem in realigning curricula. The disciplinary presumptions of Jay lead him to focus primarily on a shifting of the objects (texts) and methods (theories) of the discipline. However, the human contexts of many of our workplaces are now for the most part so crossed by the international mix of student and faculty populations, that the kinds of writing tasks, narratives, stories, and investigations need to be integrated directly into the work of curricular reform at the beginning, not after the content has been shifted.

North offers one of the few models for what he has called the fusion option for reinvigorating English studies, and I share his assessment that without the hard work of rebuilding the subdisciplinary splits that have characterized the history of the profession, we will not even be able to "*begin* the negotiations that might result in substantive change" (*Refiguring* 237). Besides healing the disciplinary splits within the field, this kind of broader institutional reform aims not only to legitimize emergent kinds of postdisciplinary academic work but to recognize many practices that are already taking place but that have been systematically devalued. Such practices may always be challenges to, and in tension with, strictly disciplinary forms of academic research, which is as it should be so long as disciplinary research does not continue to get preferential treatment.

Although the current crisis of English studies has been most commonly seen as evolving out of a need to expand the objects and methods of the discipline, my argument calls for the more fundamental task of altering the strictly hierarchical role of disciplinarity itself in determining the range of institutionally authorized labor practices of English professors. It will be best to see the range of tasks carried out by English professors along a horizontal spectrum from disciplinary to non- or postdisciplinary practices, with different kinds of evaluative criteria appropriate for different kinds of work. This argument raises large questions about the material processes whereby certain kinds of professorial labor get legitimized and authorized within our specific institutions. Significant curricular reform will depend upon our success in altering some of the basic institutional practices that we have long taken for granted. It is time for a change at this basic level.

My more ambitious claim is that, in the case of English, we may have reached the end of the 125-year history where disciplinary criteria should continue to be the exclusive measure of academic performance and curricular design. This involves more than just expanding the borders of the canon or becoming increasingly interdisciplinary, no matter how vital such practices may be to curricular transformation. Although we cannot easily alter the market forces in the current regime of "flexible accumulation," we can design curricula that more fully integrate reading and writing practices so that we can resist the isolation and exploitation of what Sosnoski so aptly calls "token professionals" *(Token)*, a large segment of our professional ranks whose labor never quite counts for much under strictly disciplinary criteria. The ultimate irony of such reforms might be that by making the range of our professional practices more flexible than the focus on disciplinary criteria might otherwise allow, we regain some of the autonomy that would enable us to heal the class differences within the profession. We simply do not have any choice about whether we will experience economic flexibility because that is a rapidly globalizing phenomenon of the contemporary social and cultural marketplace in which we must operate. We must draw on the spaces of relative autonomy still left to us to determine as far as possible the terms of how that flexibility will affect us. One would hope, therefore, that reformed and integrated curricula could better resist the "flexible accumulation" carried out by management practices that have used disciplinary justifications to further the exploitation of nondisciplinary peripheral labor. Of course, none of this will be easy, but that is the hard political work of disciplinary and curricular revision.

The arts and the humanities have always entailed more than disciplinary discourse, and this imaginative and rhetorical excess accounts for the uneasy relations in the disciplinary status of English studies.[14] Given the wide-ranging economic, social, and technological changes taking place in our culture, it becomes possible to see humanistic work as engaging a spectrum of practices that take place along a horizontal continuum from disciplinary to postdisciplinary, or even antidisciplinary modes. This continuum need not be hierarchical but differential. Obviously, hierarchies of value will continue to be exercised, because the basic evaluative task of professionals is to make such judgments, but they need not emerge on the predominant disciplinary scale. Because disciplinary constraints can sometimes foster forms of social injustice, the production of knowledge may need to be subordinated to the search for justice and understanding. We need not, therefore, require that all humanistic literacy practices fit within the system of disciplinary forms of argumentation and exclusion. Fundamental to such an integrated vision of English studies will be a thorough refiguring of the role of writing in both graduate and undergraduate education.

If our concern for reforming English studies resonates with a commitment to equitable labor conditions, this essay is a cautionary tale with a potentially happier ending. There are possibilities for retooling evaluation practices and revisioning humanities labor as running across a spectrum of disciplinary and non-, extra-, or postdisciplinary activities that need not be measured according to a single disciplinary yardstick. And the human labor involved in these practices calls for revaluations throughout our professional ranks as we reimagine the activities of reading and writing our cultures for a better future.

Notes

This chapter appeared previously as "Beyond Disciplinary English" and is reprinted by permission from *Beyond English, Inc.: Integrating Reading and Writing by Reforming Academic Labor* edited by D. Downing, C. M. Hurlbert, and P. Mathieu. Published by Boynton/Cook Publishers, Inc., a subsidiary of Reed Elsevier, Inc., Portsmouth, NH.

1. The participants were: Susan Marguerite Comfort, myself, Maurice Kilwein Guevara, Thomas J. Slater, and Roxann Wheeler from the Literature and Criticism Program; and Claude Mark Hurlbert, Donald A. McAndrew, and Gian S. Pagnucci from the Rhetoric and Linguistics Program.

2. The term *discipline* is used in sometimes contradictory ways. Although many people use the term as a synonym for the *field* or *profession,* this general use is often confused with a narrower and research-based sense of the term as it applies to academic work. In this second sense, *discipline* refers to the specific conditions of disciplinary discourse that have evolved over roughly the past 130 years (see Hoskin). For this essay, I use the term *discipline* to refer to the latter, narrower, more specific set of practices within the broader range of professional work.

3. See Bérubé, Goggin, Graff, North, and Raymond.

4. Steven Mailloux cites Hans-Georg Gadamer as a prominent rhetorician and philosopher who

> rejects the methodological model of the natural sciences as an accurate description of the disciplinary practices of the human sciences. . . . The methodological techne of the natural sciences is simply inadequate as a model for understanding the tradition-embedded phronesis of the human sciences. (14)

5. Graff complicates the general overview I have briefly summarized here, and his qualifications are crucial:

> But though the college spoke for the ruling class, it was a ruling class that felt curiously displaced from the rising sources of power and influence [since] education was not even a necessary prerequisite for the professions it trained men in. . . . Consequently, as industrialization proceeded, the gulf widened between the college and American life. (*Professing* 21)

6. For the scope of this article, I work with only three characteristics of a discipline. There are more. I have drawn especially on the works of Sosnoski, Shumway, Messer-Davidow, Hoskin, Toulmin, Foucault, and Bové.

7. Ellen Messer-Davidow, David Shumway, and David Sylvan explain in the preface to *Knowledges: Historical and Critical Studies in Disciplinarity* that "as inquiry came to assume a disciplinary form, alternative configurations of knowledge were excluded" (viii).

8. Claude Mark Hurlbert, Paula A. Mathieu, and I provide a somewhat more-detailed overview of these economic shifts in higher education in a section called "The Rise of English Incorporated" in *Beyond English, Inc.,* 4–10. See also Barrow.

9. Ohmann notes that, by 1970, there was considerable variation within English departments in America. Despite these variations, the curricula "have a common basis" (*English in America* 222), a disciplinary basis.

10. Christopher Lucas explains that

> while private colleges were left largely to their own devices, the public sector in higher education by the mid-1990s was struggling to accommodate to a level and intensity of state surveillance and supervision unlike anything to which traditionally it had been accustomed. (237)

11. A prominent composition specialist, David Bartholomae has in a recent *PMLA* article echoed the same concerns for integration rather than fragmentation of interests:

> Changes in English departments, however, will require a new politics. The divisions within English severely limit our ability to argue locally and nationally for the importance of our work. The interests of English are greater than the interests of our various field identifications, and, although the interests of English are difficult to articulate or to name, they certainly include work on behalf of 'literature in the making.' (1954)

Indeed, the difficulties of naming, articulating, and identifying our specialties are disciplinary-specific problems that need not always dominate our discussion of the labor and work we do as English professionals. The "new politics" means that we will have to take whatever relative autonomy we may have in our specific institutional locations to form bridges between different specialties and interests and the different kinds of tasks suitable for those differing interests.

12. Scholes explains his goal "to reconstruct our field as a discipline," suggesting his investment in disciplinary discourse. His answer, "to put it in grossly simplified form, is to replace the canon of texts with a canon of methods—to put a modern equivalent of the medieval trivium at the center of an English education" (145).

13. It is also the case that a wide range of professional resources must be established and developed to support all the various kinds of non- and postdisciplinary activities needed for wide-scale curricular reform. These would include new kinds of journals, Web sites, conferences, online networks, all supporting alternative kinds of reading and writing practices.

14. Although some may lament the "demise of disciplinary authority" (Menand, "Demise"), it might be better to think of it as the demise of the exclusive reign of one form of knowledge and, thus, opening university spaces for new kinds of practices that are valuable to the public in general and that are well-suited to being carried out within the more broadly conceived role of the university in the contemporary world.

5

From Adelphi to Enron—and Back

Paul Lauter

I want to begin from a slightly longer-term perspective than that provided by, for instance, the debate over whether or not to buy into the market model that now passes for common sense even in the academy. I will elaborate on what I mean by *market model* as I go along, but for now, I'll limit the definition to the idea that what sells is the only meaningful criterion of value. The question for me is when and how that idea came to be hegemonic, the interests it serves, and whether it can be displaced. In other words, can we identify the processes that put us in the pickle vat and the means for eventually climbing out?

Symptoms: It was only in the mid-1970s that "non-tenure-track positions," as they have come to be called, were instituted. Prior to that time, it was almost always the case that faculty achieved tenure or its equivalent upon appointment to an eighth full-time year of teaching at the same institution. At about the same time, retrenchment procedures that had largely been dormant and other management tactics designed to achieve institutional "flexibility" began to be deployed.[1] Similarly, the systematic exploitation of part-timers began and soon reached a scale sufficiently large to make colleges and universities, like Macy's and UPS, utterly dependent on the "savings" entailed in having courses taught for $800 to $1200 that might otherwise cost $5,000 to $8,000 plus over 30 percent for benefits.[2] These and other changes in the management of academic institutions emerged, that is, in the context of the efforts of the Nixon administration to make American business more competitive internationally by pushing downward on the standard of living even as it implicitly blamed the worsening position of American (white) working people on War-on-Poverty policies that supposedly shifted available funds to (undeserving) minorities. The mid-1970s also saw the emergence of right-wing think tanks, like the Heritage Foundation (1973), from which have flowed an endless well-funded stream of ideological statements and policy proposals justifying the "liberation" of markets from regulators (commissars) or from constraints imposed by well-meaning reformers (liberals).

I cannot offer here a thorough-going analysis of the processes by which free-market ideology and the regime of flexible capitalism have become dominant.[3] The changes taking place in the academy are part and parcel of those broader transformations reshaping other institutions in the United States. As Richard Ohmann has pointed out, the same forces have significantly altered the medical and legal professions as well. The changes underway differ from profession to profession, though a number of features are, as I will say, common. However, one in particular I want to underline at the outset: The concentration of institutional power in the hands of senior managers, or executives, at precisely the historical juncture in which larger and larger institutions—whether universities, huge accounting, consulting and law firms, immense multinational corporations, and the like—have come to play more determinative roles in the lives of people in the United States and elsewhere. Where once it was said that war was too important to be left to generals, now it seems that education is too important to be left to teachers or medicine to doctors and nurses or profit and loss to investors. The dangers of this arrangement, which I will explore in a moment, are dramatized by the Enron scandal, though academics might have come to see them earlier in small scale at Adelphi University a few years back.

I should perhaps point out here that the use of the word *executive* in the sense of a corporate manager or institutional administrator—as distinct from a main governmental functionary—seems itself to be of recent vintage. My 1971 copy of the *Oxford English Dictionary* does not include such a definition. Perhaps this new application of the term can be taken as a sign of the times, transferring to the private domain the prestige and a good deal of the authority suggested by phrases like "chief executive"—that is, president of a nation. However that might be, part of what progressives have to be about is the denaturalization of such terms—or, perhaps, the relocation of *executive* to where it is found in my dictionary, between *executioner* and *executor.*

Permanent changes in language may signal that deep historical processes are largely irreversible. You cannot go back to pre-industrial craft shops by busting up spinning jennies. All the king's horses and all the king's men couldn't put the Soviet Union together again. Nothing will reestablish Plato's academy nor that of 1968—not that, in my view, one would want to do so, given the narrowness of its curriculum, of its student constituency, and of its educational goals. Still, it is not always so clear which changes derive from tectonic shifts in the social and economic plates of human life and which others are temporary aberrations, cultural and social El Niños that will themselves alter over time. Or, more precisely, it is rarely clear which changes can successfully be questioned, resisted, or even transformed.

The changes we need to examine are variously called privatization, commodification, and marketization. Whatever they are called (and these terms represent related but somewhat different phenomena), they entail the application of "free"—minimally, not governmentally planned—market principles in every area of life, from the airwaves, to energy, to water, and, of course, to education. What this phenomenon involves is something more than turning over public facilities to private profit, though it often entails that. I am rather referring to the set of mind, the informing ideology, or perhaps what Pierre Bourdieu called the *habitus* that shapes people's ways of thinking and that underlies particular policies. That view, to say it briefly, holds, first, that the application of free-market principles is the best, perhaps the only, guarantee of efficient, sensible, indeed fair distribution of desirable commodities; second, that anything is, at least potentially, a commodity: cockles and mussels, college degrees, hearts, eyes, and livers, promises to supply as-yet undiscovered natural gas, legislation, legislators, futures of every sort; third, that market principles can best, perhaps only, be maintained by what amounts to a new class of institutional managers, whose main business it is to resist the inertial drag of other potential centers of power—employee organizations, government regulators, various publics; and finally, that other considerations are undesirable if not absolutely dangerous interferences with the operations of the market, whether they involve redressing past racial discrimination, providing a living wage, balancing public needs like the environment against private profit, or even maintaining certain traditional ideas of the ends of education.

My readers may, at this point, suspect me of believing that nothing short of some thorough-going anticapitalist revolution will bring about real change. Perhaps. But because that is not likely the day after tomorrow, my own practical goal has been to pursue a number of the ameliorative strategies discussed elsewhere in this book. At the same time, I do think that most of the problems this book engages cannot adequately be addressed unless or until the free-market ideology that underwrites current management practices is brought into serious question.

Enron and Adelphi teach us that the ability to perpetrate the most outrageous deceptions and frauds depends upon an ideology, a high level of shared assumptions among victimizers and victims alike about what is legitimate enterprise, at least so long as it works. Delegitimizing market ideology is, I believe, a necessary though not a sufficient condition of change, whether one is talking about the American economy as a whole or the current shape of the educational system.

Adelphi was, when I taught on Long Island in the 1970s and 1980s, generally thought of as the premier institution on the Island—not, perhaps, a high compliment considering the competition but a meaningful one. Until, that is, John Silber and others of his ilk came to dominate the board of trustees and in 1985 to appoint as president a fellow named Peter Diamandopoulos, who had been fired from his previous post in California and whose main talent seemed to lie in privatizing the resources of the institution, as, for example, by upping his compensation package to about $800,000 (second only to Silber's), purchasing a $1.2 million condo for his personal use in Manhattan, some twenty-five miles and an hour's traffic away, or arranging costly insurance brokerage deals and excessive advertising and legal fees for supporters on the board.[4] It is not a pretty tale nor one worth extended analysis, except to say that its reigning ideology was that of the free market—including efforts to crush faculty governance, cut courses, and force students (fewer and fewer each passing year) to pay more of the costs—at the same time raising both the endowment and, enormously, administrative costs and perquisites. Diamandopoulos also brought in large grants from the right-wing Olin Foundation to fund highly paid visiting professorships for and lectures by conservatives who presumably shared the concern of Olin's president, William Simon, over the "dominant socialist-statist-collectivist orthodoxy which prevails . . . in most of our large universities" (qtd. in Zaidi).[5] Whatever the ideology being promoted, the ruling practice was use of the institution to enrich its insiders. The regime ultimately crumbled when in 1996 the faculty union led a successful effort to get the New York State Board of Regents (a sort of educational Securities and Exchange Commission unique to New York) to intervene in an increasingly corrupt situation and to remove the malefactors—Diamandopoulos, plus seventeen other trustees, including such conservative luminaries as Silber, Hilton Kramer, and Joseph Carlino. Adelphi has been in faint recovery since, its decline perhaps symbolized by the melting away of the English department from twenty-seven faculty to about five.

Adelphi was something of an extreme, to be sure, but only in carrying certain widespread assumptions and practices of institutional executives—union busting, program cutbacks, privatization of costs, heavy capitalization, insider enrichment, a logical free-market sequence—beyond the realm of what even New York's conservative attorney-general saw as legitimate. It is not the extremity of Adelphi that was the problem but its very commonality; so is it with Enron.

Let me offer a couple of relevant Enronic examples and their academic analogies. Key to the practices of Enron were what have been called "off–balance-sheet" transactions. Once upon a time, we might have taught our first-year students that the phrase violates one of the basic laws of thought, that of contradiction. For if a "balance sheet" has any meaning, it means an inclusive summary of an organization's assets and liabilities, from which nothing can be off. Unless, of course, you're Humpty Dumpty:

> "But 'glory' doesn't mean 'a nice knock-down argument,'" Alice objected.
> "When *I* use a word," Humpty Dumpty said in a rather a scornful tone, "it means just what I choose it to mean—neither more nor less."
> "The question is," said Alice, "whether you *can* make words mean different things."
> "The question is," said Humpty Dumpty, "which is to be master—that's all."

But senior corporate managers, their Andersen accountants and pricey lawyers, and possibly key federal government players bought into this Dumpty definition—"which is to be master—that's all." Academe pioneered in such double-speak with the invention of the "non-tenure-track" line. The meaning of *line* until the mid-1970s was that a person appointed to one would in due course of time and work be fired or achieve tenure, just as a person laboring on an assembly line for a period designated in a contract would, unless terminated before, achieve an appropriate form of job security. What enabled the Humpties of our time to create such new and dangerous meanings in these phrases? The arrogance of power, in part. But most of all, I would suggest, widely shared assumptions about the market and the role of managers within it that marks today's capitalism—free-market ideology, in short.

A second instance, a set of images familiar to most Americans by now: Kenneth Lay puffing the value of Enron stock to an auditorium full of the corporation's employees—even as he is dumping millions of dollars worth of his own holdings. He is, of course, trying (desperately, perhaps) to maintain the loyalty of his troops. To say it slightly differently, he is engaged in a rhetorical exercise designed to sustain the illusion that his interests and those of employees—at least of those professionals sufficiently compensated to own company stock or stuck with it in their 401Ks—are enough allied to make common cause. This has become a problem because the "professional-managerial class," the PMC made famous by Barbara and John Ehrenreich, has increasingly fragmented. The real interests of professionals—doctors, professors, IT geeks, company accountants, even some lawyers—and of managers or executives have diverged, the more so as budgets have come under stress in recession. Perhaps Lay studied at Yale, where the letters written by the university's managers to its professoriat during the TA's grade strike, and later to a broader academic world, were similarly successful exercises in sustaining managerial hegemony by winning the assent of those whose academic and therefore largely anticorporate culture might have inclined them to sympathy with their graduate employees. To say this another way: University, like corporate, managers are able to sustain authority by the familiar tactic of maintaining the assent of those whose real-world interests might more and less overlap with but are clearly not identical to theirs. My own experience tells me that adopting management's hostility to unionization is, for most faculty, an error—not as egregious but as blind as that choice of Enron's employees to listen to Lay's lies and hold their stock.

Let me add one further element to this unseemly brew, that having to do with institutional loyalty. Enron again: most of those who actually ran the company escaped its collapse wealthy, whereas much of its staff are unemployed, its creditors empty-handed, its small stockholders and customers—like the California electricity users it seems to have cheated—a good deal the poorer. This suggests that the interests of managers, on the one hand, and of the institutions they manage, on the other, diverge as well. Indeed, that is one of the conclusions arrived at by the internal investigative committee examining Enron's demise.

This should come as no surprise. The key to the new economy of the 1990s has been the market, the stock market, that is. The stock market is at once a form of capitalization and a form of speculation. Capital markets are designed to provide funding for companies that wish to provide a product or a service, but in the new economy, no company had to produce a product or a service that actually sold. It had only to *seem* to be able to do so, and if it could sustain what might have been an illusion for a sufficient time, those who founded and ran companies like Global Crossing, who accumulated and then peddled its stock, could—and did—come away, as we used to say, filthy rich. In these cases, the operative bottom line is that of the executive's bank account, which as all Americans have come to see is very different from that of the company being managed, much less that of its employees or of the communities with which it engages, as the people of Youngstown or Houston can tell. Or even its shareholders. To say this another way, the company becomes a mechanism not only for transferring, as in traditional Marxist terms, the surplus value created by workers producing products or services into the pockets of executives, but it is equally a mechanism for transferring the investments of those who buy stock into the same pockets. As a former manager put it: "The ingrained philosophy was, me first, money counts and the government should eliminate my taxes. That's all they cared about—what impacted them personally" (Stephens). No surprise, then, that we now see the greatest disparities of wealth, and income, in the history of the nation.[6]

Universities are among the institutions involved in widening the distance between the compensation of those at the bottom—often those doing the work of teaching—and those at the top—often ignorant of classrooms. Of course, the ten- or fifteen- or even fifty-fold disparities between the compensation of TAs, groundskeepers, and secretaries, on one side, and university provosts and presidents, on the other, are small potatoes when today's corporate executives make off with millions as employees populate the unemployment office. But now a significant number of university presidents make over half a million dollars, others in the many hundreds of thousands (Lewin, "Survey"). Likewise, in other academic organizations like the Educational Testing Service, compensation is equivalent to that of corporate executives: $800,000 for its president for his first ten months on the job (Lewin, "Corporate Culture"). And in their wake, of course, come a parade of absurdly high-priced vice presidents, provosts, comptrollers, and the like, complete like football quarterbacks with $200,000 signing bonuses and other so-called incentives. Such practices in academe help legitimate the even more extreme forms now commonplace in corporate America. It is also the case that universities, like corporations, are for much of this managerial class fundamentally arenas for pursuing their own bottom lines. Such personal bottom lines often have to do, like those of Enron executives and the Adelphi trustees, with money, perquisites, connections to others who share their values, and the leg up on the next position. However, the issue is not really the personal values of academic administrators; after all, we all know excellent folks who have chosen, for whatever reasons, to work as executives. Rather, it is the way in which the institutions promote the set of corporate ideas to which I have been pointing, and even its language of markets, incentives, and the like.

Colleges and universities teach both within and outside of the classroom.

When Harvard resists paying employees a living wage, a lesson is taught. When Penn so gentrifies its immediate neighborhood that store rents there are higher than in Center City Philadelphia, a lesson is taught. When, as I have written elsewhere, Yale uses the standard corporate tools of outsourcing, cutbacks, and speed-up to "save" money at the expense of its low-income New Haven workers, a lesson is taught:

> Lessons, powerful lessons, are taught by how things are managed, and thus by the managers. . . . Indeed, the lessons of power are often those modeled by how classrooms are organized, employees managed, decisions executed— and how a college interfaces with the community it often dominates and always shapes. ("American" 58)

The free-market ideology thus being taught has to do with winning the hearts and minds of young Americans to the fantasy that their interests and those of the Lays, Skillings, and other Enronites are one. Such lessons are reinforced within the multiplying classrooms devoted to promoting enterprise,[7] marginalizing labor, submerging the realities of social class disparity, and, above all, promoting the underlying ideological tenet of free-market capital: individualism. Indeed, one way of understanding how first-year composition survives, indeed thrives, despite its costs, its dubious results, and its general disparagement even by those who do it, is to think of its ideological function, its role in teaching students that they, and they alone, are responsible for their own success or failure. I think back to English 101—and even more English 100—as it was taught at my Big Ten university in the 1950s: the flunk-out course, the one that gave students to understand clearly that failing to understand the enchantment of subject-verb agreement or the mystique of the past tense *-ed* marked them as losers who belonged elsewhere than in the university.

Perhaps we are now in a place in which we can perform a rhetorical exercise: To what question is "Enron" the answer? What is the name for some bad boys who got caught with their hands in the cookie jar? Or, what happens when there is a temporary breakdown in what is otherwise the best of all possible systems? Or, what is the logical outcome of free-market capitalism run rampant over much of the globe? These questions obviously represent three distinct, if overlapping, analyses of the current big-time scandal. What would it take to establish among a majority of Americans that the appropriate question is the last? That is, that the story of Enron is neither one of bad boys nor creaky checks and balances but of free-market ideology.

Well, what did it take to reduce the War on Poverty to "welfare queens," open admissions to racial preferences, and affirmative action to liberal condescension? What it took was organizing, arguing, and stuffing every available cultural space with sound bites and working papers, all of it designed to respond to the widespread anger of the 1970s over decaying cities, falling standards, and decreasing life chances—nicely packaged as Jimmy Carter. What the Right did was to offer apparently credible explanations for the decline of the West and concrete alternatives to what it was able to portray as the Left's emphasis on guilt, violence, leveling, and paralysis. With the elections of Margaret Thatcher and Ronald Reagan, the symbolic smashing of unionism in the breaking of the air-controllers' strike, the "setting loose" of capitalism from telephone, airline, energy, or other forms of regulation, and the adoption of a more aggressive stance toward the USSR and its clients, the America we have known these past two decades was constructed. In short, the political situation I have here signified by *Enron* was constructed in a particular way and at a particular time. In what is now clearly a new time and a rapidly changing reality, it can be dismantled, and universities *can* and *should* be instruments of that process.

Should—because the unalloyed promotion of the free market as the standard of value has, Adelphi and Enron make clear, led neither to truth seeking nor to sound education. The selling of career programs that satisfy the immediate training needs of corporate employers and donors has not prepared students for careers in a world requiring flexibility, logic, imagination, breadth, and the ability to reinvent oneself. Rather, it has slotted students, with luck, into jobs, many of the dead-end variety. A free-market curriculum has not prepared young people to survive in this tense, competitive world. It has, rather, made them into silly sheep, ready to be sheared and consumed by those who depend upon their ideological docility, their institutional credulity and their inability to ask, and to keep asking, nasty questions about ethics, truth, and even addition.

Can—because with all their narrowness and privilege, colleges and universities remain among the few institutions in American society with the resources and the intellectual space to call pieties into question. *Can,* also, because the cultural conditions within which free-market ideology became hegemonic have altered and because a renewed campus movement for change has come into being over the last few years. There is nothing especially new in deploring or anatomizing the corporatization, as it has been called, of today's university. What has changed in the wake of Enron, Global Crossing, the collapse of the dot-com bubble, and other abuses now drifting into visibility is a widespread reassessment of corporate values and practices. When, in 1997, the Council for Aid to Education called upon higher education to "change the way it operates by undergoing the kind of restructuring and streamlining that successful businesses have implemented," few and foolhardy would have been the critics of that objective. Who, in 2003, would propose that universities model themselves on corporations? What is necessary now, just as politicians and pundits are reexamining business values and procedures, is a thorough-going critique of the damaging influence of corporate culture on higher education in America.

That critique is well underway in recent campus-based movements. The organizations that have brought into question the forms of globalization impoverishing much of the world have, in part, been rooted in campus antisweatshop campaigns in which class projects have played a significant role. Since September 11, too, courses have proliferated that look critically at America in the world and the world in America—which is perhaps why anxious conservative groups have tried McCarthyite tactics to smear them as unpatriotic. The living-wage campaign at Harvard—one of many—has exposed the university as just one more greedy corporation. Such drives have begun to build coalitions between campus groups and those in the community generally excluded from the decision-making processes of corporatized universities. I do not wish to paint some rosy picture but only to suggest that developments outside the campus—from Seattle and Genoa to Enron and Global Crossing—are combining with those within to create conditions for change unimaginable even just a few years ago.

Notes

1. See Paul Lauter, "Retrenchment—What the Managers Are Doing."
2. See Paul Lauter, "A Scandalous Misuse of Faculty: 'Adjuncts.'"
3. See Serge Halimi for a very useful analysis.
4. See, for example, http://www.courts.state.ny.us/nycdlr/issue2/adelphi.htm or at http://www.courts.ny.us/nycdlr/issue2/vacco.htm. See also analyses provided by Ali Shehzad Zaidi and by Lionel S. Lewis.
5. Not incidentally, Simon had been a major player in the practice of hostile corporate take-overs financed by junk bonds, often followed by selling off the assets of companies to enrich those who had seized them.
6. See for example, Neal Peirce:

Labor Day and a nine-year peak in worker layoffs helped focus attention on a report that compensation for America's top corporate brass is running out of control—now 531 times the pay of the average worker. Not only did CEO pay rise a stratospheric 571 percent from 1990 to 2000, the liberally oriented Institute for Policy Studies and United for a Fair Economy said in its report, "Executive Excess 2001," chief executive compensation continued to soar last year even while many of the same executives were firing workers by the thousands and corporate stocks lost 10 percent of their value.

7. I was charmed to read recently about an "Entrepreneurial History Tour of Manhattan" being provided for students at one of our elite colleges. The tour will visit "5th Avenue, see Park Avenue and Rockefeller Center before reaching Grand Central Terminal. After lunch we will visit the Main Library and Times Square before taking the subway to Lower Manhattan. In addition to the Battery, Wall Street, the Woolworth Tower, and City Hall, we will pass Ground Zero." The items and the sequence are perhaps inevitable—and probably appropriate. But when was the last time a college provided a tour of labor history sites in New York or, so far as I know, anywhere else in the United States outside, maybe, of Detroit?

Part Two

Putting Labor First

6
Making a Place for Labor: Composition and Unions

Bill Hendricks

College English teachers have been describing (and often bemoaning) their working lives ever since there were English departments. In the last quarter-century, however, public considerations of the conditions of academic labor in English have greatly multiplied—ironically, but not coincidentally, during a time of unprecedented academic unemployment and underemployment for Ph.D.s in the humanities. Some of these considerations, like Gary Rhoades's *Managed Professionals: Unionized Faculty and Restructuring Academic Labor,* or Randy Martin's edited collection *Chalk Lines,* touch on English studies only peripherally and thus may still be unfamiliar to many English faculty. Probably better known is work like Richard Ohmann's *English in America,* Gerald Graff's *Professing Literature,* Evan Watkins's *Work Time,* and Richard E. Miller's *As If Learning Mattered.* And seemingly most relevant of all for my purposes in this paper is the recent flurry of publications in Composition studies connecting the teaching of writing to the institutional and material positions of writing teachers (e.g., Sharon Crowley's *Composition in the University;* Bruce Horner's *Terms of Work for Composition;* Eileen E. Schell's *Gypsy Academics and Mother-Teachers;* Frank Sullivan et al.'s "Student Needs and Strong Composition"; Jennifer Seibel Trainor and Amanda Godley's "After Wyoming").

This work is difficult to characterize in the aggregate. It has been diverse and multiply motivated. An important impetus for some has been the (perhaps inevitably) belated recognition that the academy is not a privileged realm. The attacks on labor since the early 1970s—driven by American capitalism's scramble to maintain its markets and profits after the post–World-War-II boom petered out—have spared no one (see Ohmann, "Historical Reflections"; Zweig 74–75). What we are now beginning to see is less astonished outrage at the corporatization of the university and more attention to fighting back—in a variety of ways and from various political perspectives. Especially for composition teachers, one factor motivating writing about the workplace has been troubled reflections on access to postsecondary education (e.g., What are the connections between educating our students and credentialing them? or, In what ways might writing courses function to limit rather than expand what students can know and do?). And, again, especially in Composition, recent writing about the academic workplace has often been spurred by a desire to insist that teaching and learning are ineluctably tied, for both students and teachers, to the social and material circumstances of their enactment.

Even in Composition studies, however, writing about the academic workplace, despite its recent proliferation, has to date had relatively little influence in improving the working lives of teachers. More surprisingly, even in Composition (the field, not the educational enterprise), labor is still often ignored. In much of the recent literature on composition reform, labor continues to be invisible in two ways. First, proposals for reform are often propounded with a seeming blindness to human activity—who will do what, how, under what conditions, and with what negotiations among students, teachers, and other actors. (For notable exceptions to this tendency, see Rodby and Fox; Sullivan et al.) Second, mainstream Composition (again, the field) seems to be remarkably uninformed about organized labor. When unions are mentioned at all, they are most often treated as tangential rather than as the centrally important player that I believe they must be in successful transformations of the academic workplace. I think that composition's double blindness to labor is unfortunate for three reasons. The neglect of labor is unfortunate insofar as it frustrates and vitiates efforts to improve the teaching and study of writing in college. Second, blindness to organized labor is unfortunate because academic unions offer a collective strategy that can make some of the problems of composition teachers not only more tractable but actually solvable. Finally, the relative disregard of unions in mainstream Composition is also unfortunate because to set unions aside is to relinquish the single most important instrument that composition teachers and other workers have to effect social justice. Unions link desire to power.

My aim in this paper is to contribute toward making a larger place for labor in Composition theory and practice. I will be attempting—roughly, but not exclusively, in this order, (1) to demonstrate that, despite the new climate of interest in the material conditions of our jobs, Composition often continues to ignore both the work of change and the existence of academic unions; (2) to explain what I take to be the major causes of this neglect; and (3) to outline what I believe greater appreciation for and participation in organized labor could mean for composition teachers and their work.

Forgetting Labor in Composition Reform

> Many representations of school in our reform literature—and, for that fact, in the various forums of our culture wars—are static ideological

abstractions. And teachers are either the focus of blame or, despite all the talk about "teacher empowerment," are impotent shadow figures. We lack adequately complex models of schools as institutions in which both limiting and liberating forces contend.

—Mike Rose, *Possible Lives*

The spring 2000 issue of *Writing Program Administration* includes an article by Keith Rhodes on "Marketing Composition for the Twenty-first Century." Rhodes believes that curricular and programmatic debates in Composition generally proceed at some ivory-tower distance from the material facts, which are, as I understand Rhodes's argument: (1) that writing teachers (and all other faculty) are laboring in a "market-driven institution"; (2) that required composition generally does not respond in strategically beneficial ways to the powers that ultimately sponsor it (basically business and industry); (3) that this is so *partly* because composition does not uniformly produce what employers want but *mainly* because composition has failed to demonstrate to employers that it does have that which they are seeking; and that, consequently, (4) composition could better respond to existing demand—and also go a long way toward ending exploitative conditions in composition teaching—by aggressively marketing fewer (because not required) but "fully rhetorical composition" courses, courses taught by better-educated and better-paid teachers and designed to fill the market niche of employers looking for rhetorically skilled workers and managers.

While, in common with some other recent work in Composition (e.g., Gleason; Graham, Birmingham, and Zachry; Schell), Rhodes's article has the virtue of insisting that the teaching of composition must not be seen apart from its material circumstances, it tends nonetheless to ignore labor. Despite his insistence that composition teachers ought to be paid a whole lot more, in money and respect, than they generally now get, Rhodes makes no place for labor in two ways. Rhodes erases the struggle between capital and labor by assuming that "the market" is really the only game in town, as if academic workers have no interests, agency, or power not subsumed by market forces. And Rhodes also ignores labor in a different but related sense by almost completely eliding the multiple and very long negotiations between social actors (faculty, administrators, boards of trustees, legislators, corporate managers, and others) that would be necessary in order to enact the sort of marketing plan he has in mind. It is as if for him the labor, the work, of such negotiations is not that significant; just get WPAs and theoretically informed compositionists in line, and the rest will be merely a mopping-up operation.

"Marketing Composition for the Twenty-first Century" can be seen as a contribution to the larger and more general "abolition" debate currently consuming Composition—the idea, first articulated by Crowley a decade ago, that *required* freshman composition ought to be abolished (*Composition* 241, 249). How to read the abolitionists' arguments? Toward what ends are they intended? As Maureen Daly Goggin and Susan Kay Miller have recently cautioned (95), the arguments are not all the same. Let me suggest their variety. *Pedagogically,* for example, it has been said that required first-year composition must be abolished because of the twin barriers to its efficacy brought about by insufficiently trained teachers and insufficiently motivated students. From an *ideological* perspective, it has been claimed that required first-year composition must be abolished because it tends to inculcate political quietism and cultural conformity in those forced to undergo it. *Instrumentally,* required first-year composition must be abolished because it does not well serve either writing in upper-division courses or the writing that students must/will do when they graduate. *Ethically,* required first-year composition must be abolished because it has often tended to create and maintain unjust working conditions and compensation for writing teachers.

Each of these warrants (and there are others) for abolishing required first-year composition has been responded to in various ways. For instance, Marjorie Roemer, Lucille M. Schultz, and Russel K. Durst argue that composition teachers are generally well-trained (385). Horner questions Crowley's view of first-year composition as cultural cop (126–27). James Sledd thinks that "general-purpose prose" is both teachable in first-year composition courses and can provide a valuable foundation for writing in the disciplines and the workplace (27). But I have no interest here in keeping score or declaring a victor. For what I have found to be most puzzling and troubling in the Great Debate is the way in which it is often implied that readers of this textual combat (mostly people with professional interests in Composition and the teaching of composition) have intellectual and ethical obligations to *take a position* on the question of whether first-year composition should be required or at least reconceptualized (see Crowley, *Composition* 241; Goggin, "Disciplinary" 42–44; Roemer, Schultz, and Durst 382; Sledd, "Return" 24–28). What seems obvious to me, however, from my perspective as an advocate for the rights of academic labor, is that I have an obligation *not* to take a position on this question, save within my own workplace. It seems to me both ethically dubious and logistically deluded that I should offer to teachers in other workplaces dicta about how (or whether) they should do the work of composition.

When it comes to abolishing required first-year composition at California University of Pennsylvania, my workplace, I'm against it, for now. Two years ago, the university began a general education program that requires various things of undergraduates (everyone now has to take some mathematics, for instance, and everyone now has to take a laboratory course). In writing, the requirement is Composition I (an introduction to rhetoric), Composition II (an introduction to research writing in the disciplines), and two upper-division writing-intensive courses in the major. For me, a significant feature, probably *the* most important element, of the new gen ed program is that it is the result of long (don't ask how many years) faculty deliberations and a final ratification vote by all faculty. Even if I were to become uneasy about any part of the new writing requirement, I would be very reluctant, at least near-term, to argue against my colleagues' democratically expressed desires. In this instance, those who must produce were those who decided. Like my colleagues across campus, I'm curious to see what the results of the new program will be.

Although each of the abolitionists' rationales for abolishing required first-year composition has been responded to in various ways, I think that the ethical warrant (that required first-year composition must be abolished because it has often tended to create and maintain unjust working conditions and compensation for writing teachers) has been countered least successfully. Though I have said that I do not think Composition has the right to specify how—or whether—composition should be taught in other people's workplaces, I also think that labor advocacy requires continuing collective efforts to ensure that composition be taught (whenever it *is* taught) with justice for labor.

On the Difficulty of Beginning with Labor

> With a few exceptions—for example, the State University of New
> York system—research university faculty (who do the most writing
> about higher education) are not unionized. . . . [One] can read much
> higher education literature and not discover that faculty unions exist.
> One can read many of the most widely read books on higher education
> and not learn that faculty unions exist. One can get a master's or
> doctoral degree in many Higher Education programs, and gain no
> knowledge of faculty unions.
>
> —Gary Rhoades, *Managed Professionals*

To date, corporate restructuring of the academic workplace has not made much progress in figuring out how to replace writing teachers with machines. At least in the near future, writing instruction will remain largely labor intensive, a matter of teachers and students working together, though not always in classrooms. The essential task for composition teachers is thus not to stay employed but to carry on collective deliberations about how the work of teaching writing can be made not just more remunerative but more intellectually and emotionally rewarding for the human beings involved in it. Within a capitalist framework, our framework, to say that those who must produce are those who must decide is not *only* an ideal. As a principle of labor advocacy, it has a present as well as a future. It is a way to begin negotiations with those who believe that deciding for others is their work.

Academic labor unions have been around since the 1960s (Tirelli 182; Rhoades, *Managed Professionals* 10), but it is particularly in the last decade that labor activism among college teachers has evolved from a fairly site-specific activity into a national phenomenon that has reoriented notions of professionalism in higher education. While in recent years union membership among tenure-track faculty, contingent faculty, and graduate students has continued its steady growth (Leatherman, "AAUP Reaches Out"; Rhoades and Slaughter 44; Smallwood), the new organizing activity has not simply been more of the same, not just more teachers getting organized. Rather, the recent organizing gains have also often been accompanied by a new discourse of labor militancy that links justice for academic labor to an examination of what sorts of educational practices in what kind of university are best suited for students and teachers to work together (see "Casual Nation"; Cox; Harney and Moten 168–72; Leatherman, "Part-Time Faculty Members"; Leatherman, "Union Organizers"; Thompson, "Ultimate" A22–23; Trainor and Godley).

The new labor activism connecting conditions of work to the quality of educational results has been especially notable among composition teachers. This is hardly surprising. Composition teachers are unusually heavily represented among the ranks of graduate-student T.A.s and contingent faculty. They are keenly aware of the links between the terms of their employment and the achievements their students can make and have therefore been especially attracted to and actively concerned with questions of labor organizing (see Horner, *Terms* 22–24, 179; Kavanagh; Schell, *Gypsy Academics* 109–12).

As Rhoades makes clear in his *Managed Professionals,* unionization has been of substantial economic benefit to U.S. college teachers. In English, for example, unionized faculty make on average 30% more than their non-unionized colleagues (78). And, though apparently unknown to some in higher education, unionized faculty are by no means a marginal group. Already by 1994, 44 percent of full-time faculty (and 26 percent of full- and part-time faculty combined) were unionized. If only *public* colleges and universities are considered, by the mid-1990s 63 percent of full-time faculty were union members. If a further selection is made to include only *nonresearch* public universities, by 1995 89 percent of full-time faculty in public nonresearch universities were unionized (9–10).

Yet, despite the obvious interest of composition *teachers* in academic unions, I think that we often see in the *field* of Composition today indications of, or perhaps an analogue to, the relative silence about faculty unionization in the literature of higher education that Rhoades has noted. Crowley has for the last decade been a vocal and persistent critic of required first-year composition courses. One of her arguments for getting rid of what has become the only almost-universally required part of the undergraduate curriculum is that required composition tends to perpetuate the inequitable pay and working conditions that most composition teachers labor under:

> Today, first-year composition is largely taught by graduate students and temporary or part-time teachers. Full-time permanent faculty regularly teach the course only in liberal arts colleges, two-year colleges, and the few four-year universities that still privilege teaching over research. (*Composition* 118)

Furthermore, "[P]eople who labor overlong at teaching composition find themselves shut out of tenurable positions in English departments" (*Composition* 131).

However, it is puzzling to read that full-time permanent faculty regularly teach required composition courses *only* in liberal arts colleges, two-year colleges, and four-year universities with a primary commitment to teaching—*only,* that is, in the vast majority of colleges and universities in the country. The *Chronicle of Higher Education*'s "Almanac" for 2000–2001 puts the number of U.S. colleges and universities at 4,096, of which only 261 are listed as "doctorate-granting institutions" (7, 51). Crowley may have good reason to believe that only a "few four-year universities . . . still privilege teaching over research," but she offers no explanation for this claim in *Composition in the University*.[1]

Equally strange, to me, is Crowley's contention that faculty who spend too much time teaching comp reduce their chances of getting tenure. In my department at California University, for instance, where there are currently seventeen tenure-track, four full-time adjunct, and one part-time adjunct faculty, all twenty-two English Department members regularly teach our required composition courses, and sixteen of the seventeen tenure-track faculty are tenured. To move beyond my own workplace, what of all of the full-time permanent faculty that, Crowley acknowledges, are teaching composition at community colleges, liberal arts colleges, and nonresearch universities? Few of them are tenured or likely to get tenure?

There is what I take to be another instance of Composition's obliviousness to the pervasiveness and power of faculty unions in Joseph Harris's "Meet the New Boss, Same as the Old Boss: Class Consciousness in Composition," published in the September 2000 issue of *College Composition and Communication*. Harris calls for improvements in pay and working conditions for *all* teachers of composition, including T.A.s and adjunct faculty. "We" must, he says, "find ways now of supporting good teaching for undergraduates and fair working conditions for teachers—*including . . . full-time non-tenure-track instructorships*" (56, my emphasis). But why consign *any* composition faculty to non-tenure-track instructorships (in which, for one thing, opportunities for promotion might never materialize)? As Harris sees it, this is simply a consequence of the current economic reality in higher education, where tenure-track jobs will inevitably shrink everywhere (56, 60, 64, 66n4). Yet, this is not the reality I am familiar with in my everyday working life. The current contract that my union, the Association of Pennsylvania State College and University Faculties (APSCUF), signed in November 1999 with Pennsylvania's State System of Higher Education (SSHE) provides opportunities to not only halt but reverse the erosion of tenure-track jobs (Pennsylvania 20–22),[2] opportunities that are currently being realized, though not without considerable struggle, at California as well as at other SSHE schools.

Harris says that if composition teachers and their students are to do good work together, we will have to wean ourselves from the delusion that "composition can become part of what English professors routinely study and teach—and thus that the need to maintain small armies of contingent instructors to staff first-year writing courses will eventually disappear" (56). While I don't want to overgeneralize from my own work situation and while, further, I realize that, despite that SSHE faculty at all fourteen schools are working under a uniform contract, the situation for composition teachers varies from school to school, still, I know that, at California, composition already *is* part of what all English professors regularly teach and study and that there is reason to expect that adjunct positions, already few in number, will continue to be converted into tenure-track jobs. At nonunion research universities, perhaps, Harris's vision of a better-supported but still second-tier composition workforce might seem attractive, but I think that few non-research university faculty are likely to succumb to its putatively hard-nosed logic. This is especially true at SSHE campuses, of course, because all faculty, tenure-track, and non-tenure-track are part of a single bargaining unit working under a unified collective bargaining agreement, an advantage that was not in place at Eastern Michigan University in the fall of 2000 when striking full-time faculty found that they had to settle for a mediocre contract because they and their part-time colleagues were in different bargaining units (Leatherman, "Tenured Professors").[3]

What makes unions so hard to see? Why is organized labor so often ignored in the discourses of Composition? Maybe the first thing to say is that the answers to this question must be social, not personal. Obviously, I do not believe for one instant that Crowley and Harris covertly harbor anti-union sentiments. But good intentions are not the issue. We are not dealing here with individual failures of moral imagination. Rather, I think that what makes it so difficult for Composition to begin with labor is a cluster of cultural, professional, and political factors, most of them not exclusive to Composition or the teaching of composition.

Academic Culture

Much in the social imaginaries, or ideologies, of capitalism and professionalism conspires against the move to begin with labor. In an opinion piece in May 2000 in the *Chronicle of Higher Education,* Catharine R. Stimpson, dean of the graduate school of arts and sciences at New York University, explains her opposition to the drive among graduate students at NYU for unionization ("A Dean's Skepticism"). Stimpson is angry that NYU's graduate students would identify themselves as "workers," and she seems especially angry that they want to affiliate with the United Auto Workers, thus seeing themselves, according to Stimpson, as "industrial workers." Stimpson adduces her own experience as a member of the unionized faculty at Rutgers University, an experience that for her was mixed. While acknowledging the benefits of unionization for her own working life at Rutgers, Stimpson also recalls that the union was sometimes harmful, most egregiously by "sometimes promoting the belief that the union mattered more, and deserved greater allegiance, than the university." That, I take it, is the rhetorical center of Stimpson's piece: What must we think of an academic union that would promote the belief that it mattered more than the university?

Setting aside the specious binary opposition (the union is, after all, a part of the university), it is interesting to speculate whether Stimpson would find equally nonsensical the position that advocacy for feminism and justice for women could be harmful by "sometimes promoting the belief that feminism and justice for women mattered more, and deserved greater allegiance, than the university."

Actually, we do not need to speculate because Stimpson has argued elsewhere that feminism and justice for women *are* sometimes more important and deserve greater allegiance than business as usual within the academy (see her essay "Feminist Criticism"). I am not accusing Stimpson of conscious bad faith, only trying to suggest by her example how conceptually difficult it is in our culture to begin with labor, especially for academics. In common with many liberal academic enterprises, Composition, because it has serious difficulty imagining what *collective* self-interest might be, tends to counterpose against the bad guy of *individual* self-interest the good guy of professional responsibility and solicitude, a social-work perspective that keeps organized labor out of sight.

Professional Positioning

Perhaps the most obvious reason for Composition's neglect of organized labor is what Rhoades alludes to in the epigraph to this section. Because so much of what is published in the field's mainline journals is by faculty working at research universities, the labor situations at these sites start to look like the norm.[4] True, faculty unions are relatively scarce at research universities and at private liberal arts colleges. Elsewhere, however, faculty unions are quite common.

And there are other phenomena of professional positioning that also tend to militate against a deep knowledge of or concern with organized labor. By their nature, unions involve collective activity, often anonymous. Unions are promiscuous, everyday, open to all. They are thus not particularly academic. They are not fertile sites for professional distinction. There is no easy way out of what, to many, will be seen as this deeply uncomfortable bind. I am obviously not the first to notice this; some important work in Composition has been done recently on the not-necessarily reconcilable conflicts between academic professionalism and academic labor (e.g., Horner; Spellmeyer; Trimbur).

Moreover, writing program administration, which employs many who see themselves as compositionists, almost inevitably calls upon WPAs to start to think of administering labor as akin to, though secondary to, administering program goals or curricula. All is manageable (or had *better* be manageable if WPAs are to receive favor from those above them in the university hierarchy). Even on unionized campuses, putting labor first can be difficult for WPAs as they work (though not always harmoniously) with university administrators who almost invariably see faculty unions as strictly an impediment to correct management.

The social factors I am attempting to describe are not the exclusive burden of WPAs or prominent compositionists. I think that an important motivation for *all* composition teachers—currently in unions or not, pro-union or not—to want to hold unions at arm's length is that unionized academic workplaces are often not comfortable places to be. When they are working right, faculty unions are a pain in the ass, a constant irritant. Academics do not shrink from professional conflict, but we expect, in our working lives, that our opinions will be respected, that *we* will be respected. We expect, as we say, collegiality. But unionization tends to redefine "collegiality," which has become the term most often extended by management to faculty on unionized campuses as an invitation to forget about the rights of labor.

Class, Organized Labor, and Power

Another potential barrier to composition teachers' identification with the labor movement may be too little understanding of organized labor's twentieth-century *successes*. In a recent *CCC* article, Debra Hawhee laments that our "working class status" is something composition teachers may never escape (522). Yes, many composition workers are grossly exploited, but, as the twentieth-century history of industrial, craft, and professional organized labor might suggest, there is nothing *inherent* in "working class status" that ought to connote penury.

Power, on the other hand, is another matter, more problematic. Though Hawhee at the end of her essay says that it is composition teachers generally, not some segment of composition teachers, who may never escape their working-class status, her article as a whole suggests that in her peroration she may really be thinking of non-tenure-track composition teachers. From *that* perspective (teachers of college composition = contingent academic labor), what Hawhee says makes sense. Also, though partly this is a matter of pay, mostly (and here I follow Michael Zweig's delineations of class,) it is a matter of "the power and authority people have at work" (3). For the most part, contingent faculty in composition have not just lousy pay and working conditions but relatively little say in determining the shape of their working lives.

In contrast, however, tenure-track faculty teaching composition continue to have considerable workplace autonomy. They (we) may also have (and certainly this applies to tenure-track faculty teaching composition at every campus of Pennsylvania's state system) job security, good benefits, and excellent pay. Though some of us have working class identifications, we are, systemically, middle class. The irony is that tenure-track faculty at public nonresearch universities owe much of what they have to labor unions, the vehicle connected by many to working-class labor. The concomitant scandal is that unionized tenure-track faculty (including many unionized tenure-track teachers of composition) have often been way too slow to identify themselves as part of the labor movement and far too amenable to maintaining (or acceding to) barriers between themselves and non-tenure-track faculty—one of the results of which is that non-tenure-track faculty are much less unionized than tenure-track faculty and often, even when they are unionized, work under inferior contracts.

Though class is almost inevitably linked to any considerations of labor, I am in this chapter concerned with class only secondarily. I am primarily talking about the labor movement. I am not speaking primarily of "studying" the labor movement, though I think that is a good idea. I am not even speaking of "supporting" the labor movement (thus maintaining a respectful distance from it). I am speaking, rather, of a combination of self-identification and direct political action, of composition teachers *belonging* to the labor movement and working collectively toward expanding its, our, range and power.

Making a Place for Labor

> Management under globalization can destroy the concept of seniority and the memory of its life-course benefits only if the public becomes passive or hostile. One way to produce these reactions is to convince people rhetorically that there are no alternatives to lifetime insecurity. The complementary way is to eliminate the existing alternatives by making people feel that Sisyphus's situation ought to be more broadly shared.
> —Margaret Morganroth Gullette,
> "The American Dream as a Life Narrative"

I think that the "Report of the ADE Ad Hoc Committee on Staffing," the "Final Report of the MLA Committee on Professional Employment," and "Who Is Teaching In U.S. College Classrooms?" by the Coalition on the Academic Workforce are at once fundamentally accurate and significantly incomplete. They are accurate in their depiction of the massive casualization of academic labor that has occurred in the U.S. over the last thirty years, but they are incomplete in their silence about organized labor's (sometimes successful) efforts to fight back. A somewhat different picture of the crisis in academic labor emerges from reading documents such as the American Federation of Teachers' "The Vanishing Professor" or the Coalition of Graduate Student Employee Unions' "Casual Nation," both of which paint the same bleak scene as do the ADE, MLA, and CAW reports but also detail recent successes in academic labor activism.

But academic labor can not afford to confine its efforts to unionization (see Kavanagh). "Organized labor" includes more than unions. I think it is significant that at the MLA's December 2000 convention delegates voted to "create . . . a system in which the association would give its stamp of approval to departments in which at least half of the credits are taught by tenured or tenure-track professors" and that the delegates also passed "resolutions to encourage professors and graduate students to unionize, and to censure colleges that do not recognize the results of collective-bargaining votes"[5] ("MLA Moves"). I am very encouraged that for the past six years *CCC* has included within its pages *Forum*, the semiannual newsletter of the Non-Tenure-Track Faculty Special Interest Group. I think it is of the utmost importance that within the last few years the National Labor Relations Board has ruled that both faculty and graduate students have the right to collective bargaining at private colleges and universities (Leatherman, "NLRB Lets Stand," "NLRB Rules"; and see Abram), thus beginning to dismantle the twenty-year-old barrier of the Yeshiva decision (especially, for now, for graduate students). Organized labor includes for composition teachers more than union organizing. It includes work within the courts (in some states, it is illegal for *public* college faculty to unionize); work in professional advocacy organizations; work in public relations (see the public-relations campaign described in "The Vanishing Professor"); lobbying in state legislatures and state educational bureaucracies; agitation for and within faculty governance on campus; and work within the larger labor movement. In what follows, then, as I outline some implications of what I believe greater appreciation for and participation in organized labor might mean for composition teachers, I will sometimes be ranging beyond unions.

Inclusiveness

We all have multiple identities. In what may be a disappointment to some, I think that in advocating that one of composition teachers' self-identifications be with the labor movement, I am proposing nothing that is either revolutionary or utopian. In fact, I mostly agree with Richard Miller's idea that compositionists must work within the system ("'Let's Do the Numbers'"). It's just that, while I acknowledge the value of our being canny bureaucrats, I place greater value in our being academic workers who are committed to the labor movement—which is also part of the system as its permanent opposition.

James Sledd says,

> Working people see [academics'] claim to tenure as a claim to unique job security in a world where mergers and downsizing have made job security a bad joke. . . . If we really meant what we say when we talk virtuously about the evils of frozen hierarchies, we'd work to abolish . . . tenure. ("Return to Service" 26)

I do not see why this follows. Why would we not work instead for greater job security and economic justice for all, especially on campus? I do not think that equal-opportunity suffering is the road to labor justice, and I doubt that working-class people are eager to see college professors have less job security. In the fall of 1999, my union, APSCUF, almost went out on strike. That we did not, that a settlement was reached, was the result of many factors, one of which was a pledge by transport unions not to cross faculty picket lines to make deliveries in the event of a strike. In the November–December 2000 issue of *Steelabor* appears a letter in which John F. Goodman, Local 338 of the United Steelworkers of America, reflects on the two-year strike and lockout he had just been through at Kaiser-MAXXAM in Washington state:

> When I looked into the eyes of my sons and granddaughters, and thought of what the future may hold for them if we were not successful in this battle for human rights and dignity, I knew I had to go on. Jodi Viabrock, a sister Steelworker, once said with conviction, "These are our jobs and we deserve them," and she was so right. (2)

I would say that not only is the labor movement as a whole not waiting expectantly for college faculty to weaken their own job security but that it would be considered madness if we tried to—madness and also perhaps a kind of betrayal, since less job security for some workers tends toward weakening it for other workers. As I've argued above (and see endnote 3), faculty unions are strongest and fairest when they include tenure-track faculty and non-tenure-track faculty in the same bargaining units, so I think that Sledd is dead-on in his advocacy for "inclusive unions of faculty" ("Return to Service" 12).

However, I think that in advocating inclusiveness, Sledd is not being as inclusive as he should be. Specifically, I think that Sledd is mistaken, politically and rhetorically, in the contempt he lavishes on "boss compositionists," by which term he seems to mean sometimes writing program administrators and sometimes composition theorists who have been theorizing in ways that Sledd does not like:

> Who or what imposes [the] wretched conditions of the teachers and teaching of the basic course that so many institutions require and so few properly support. . . . [The] obvious answer . . . [is] hierarchy and the hierarchs, including the hierarchical assumption that research is superior to "mere" teaching and that service is beneath the dignity of brahminical theorists. ("Return to Service" 28)

Although, as I've suggested earlier, Composition and compositionists are not immune to the institutional assumption that would place research above mere teaching, I do not think that in "Return to Service" Sledd establishes the existence of a group of theorists/WPAs in Composition who, in the aggregate, really are unable in their working lives to overcome this assumption, or who, worse, let this assumption control absolutely their leadership roles in composition programs.

Is the struggle really between composition teachers on one side, hierarchy and hierarchs on the other? I would define it differently. I think that the struggle now, as it has been for quite some time, is between capital and labor. Faculty governance in the academic workplace is worth fighting for. If writing programs benefit from leadership, and I think they do, that leadership ought to come from justly compensated faculty, not from administration. In working toward establishing or strengthening the collective structures necessary for labor ascendancy and workplace democracy, composition teachers can be in a distinctly more advantageous position by working with, if sometimes challenging, those who generally share these goals than they would be if they were only working against those who assuredly do not.

Composition as Unspecial

I suppose that both my general orientation in this chapter and many of the points I make along the way would be different if my working life had been different. In the last three decades, I have spent all but four years working in unionized jobs, not all of them teaching jobs. Chronologically: one year in the National Education Association; two years in the United Electrical Workers; ten years in the United Steelworkers; two years in the Temple Association of University Professionals; eleven years in the Association of Pennsylvania College and University

Faculties. (Right, the UE and USWA stints were the nonteaching jobs.) Good work. With the exception of one year (as a high-school teacher in a small town in Ohio), always a living wage. Conflicts unending, but I have never felt particularly oppressed. Unions have not made my working life smooth, but they have made it doable, survivable with some measure of material reward, dignity, and satisfaction.

Now, in my current job, if I am less worried than some about academic pecking orders, it is probably in part because in my workplace the usual (at least in research universities) English Department hierarchy (literature first, other fields of English studies next, composition always last) is not much in evidence. Collectively, my colleagues and I have agreed that we will each teach two courses a semester in composition and two courses a semester in other things (though, for me, every course becomes a kind of writing course). So, I have taught courses in English education, in professional writing, in literature and critical theory, and in composition theory. For me, this has been a stimulating mix. My colleagues and I are all essentially generalists, each of us working in many rooms of the House of English and meeting from time to time in the commons area of the composition courses that we all teach.

Thus, it may be all too easy for me to say that I think that advancing labor justice for composition teachers will probably require letting go of some of our *professional* grievances as composition teachers, an effort to soft-pedal the feeling that we get no respect, that we are special because we have been specially victimized. Yes, nationally and numerically, all non-tenure-track composition teachers *have* been especially victimized, but that is probably beside the point. Though I may be just reacting to an elliptical way of talking, when I occasionally read proposals that composition teachers *as a discrete group* should unionize, I wonder whom it is thought they will bargain collectively *with*. It is the collective that matters. Working to create or strengthen faculty and graduate student unions means working together with all faculty (full-time and part-time) and graduate students in the bargaining unit, proposed or actual: the sheep and the goats, people we like and some we don't, people who have supported us and some who have not, people who know and love what they're doing in the composition classroom and some who hope never to teach composition again.

When I taught at Temple University (1988–1990), I was introduced to what was for me a new term, *salary compression,* which signified the phenomenon of some new faculty being hired at salaries significantly above some veteran members of the same departments. The faculty union (TAUP) declared itself against salary compression and attempted to reduce it in negotiations for the 1990–1992 contract. In contrast, APSCUF, my union, has made it a goal in recent years to *increase* salary compression, though here the term has a different meaning. In APSCUF bargaining with Pennsylvania's state system, the union has had some success in "increasing salary compression" by *reducing the ratio* of the highest salary to the lowest.[6] Salary increases for those at the top of the scale have continued, but salary increases for those at the bottom have been much greater. The significance of this strategy is partly that it increases labor equity (and union solidarity) by flattening the financial hierarchy among currently employed faculty. Equally important, however, this strategy works toward altering the *future* composition of the faculty workforce—both by helping to attract good candidates for new tenure-track slots and by continuing to make it only marginally cost-effective for management to attempt to hire more part-timers instead of new tenure-track faculty (because per-course payments for all non-tenure-track faculty are prorated to the bottom steps of the full-time salary scale). Obviously, it is not only the union that foresees these results. One of the more dramatic moments of the last contract negotiations was an eleventh-hour attempt by SSHE to offer higher wage increases to full professors if the union would modify its demands for big increases at the lowest levels, a bribe that was flatly rejected. So yes, in some ways, and at some times, hierarchy is the enemy.

Putting Labor First

Where I work, whether compositionists, or any other faculty, ought to "return to service" is a question that, frankly, has never come up. Always it is assumed that faculty's primary job is to serve our students.

There are, of course, some disagreements about how this might best be done, about what it might mean, for example, to teach "the general-purpose prose that our students need and our colleagues want" (Sledd, "Return to Service" 11). I think that in imagining at the end of "Return to Service" that compositionists might return to that unproblematical historical moment before the seductions of disciplinarity had infected them with the researching and theorizing bugs, Sledd is asking for a return to a consensus (a consensus about what college students need in the way of writing instruction) that has never existed. Back in 1956, before Composition had lost its predisciplinary innocence, John C. Gerber, in a retrospective look at the first seven years of the Conference on College Composition and Communication, regretted that the organization was no closer than it had been in 1949 to agreeing on standards for freshman writing:

> I could name five instructors who do not think writing is any good until it sounds like E. B. White's, and I could name five others who think the letter-writing of the typical small business man is a reasonable goal for good writing. . . . In all candor we must admit that we are confusing our students, we are confusing the public, and we are in many ways confusing ourselves. (119)

I am sorry to report that, at California University of Pennsylvania, such disagreements continue to this very day.

However, it may be that at the end Sledd is primarily thinking of something else, that he is not so much invoking a chimerical golden age as proposing that composition faculty *within their own workplaces* (like the University of Texas–Austin or like Cal U) have an obligation to confer and debate with faculty across campus about what we value in student writing. If this is what Sledd has in mind,

I cheerfully concur, having always found such labor to be intellectually and pedagogically rewarding. Not that my colleagues and I have ever reached consensus, not that I think we ever will (fortunately, because it is writing's very incapacity to be so contained that sustains people's engagements with teaching it, studying it, and doing it).

But I've strayed from my subject. I doubt that it is really necessary to choose between Composition and composition teachers. Yet I understand that respect for Composition is not the same thing as justice for academic labor (including composition teachers) and that, if we must choose, working for the latter is more important than working for the former. I think that, along with greater attention to and respect for workplace democracy (in which no one, no individual, always wins), composition teachers' affiliation with the labor movement can provide a much more promising field for a progressive public agenda than can, for example, our largely hidden efforts to uncover the hidden workings of ideology. And I think that another important consequence of seeing ourselves as part of the labor movement is that doing so can give a new focus to our working lives, a focus that makes visible the perhaps unexpected degree to which academic labor's battles are winnable—not easily, and not once and for all, but winnable nonetheless.[7]

Notes

1. But doing a count by type of institution is of course not a reliable way of identifying the total workforce for composition teaching, particularly considering the enormous size of many doctorate-granting institutions. The Association of Departments of English's "Report on Staffing," based on "a stratified sample of 123 English departments in four-year colleges and universities" ("Executive Summary" 1), concludes that contingent labor (graduate students + part-time faculty + full-time non-tenure-track faculty) is teaching 59 percent of undergraduate sections in English nationwide in departments having graduate student T.A.s and 31 percent of undergraduate sections in departments without T.A.s ("Executive Summary" 2). Using a much larger database, the MLA's "Final Report on Professional Employment" concludes that in Ph.D.-granting English departments, contingent labor is teaching 96 percent of first-year composition sections. The comparable figures for "departments where the M.A. was the highest degree" and for "departments where the B.A. was the highest degree" are 64 percent and 50 percent (1157).

2. Article 11.G.1 provides that full-time temporary faculty who have worked for five years in the same department will be "placed in tenure-track status." Article 11.H.1 provides that the existence of any courses that have been staffed by temporary faculty for four years in such a way as to equal a full-time workload (four courses a semester) for one or more tenure-track faculty shall constitute grounds for creating new tenure-track positions. Thus, two kinds of conversions have been instituted, conversion of persons to tenure-track (11.G.1) and conversion of positions to tenure-track (11.H.1).

These two new contract provisions supplement a continuing provision (Article 11.F.1) that mandates that the number of part-time temporary faculty members not exceed 7 percent of the total number of tenure-track faculty. All three provisions are the subjects of ongoing interpretive and implementation wrangles between the union and the administration. As any faculty with experience in a unionized workplace know, getting a good contract is only half the battle; monitoring and implementing the contract never end.

3. I think that unified contracts (tenure-track and non-tenure-track faculty working under the same bargaining agreement) are absolutely critical, for one thing, as a strategy for "[decreasing] the economic incentives for colleges and universities to employ part-timers" (Harris, "Meet the New Boss" 61). One advantage of unified contracts is that per-course payment for part-timers goes up, being pro-rated to what a tenure-track faculty member (though often an entry-level tenure-track faculty member) would make for teaching the same course. At SSHE universities, which have unified contracts, the minimum per-section compensation for composition (or any other) instructors without a terminal degree is currently (January 2003) $4,785.

4. For a trenchant analysis of how "the experiences and practices of elite universities and liberal arts colleges" are often taken "as the norm for higher education" (563), see John Alberti's "Returning to Class."

5. Even more important in my view (though the *Chronicle* report doesn't mention it) was passage of a more radical and wide-ranging resolution (submitted by Leo Parascondola, Cary Nelson, and Marc Bousquet, with cosponsorship by the Graduate Student Caucus and the Radical Caucus in English and Modern Languages) calling for national minimum salaries for full- and part-time faculty, together with health-coverage and retirement benefits.

6. At the end of the last contract (1 July 1996 through 30 June 1999), the highest base salary step for full professors was $77,889, and the lowest base salary step for instructors without the terminal degree was $30,823, a ratio of 2.53 to 1. At the conclusion of the current contract (1 July 1999 through 30 June 2002), the highest base salary step for full professors will be $87,706, and the lowest base salary step for instructors will be $37,332, a ratio of 2.35 to 1.

7. A somewhat longer version of this chapter was published in *Workplace* 4.1 (Spring 2001) in a special issue on "Composition as Management Science" edited by Marc Bousquet, Leo Parascondola, and Tony Scott (www.workplace-gsc.com).

7

Toward a New Labor Movement in Higher Education: Contingent Labor and Organizing for Change

Eileen E. Schell

On 30 November 1999 in Seattle, Washington, thousands of union members, non-governmental organizations (NGOs), students, community and religious activists, farmers, Zapatistas, Cuba supporters, gay and lesbian activists, and a plethora of others gathered to protest the World Trade Organization summit. In Washington, D.C., a few months later, protests continued. The World Trade Organization protests signaled a shift in awareness of labor issues and a building up of strategic alliances between workers and national and international labor organizations. As Rich Daniels puts it:

> Common ground and common cause have been and are being mapped out; everyone is focused right now on the structure of the internationalizing economy and thinking about how to shape alternatives that work for working people and the environment everywhere. (1)

Even in rural areas, workers are organizing. In Chelan County, Washington, the self-proclaimed Apple Capital of the World where I grew up on an apple and pear orchard, migrant farmworkers, many of them recent immigrants from Mexico, have unionized at local warehouses. Apple and pear growers, patterning their protests after French farmers, recently held tractor rallies to protest corporate grocery stores selling their fruit at well below production costs, thus forcing small farmers into bankruptcy and foreclosure. In communities both large and small, many workers are speaking out against the ways in which corporatization and globalization in the name of progress and the so-called new world order have undermined the rights of working people. As a result, what was once thought to be disparate groups are building strategic alliances in many sectors of the international economy.

The revitalization of academic unions and growing regional, statewide, national, and international coalition-building efforts among various groups concerned with contingent labor coupled with localized legislative action can affect change. In this chapter, I will report on and analyze campus, municipal, statewide, national, and international organizing campaigns to address the working conditions of part-time and non-tenure-track faculty, many of them first-year-writing teachers. After that, I will discuss an international action, Campus Equity Week and will conclude with a discussion of the rhetorical strategies that literacy workers and others agitating for change can best adopt to achieve coalition building and organizing toward improved working conditions.

The International Economy and Literacy Workers

In the U.S. and Canada, growing unionization of graduate students and contingent faculty, coupled with campus, municipal, statewide, national, and international organizing efforts, are creating the momentum for a revitalized academic labor movement among a range of university workers, including staff, cafeteria, and physical plant workers. As labor historian Robin D. G. Kelley describes, universities employ a "vast army of clerical workers, food-service workers, janitors, and other employees whose job is to maintain the physical plant" (146). Many of these employees are women and people of color, which, contends Kelley, necessitates that unions must resist low-paid wage work *and* resist race and gender-based oppression as part and parcel of class oppression (150). Coalition building among all university workers and the recent local and national campaigns for the Fair Wage Initiative are indicators of an important shift in business as usual at American colleges and universities.

Even professional associations, which are prone to issue statements and to stay out of the fray of labor politics, are beginning to collect wide-scale data on the transformation of the academic work force from full-time jobs to contingent jobs. After the Conference on the Growing Use of Part-Time/Adjunct Faculty in November 1997, a number of professional associations, including the Organization of Historians in America (OHA), the Modern Language Association (MLA), and the NCTE/CCCC hired the Roper-Starch Research agency to conduct institution-wide surveys on part-time and non-tenure-track faculty's working conditions in the individual disciplines. Prompted by activist graduate students and faculty in the MLA Delegate Assembly, the MLA not only conducted the survey but it committed the unprecedented act of publishing the salaries and working conditions at particular institutions on its Web site. Not to be outdone by MLA, CCCC has conducted a study of labor practices in independent writing programs, which the CCCC Committee on Contingent, Adjunct, and Part-Time Faculty Issues has summarized in a report and recommendations released in the December 2001 issue of *CCC*.

Those of us who teach in writing programs or administer them will say that despite widespread acknowledgement of the problem, the part-time and non-tenure-track situation has worsened. On the one hand, our field has burgeoned: graduate programs in rhetoric and composition have sprung up, assistant professorships are still advertised and filled; established journals, books, and even presses specializing in rhetoric and composition titles have grown. On the other hand, first-year composition is still overwhelmingly staffed by part-time and non-tenure-track faculty, many of them women, whose wages and working conditions are exploitive. The national statistics remain dire.

According to a survey by the Coalition on the Academic Workforce (CAW), a group of twenty-five disciplinary associations, part-time and non-tenure-track faculty comprise a large percentage of those responsible for first-year writing instruction. In the CAW/MLA survey, nearly one-third (32 percent) of those who teach introductory writing courses situated in English departments are part-time faculty. An additional one-tenth (9.5 percent) are full-time, non-tenure-track faculty, and 22.2 percent are graduate student teaching assistants ("MLA Survey," table 2). Thus, in English departments, only one-third (36.3 percent) of all instructional staff who teach writing courses are full-time, tenured, or tenure track faculty. In the CAW/CCCC survey of freestanding writing programs, those that constitute a department with a separate budget and instructional lines from English departments, approximately one-fifth (18.2 percent) of first-year writing courses are taught by full-time, non-tenure-track faculty; one-third (32.5 percent) are taught by part-time faculty, and almost half (42.5 percent) by graduate teaching assistants. Only 6.9 percent of introductory writing courses are staffed by tenured- and tenure-track faculty (Cox A13–14). Clearly, part-time and non-tenure-track (or *contingent* faculty as I will refer to faculty working off the tenure-track) comprise a significant percentage of those responsible for teaching general-education writing requirements. Thus, the professional success narrative of composition is tempered by the continued exploitation of non-tenure-track faculty.

Moreover, in CCCC, in the late 1980s and early 1990s, we experienced a critical impasse in organizing around contingent faculty issues when the 1986 "Wyoming Resolution," with its proposed grievance and censure procedures, was not implemented—although it was endorsed by CCCC. Instead, the CCCC "Statement on Principles and Standards for the Improvement of Postsecondary Writing Instruction" with its focus on converting part-time and non-tenure-track positions into tenure-line positions was issued. Many in our organization were angered and discouraged that CCCC did not enact the "Wyoming Resolution" (see Gunner; Sledd). As I have argued in *Gypsy Academics and Mother-Teachers*, we learned many important lessons from this impasse, one of which is that we cannot remain in it. Instead, we must build coalitions with organized labor and other professional associations and take action, a point Lester Faigley underscores in his 1996 CCCC Chair's Letter:

> From the Wyoming Resolution and the ensuing debate with CCCC, we have learned that we will have to do more than write statements and that we need

to form alliances with other organizations if we expect to address issues of working conditions in any substantial way. We also should recognize that "working conditions" lumps together many broad issues and that we need to learn more about community organizing, the economics of higher education, and the impact of changing technologies on literacy education. (1)

Organizing writing faculty as a bloc to address working conditions is no easy matter. Many part-time and non-tenure-track faculty already feel burdened by their teaching loads, and some fear that speaking out may cost them their jobs. Many writing program administrators, too, feel overworked and implicated by their perpetuation of the non-tenure-track system, although a number of activist WPAs have emerged as well. I believe, however, that it is unionized and politicized graduate students and part-time and non-tenure-track faculty who will lead the way in efforts to address labor issues in the field. The electronic journal *Workplace* chronicles the efforts of graduate students, contingent faculty, and tenure-track advocates to speak out and take action toward labor justice in higher education. Authors link their labor struggles to struggles undertaken by workers in other sectors of the national and international economies. I am hopeful that the activist-organizing–oriented scholarship modeled in journals like *Workplace* will take hold in the mainstream scholarship on labor issues in composition, which tend to be caught up in describing and narrating labor problems rather than addressing how to organize and effect action. Indeed, there is currently a strain of scholarship in composition that advocates that we make do with what we have and make some small improvements because there is not enough funding to better working conditions overall (see Richard E. Miller). Such arguments tend to follow the reasoning that the American public will not use more of its tax dollars to go toward higher education and that we must simply adapt to the post–Cold War funding system and do what we can to make localized improvements. Certainly, local improvements can make a difference, but what happens when there are no legal and contractual protections built into those improvements? What happens when the benevolent administrator making the improvements is let go, retires, leaves for another institution, or is replaced by a less benevolent administrator? What happens when those working above the benevolent administrator erode his or her hard-won reforms or when faculty themselves sabotage them? (see Anson and Jewell 71–73). What happens in a time of budget crisis or freeze if those localized improvements are not protected through a union contract or through any sort of legal protections? Although local reform remains a path toward initiating change, such efforts must be buttressed by organized change movements that involve unionization and revitalization of existing unions or professional associations, coalition building with other workers, academic and nonacademic, and a critical understanding of the changes and challenges facing higher education.

A local reformist agenda, if it is to have credibility, must keep in mind the big picture of higher education funding and a vision of a democratic higher education. Within many university budgets, monies allocated toward administrative costs, student services, and distance learning have increased, while money for instructional budgets has not. In addition, many of us have watched with dismay as our state legislatures have built up the prison-industrial complex and systematically defunded higher education to do so. We have watched as our police forces and court systems have systematically locked up poor, working class African American and Latino/a men and women instead of creating real economic and educational opportunities (Reiman, *And the Poor Get Prison* 98–99). As literacy workers in the system of higher education, we need rhetorics and organizing strategies that will put us in a position to advocate for higher education's continuation and democratization, not its demise.

Organizing Models: From Campus to International

Since the mid- to late-1990s, campus organizing, municipal organizing (in cities like Boston, New York, and Denver) statewide organizing (particularly in California and Washington), and national and international organizing efforts around contingent labor issues have grown. In January of 2001, the Coalition of Contingent Academic Labor, an international group supporting equity in pay and working conditions, met in San Jose, California, at the fourth annual national conference on labor organizing. As Chris Storer, executive director of the California Association of Part-Time Faculty, notes, the COCAL IV conference allowed a national group of activists to give voice to a movement

> that has moved far beyond anger to the practical politics of healing the profession and uniting around the common cause of improving the educational opportunities of our students through a reinvigorated faculty professionalism which returns all faculty to the center of institutional governance and educational policy deliberations.

Storer's use of the word *healing* is important. All too often, we think of labor issues as a site of struggle, a fight, a battle; however, the language of healing and empowerment is crucial as well, especially as it pertains to working across lines of difference to achieve commonly held goals. Those of us who attended COCAL IV realized we were seeing a watershed moment in contingent academic labor organizing. We saw, for the first time, the seeds of national and international movements coming to fruition. These movements, however, are part of a larger revitalization of the academic labor movement and coalition building among diverse workers. On some campuses, unions and progressive coalitions of university employees have begun to bridge the gap between white-collar workers and blue/pink-collar workers. Kelley argues that this bridging is essential if we are going to address the root issue of exploitation in a global economy, an economy where women and people of color often experience the worst of "low-wage service work, part-time work, or outright joblessness" (151).

Campuswide Coalitions of University Workers

On many campuses, undergraduate and graduate students and faculty partners are waging campaigns against university patronage of prison labor and sweatshop manufacturers. Moreover, as mentioned earlier, alliances of university workers are growing through campuswide organizing. For example, on Syracuse University where I work as a tenure-track faculty member, a fall 1998 Service Employees' International Union (SEIU) strike over contract issues regarding wages and subcontracting for SEIU members galvanized faculty, staff, and students to create a faculty support group for SEIU university workers. Public meetings were held between SEIU representatives and faculty, students, and staff. A faculty support group listserv kept supporters up to date on mobilizations and actions. Tenure-track faculty, undergraduate and graduate students, and part-time faculty raised money for a strike fund, organized a support rally, wrote letters and signed a petition urging the chancellor to settle the contract fairly, walked the picket lines with the strikers, and held a teach-in rally at the local campus chapel. Some of us also invited striking SEIU workers to our classes to speak with students. I invited one of the picket captains, a janitor and part-time returning student, to attend my first-year writing course, a valuable opportunity for first-year students who, in their first week on campus, were unclear about the purposes behind the strike.

Thanks to the work of this faculty–university worker coalition, the strike was ended soon; moreover, this action raised consciousness on campus. A newly formed Student Coalition on Organized Labor (SCOOL), inspired by a similar student group at Cornell University, continues to actively lobby against sweatshop labor and agitate on behalf of organized labor in the university and the city of Syracuse. Faculty continue to notify one another of labor actions and needed coalitions. Syracuse University, however, is not unique; other campuses have held similar actions, and there is a rich history of such actions that is largely unknown by many academics (see Nelson; Kelley). Campus organizing around local and highly specific campus issues like union-contract struggles and the campus's use of sweatshop and prison labor are highly effective points of galvanization. Yet, municipal campaigns, largely conducted in urban areas, are also effective means of change.

Municipal Coalitions

One of the most successful municipal campaigns, and a model applicable to the national contingent labor agenda, took place in the greater Boston area in 1998 when part-time faculty activists spearheaded an organizing campaign at the University of Massachusetts–Boston. The campaign resulted in numerous gains: "half time status; full medical, dental, and pension benefits; and a floor of $4,000 per course" (Boston, "Adjuncts" 1). After winning these gains, UMass–Boston adjunct activists joined forces with professional associations, along with other union members and leaders, to found the Boston chapter of COCAL with the goal of municipal organizing—an important move in a city where one out of every four people is a college student, a population that makes adjunct faculty almost as common as college students. Cosponsored by the American Association of University Professors, local labor organizations, and undergraduate students, the Boston COCAL activists have conducted informational pickets at target colleges with problematic labor practices, held meetings to organize part-time faculty at area colleges (both public and private), and worked to help graduate students as well as contingent faculty organize (Boston, "Ten-Point Program" 1–2). Boston's COCAL's ten-point program connects quality working conditions to quality learning conditions:

1. Equal pay for equal work at the appropriate academic rank
2. Full medical, dental, and retirement benefits for those teaching two or more courses per term. Prorated benefits for those teaching fewer. Tuition remission for family members
3. Job security. No one terminated without just cause and due process
4. Adequate office space and facilities
5. Full participation in department and college or university governance
6. Opportunities for professional development, including financial support for research and creative work
7. Promotion of part-time faculty to full-time positions
8. Narrowing of salary disparities within the faculty
9. Full protection of free speech rights and all other forms of academic freedom
10. Recognition and respect as vital members of the academic community (Boston, "Ten-Point" 1)

Efforts at municipal organizing are being made in New York City and in Denver. David Rosman and others at the Auraria Higher Education Campus (AHEC), which includes the University of Colorado at Denver, Metropolitan State College of Denver, and the Community College of Denver, are organizing. In New York City, adjunct faculty at the City University of New York organized and sponsored a public hearing before the Higher Education Committee of New York State and the Labor Committee on 9 March 2001. The goal of the hearing was to "awaken public consciousness," "gain public and legislative support for increasing funding of higher education in New York State," "highlight budget items that will improve the status of adjunct faculty," and to create "legislation on unemployment and disability insurance for adjuncts" (CUNY). The AAUP, along with COCAL, has encouraged these municipal organizing efforts, connecting them to unionization and bringing together citywide groups of adjuncts to defend and protect basic worker rights.

Statewide Coalitions

Another arena for organizing has been through statewide efforts on the part of unionized faculty. Two coalitions of community-college faculty, the California

Part-Time Faculty Association (CPFA) and the Washington Part-Time Faculty Association (WPFA), have led successful statewide organizing campaigns to improve part-time faculty salaries and health benefits. The CPFA, newly revived in 1998, promotes "professional equity for all faculty in the California Community College System by ending the exploitation of part-time faculty" (Brasket 1). The CPFA's goal is three-fold: (1) to foster communication and resource sharing among part-time faculty; (2) to educate multiple publics about part-time faculty issues; and (3) to work to improve the quality of education through improving part-time faculty working conditions (Brasket 1). The CPFA, banding together with unions, professional associations, local activists (who sponsored Part-Time Faculty Equity Week April 2000, an event they refer to Action Coalition 2000 or A2K), and A2K activists engaged in a petition-drive campaign around equal pay for equal work, urging the state to set aside funds ($75 million) for improving part-time faculty salaries (Baringer 1). This campaign was successful. California Governor Gray Davis in 2001 earmarked $62 million for improving part-time faculty salaries, a significant victory (Leatherman, "Part-Time" A13). Washington State has seen similar gains. Keith Hoeller, a part-time adjunct philosophy professor at Green River Community College and cofounder of the WPFA, which represents the needs and concerns of part-time faculty statewide, has used the courts, petition drives, lobbying efforts, and organized actions to get the issues of contingent faculty's wages and benefits on the statewide agenda (Leatherman, "Do Accreditors" A12). The CPFA and WPFA are two key examples of broad-based coalitions among staff and graduate and undergraduate students as well as those outside the academy; however, the organizing of adjunct faculty is moving into national and international arenas.

National and International Coalitions

In many of the above-mentioned coalitions and campaigns, COCAL has been a major force. The coalition was formed as a result of three academic conferences held in 1997–1999 (Boston, "Adjuncts" 1). COCAL is now a national and international network of activists who work to improve the working lives of the growing ranks of part-time and non-tenure-line faculty, graduate teaching assistants, and research assistants. COCAL every year since 1998 convenes an annual conference, bringing together adjunct activists, union organizers, full-timers, scholars, and others to address working conditions and to create a national agenda. COCAL sponsored Campus Equity Week in fall 2001 and is sponsoring a second Campus Equity Week in fall 2005, organizing teach-ins, petitions, protests, and other actions to call attention to the overuse and exploitation of contingent faculty (Leatherman, "Part-Time" A12). During October 28–November 3, 2001, the first Campus Equity Week took place in Canada, Mexico, and the U.S. and included rallies, teach-ins, information tables, union drives and card-signing campaigns, and a collecting of signatures to petition for local adoption of a common campus charter or professional working conditions bill of rights.

The event was coordinated by a campus equity week steering committee who developed organizing materials (Storer 1).

Rich Moser, the chief organizer of the Campus Equity Week steering committee, describes the event as

> a decentralized effort, that means that each campus or region or organization calls their own shots and choose a level of activity that's appropriate. The committee will provide a slender packet with some core materials but this is really about local initiative as part of a national movement or the old think globally act locally approach.

Campus Equity Week is particularly important for those of us in the fields of English and writing because we have, by far, the greatest reliance on part-time and non-tenure-track faculty. The issue of working conditions, though, goes beyond the bread-and-butter issue of salaries and contracts; CEW is also about the fight to maintain adequate public funding for higher education and about the right to keep higher education affordable and accessible to diverse populations of students.

In 2001, the CCCC Committee on Contingent, Adjunct, and Part-Time Faculty, which I then cochaired with Karen Thompson from Rutgers University, put forward a resolution asking CCCC to support CEW. The resolution unanimously passed at the 2001 business meeting at CCCC, and the committee held a rally to help the CCCC membership strategize plans for CEW. In conclusion, I will briefly describe the rhetorics we can best adopt to achieve coalition building and organizing toward improving working conditions: the rhetoric of costs, the rhetoric of common cause, and the rhetoric of coalition building.

Costs, Common Cause, and Coalition Building

First, we need to make arguments for improvements in working conditions that are based on presenting the costs of contingent labor, not the cost-savings. We have heard plenty about the cost-savings that reliance on contingent faculty provides but what about the costs to students, to higher education, and the local economy? Students, parents, and taxpayers deserve to know what the educational costs are to students when their college instructors do not get compensated for office hours or when their instructors are notified two nights before the term begins that they are being hired back. These issues must be presented respectfully, without denigrating the work of part-time and non-tenure-track faculty, but, at the same time, we cannot pretend that instructional quality is not affected by working conditions. We have to make the costs visible to our multiple publics through editorials, petitions, legislative hearings, and lobbying efforts.

We also need to develop a more sophisticated rhetoric of common cause. All too often I hear tenure-track colleagues argue that we cannot improve working conditions for part-time and non-tenure-track faculty because to do so will solidify a second or third tier of faculty, thus eroding tenure. I believe this is a defeatist logic that has the potential to lock us into permanent inaction. Instead of a two-tier system, we now have a four- or five-tier system: tenure-track–tenured, permanent non-tenure-track faculty, temporary non-tenure-track faculty, part-time permanent faculty, and part-time temporary. Improving working conditions means closing the gap between exploitation and stability. As Linda Ray Pratt, former president of the American Association of University Professors, argues, we must reduce the "cheapness and convenience" of part-time labor by putting "more money into it and more stability behind it, two conditions that negate the attractiveness of part-time over full-time positions" (273).

In a recent article in *Workplace: The Journal of Academic Labor* entitled "Medieval or Modern Status in the Postindustrial University," Gary Rhoades, a sociologist of the professions, urges that graduate students and other academics who wish to organize should adopt a

> post-modern approach to agency and action, . . . [thus] [r]eject[ing] the implied forced choice between competing metaphors and mechanisms, between apprentice or employee, between private, individual negotiation and public collective bargaining. (4)

To this I would also that we need to resist the divisions among full-time, tenure-track faculty, and contingent faculty and the binary between academic workers and other workers.

Finally, we need rhetorics that enable coalition building. In "Making Better Connections: Some Thoughts on Rhetoric and Solidarity as We Struggle for Academic Unionization," Jamie Owen Daniel argues that we need to avoid rhetorical strategies that reinforce the idea that academics as a group are more entitled to fair wages and benefits than other groups of workers. It is certainly true that academic training is specialized, and it is often the case that our apprenticeships are longer than many workers; but is this information useful when we are making arguments to the automobile assembly-line worker or the teacher in a public school about the role of working conditions in higher education? Will he or she want to hear how specialized and educated we are? No. He or she will want to know what common cause exists among our situation and theirs. If we are going to build coalitions with other workers, we need a rhetoric of common cause, not a rhetoric of entitlement.

Daniel also advises that we avoid one-way analogies, statements that compare adjunct teachers to migrant workers for instance. Although it is important to point out exploitation, and the migrant-labor analogy is a particularly dramatic, evocative, and frequently used one, it is a one-way analogy. Few migrant workers would say they are like adjunct teachers, especially as "they risk machete wounds or rat bites or heat stroke or the possibility of being reported to the INS and then deported because they've demanded a legal days' pay or a bathroom on site" (Daniel 3). We need to be careful about analogies that compare us to other workers, using the oppressed status of others to signify our own.

Eileen E. Schell

With a rhetoric that opposes binaries and encourages agency and coalition building, we are in a good position to articulate a broad educational agenda that acknowledges worker rights and the fundamental need for a democratic, accessible, and diverse system of higher education. As the narratives and case studies show in *Moving a Mountain,* the "organizing strategies that will work best [toward achieving that goal] must be adaptive and multiple" (Schell, *Moving* 337). Literacy workers can play a significant role in this movement for change, especially if we use our considerable critical and rhetorical skills as a platform for organizing and agitating for change.

8
Teaching Writing in a Managed Environment

Eric Marshall

(A) academics are managed professionals and are increasingly so. Managerial discretion is broad and expanding. Professional involvement in decision making is limited, as are professional constraints on managerial discretion;

(B) academics are highly stratified professionals and are increasingly so. Managerial flexibility serves to heighten the hierarchy and divisions within the academic profession, which are already considerable, and are growing

—Gary Rhoades, *Managed Professionals: Unionized Faculty and Restructuring Academic Labor*[1]

The Making of an Academic Unionist—Part I

When I began teaching at the City University of New York, in the English Department of Kingsborough Community College, out at wind-swept Manhattan Beach, Brooklyn, in October 1991, I had exactly four weeks of doctoral education under my belt and no college-level teaching experience. I arrived, as instructed, on the first day of classes, was handed the course rosters for my two developmental writing seminars, pointed in the direction of my Monday morning building (which was different from my Monday late-morning building, which was likewise different from my Tuesday buildings, and so on), and given a supportive (albeit figurative) pat on the back. I had selected my textbook a week earlier, just after a rather pro forma interview, from among the few available readers on the old gray-metal bookcase in the storage/mimeograph room. I had little contact thereafter with my department chair, who was nevertheless a nice-enough person, and even less with the other full-timers in the department, save one who had been assigned as my mentor for the semester and who, seemingly gladly, carried out his undefined responsibilities with reliability and felicitous wisdom.

The Kingsborough students were a wonderfully diverse slice of South Brooklyn life: Italian-Americans, Hispanics of many nationalities, Orthodox Jews, Russian and Caribbean immigrants, seventeen-year-old freshmen and seventy-year-old retirees. I loved teaching them, even while I felt my inexperience. Somehow I always suspected that they felt it, too.

I also felt grateful to have a job, proud (if largely unqualified) to be teaching college, and relieved to be able to subsidize my own graduate education, however insufficiently, without venturing outside the academy too much. Apart from the thrice-weekly trek out to Brooklyn from my Manhattan apartment (ninety minutes via two subway trains and a bus for a not-insignificant fourteen dollars per week), there seemed to be few negatives to the situation. The last thing on my mind was a consideration of the conditions under which I dutifully labored, even as I regularly conferenced "confidentially" with students while one (or more) of my several office mates sat close by grading papers in our six-by-eight-foot, one-desk office.

As it turns out, it did not take long for me to realize the extent and degree of the exploitation to which I, and thousands of my CUNY adjunct colleagues, were being subjected on a daily basis. Sub-livable wages. No health insurance. No pay for the office hours I religiously maintained. Too many adjuncts crammed into too-small an office space (though at least we *had* an office, unlike many CUNY adjuncts). Too many students producing too many papers to respond to effectively. No job security. No say in what or when I would teach.

That first year at Kingsborough, I taught four sections of a remedial English course designed expressly to prepare students to pass the critical CUNY Writing Assessment Test (so critical that even though faculty referred to the exam as "the WAT," my students referred to it more synecdochically as "the CUNY"). This fifty-minute, prompted essay on fairly innocuous, if nevertheless controversial, topics stood as the gateway to students' academic futures. My own assessment of their academic progress mattered comparatively little. The students understood the equation quite clearly: pass the WAT, move out of remediation and on to the required English curriculum—indeed, out of Kingsborough and, perhaps, on to a senior college; fail the WAT again (it was used as both placement and exit exam), remain in community college and in Developmental Writing. I do not recall anyone explicitly telling me to teach to the exam, though I knew my success as a teacher would be judged at least in part by my students' passage rate. The more students I got through the exam, (which in those days was scored by other members of the department who were paid for each scored exam), the better the department looked to college and CUNY administration, and, hence, the better I looked to the department. Though I resisted the urge for most of the semester, as the exam date approached I found myself talking to the students about test-taking strategies and giving them WAT-like practice tests.

Soon I learned that the conditions under which I labored at Kingsborough were not local to CUNY, or even New York City, but were nearly universal to the nation's large and growing part-time, contingent academic labor force, which, even then, comprised nearly half all higher education instructors in the country. What it came down to, it seemed to me, was *control,* who was making the decisions that affected the conditions—both within the classroom and without—under which I labored. As I began talking to friends and colleagues around CUNY and elsewhere, several questions repeatedly surfaced: Why were we being paid so much less per course than our full-time colleagues often teaching the same courses? Why did we often wait six weeks or more from the start of the semester before receiving our first measly paycheck? Why did we often have to wait until days, or even *hours,* before the start of the semester to learn if we even had a teaching assignment? Why were we not being paid to maintain office hours to meet with students—an essential component to composition education—although we were often directed to maintain them? Why were we given insufficient (or no) space in which to meet privately and confidentially with students? Why did we have to labor so long without any health benefits?[2] Why were we not given appointments longer than one semester at a time so that we might build some continuity and familiarity within a program and gain with the confidence to create new pedagogies and methodologies, as well as the freedom to plan a course in advance of the first day of class? And, ultimately, how were we supposed to provide the best education to our students under these conditions? Indeed, how could it possibly be in the best interest of the students to have more than half of their instructors (*far* more at the community colleges like Kingsborough) trekking among several different jobs, leading a precarious professional existence from one term to the next, incapable of devoting the time and attention both needed and desired to perform most effectively? The more frequently the questions arose, the more conspicuous was the absence of answers.

Case Study: The City University of New York

Perhaps nowhere in the country are these conditions more prevalent or extreme than on the large urban campuses in our largest cities. Nowhere in the academy are they more apparent than in the instruction of composition. The City University of New York is the oldest, largest urban university system in the country, with 200,000 students and about 5,500 full-time and 7,000 part-time faculty in 2000. As is common throughout higher education in this country, CUNY's composition programs are among its largest employers of part-time faculty, although former Mayor Rudolph Giuliani's über-management efforts to remove remedial instruction from the university—despite organized protest from the faculty and students—have cut into those numbers over the past two years.[3]

In an attempt to begin redressing decades of neglect and disinvestment in the university, the Professional Staff Congress (PSC)—CUNY's faculty and professional staff union—compiled in the summer of 2000 a set of progressive contract demands designed to reinvigorate CUNY and prepared a budget proposal designed to return CUNY to excellence and national prominence. For adjuncts, this PSC budget included a request for $12.8 million in additional state funding to pay for adjunct office hours (*PSC/CUNY* 18), as well as increased access to travel funds, additional graduate fellowships, and tuition remission for all doctoral students who teach at least two courses. The initial set of contract demands, released in fall 2000, continued a section of specific demands for adjunct faculty, including: prorated pay and benefits, job security provisions, establishment and utilization of seniority lists, annual appointments, written explanations for non-reappointments, accrual of sick leave, guaranteed consideration for open full-time lines, and offices with computers, telephones, and other necessary equipment with no more than three people to an office.[4] Moreover, the union is engaged in massive organizing and mobilization efforts, designed to recruit part-timers into the union as active members.

I taught at CUNY for nearly two years before I even learned that there was a labor union representing faculty. My academic political awakening was not an epiphany but developed over the course of several years, commencing in the fall 1993, when I and five of my graduate-student adjunct colleagues at Queens College were unfairly treated by the college. It was not a major violation, but it sufficed to demonstrate for me the degree of my vulnerability in the university. This episode not only led me to find and become involved in the PSC but also to become more active in the CUNY Graduate Center's student government and help make it more politically active by creating the CUNY Adjunct Project to educate doctoral students about their rights as workers and encourage them to join the union. This work led me to join the New Caucus—a group of then-insurgent faculty seeking to challenge the union's long-sitting leadership for control of the PSC.[5] It also led me to help found CUNY Adjuncts Unite!, a coalition of CUNY adjunct activists committed to educating the faculty, both full- and part-time, about the conditions under which CUNY adjuncts labored and to agitating for better representation and more equitable working terms and conditions. In April 2000, the New Caucus won eighteen of the twenty-one executive offices at the PSC. As vice-president for part-time personnel, I sat with the PSC at the contract-negotiating table, fighting for a set of demands that I helped to compile and represented fellow adjuncts when their contractual rights were violated.

Almost immediately upon taking office at the PSC, I conducted the first-ever survey of CUNY's part-time faculty assessing their demographics, working conditions, and contract priorities. What we learned from this survey was edifying, though not particularly surprising. Based on this survey (which had an exceptionally high return rate of 40 percent) of approximately 4,800 adjuncts and graduate assistants, we identified the following about the CUNY part-time faculty: In 2000, they are older (median age of 50), more long-term (while the average tenure was five years, a substantial number of adjuncts had tenures of more than ten years), more full-time (average workload is nearly two courses per term at CUNY; only about one-third indicated having a full-time job elsewhere), more professionally credentialed (25 percent hold doctorates; an additional 60 percent hold masters degrees), and yet more poorly paid (average annual adjunct income of under $10,000; three-quarters earn less than $15,000) than many imagined. In addition, CUNY adjuncts reported a great deal of "subway surfing." One in twelve was teaching at more than one CUNY campus; one in four was also teaching outside of CUNY. CUNY adjuncts described having minimal input in determining the number, type, and schedule of courses they teach. Nearly one-third reported having no office space at all; nearly two-thirds reported no computer access on campus; nearly three-quarters reported no Internet access on campus. Finally, when it came to contractual priorities, CUNY adjuncts fell right in step with their colleagues around the country, identifying pay, health benefits, job security, and scheduling as their chief concerns.[6]

The Bigger Data Picture

In spring 1999 (about a year before the PSC survey and following the 1997 Conference on Growing Use of Part-Time and Adjunct Faculty held in Washington, D.C.), the Coalition on the Academic Work Force (CAW)—an amalgamation of twenty-five academic societies—conducted a survey of humanities and social science disciplines across the country on the use and treatment of part-time faculty. CAW reported that the number of full-timers has been declining and confirmed that part-timers now constitute more than half of the instructional staff in most disciplines.[7] Further noted was that most part-timers

> could earn comparable salaries as fast food workers, baggage porters, or theater lobby attendants. . . . [The] terms and conditions of such appointments are too often inadequate to support responsible teaching or a career, . . . [and] terms and conditions of part-time and adjunct faculty appointments, in many cases, weaken our capacity to provide essential educational experiences and resources. ("Summary of Data")

Data also indicate

> that part-time faculty members are not integrated into the life of the programs in which they are teaching (by invitation to department meetings) or the academic community (by support for their research and professional development). ("Summary of Data")

This, of course, is especially troubling considering that part-time faculty are most students' initial contact with college and that these faculty often teach the introductory courses that lay the groundwork not only for more advanced study but also for the entire higher educational experience.[8]

For years, academic professional associations and labor unions have decried the overuse and exploitation of adjunct faculty but rarely have they taken the offensive in remedying the situation.[9] Numerous effects of this overuse and exploitation have been repeatedly identified: adjuncts often teach an excessively heavy course load, with larger classes, often at several different campuses, necessitating costly and time-consuming travel and significantly limiting the time available to prepare, grade, meet students, and rest. Adjuncts forced to travel between jobs have depleted energies to devote to their teaching. Graduate student adjuncts forced to teach to pay their bills—often full course loads, often for years without a break—frequently take years longer to complete their degrees, if they finish at all. Adjuncts seeking full-time employment, who are forced for economic reasons to teach four, five, six or more courses per term, have little if any time to maintain their scholarship, and thereby their competitiveness, for those increasingly rare tenure-track positions. Adjuncts are typically far removed from the curricular decision-making processes, to their detriment and that of their students. The situation is generally recognized as untenable but, besides issuing statements, little has been done by the various professional associations.

Teaching Writing in a Managed Environment: Preparation

As an undergraduate at the University of Pennsylvania in the mid-1980s, I studied economics and English. Penn was just then developing a writing across the curriculum program, and so I had my writing scrutinized only slightly more than usual (which was little) in just one economics course. I took no writing classes in college, and I do not even know if any were offered at that time. In my first year of graduate school, I took courses in Old English, scholarship and criticism, seventeenth- and eighteenth-century satire, nineteenth-century British novel, Dickens, Emerson, and Wallace Stevens. Although they all required me to produce the standard twenty-page term paper, effectively training me in British and American literature, there was nothing to prepare me (much less *qualify* me) to teach writing. I was training as an academic reader and writer to do literary scholarship. I often wondered what I was doing standing in front of thirty students who desperately needed to acquire basic college-level reading and writing skills but even more desperately needed to pass the university's monolithic WAT in order to move on and out. I sought a connection, which I (rightly) suspected existed, between what I was studying and practicing and what I was teaching. My academic preparation and practice could not, after all, be completely divorced from my academic labor. The answer, I would learn, was as much political as academic.

Teaching Writing in a Managed Environment: Praxis

More perhaps than any other academic discipline, composition remains a primary site of managerial opportunism and labor exploitation. It has been in the classrooms of basic writing instruction that this fight between academic freedom and managerial control has been playing out most emphatically and destructively.

Composition instruction is (or is at least perceived as being) highly manageable. First, by the very nature of the discipline, composition instruction is problematic. Writing well and teaching writing well are two *very* different enterprises. Success in the former by no means ensures success in the latter. Of course, this observation applies in other disciplines as well: A skilled practitioner is not necessarily a good teacher. However, composition is different. Most academics, including administrators, consider themselves able writers. Many, perhaps most, consequently undervalue the skills involved with teaching writing well—believing that anyone who can write well can teach writing well. In some institutions, virtually all faculty, even full-timers, take their required (often grudging) turn with an obligatory composition section or two. Can one imagine that attitude being extended to literature courses or to other disciplines?

The modern academy, as I have argued elsewhere,[10] privileges specialization over generalization, and composition—the quintessential basic skill—suffers for this. All students need to be able to write well to succeed in school. "It is *because* composition is needed in *every* college course, in *every* discipline, that it languishes in the educational basement, not *despite* that fact" ("Abolish or Perish"). Moreover, the modern academy, as it further corporatizes, privileges—at least in terms of compensation—disciplines whose practitioners have greater corporate utility and hence economic value, business and computer science, for instance, at the expense of others.[11] "Policies driven by a concern with enhancing corporate competitiveness," note Gary Rhoades and Sheila Slaughter, "concentrate resources on fields that are seen as potential wealth creators" (27). Composition is not one.

Like physicians in HMOs, Rhoades argues, faculty have become salaried employees of large profit-seeking corporations, not independent practitioners (*Managed Professionals* 2). In health care, however, overly managed conditions have had demonstrably (and publicly debated) negative impacts. In academia, we have never made that conceptual leap to argue, publicly, that one consequence of our over-reliance on part-time instructors has been a diminished or inferior product. Sure, it is not as good as it *might* be, but that is hardly the same as arguing that it is not as good as it *must* be.

At the end of the day, we are one faculty. What is good for part-timers is good for full-timers. Raising the professional status and conditions of adjuncts has (and will continue to have) a markedly positive impact on the status and conditions of full-timers. In *Managed Professionals,* Rhoades notes:

> The suspicion, resentment, and distrust generated bidirectionally in the two-tiered system is probably its most destructive aspect. It complicates the possibility of forging a collective identity among faculty. . . . However, given that a large number of adjuncts in any department increases the administrative workload of the full-timers, and that the growing lower tier will, over time, diminish the collective-bargaining power of all faculty, then it stands to reason that there is an increasing convergence of interest between the upper and

lower tiers, and it is that convergence of interest, if properly understood, that will provide a basis for dialogue and for mobilization. (86)

We are far, however, from universal recognition—much less acceptance—of this reality. There remains much education that must take place, both within the academy and with the public. Part-timers must recognize the extent of their exploitation as well as the possibilities for improvement and educate their full-time colleagues about their conditions. Full-timers must be educated to appreciate the adjunct conditions and must be mobilized to help improve those conditions as part of a process of improving their own, along with the general health of the profession. Unions must organize and mobilize faculty and staff, full- and part-time, to begin to change public attitudes towards higher education, convincing people, for instance, of the fundamental need to subsidize public higher education. Then, *only* then, can we return to an academy where a united faculty regains its historic prerogatives and best serves the students.

The Making of an Academic Unionist—Part II

So my Kingsborough students did well on the WAT that year, and I was invited back for the following year. But that reappointment offer was for a four-day-per-week schedule, one day more than I had been teaching. I was a full-time doctoral student still taking classes, and, besides, by then, I knew that the rest of CUNY, for the most part, was on a two-day schedule. I told the chair I could not work a four-day schedule, and he wished me the best of luck in my future. Never have I felt more dispensable. After taking a semester off from teaching at CUNY, I arrived at Queens College in spring 1993, wiser perhaps and rejuvenated, having accepted their offer of a graduate teaching assistantship. Unlike Kingsborough, at Queens I had a great deal of contact with my chair and a great deal more with the director of composition. I enjoyed more academic freedom, taught a wider range of courses, from English 95 (their now-defunct version of remedial writing) to Shakespeare, shared a two-desk office with only one other adjunct, interacted collegially with the full-time faculty, was invited to department meetings, and generally felt like a valued, appreciated member of the department. I was regularly asked what I wanted to teach and when and almost always had those requests honored. Although my English 95 students had to pass the same WAT as my old Kingsborough students in order to move on to the required English curriculum, I never felt judged as an instructor by my students' pass rate, which nevertheless remained high. Consequently, I never felt compelled to teach to the test and believe much more was accomplished in developing students' reading, writing, and learning skills and confidence as a result.

I taught at CUNY for eleven years and have reflected much on my teaching, and on my life, through those years. My experiences as a union officer, negotiator, and representative have given me a much richer, deeper sense of teaching and what teachers can and must do. As an adjunct and graduate student, I have been able to identify more meaningfully with my students, my *fellow* students, and have fought diligently to remedy *our* problems, truly understanding that in education what is good for the teacher is generally also what is good for the students.

The eight years I spent in academic labor politics in CUNY took me around the country to speak at conferences and to meet with adjuncts at many other institutions. It also led me to work for the American Federation of Teachers for a year and a half, which I did full time in addition to my CUNY work, organizing and educating adjuncts. After getting involved with the PSC and especially after becoming an officer, I began and continued to view my role in the academy much more expansively. I considered my work in the classroom and my obligations to students as well as my responsibility to the profession in a new light. They are integrated and interdependent. I was no longer simply a teacher of writing or of Shakespeare but an educator more generally, as I believe we all must be educators in a collective agenda that extends beyond the scope of a single syllabus, past the parochial interests of discipline, and beyond the walls of the classroom.

Notes

1. Gary Rhoades argues, "Evidence of managerial discretion takes three forms . . . (a) absence of conditions . . . (b) statements of management rights regarding workforce matters; and/or (c) exceptions to particular rules—for example, order of layoff" (*Managed Professionals* 141). The record of National Labor Relations Board rulings on higher education unionization rights since 1950 provides a useful historical backdrop to this discussion.

2. In 1991, when I began teaching at CUNY, adjuncts had to wait three years before becoming eligible to receive health benefits through the union. As a result of adjunct organizing, however, that waiting period was reduced in the 1996 labor agreement. Adjunct lecturers are now eligible to receive free health benefits in their third consecutive semester of teaching, providing they teach at least six credits per term. Graduate students serving in graduate assistant and graduate fellow titles, however, are ineligible for benefits, despite teaching the same courses as their adjunct colleagues, many of whom are likewise graduate students but who are not on assistantships or fellowships.

3. Giuliani was not the only political enemy of CUNY, however. Through the 1990s, New York state and New York City defunded CUNY by $375 million (inflation adjusted), a 30-percent decline in funding, according to data published by the National Center for Public Policy and Higher Education (*PSC/CUNY* 3). New York state ranks last in state and local appropriations for higher education, in terms of percent change between 1990 and 1999 in constant dollars (*PSC/CUNY* 5). Full-time faculty declined more than 50 percent between 1975 and 2000, as student enrollment increased (*PSC/CUNY* 9, 10). The percentage of part-time faculty peaked in 1997 at 57.7 percent and remains near that level. Moreover, in 1999, 56 percent of undergraduate instruction was done by part-timers at the community colleges and 49 percent was done at the senior colleges, compared with 46 percent and 38 percent respectively in 1990. For the period 1990 to 1999, New York state is last nationwide in the increase in state and local appropriations for higher education. The state also ranks last in the percentage of income that poorest families need to pay for tuition at the lowest-priced colleges; new York's poor families pay a share of 33 percent; the national average is 15 percent of income (*PSC/CUNY* 5).

4. See the PSC Web site (www.psc-cuny.org) for the complete set of bargaining proposals.

5. Among the New Caucus's many complaints with the union's former leadership was its demonstrable lack of interest in the part-time faculty, both at the bargaining table and as union members. In its successful campaign to take over the union's executive offices, the New Caucus ran on a platform centered around issues of equity, such as pay parity and paid office hours for adjuncts. Since the change in PSC leadership, part-timer membership in the union has more than tripled.

6. While PSC vice president, I spent much time poring over the NEA–AFT Higher Education Contract Analysis System (HECAS) 2000 database of more than six hundred contracts. In *Managed Professionals,* Gary Rhoades similarly analyzed the 1997 HECAS database, then containing just over two hundred contracts. Rhoades's findings led him to conclude that the "absence of provisions about general personnel actions is striking." In particular, he cites the lack of provisions for conditions of appointment and release for part-time faculty as well as the silence on priority hiring of adjuncts for full-time positions (142–55). Rhoades further notes that "nearly two-thirds of HECAS contracts do *not* accord part-time faculty *any* of the rights/perquisites accorded full-time faculty." Of those that do, of the seventy-four contracts that define some rights/perquisites for part-time faculty, several involve "negative references, explicitly denying part-timers certain rights/perquisites" (157). The most common categories Rhoades observed concerned leaves and health benefits, with professional development, tuition waivers, and work space a distant third, fourth, and fifth, respectively (158). Based on his study of the HECAS contracts, Rhoades concludes that, in regard to part-time faculty professional rights, "Managerial discretion . . . is virtually unconstrained in the contracts" (146–47). In the current HECAS database. there are 106 contracts for two-year institutions representing both full- and part-time faculty, thirty-two contracts for four-year institutions representing both faculty groups, sixteen contracts for two-year institutions, five for four-year institutions representing only part-time faculty, and seven contracts representing only graduate assistants. All told, they once again paint a bleak picture of the professional landscape for the nation's adjunct faculty and an especially bleak one for those in the humanities and social sciences.

7. According to the survey, in freestanding programs in composition, full-time tenure-track faculty constitute under 15 percent of classroom teachers. English and foreign language departments employ full-time tenure-track faculty in just over one-third of their staffs. In most disciplines, graduate students make up 15 to 25 percent of the instructional staff. The numbers are much higher in composition; for example, graduate students taught 42.5 percent of courses in freestanding composition programs. Full-time tenure-track faculty taught less than half of undergrad introductory courses in nearly every discipline; in freestanding composition programs, they taught less than 7 percent. While full-time non-tenure-track faculty, by and large, were determined to receive "a viable standard of living," part-timers received less than $3,000 per course, with nearly one-third earning $2,000 or less ("Summary of Data").

8. CAW's conclusion does not elaborate on how the "capacity to provide essential educational experiences" is weakened. The report might have noted, for instance, the impact of failing to compensate part-timers for maintaining office hours (thereby effectively discouraging them from doing so).

9. Compare the comments of the NEA quoted below from Rhoades; the AAUP Committee G Report, published in *Academe* 1992 and elsewhere; and AFT statement issued in 1979. In its 1992 amendment of the 1976 resolution, Resolution F. 41, the NEA, for instance, declared

The National Education Association believes that part-time education employees should receive the same salary and benefits as full-time education employees prorated according to the workload. The Association deplores the practice of employing part-time education employees for the primary purpose of reducing instructional budgets or for the purpose of reducing the number of full-time education positions. (qtd. in Rhoades, *Managed Professionals* 139)

In *Part-Time Faculty: Higher Education at a Crossroads* (1984), Judith M. Gappa concludes simply that "the three national faculty unions [AFT, AAUP, and NEA] want to minimize and control the use of part-time faculty. They argue for fewer part-time faculty members and greater economic and professional security for those few" (58).

10. See Tony Baker, "Abolish or Perish? Managed Labor in Composition: A Roundtable Discussion with Sharon Crowley."

11. Across disciplines, faculty salaries collectively bargained are higher than those not—by as much as 44 percent in one discipline, according to *The NEA 1995 Almanac of Higher Ed* (qtd. in Rhoades, *Managed Professionals* 78).

9

The Role of Writing
Programs in Labor Relations

Steve Parks

Writing programs traditionally have been defined by a set of components—
first-year writing courses, upper-division writing courses, a writing center, and faculty development. Becoming a full-time tenured professional in the
field means learning how to negotiate and understand those components. For instance, part of a graduate student's career involves learning how to teach and tutor
the students in basic writing courses. Later, as the graduate students assume managerial responsibilities (either in or outside the tenure stream), they also learn how
to assign courses, battle within departments for more instructors, and develop
faculty training seminars.

Through these different avenues, such faculty begin to develop sensitivity to
the economic structure that grounds our work (such as part-time labor) and its
connections to the larger economic system. The discussions that grow from these
insights, however, occur in closed meetings with deans, department chairs, or
faculty committees. The discussions do not enter the classroom or the curriculum. They typically do not include labor activists or community organizers. I
would argue that, as a field, there is little or no expectation that writing programs
should engage in systemic work concerning economic questions, nor is it generally expected that writing programs should undertake such work with individuals or labor organizations outside the university community. In effect, the "we"
of composition often gets represented by the work of full-time, tenured compositionists, typically at large research universities, who produce scholarship and
oversee a body of courses dedicated to the production of academic writers.

Speaking as someone who fits into that representation, I believe that such a
limited focus and limited definition of community represents a failing on the
part of myself and those with similar institutional profiles to engage with the
needs of our students or the possibilities of collective writing. It represents a model

of professionalism that ultimately restricts our ability to be full citizens in our own community or region. As professionals in the field, we need to bring the economic struggles of our students and neighbors into the center of our work. To do this, however, will mean reconfiguring the traditional components of our writing programs to include voices other than our own and ultimately to integrate our voices into the larger struggle for economic justice—a struggle, that is, against an economic system of which our labor is but one part.

It is the task of thinking through what such a reconfiguration of a writing program might look like that I have set myself for this chapter. In the following pages, then, I want reflect upon work I have undertaken at Temple University as a framework to suggest some strategies for revising the four components of a traditional writing program and to respond to the economic questions that are the focus of this book.

First-Year Writing

If we believe in bringing economic literacy into our writing classrooms and working toward building a common labor identity, an initial commitment might be to developing a connection among high school students, college freshman, and laborers. Such a connection might not only be a way to increase the quality of education in high schools but also to provide each student population with a way to understand their common economic situation.

For instance, in Philadelphia, a typical comprehensive high school near Temple University begins with a freshman class of one thousand. All of these students will originate from a family that lives below or at the poverty line. The student population itself will be almost 95 percent African American, Latino, or Asian/ Pacific. Of the original thousand students, only two hundred will graduate. Of those two hundred, a significant number will go on to attend some institution of higher learning. Most likely, they will be required to take a basic or remedial writing program. If they succeed, they should earn on average $10,000–15,000 more a year than their former high school colleagues. Yet, they will attempt to do so in a city with high unemployment and low resources. In such a situation, many will follow the decision of others and simply leave the city. The model of education as escape means that the cycle of neighborhood poverty will continue. I believe a writing program should serve as a vehicle to create a collective identity among these populations.

To effect this goal, a collective identity would have to be based upon alliances amongst laboring populations that create not only a sense of purpose but a common agenda. For instance, Philadelphia's public school system was recently taken over by the state. At the outset of this takeover attempt, Edison Schools was selected to analyze and eventually take over a significant portion of the schools in the district. In response to this privatization effort, a coalition of public school students, college students, city advocates, literacy teachers, public schoolteachers, university faculty, union locals, and community organizations launched a campaign to alter any such takeover deal. Participants included all segments of the Philadelphia region, crossing neighborhoods and communities. Here the primary emphasis was that even those without the ability to send their children to private school deserve a voice in the policies designed to ensure a quality public education. As importantly, this basic civil right also became a vehicle for supporting the blue-collar unionized workers who are often displaced by an Edison takeover.

For such collective politics to have long-term viability, however, there needs to be a consistent and wide-ranging education effort—an effort that continually researches and shares data on a particular issue as well as works to educate participants about the diversity of the Philadelphia community. One place for elaborating and supporting this collective identity is emerging at Temple University. As part of a coalition effort sponsored by New City Writing (www.newcitywriting.org), students in our basic writing course studied the debates surrounding the industrial revolution. Using the textbook, *Negotiating Differences,* students read selections from Horatio Alger and Andrew Carnegie as well as testimony from government hearings. As the course continued, students were asked to consider the situation of a postindustrial city and to consider what language best describes the current economy. More to the point, they were asked to think about what coalition of forces might be needed to revise the current situation and what role language/writing might play in creating that coalition.

Simultaneous to this class, members of the writing program and the university's Office of School and Community Partnerships were asked to develop assignments that asked high school students to write about the connection between education and income. One of the assignments asked students to analyze a graph detailing this information.[1] As part of the work, students were asked to imagine how many years they would have to work to earn a million dollars. The whole class was then asked to stand up. As each year was counted off, students could sit down when they reached a million dollars. They were then asked to write about this experience:

> How many years were you able to rest while that student was still working? Why do you think that student had to still work? How much education do you think that student's salary required? If you had to stand longer than others, how did you feel when you had to work while others sat? Do you think it was fair that the student had to work so much longer than you?

Out of these assignments, discussions were held about whether a person's primary identification should be economic, educational, communal, or ethnic. Each category implied a different set of values and responsibilities. Each led to a different set of actions by the individual as part of a collective. In effect, these two classes were engaged in the same type of work—coming to terms with how their own economic situation fit into larger trends and attempting to understand their role within that economy.

Through this work, professors, teachers, educational activists, and labor organizers were able to have sustained conversations about what it meant to bring students into a collective understanding of the labor market. These conversations themselves helped to create a better sense of how to engage students in issues of the working world. In summer 2002, these two unique student populations were combined into a special writing course that not only drew the two populations together but also brought the students into writing projects about labor unions, museums dedicated to labor history in Philadelphia, and organizations working for economic justice. That is, the next stage was to bring the students into a working relationship with the collective that originally sponsored the project. A series of publications and research reports were planned. From this work, it was hoped the participants would gain an understanding of the pressures placed upon writing within different economic/political spaces.

Through engaging in collective writing, the participants also gained a sense of how a new rhetoric must be created to allow them to speak across their own economic positioning. They began to see how campaigns for locally controlled public schools must develop a way of speaking that unites seemingly disparate interests and audiences within the city—an audience that includes city planners, recent immigrants, community organizers, labor activists, community residents, and more. To do so, they had to move beyond their own seemingly unique subject position, their own economic position and had to begin to see how and where they stand within the city collective.

Of course, such a program was a limited first step. It did not bring such an emphasis into the entire first-year writing program, nor, I suppose, does every class need to tackle these issues. I do believe, however, that first-year writing programs need to consistently develop programs that challenge students to see how their writing is part of a collective moment. To return to the students reading Horatio Alger in the first-year writing program: In an environment where economic success is too often gauged as the result of individual effort and writing is seen as the mark of individual genius, writing programs that emphasize collective effort serve both a social and pedagogical goal. It serves as an engine for a more sustained debate throughout the writing program about its social purpose and its relationship to the economic structures that ultimately limit the aspirations of the urban poor.

Upper-Division Writing Courses

I think it is equally important to agree that upper-division "writing-intensive" ("w") courses ought to take the university itself as a subject of investigation. For one thing, students need to understand the economic system that their tuition dollars and activity fees support. In many cases, upper-division classes are an opportunity to ask students to begin thinking about the impact of a long-held economic identity. What does it mean, for instance, to spend your life as a mechanic, public schoolteacher, or secretary? What opportunities do you obtain from this position? What opportunities are lost? In addition, as students approach a stage where most will begin to actually enter the full-time work world, it is important to continue exposing them to the way an individual career forms part of a larger economic structure.

In effect, I am arguing that the "w" designation stand not only for a writing emphasis in a course but for an emphasis on *work* as well. Such courses would turn the pedagogical topic of the course into a simultaneous discussion of how the work world structures that course as well as that working relationship to other environments. For instance, a course was recently offered at Temple around the theme of Philadelphia. As part of the course, students read historical and fictional accounts of the city. Simultaneously, however, students engaged in oral history projects around the issue of work. Stories were collected from Temple employees, city workers, taxi drivers, and small-business owners. As the stories were collected, students were asked to reflect upon their own economic relationship to the participant as student, part-time worker, or city resident. The texts that emerged from this course were then placed within a set of economic data being studied. All these other texts were then placed in relationship to each other in an attempt to gain a sense of the languages that create our sense of the city's identity. Through such work, I would argue, students were formulating a collective sense of where they fit into the larger economic terrain of the city.

Such work could occur in other classes as well. For instance, in an urban-anthropology course, students would study the tools used by anthropologists. They would also study how the working community of the professor is structured differently from the urban communities being studied. Within such a situation, the question of part-time instructors at major universities would become a question organic to the course. Questions of economic relations would inevitably intrude upon the professional distance often accorded academic study. In doing so, not only would students gain an insight into how a professor's life differs from the community being studied but also how each is mutually integrated within a larger economic system.

Within this course, then, the writing studied would not only be textbooks but contracts between the university and the community concerning research standards; labor contracts from the university and public schools; and, economic studies of where these contracts put the faculty in relationship to the students in each institution. Throughout, the writing done by students would be problematized by the need to negotiate such a variety of rhetorics. Such a course would further an academic course of study but also produce a sense of the working world in which that study occurs.

Writing Centers

I have been arguing writing programs must present writing as a negotiation between a variety of communities and community interests. To some extent, teaching writing becomes teaching students how to become skillful at code switching and code adoption. With writing centers, however, the work changes to some extent. Typically, writing centers are portrayed as a resource for the student population (across degrees and colleges) to secure help in passing a particular course or program requirement. The staff at such a center will often be volunteers, part-time labor, work-study students, and perhaps one or more full-time administrators (if the program is well funded). The focus on degree-based writing, however, fails to allow other writing communities access to university resources or to negotiations about the goals of a writing center.

At Temple, a coalition of faculty and community organizations in Philadelphia is developing a network of community-based writing centers. Governed by the coalition, we are developing centers in public schools, religious institutions, ethnically based community programs, and government housing projects. This network of centers (of which the university writing center is but one) has agreed to share their combined literacy resources to develop programs that address the economic and cultural issues facing their communities. For instance, the ethnic community center will provide a community connection through which the university can understand the culture of ESL students. The university will supply tutors who can explain the culture of university writing to students first entering college. A housing project will share their welfare-to-work materials. The combined insights and stories this writing tells will gain a public performance aspect by through a connection to a community press.

In this model, writing centers become sites through which the individual, community, neighborhood, and university work in alliance to foster cross-institutional programs. Through such work, a new set of publications emerges marking the creation of a new community. Not incidentally, these different sites also become a place to connect individual writing courses (freshman through senior seminars) with a community working towards a collective goal. All the pieces of a writing program begin to interact with surrounding organization for the production of a new collective writing space and a new urban center.

Faculty Development

Faculty development is often framed around pedagogical issues. Workshops are held on how to design an effective writing assignment or how to mark student papers. This aspect of our work as teachers is vital and should not be underestimated. It is, however, only one-half of our work. Writing moves across the curriculum and across the university. Not only is it the case that everyone at Temple from the staff to student has to write in one form or another, it is also the case that a significant portion of this writing occurs within a particular economic situation. At Temple University, there are many discrete labor units: full-time faculty, full-time maintenance/secretarial workers, teaching assistants, research assistants, part-time faculty, undergraduate workers, and contract workers. Most are asked to write daily and to have their writing evaluated.

Just as a writing committee will oversee a writing program, a similar committee, consisting of representatives from the different labor segments of the university, should form a workers' writing council. The goals of this council would be various. First, at the most basic level, it would work to coordinate the variety of professional-development opportunities around writing to include more than faculty and students. Workshops should be provided that not only allow individuals to become better writers for their jobs (a form of business writing) but also to create connections between the different labor populations. For instance, a workshop in memos might include not just faculty but maintenance and administrative staff. Discussions could include not only about form but also about different senses of authority, power, and privilege. Out of these discussions could emerge a greater sense of how writing can be a tool to bring diverse populations into accord over the connections between language use and a common agenda for economic justice.

This council could support graduate student unionizing efforts. It could move towards taking stands against curricular or admission standards that unfairly impact working students. Out of this unique coalition of workers could emerge an analysis of how the curriculum or writing program fails to speak to the economic situations or the interests of student, self-identified community, or neighborhood participants. In a profound sense, such a council would serve as a space from which the workers at the institution could attempt to create the laborers across the curriculum program.

(such as part-time labor)

At the outset of this chapter, I made an indirect allusion (in parentheses) to the labor upon which composition is based—part-time, contingent, or contract labor. With almost the blink of an eye, I moved from that hard economic fact to a series of programs and ideas for connecting the university writing program to the community. This quick wink towards the economic hardships of our fellow teachers is not unusual. Much of the recent scholarship arguing universities should play a role in community development does not touch upon the rising numbers of poorly paid workers in our own community. There are books on pedagogy and books on community partnerships. There are books on the economics of universities. Rarely do these multiple worlds collide in a single book.

Yet, if the university is to imagine itself as a model community citizen, it cannot perpetuate these labor practices. Community-partnership meetings where only tenured faculty and fully employed community directors hold court models the liberalism of the professional-managerial class. There are no voices representing the economic needs of those working in the program or suffering from economic injustice within the university itself. In that environment, programs are developed in which underlying economic questions are pushed into another realm. While people are taught to read, the economic injustices that produced their illiteracy are perpetuated.

Without a well-paid and supported teaching staff, many of the ideas discussed above will simply fail to materialize as actual policy. Structural reform and long-term community partnerships cannot be based upon exploited labor. The laborers will simply move on and find better work. Even those most deeply committed to a project will be worn down by the need to work multiple jobs to keep "bread on the table." In such a labor environment, there is the constant need to find new individuals to keep a project running. Time is wasted reestablishing the personal connections that make an effort successful. On a basic level, it is difficult to argue that the institution has a long-term commitment to an area when it has only a marginal commitment to the employees doing the work. It is difficult to set ourselves up as model partners to the community when we perpetuate many of the wage practices being protested by that community.

Ultimately, the work outlined in this chapter implies (and necessitates) work to unite and organize the contingent labor within a region and highlights the importance of signing labor agreements with the principal employers in the area. For instance, an alliance of writing directors in Philadelphia has developed an outline of what different universities and colleges pay part-time writers and is working on developing an on-line job board. This information should serve as the first step for contingent teachers to press for standard course pay and a benefits package across the region. In making this claim, the tenured and full-time writing teachers and the unions that represent them should lobby their institutions to support fair labor practices for all workers in the institution. Ultimately, this struggle should be linked to the needs of the mass of part-time contingent workers in an urban environment such as Philadelphia, where full-time unemployment is high.

I realize that it is important to keep the educational role of teachers in our sights as we work towards economic justice. Arguing for the need to do organizational work, support picket lines, and bring contingent workers onto our committees appears to some observers to take us away from our classrooms and our research. Yet, the recognition of our collective identity with these fellow laborers is the insight upon which all the pedagogical and research programs discussed above are premised. I would argue we cannot be collective in our pedagogy and individualistic in our politics. Or rather we can, but it is that very split consciousness that has enabled the current economics of the university to take hold. To be a transformative teacher, then, is to be fully involved in the transformative economics that support that teaching.

In Dreams Begin Responsibilities

I recognize that the above is schematic. It is the narrative my colleagues and I like to tell ourselves about our work. It enables us to get up each day and work. It probably represents more of a set of promises than facts, more fiction than reality. Yet, I would imagine that it is a dream that many of the readers of this book share—a dream of a writing program linked to larger struggles for economic justice. Rather than end with the harsh lens of reality—a lens of hostile opponents, limited possibilities, and few resources, I want to end by asking a question. Suppose for the moment, we believe the story or at least in its possibility. How would holding onto that illusion frame the work that follows? How might we begin to alter in small ways the programs we direct or the classes we teach? To some extent, all of the above has been an extended dream, but in the words of Yeats, "In dreams begin responsibilities." What is our responsibility to bringing alive the dream of a writing program connected to economic issues? What is our responsibility to instantiating the dream of economic justice?

Note

1. The full assignment read as follows and was part of a six-part thematic unit coauthored with Lori Shorr, director, Office of School and Community Partnerships.

So You Want to Be a Millionaire?

It seems everyone wants to be a millionaire. Who wouldn't?

Our ability to be a millionaire, however, depends upon the jobs we have as adults. While we might dream of being Donovan McNabb or Mia Hamm, it also wouldn't hurt to have a solid education. (Both Hamm and McNabb are college graduates.) In fact, some people argue how much money we make as adults will depend upon our education. Today we are going to try an experiment to see if there is any relationship between education and our ability to make money. To do this experiment, you will have to solve mathematical problems, keep notes, and record your personal feelings. This "data" will be important when you write up your final report.

First, your teacher is going to pass out "career" slips. Each career will have an annual salary (how much money you would receive a year). Based upon that salary, we would like you to calculate how many years it will take you to earn one million dollars. Looking at the graph, "Annual Family Income by Educational Attainment, 1997," how much education do you think such a salary requires? Do you need a high school diploma, a college degree, a master degree (college plus two extra years), or more? What type of job might you have? Would the job be physically demanding? Might you get hurt on the job? Pretending you start working at the age of twenty-five, how old will you be when you become a millionaire? Based upon you age at that time, what do you want to buy with the money?

Next, we would like you all to stand up. Your teacher will start counting years of work ("You've worked one year, two years, three years . . . "). When she reaches the number of years it takes for you to reach a million dollars, sit down. When the last person sits down, write down how many years that student had to work. How many years were you able to rest while that student was still working? Why do you think that student had to still work? How much education do you think that student's salary required? If you had to stand longer than others, how did you feel when you had to work while others sat? Do you think it was fair that the student had to work so much longer than you?

Of course, in real life, you're not handed a career. You get to choose. You decide when to stop attending school. Based upon the information you collected, write a short essay explaining how education impacts a person's ability to make one million dollars. How might you start planning to be a millionaire? What advice would you give to the last person standing in our experiment? What advice would you give to society about how to produce millionaires?

Assignment Benchmark Standards

Writing Content Standards #3: Write in a variety of forms including journals, essays, stories, letters, plays, poems, and reports using figurative descriptive, literary, and technical language.

Math Content Standard #7 Applications and Connections: Incorporate the fundamental elements of mathematics and integrate mathematics with all disciplines while relating the results to the everyday world.

Math Content Standard #8 Mathematical Communication: Express, discuss, and justify solutions to mathematics problems to a variety of audiences.

10
When Critical Pedagogy Becomes Bad Teaching: Blunders in Adjunct Review

William H. Thelin and Leann Bertoncini

Critical pedagogy, to us, clearly offers students the best opportunity to develop as writers, resist oppressive discourses, and take an active interest in learning. The intellectual rigor of critical pedagogy, if not the political commitments tied to it, often appeals to educators, some who believe process or expressivist approaches to composition are too soft and compromise standards.

Yet, critical pedagogy takes committed and knowledgeable educators, ones willing to put extensive hours into teaching. Even if instructors have three sections of the same course, frontloading the students' interests (see Shor) often requires three preps, and adjusting to the needs and challenges brought up by students demands an open syllabus or a willingness to reshape the course schedule. Doing the job of critical pedagogy well constitutes an arduous task. The conditions under which adjunct faculty work in English departments, though, can undermine attempts at implementing critical pedagogy, especially on a department-wide basis, as adjuncts teach the majority of composition across the United States.

Our experiences tell us that most adjuncts survive their difficult schedules, often at more than one campus, by adhering to tenets of current-traditionalism, which makes the job of teaching composition much easier. Current-traditionalism also feeds into the sense of fulfillment many instructors receive from teaching, as the banking model of education casts them in the role of a transmitter of knowledge who saves students from the doom of illiteracy (see Helmers for a discussion of the hero role in composition testimonials). Many teachers can overlook their own exploitation by turning what should be a narrative of their own oppression, perhaps an oppression shared with their students, into a tale of dedication and martyrdom. Current-traditional pedagogy is further encouraged by corporate ties to universities. As Lawrence C. Soley shows, administrators devalue teaching in favor of the agendas of donors and corporate business partners. Universities and colleges have a disincentive to hire critical pedagogues to teach writing, relying on the powerlessness of adjunct faculty to teach sanitized versions of composition.

This situation leads to what John Campbell calls the "dry rot" in academia. University and departmental leaders, some well-intentioned, lead a college astray from legitimate goals of scholarship and teaching while seeking to maximize revenue. Profit-seeking administrators do not challenge the exploitation of adjuncts and a vicious cycle emerges. Composition directors and department heads, themselves sometimes lacking any formal education in rhetoric and composition, must put together standardized syllabi with the goal of enabling the undertrained to perform their jobs. As adjuncts grow experienced in this downsized mode of teaching composition, they espouse, even aggressively defend, aspects of this current-traditional pedagogy such as grammar lessons, vocabulary quizzes, and modal assignments. Process-writing advocates find it difficult to negotiate such dry rot. Critical pedagogues face a near impossible situation when mired in it. We will demonstrate the outcome of this corporatized traditionalism through a narrative of Leann's teaching experience as an adjunct lecturer, tying it into the theory Bill created with John Paul Tassoni called *blundering*. We feel the perpetuation of current-traditionalism and the intellectual poverty of textbooks associated with it (Crowley, *Methodical Memory* 140) stand as testament to universities' noninterest in teaching.

Bill: Adjunct teachers of composition have a hard time finding themselves represented in the literature of critical pedagogy. When they are allowed to become part of the story, their plight is often the topic rather than their teaching (see Gillespie; Singleton; Slevin). When they do write as teachers, the constraints they teach under are rarely addressed adequately. So, adjunct instructors wanting to teach critical pedagogy look to the theories and practices of those who are safe with tenure and take chances with fewer repercussions.

When thinking about this seeming exclusion, I looked back at my own theory of blundering. John Tassoni and I developed this theory as a response to the teacher-hero narratives so prevalent in the discipline of composition. We felt that too often, practitioners of composition represented their pedagogies as smooth, sure-fire solutions to problems that were obviously much more complicated. We felt a more honest and stimulating approach, especially to the teaching of critical pedagogy, would be to show the mistakes and not settle for pat conclusions about what worked and what did not. Therefore, we championed the blunderer—the critical pedagogue who either failed to accomplish his or her goal or *looked* like he or she had failed, due to dominant perceptions of the form teaching should take. We now view blundering as essential to the understanding of critical pedagogy, as it demands that an instructor analyze the whole situation under which teaching occurs, rather than trying to isolate one or two variables, and realize that learning—both for the student and instructor—involves forces well beyond our ability to control easily or thoroughly. Yet, the consequences for blundering were not discussed much in the collection of narratives we gathered. Leann's tale forced me to see that the authors in our book were relatively privileged. They were free to learn from their mistakes: to reflect or mope or laugh or simply move on. No one penalized the risk-taking involved in democratic, critical pedagogies. Many other teachers are not so fortunate.

Leann's tale, at one level an example of the powerlessness of adjuncts, can be better understood as evidence of deeply embedded, institutionally wrought blunder at the systemic level, revealing the general bankruptcy of composition instruction and administration, due to workplace conditions. At the time of this episode, Leann worked in a large, Midwestern university that had a separate college on the main campus to house open-access education. The English department within the college contained only two professors with doctorates in rhetoric-composition, and neither were involved in administering the composition program. The other tenured or tenure-track professors held master's degrees, doctorates in education, or doctorates in literature. The salaries fell well below the standard for other colleges on the main campus, and the teaching load for all full-time faculty was 4-4-4. Many members of the full-time faculty felt as exploited as the adjuncts who worked there. Nonetheless, the faculty prided itself on its dedication to teaching and its mission of helping previously unsuccessful students. This help, though, often ran counter to contemporary composition theory.

Leann: The official record of my "blunder" states the following: that I am incompetent, that I need to take courses in how to teach, that I do not know how to run a classroom or lead a discussion, that I do not teach lesson plans relevant to writing, and that in my examples to the students, I unfairly characterized people by their class affiliation. As I look back, I think my blunder started with my graduate education.

As a master's student at Indiana University of Pennsylvania, I was schooled under notable critical pedagogues C. Mark Hurlbert and David Downing. Both had edited collections out at the time that addressed the need for and the struggles of implementing critical theory into our classrooms. Among the influences of many of the contributors (and Mark and David themselves) were James A. Berlin and Paulo Freire. Berlin impressed upon me the importance of language in constructing reality. Freire's well-known critique of the banking model of education and emphasis on dialogic methods of teaching showed me that our classes had to work harder to integrate our students' knowledge, concerns, and environments if we were to make our classrooms meaningful. I also learned to be critical of the deficit theory and the cognitive disadvantage it expounded regarding dialect speakers (Trudgill 132–38).

When I started teaching, I tried to integrate Freire and Berlin into a pedagogy for the basic writers I was teaching in the open-access arm of my university. I taught in a way that denounced deficit beliefs and developed a cultural-studies curriculum that eschewed the concentration on five-paragraph structures, grammar, and modernist concepts of style and fluidity that made up the status quo of the department. In so doing, though, I was also veering away from the perception of good teaching held by powerful members of the department. This perception did acknowledge student-centered activities and collaboration as valid forms of teaching, but the administrators in charge fiercely clung to models of order and clarity that did not take into account the messiness that often develops as a result of truly taking the students' input seriously. Furthermore, many of those professors in charge of faculty observations maintained a fairly rigid view of what constituted teaching writing and what was going beyond those boundaries. My preparation in graduate school did not teach me how to respond when administrators disagree with Freirean and social-epistemic methods. Still, my first two annual observations seemed fair, and the professors involved recommended my continued employment.

Going into my third year of teaching, a new director of basic writing was appointed. Although some of her ideas were thoughtful and coherent, such as allowing for multiple revisions, she herself was unschooled in composition theory, much less critical pedagogy. Her agenda sounded liberatory when she spoke about teaching writing, but if the new standard departmental syllabus was any indication, she either did not fully understand critical-pedagogical practices or did not trust the adjuncts to implement them properly. For instance, the syllabus was called a contract, and students and instructors were supposed to agree to its terms and sign; however, it did not resemble the method of contract grading that Ira Shor discussed (98–101), as it contained no student input and no mechanism for students to disagree—other than dropping the course. Even her view of writing processes seemed static and controlling, relegating each part to a certain stage and using peer groups to get the students to agree with the teacher's agenda, a tendency C. H. Knoblauch and Lil Brannon warn against (148).

Four days before the fall 1996 quarter began, I received my assignment to teach two sections of basic writing. On this day, all adjuncts attended a meeting, where we received our course syllabus and the text we were going to use for the course, *Voices and Visions* (Meyer and Mylan), which was set up in worksheet fashion, complete with perforated sheets to attach to assignments, fill-in-the-blank–type questions, and step-by-step activities purported to make the students proficient in the writing process. I remember looking at the book and not having a good feeling at all. The types of assignments and busywork the students were required to do left little room for the cultural-studies approach I had been developing. Every single class plan and every last assignment had been constructed for us.

I assumed too much, perhaps. I remember someone saying we could bring in supplemental materials and tweak the syllabus to accommodate our needs. Therefore, I looked at the syllabus as a basic guide, one designed to aid last-minute hires and provide departmental goals. It wasn't meant for me, I reasoned. I remember making jokes with other adjuncts about especially bad parts of the daily schedule and talking about how I was going to change it for my class. As the quarter began, though, the suffocating nature of the syllabus interfered often with my goals. Some of my changes were contradicting instructions in the text, and I tripped over myself in class. I stopped joking and started griping, even complaining to the basic-writing director during our earliest portfolio-norming session. She took offense at my request to dump the remainder of the syllabus and wondered why I could not just follow the daily schedule. It would work, she insisted, if the adjuncts would just adhere to it. The remedial students, she told me, would not profit from the type of cultural studies or social-epistemic approach I wanted. They needed the basics. Clearly, then, the departmental syllabus was not meant as a mere guide.

The real reason for the syllabus, though, came back to the adjuncts later through tenured-faculty gossiping and inadvertent eavesdropping. The department members felt they had had difficulty finding stable and experienced part-time faculty. The new basic-writing director especially felt that the department was scraping the bottom of the barrel. She believed that she needed to ensure that the poor quality of the adjuncts did not seep into the classroom, and she implemented the syllabus in an attempt to keep up the departmental standards. Like the students taking developmental writing classes, then, we were viewed as having deficits that only administrative direction could remedy. The deficit theory was now being extended to adjuncts! She did not want us to have any input into the teaching because she had constructed us as not capable of giving knowledgeable input or making our own pedagogical choices. In her defense, there were some adjuncts on staff who espoused the most traditional views of the writing classroom, such as a concentration on grammar lessons, and others who were unsteady in their approaches to the students. These teachers probably improved by following *Voices and Visions*. But where was I in all of this? Was I one of those scraped from the bottom of the barrel?

Bill: It is important at this juncture of the story to understand the thinking that creates teacher-hero narratives and ignores workplace imperatives. The basic-writing director saw a problem that had its roots in economics. The department could not fill all of its sections of developmental writing with what it perceived as competent instructors due mostly to the low compensation and odd hours those instructors would have to work. The basic-writing director had to save the day somehow, so she came up with a book that she believed would teach itself. Her "teacher-proof" syllabus allowed her to fill classes headed by teachers she felt were substandard.

Leann: After having a terrible time with one assignment based on describing an object and another trying to turn an interview with a classmate into a critical essay, I decided to redesign the next essay, which at least had the promising premise of television talk shows. The assignment as written seemed to contain readily found answers to its questions, so I modified it to make the students look at political ideology. I drew on material I had found in *The Progressive* to supplement the assigned reading, and I showed clips of talk shows during class hours to ask serious questions—ones I did not know the answers to. Who gained and who lost by these shows propagating a different side of American society? Was the fact that the shows made use of voices not normally heard an empowering act for people in the working class? Was the status quo only being challenged at the outer margins, or was it being more seriously ruptured? Although my students and I agreed to abandon the mandated discovery drafts and prewriting activities, we were still generating content and engaging in real dialogue about the text in front of us—the shows.

My annual observation came up at this time. I knew and liked the senior professor assigned to do it, a woman I will call Professor Jones. But she was closely aligned to the basic-writing director and had a tendency to be dismissive of people she disagreed with, using the term *idiot* to describe her opponents. She was serious minded, intimidating, and very intelligent—all of which made me nervous. Furthermore, she knew little about critical pedagogy or cultural studies. According to the syllabus, she was supposed to be observing peer-group review, but because the students' drafts were not due in my revised schedule, I had devised a plan about language use to assist the students in recognizing clichés and interrogating seemingly innocent turns of phrases they might encounter in their reading and viewing.

On that Monday morning, Professor Jones arrived a few minutes early and sat down outside the circle. Also present were two tutors from our Writing Center, who regularly attended on workshop days to help facilitate the peer-group review. The students noticed Professor Jones right away, sneaking glances at her and feeling, I believe, that they had to be good. She did not smile or interact with any of the students, producing an icy feeling as I began. I started off with a handout about clichés and euphemisms. I do not know what happened, but throughout the handout I misspelled *euphemism* as *euphemisn*. Professor Jones claimed in her report that I mispronounced it as well, but I know I did not. Still, the misspelling was a careless mistake to make in this situation.

After discussing the handout, I read an example of deceptive language use from *Doublespeak Quarterly* and had the students write briefly about what the passage seemed to be covering up. After I called time, one student named Liz appeared excited and wanted to talk about the manipulations she saw in the example and elsewhere in her life. It did not follow directly from what I had asked them to write on, but she was on the right track. I felt that maybe her ideas might be more relevant than mine, but as she redirected the class, suddenly the dynamics felt all wrong. My usually vocal class clammed up. One of the tutors responded to her, but that was about it. As Professor Jones sat and wrote and watched, my students looked bored. I felt forced to call on students to answer questions, or I would have been reduced to lecturing to Liz. I was losing the class and blowing the observation. I thought about shifting into group work, but nothing came to mind in terms of what to do. I repeated the importance of looking closely at language and talked about the connections to talk shows. I realized, though, that I had indeed slipped into lecturing! I asked them again to write something about language in an attempt to stimulate some conversation. I shuffled around the class, prodding reluctant students to write, but little happened. Mercifully, the class ended.

In my two previous observations, the professors had reviewed my performance with me immediately after the class concluded. Professor Jones did not. She just walked off, not mentioning a thing. Physically ill, I went to the restroom and vomited. I might have gone off immediately and drank myself into a stupor if not that I had to work. No, not teaching. I had an afternoon shift at Kroger, where I toiled as a cashier part-time to supplement my income. I never imagined I would soon have to begin working there full-time.

Bill: Leann's assumption that the observer was looking for more student input than lecture demonstrates the tremendous chasm between her training and that of Professor Jones. The syllabus had been arranged to mute the instructor's voice as an authority. On one level, then, Leann violated expectations by showing a developed, scholarly knowledge of language and *leading* a class discussion about it when the type of instruction desired, the reading of drafts in group, did not require her to do more than keep the students on the task of attending to all of the questions posed to them in *Voices and Visions*. On the other level, though, she panicked when the students did not control the classroom through vocal responses to her questions. She felt too teacher-centered and did not want to continue what had become a lecture. She wanted to have her voice muted but in favor of the students' participation, not the text's.

Had she kept students obedient during fifty minutes of textbook-centered group work, Leann probably would have received a positive if not glowing recommendation in her observation report. Professor Jones might have complained about the changes to the syllabus while signing off on a recommendation to re-hire. Had Leann proceeded with a lecture, Professor Jones could have commented on her preparedness and ability to deliver information in that format. Clearly, the lack of decisiveness in executing the class plan made Leann look unsure of herself and her goals blurry. The interesting question, though, centers on what would have happened if the students had responded enthusiastically to the assignment. How important was Leann's ability to *control* the classroom?

Leann: Working at Kroger for eight hours gave me plenty of time to reflect on the class, and I started to feel better about it. If confusion caused the students to keep quiet, I could build on any seeds I had planted. If resistance triggered the silence, then I had struck a chord. So, when I was summoned to Professor Jones's office that Wednesday to discuss the results of my observation, I expected to have a lukewarm but passable evaluation. Her reaction shocked me. The problems I had getting the students to respond were downplayed. Rather, she could not understand how my lesson plan had anything to do with teaching them how to write. Why had I not done the peer-review activity? Professor Jones had been so concerned about my deviation from the syllabus that she had already filed the report with the chair. I explained I wanted the students to think critically because they often had the habit of reverting to abstract language to avoid in-depth thought. Clichés and euphemisms were easy substitutes for serious thinking. Ah, but the book covered issues on critical thought, she said. I did not need to rearrange the schedule to get the students to think. She expressed doubts that I should continue teaching and recommended that I take a course about teaching from a friend of hers. After consulting with the basic-writing director, though, Professor Jones agreed to a two-class, follow-up observation. I could save myself by showing I could follow the syllabus.

The fourth paper dealt with a time that language made the writer feel left out. Again, the assignment had potential, but the processes around it disconcerted me, and I feared the students would interpret it without a multicultural bent. I dreaded seeing a stack of papers about how everyone should speak English only or how foreign-born professors should not be allowed to teach at American colleges because of their accents. The material in *Voices and Visions* did not give enough content to assist the students in moving away from such common but prejudicial sentiments. So, although I left the assignment alone, I again constructed a different class plan.

For the first of the two observations, I introduced the topic of language barriers as encompassing all walks of life—or that is what I intended. I brought in some exotic produce from Kroger such as litchi nuts, star fruit, and persimmons—not stuff readily available or familiar to most people. Students sampled these and were to taste, describe, and define them by name. Few students could identify the fruit. One woman who worked in a market did know most of them, though, as did an older, returning student experienced at cooking. It seemed obvious that those who were unfamiliar with the fruits would not be conversant at a produce market or at a dinner where the fruit was served, and I hinted at class differences associated with language. The sampling and defining led to a discussion about being left out because of language. I thought I had really hit on something, as I had the students freewrite for ten minutes about this connection.

This sharing of writing led us to times the students had come in contact with a foreign language. I wanted to be careful here because of the possibilities of ethnocentricity or jingoism taking over the discussion, but I did not want to silence the students either. One student named Gary mentioned a time when he visited Miami and got lost in little Cuba. He tried to get instructions at gas stations, but no one spoke English, so he felt more lost than ever. He concluded that people living in the United States should speak English, especially if they own a business, as English is the most common language in commerce. Before I could vocalize an analysis of his statement at all, Professor Jones spoke up. She corrected the student and asserted that Chinese is spoken by more people than English. I was dumbfounded. I wanted a good observation, so I nodded my head and agreed, even though I was incensed that *my* student had been rebuked in an entirely undialogic manner in *my* class.

I tried to move forward by discussing our experiences with accent and dialect. I used my accent as an example, explaining how my *steel* sounds like *still* (as if they couldn't hear it themselves), and my *oil* is confused with *all*. Faltering a bit, I got back to the idea of class and language by providing a story about the wealthy shoppers in Kroger who tell the African American cashiers exactly what they are buying—"that is celery" or "this is a pear." The students enjoyed and related to this example, and we talked about the power structure involved in communication. The students were lively and perhaps a bit out of control, but the discussions elevated the level of discourse from what the book had settled on and worked as a lesson in invention.

Professor Jones was congenial, saying she enjoyed the class, but there was a look in her eye I did not trust. I tried to dismiss my suspicions as paranoia, but they clung to me. I decided to be safe and follow the assignment criteria exactly for the second observation. I typed out instructions verbatim. I thought Professor Jones would like my conformity and foresight in typing up the assignment so the students could show the tutors when they visited the writing center, something we received memos about throughout the quarter. Instead, her final report would state that my efforts were a waste of time as all of the information could be found in the book if the students looked. She also dinged me for reading the assignment instructions aloud, another waste of time, I assumed.

At the beginning of the second observed class, I picked up from the previous day and summarized the discussion, as many of the students had been absent. We exchanged more ideas about language barriers, and the students added their stories, many of them based on class distinctions. I thought Professor Jones looked unhappy at the chuckles the stories drew, but it was hard to tell. I wanted us to move forward to try to remove the scowl from Professor Jones's face. We took out the freewriting we had done the previous session and selected one sentence for the students to use as what *Voices and Visions* calls a *focusing sentence*. I could not stand giving such formulaic prescriptions, though, and when I saw students staring blankly at their papers, I turned to small group work, where I had the possibility of having more productive discussions about getting drafts started than focusing sentences would allow. Indeed, the students batted around ideas, and I had extensive conversations about paper topics with several students. However, Professor Jones sat in her place outside the circle, not knowing what was actually said, only noticing the volume level and speculating that something was not quite right. The class ended in a sort of frenzy, as students were still talking to me while others were anxious to leave. I did not see Professor Jones exit.

Bill: Leann was a cashier teaching composition. Her work as a Kroger employee materialized as an essential, critical point of departure for her critique of language. Within the confines of a regressive syllabus, she tried to be creative in forging understanding and led the students in a critical analysis of the topic. Her status as an adjunct instructor and the disparity with the assumed class privilege of the typical professor became evident. Although Leann's students could join the conversation, Professor Jones occupied an incredibly uncomfortable position, even physically staying outside the circle of discourse. Leann had more in common with them than she did with Professor Jones. As such, she had betrayed her profession.

I found the correction of the politically incorrect student to be indicative of this betrayal. Professor Jones's motives for speaking out could have been outrage at what she perceived to be a racist remark. They could be rooted in her need to get the facts straight, though Leann's record of it seemed to indicate the student was speaking about English's rise as the language of power in the business world rather than it being the most widely spoken language in the world. But Professor Jones's quick response made me believe she felt she was the only authority in the classroom. Leann was not acting her part as a college instructor and could not be trusted to engage the student's statement critically. Thus, Professor Jones had to speak and reclaim the classroom from ignorance.

Leann: Professor Jones's revised report noted improvement in the last two classes. However, she nonetheless was still quite concerned. She saw virtually nothing that she connected with the teaching of writing and thought I unfairly made use of class-based stereotypes, such as the "matrons" who shopped at Kroger, although I never used that word. She felt I was not well-acquainted with *Voices and Visions,* which, she said, walks the students through various writing topics based on ascending skill sequences. I was not having the students do any of the exercises from the book that led up to the essays. She claimed I repeated activities instead of doing concrete preparation for the draft that was due. And, she added, I did not discuss process with the students. Plainly put, I was unprepared, had dubious goals, and delivered the materials poorly. Therefore, I was terminated.

When we reflect on Leann's blunder narrative, the loyalty the department gave the syllabus and the book strikes us as incredibly ironic. Devised as a solution for the adjunct problem, the syllabus took on a life of its own and became the standard by which adjuncts would be judged. An orderly application of the lesson plans equaled good teaching. A failure to conform or to implement the plans equated to bad teaching. The limited expectations placed on the students turned into legitimate goals. We are also amazed at how Leann's status as a worker fits into her narrative. In many ways, she laid bare to the students the dry rot in academia, the systemic abuse of labor that forces an educator to supplement her teaching income with service work and from Professor Jones's perspective, we are sure, forced the department into hiring a cashier to teach its basic writing courses.

We see, then, a serious pedagogical consequence of the exploitation of adjunct labor as, although Leann's situation might have been extreme, elements of it exist in almost every English department. In many universities and colleges, adjuncts are not allowed to choose their own textbooks or devise their own syllabi. Most department heads scramble to fill odd sections of basic writing and composition, relying on teachers with limited knowledge of current composition theory and practice to run the classroom. Composition and basic-writing directors often claim expertise in the subject on the basis of teaching writing for several years rather than on educational backgrounds or sustained professional activity. Although most professors would not have put such a negative spin on classrooms like Leann's, harsh evaluations and agendized observations are a reality in our field. And, we contend, the majority of departmental syllabi maintains current-traditional precepts, gives lip service to process, and contains few if any elements consistent with critical pedagogy.

Academic freedom guards tenured professors who choose to implement critical pedagogy in a composition classroom. But with more and more tenure-line positions being eliminated in favor of short- or long-term adjunct positions, critical pedagogy's potential impact on composition practice will be minimal. Standard syllabi will gain momentum, as will their adherents, and the practitioners of the various methods of critical pedagogy will be the ones outside the realm of the norm—perhaps even being labeled as bad teachers. Thus, the decision of universities across the nation to continue to stock classrooms with adjunct labor works as a form of political oppression, as the dissent against the status quo contained in most critical pedagogies will be further marginalized in the halls of academia. The plight of adjuncts, then, is not only an egregious demonstration of exploited labor; it is a labor situation that threatens progress in the field of composition.

Note

The authors would like to thank John Paul Tassoni for looking at early drafts of this essay and to thank Mark Lause for steering us to *Dry Rot in the Ivory Tower.*

11

The Politics and Economics of
the Super-Exploitation of Adjuncts

Ruth Kiefson

In recent years, adjunct faculty have won some economic victories across the country. In California, a massive organizing effort by groups such as the California Part-Time Faculty Association (CPFA) and the Coalition of Contingent Labor (COCAL), has resulted in a law that grants health and retirement benefits to adjunct faculty. Parallel organizing efforts by graduate students throughout the University of California system to affiliate with the UAW have been successful. There have also been other successful organizing campaigns at New York University, Temple, Brown, Columbia, University of Kansas, and more. At University of Massachusetts–Boston, any adjunct teaching a total of four courses in two consecutive semesters is now entitled to half-time status with accompanying benefits. The Massachusetts Teachers Association (MTA) has recently sponsored a bill in the Massachusetts legislature that would spread these benefits to adjuncts across the state. Although these changes will ease the economic pressure on the growing number of adjunct faculty, they will not alter management's increasing reliance on part-time labor within higher education. Ironically, this may be the kind of adjustment or refinement of the two-tier system that is needed to stabilize it as a permanent feature of higher education. Whereas this is certainly not the goal of those involved in the adjunct-organizing campaigns, nonetheless, considering this possibility should provoke serious thought about the scope of the struggle in which faculty find themselves. Those who are motivated to organize against the growing injustices in higher education must consider the nature of the beast we are fighting, and what it means to be winning the struggle.

Globalization is the popular term used to describe this beast. However, 150 years ago, Karl Marx first exposed it to the world as *capitalism,* a system that requires each capitalist to maximize profits and lower the cost of production by revolutionizing the means of production as well as seeking sources of cheap resources and cheap labor. Marx showed how this process led inevitably to wealth being concentrated in fewer and fewer hands, wars to safeguard investment, and a crisis of overproduction. We see these developments unfolding today as domestic markets become saturated and the pressure on the capitalists to expand into foreign markets becomes more and more intense. To compete in this new globalized environment, the capitalists are forced to pursue two strategies.

Domestically, they close factories and condemn millions of workers to unemployment, and at the same time, they drive down the wages of the workers who are still employed. What the capitalists do in industry, the politicians and legislators dutifully carry over into the public sector—taking down all the safety nets (e.g., welfare and, eventually, social security) in order to beat working people into passivity and submissiveness and reduce the percentage of profit that is allotted to social wages. Their domestic strategy constitutes a form of class rule in which the government passes laws and policies that directly benefit the capitalist class.

The economic boom of the 1990s, enjoyed only by a tiny percentage of CEOs and other stockholders, came from grinding down the U.S. working class as well as the working class internationally. Millions of U.S. manufacturing jobs have been replaced by low-wage jobs in the service sector. The current recession, deepened by the events of 9-11, only intensifies the impoverishment of the working class that began twenty-five years ago. In an Economic Policy Institute journal, the loss of economic strength of the working class was assessed: "In 1998, the U.S. poverty rate was 12.7%, higher than the 11.7% rate of 1979"; the "employer-provided health insurance coverage" has dropped from 70.2% in 1979 to 62.9% in 1998 (Mishel, Bernstein, and Schmitt, introduction). The Bush administration continues to wage class war against working people with the recent tax cut that provides the top 1 percent of the population with nearly 40 percent of the proceeds.

Globally, the capitalists move their operations overseas in search of cheap labor and cheap raw materials. From Vietnam to Mexico, sweatshops produce cheap goods to be sold at huge markups on the world market. Fourteen-year-old Vietnamese children work for a few dollars a day to produce Nike sneakers that will sell for $120. The U.S. politicians do their part by negotiating trade agreements that guarantee access to cheap labor zones—NAFTA and the Free Trade Agreement of the Americas (FTAA). Over the past few decades, globalizing capitalism has carried out a massive impoverishment of the world's workers. According to the Economic Policy Institute, "75% of the world's population makes less than $2 a day" (Mishel, Bernstein, and Schmitt 5). What is more, the competition over markets and cheap resources, particularly oil, will inevitably turn into trade wars. The trade wars will just as inevitably turn into shooting wars.

Preparing for this eventuality means the U.S. rulers must exercise more rigid control at home and militarize all aspects of society. Many months before the atrocity of 9-11, during the winter of 2000–2001, the bi-partisan Hart-Ruddman Commission issued its recommendations to secure the United States in the new millennium. The commission called for centralizing all policing and regulatory agencies, dramatically broadening police powers, and gearing up for a succession of oil wars, as well as wars with Russia and China. The Patriot Act, passed in the wake of 9-11, contained virtually all of the key features of the Hart-Ruddman Commission's recommendations. Thus, the rulers' necessity of militarizing society was expedited by the tragedy of 9-11, ushering in the basis for legal fascism.

In the last decade, the U.S. government has been restructuring health care, the welfare system, and now education. The overall goal of the restructuring of education is to bring all levels of education into closer sync with corporate needs. Internationally, this process is being executed by the International Monetary Fund and the World Bank. For example, they are requiring changes in higher education as part of the restructuring of developing economies—hiking tuition in public colleges and more (LaFranchi 1). (This development is what sparked the year-long student strike at UNAM, the National Autonomous University of Mexico, Mexico's largest public university, in 2000.) In this country, too, the tuition of public higher education has increased many fold, liberal arts programs are being slighted in favor of science and technology programs, which more directly serve the needs of the capitalist economy, and since roughly 1970, the reliance on adjuncts has become policy throughout higher education. The growing use of adjuncts is part of the grinding down of the working class; they are among the 43 million U.S. citizens without health insurance. In order to fight effectively against this super-exploitation in our midst, faculty must recognize it as a consequence of capitalism's imperative to lower the cost of labor and not primarily a result of the greed or "oversight" of management.

Until recently, organized labor has done nothing to challenge the increasing use of adjunct labor. Now, the adjunct organizing campaigns are forcing labor unions to take a stand in organizing and defending adjuncts. In general, however, these campaigns are defensive in nature and keep the participants submerged in the immediacy of the crisis. They refuse to see that this is class war, and it cannot be beaten back without a massive revolutionary response. The super-exploitation of adjuncts, which is so grossly unjust and educationally counterproductive, represents a vulnerability of capitalism. Therefore, the organizing drives are an important opportunity to assemble the forces for the long-range battle against all exploitation. They are an opportunity to build solidarity among full and part-timers, campus workers, and students, which is vitally necessary if we are to go on the offensive against both the growing fascism that the rulers need to control the working class and the crisis of capitalism.

This systemic crisis has created a tough contradiction for the three thousand U.S. colleges and fifteen million college students (70 percent of whom attend public institutions). Despite the frequent talk in the mainstream press of the need for advanced technological training, outsourcing and relatively slow economic growth, together with computerization, have reduced the skill requirements of many jobs as well as the demand for many types of managers and professionals. A case in point is the rapid growth of distance-learning programs that threaten to replace faculty with computers and telecommunications. State governments and their corporate advisers see an overabundance of four-year-college students as a drain on their budgets. Their response is detailed in an internal survey conducted by the Association of American Universities, which finds that "nearly 60% of its U.S. members are consolidating, eliminating, or reducing academic departments" (Barrow, "New Economy" 43). College students, especially students of color, are being eliminated by standardized testing, more stringent financial aid rules, and rising tuition. Certainly, in the meantime, until supply is pared down to meet demand, the goal is to serve this overabundance of students as cheaply as possible.

Thus, the federal government cut its allotment to the states dramatically between 1980 and 1993, which has led to an accompanying cut in state funds to higher education. According to the Government Accounting Office, the revenue coming from the states to higher education has dropped by 56 percent since the mid-1980s (Aronowitz 33). Changes in the form of federal funding have also occurred, with a de-emphasis on block grants and an emphasis on grants that can be tailored for specific research agendas. A case in point is President Bush's recent call for universities and research laboratories to rapidly develop technologies that would aid the war against terrorism. Heeding this call, the National Academies called an extraordinary summit in October 2001 of "some of the nation's top scientific minds" to plan to "submit recommendations to the White House for ways the research and academic communities can fight terrorism threats" (Donnolly). Clearly, funding sources must be flexible in order to meet the requirements of the U.S. rulers both in wartime and in a globalized economy. Although the changes in federal-to-state funding affects primarily public higher education, private colleges are also affected by sharpening competition for students and rising costs. Thus, both private and public colleges are being forced to supplement their budgets from the private sector and to adopt a corporate model of operation in order to survive this harsh environment.

One specific outcome of this is for colleges to sell pieces of their curriculum to private corporations. Logically, the ideological content of the curriculum would be reshaped to more overtly reflect the needs of the corporation that funds the program. Several months ago, representatives from Stop & Shop, a regional supermarket chain in Massachusetts, were invited to a faculty meeting at Roxbury Community College (RCC) in Boston. The RCC administration used typical corporate tactics—intimidation and bribery—to get faculty to attend the meeting and to buy what they were selling—a partnership between Stop & Shop and RCC. Shortly before this meeting, faculty received intimidating letters (which were also sent to Human Resources) from the acting provost, reporting how many and which meetings each faculty member had missed during the year. At the luncheon, faculty were enticed with fancy sandwiches and drinks and then listened to the Stop & Shop representative talk shamelessly about students as "customers" and how we have to use business strategies to "attract and retain them."

As the federal government reduces its commitment to the public sector, it has created the conditions for corporate control to assert itself within these public institutions, also a feature of growing fascism.

College administrators in keeping with the corporate model are studying and applying the latest managerial strategies, the most comprehensive of which was pioneered by Japanese automobile manufacturers. In his essay "Lambs to the Slaughter," Michael Yates points out that "lean production" is

> based upon the twin ideas that every aspect of work must be controlled to the greatest degree possible and that employees must be led to believe not only that this is good for them, but that they have some real say in directing their enterprise. (3)

This is reminiscent of the directive that is coming down from the Massachusetts Board of Higher Education that community-college faculty produce a list of student proficiencies that must be attained by the time of graduation. How far away are we from a mandate that these proficiencies, *which faculty, themselves, have designed,* be made measurable by standardized tests? Then, how far away are we from looking back to see that we have been duped into participating in our own and our students' defeat, as faculty performance is evaluated by our students' achievement or lack of achievement.

Another management strategy that is becoming popular with the higher education bosses, the Babbage Principle—was named after the mathematician and entrepreneur Charles Babbage, the inventor of the analytical engine, the precursor of the modern computer. The idea is to substitute less-skilled or cheaper labor for more-skilled or more-expensive labor whenever possible. As Yates indicates, this is happening with a vengeance in higher education: "As more expensive faculty retire or leave, they will be replaced with cheaper and less secure people" (5). The mean income for adjuncts at a two-year college is $8,178, and the national average for full-timers is $40,000 plus $10,000 in benefits. A little math will tell us how many part-timers can replace one full-timer. The growth of part-time labor in colleges is therefore both a cost-cutting practice and a way to control the work force. Adjunct faculty, with absolutely no job security, are not inclined to create waves. Having thousands of fully qualified adjuncts, desperate for full-time jobs, standing in the wings as lower-priced replacements, objectively undercuts the bargaining position of full-timers. The faculty unions have accepted this two-tier wage system, which is an objective basis for division between full- and part-time faculty. During the last contract negotiation for community-college faculty in Massachusetts, the state's Board of Higher Education took advantage of the weakened state of faculty to increase the workload of full-timers and impose post-tenure review, further eroding job security. For many years, the state's agenda as expressed both at the negotiating table and through the exhortations of college administrators like James Carlin, the former board chairman, has been to reduce the power of faculty and increase their productivity. Several years ago,

Carlin addressed the Greater Boston Chamber of Commerce (as reported in *MTA Today,* 28 November 1997) calling for an end to the "divine right" of faculty, search committees, and tenure. He called for the president of a college to have the "authority to run his or her campus" like a CEO and that the solution to bringing down costs is for full-time faculty to "work more."

Nationwide in every major industry, the same strategy of part-time and two-tier wage systems has been installed over the past twenty-five years. A new worker for DaimlerChrysler earns half of what a twenty-year veteran earns. In mass transit, new workers get hired at a fraction of the salary of veteran workers, and they are assigned split shifts that make their working days unbearably long. For steel, health care, and postal workers, the situation is the same. New workers in all these industries get IRAs instead of pension funds, further dividing their interests at the bargaining table. Instituting multi-tier wage systems has been a comprehensive and most lucrative strategy on the part of the capitalist class to drive down the cost of labor, divide the work force, and weaken the unions.

The AFL–CIO leadership has succumbed in the face of this massive attack. Their whole strategy since the 1950s has been based on the premise that workers cannot be motivated to fight for anything beyond their immediate, narrow self-interest. This was a political and strategic shift that didn't happen by accident. After World War II, laws such as the Taft-Hartley Act were passed amending much of the pro-union Wagner Act of 1935. Taft-Hartley gave employees the "right" not to join unions (outlawing the closed shop), permitted union shops only where state law allowed, gave the federal government the right to impose injunctions on a strike if it deemed the strike as threatening to the national interest, and required union officials to deny under oath any communist affiliation. Communist leadership was thereby ejected from the unions and replaced by leaders loyal to the goals of the financiers and industrialists. Taft-Hartley, as well as other laws, also redefined the bargaining units very narrowly to restrict the scope of class struggle. The Hawaii Teachers' strike in spring 2001, in which all the teachers from kindergarten to university shut down education in the state, gave us a glimpse of what workers can do when their bargaining units are *not* so narrowly defined.

Within this context of an unfolding general crisis for working people, how are full-time faculty reacting to the specific crisis in higher education? Mainly with passivity and cynicism. Most feel that they are up against a force too formidable to be confronted. They fail to see themselves as part of the working class and that they are being assaulted by the same processes that are creating economic and social instability and misery for millions. In general, the individualist training that they received as professionals, which is reinforced by the narrow trade-union approach of the faculty unions, dominates their decision making and outlook. A case in point is the last contract that was voted in by Massachusetts community college faculty. In exchange for a big (and much needed) wage hike, the contract increased faculty workload, weakened tenure, put the jobs of part-timers in jeopardy, and attacked quality of education for students. Disturbingly, it was approved by over 60 percent!

Part-time faculty, on the other hand, have been thrust into struggle by the extreme levels of exploitation they have been forced to endure. They are beginning to push full-time faculty out of their denial and passivity and to force faculty unions to organize and defend part-timers. The point of departure of these struggles should be that the crisis in higher education emanates from the crisis of capitalism and that it is not going away! Much worse is in store as the economic contradictions continue to sharpen. The adjunct movement can and should play a leading role in winning all faculty and students to think strategically. It should fight for faculty unions to attack management's reliance on part-time labor *as a contract demand.* It should expose the role of colleges as "ideology factories" that serve the capitalist class. It should attack the restructuring of higher education as an attack on students, particularly minority students. Most importantly, it should forge unity with students as fellow workers and use the struggle against the super-exploitation of adjuncts as an opportunity to build a movement that can ultimately transform society.

PART THREE

CRITIQUE OF MANAGERIALISM

12
Managing Labor and Literacy in the Future of Composition Studies

Tony Scott

Over the past decade, discussions of the working conditions of writing teachers have slowly begun to move from the margins of fringe journals and conference caucuses into mainstream venues. Interestingly, even a cursory review of these discussions reveals that they rarely focus only on labor issues. The labor discussion in composition often quickly veers into issues as varied as the continued viability of tenure; the service ethic; the value of pedagogy relative to scholarship; the character of composition research; the abolition of first-year comp; the relationship between composition and literature in English departments; and the position of composition within academic institutions (including writing-across-the-curriculum discussions). The wide scope and urgent tone of this discussion suggests a general recognition that this issue is consequential and bears not only on the future of composition studies but on the way academic work is done more generally.

Ironically, the emergence over the past three decades of composition as an established discipline distinct within English studies has not led to improvements in the percentages of composition courses taught by contingent faculty. Indeed, the proportion of contingent and contract teachers to full-time, tenure-track teachers has steadily increased during this period. Most of the people who teach college writing in America continue to be contingent laborers whose salaries and working conditions do not even come close to meeting any reasonable minimum standards for professionals. Among those institutions that participated in the 1999 CAW–CCCC study of part-time and non-tenure-track faculty working conditions:

- Only 7 percent of those who teach introductory undergraduate courses are full-time, tenure-track faculty.

- Of the remaining 93 percent, 18 percent of introductory undergraduate courses are taught by full-time, non-tenure-track faculty, 33 percent are taught by part-time faculty, and 42 percent are taught by graduate teaching assistants.
- Departments that grant doctorates have the highest percentage of introductory courses taught by graduate teaching assistants (85 percent) with 5 percent of those introductory courses taught by full-time, non-tenure-track faculty and 7 percent by part-time faculty.
- Sixty percent of full-time, non-tenure-track faculty make less than $28,000 dollars a year.
- Twenty-one percent of part-time faculty earn less than $2,000 per course, and 60 percent earn less than $3,000 per course. (Faculty earning $3,000 per course, what some have described as "reasonable compensation," would only earn $24,000 per year if they taught a full course load.)
- Less than half (47 percent) of part-time faculty paid by the course get six weeks' notice of their teaching assignments.
- Only 26 percent of part-time faculty paid by the course receive funds to attend professional meetings.
- Less than half of part-time faculty paid by the course (37 percent), as compared to 100 percent of full-time, tenure-track faculty, have access to a health plan through their work.

Of course, these statistics will not shock anyone who has been teaching college composition for long. The numbers are very consistent with other studies published over the past decade and only quantify the conditions and terms of labor that most in large English departments—regardless of rank—have come to take for granted.

However, curiously, in spite of the pervasiveness of the labor problem in most of our everyday lives and the mounds of statistics and published narratives that consistently present a fairly bleak picture of writing instruction as a profession, labor conditions have never been at the forefront of composition scholarship. We now have a very broad and substantial theoretical foundation in composition, and we are doing empirical research that uses increasingly sophisticated methodologies to contextualize writing and pedagogy and explore the varied factors that affect public literacies, the production of texts, and classroom instruction. It is troubling that the everyday working conditions of most writing instructors— basically, the material conditions within which literacy instruction occurs in postsecondary education in the U.S.—have so rarely surfaced as a concern or focus in our research. I often marvel at the difference between the portrait of writing instruction I see in most of our scholarship—where the teacher is typically assumed to be a full-time teacher with her own office—and the material reality I encounter in my everyday working life as a writing teacher. We publish research concerning issues as varied as class dynamics, workplace genres, and the relationship between our literacy missions and the universities and communities within which we work. We have ongoing and rigorous discussions in our journals and at our conferences concerning how issues associated with race, gender, and technology impact the work of teaching writing. We have nevertheless been unwilling to develop a body of research that explores how universities' historic reliance on a contingent labor force to teach composition classes affects literacy education. I wonder how different our discipline and its scholarly conversations might look if we shined more of the light of our research on the basement offices of our contingent instructorate.

Myriad reasons exist for composition's evasion of its labor problems, but some of the avoidance might stem from the situation that addressing our own labor issues forces us to ask the most basic and existential of questions: "Who, or what, is composition?" and "What are we going to do now?" The discussion of labor issues emerging in composition's mainstream journals does the necessary work of ensuring that when we talk about labor issues, we recognize that we work within complex, economically accountable bureaucracies. However, the implicit ideologies of these approaches has gone largely unacknowledged and unexamined. A significant element of the emerging labor conversation in composition employs a business-management logic that, if adopted as the natural way of thinking within our profession, will have a profound impact on the way that compositionists view the work of teaching and our goals as literacy educators and scholars.

The specifics of the management-oriented models that have been proposed and enacted certainly vary, but they are generally characterized by

- the advocacy of coping tactics within externally imposed economic/institutional frameworks represented as "inevitably" defining our labor structures and our pedagogy—frameworks whose terms and logic are typically justified, rather than questioned
- the explicit or tacit advocacy of casualized or para-professional labor structures that usually include a tenured class of manager-scholars who make policy and are invested in the long-term interests of the institution and an efficiently maintained and variously contingent class of worker-teachers (including full-time, non-tenure-track "renewable" instructors)
- an approach to our literacy mission that tends to promote literacy education exclusively within the context of job training—a task that can be accomplished by people with widely varied backgrounds as long as they are well-trained and efficiently monitored

Complicit with broader trends toward casualization that have been underway in academia for some time, these approaches seek to legitimize workplace models in which a small but tenured and institutionally empowered class of scholar-bureaucrats do research, set policy, and manage the work of a large, permanently subordinate class of teachers whose primary virtues are that they are at least minimally competent, cheap, and willing.

Producing, Consuming, and Finding a Niche

Composition jobs often require that we juggle various institutional roles—as teachers, scholars, and administrators who are variously situated within academic bureaucracies. It is therefore perhaps not surprising that the logic of management and administration is an increasingly salient feature of our discourse. For instance, Richard E. Miller has called for an "entrepreneurial spirit" among composition's managers when proposing a model for the efficient administration of inexpensive teaching labor ("Let's Do the Numbers" 104), and in an article in *College Composition and Communication,* Joseph Harris co-opts the term "boss compositionist" and argues for the legitimacy and normalization of his own version of a two-tier system of managed labor. Miller and Harris are engaging in an emerging conversation that is conspicuously management-oriented. Indeed, many of the labor models that have recently been proposed include measures that solidify the institutional constancy, authority, and "flexibility" of professional academic managers and relegate large portions of the literacy work force to a permanently subordinate, para- or nonprofessional status. Teachers and teaching work are pushed further to the margins of "composition" as "our" work is defined primarily as teacher management. Harris's model would enable composition managers "to interview, hire, and train a teaching staff, to fire teachers who don't work out, to establish curriculum, to set policies, and to represent the program as he or she sees best." Composition's managers would still get tenure "because the individuals who run composition programs and train writing teachers need the security and leverage of tenure," but the "staff"—while getting more pay and benefits than they do now—would not get tenure. Harris claims that "what teachers want are reasonable salaries, benefits, working conditions, and job security; autonomy over their work; and to be treated with respect as colleagues" (57). Miller has proposed a model that uses graduate students from across the disciplines to staff first-year writing courses, as long as the students are trained and supervised by a professional compositionist. He even envisions graduate programs in composition as a type of administrative training (102).

Although these models are proposed as a means of improving present conditions, the managerial imperative of filling sections cheaply remains an important, if not primary, goal. Very limited budgets are certainly a fact of life for most of us, but when we make budgetary concerns paramount and discuss outcomes only in terms of courses filled and money saved, the practice of maintaining a permanently subordinate class of teacher-technicians becomes the "only" possible solution to the problem. Some even come close to *advocating* the practice of using semi- or nonpermanent teachers for literacy instruction in higher education. For instance, Michael Murphy, a WPA who has been an adjunct for a number of years, claims that composition managers can learn from, and even build upon, a system that has survived for decades on a foundation of flexible, cheap labor. He argues that the "teaching substructure" in which he has worked is not as bad as it is often portrayed; indeed, it should be seen as a potentially important part of the future of composition. Leaving issues of justice and equity on the periphery, Murphy asserts that universities have come to rely so heavily on contingent labor only because it makes good economic sense for the institution:

> In a sense, a really reliable, talented part-time teacher—one willing to teach the same number of courses for a fraction of the pay and who teaches them well—is actually worth more to the fiscal health of any given academic department than a talented traditional faculty member. ("New Faculty" 20)

Some have even attempted to employ a cost-yield-focused economic analysis to pedagogy itself as they suggest that we should determine how composition can best respond to the marketplace. In a recent issue of *Writing Program Administration,* Keith Rhodes draws on total quality management (TQM), a theoretical framework designed for analysis in business, to plot the future of composition. According to Rhodes, the true "customers" of the "business" of composition are America's employers, who merely use students and parents as "buying agents" (61). Compositionists would be more happy, respected, and highly paid if we focused on determining what the marketplace expects from our students and delivered it to them as expertly and efficiently as possible. If we more fully embrace market ideology and processes, the market will solve our labor problems because our obvious utility as trainers of effective workplace communicators will enable access to a greater share of the institutional pie. Rhodes further argues that "composition's best marketing plan, the one with the best ratio of reward to risk, entails a radical, seemingly dangerous, change in how composition's 'managers' do business" (52). He believes that the mission of higher education is being redefined. Students are not coming to the university for enlightenment; they are coming to escape the low-paying, dead-end jobs that they will face in the new information-age economy without a degree. We should define our literacy mission accordingly, and in order to respond to our market most effectively, Rhodes encourages composition's managers to break from English departments and the "elitist literacy dreams of the university." We should retool ourselves to educate a loyal and efficient work force. The "consumers" of higher education will require proficiency with "basic information handling," entailing instruction in "'basic' literacy and numeracy," what Rhodes calls "education for followership" as opposed to education for leadership (53).

Also taking an approach that emphasizes market forces, Murphy believes that academics are workers who produce a product—education; we therefore have to make sure that we are accountable to the "*education-consuming* general public" (18) (italics mine). Generally, the position is that if composition is going to survive and prosper as a discipline, we have to face facts about the future health of our own bottom line—that means finding our place in what Murphy terms the "product-oriented educational marketplace" (17). While existing working conditions among non-tenure-track faculty are often bad, Murphy feels that many have been "professionalized" while filling their "niche," and further that niche-filling serves as a good model for the new academy. My experience during my years as an adjunct and as a graduate teaching "assistant" working among adjuncts has been very different from Murphy's, and I do not see any reason to believe that basement faculty are any more "professionalized" than they were ten years ago. The way that Murphy describes the niche that part-time faculty have "come to fill in academia" might lead one to believe that the niche and its filling are a natural and inevitable process, rather than the academic version of downsizing, a consciously enacted management strategy that is designed to get more work for less money. Murphy's version of academic reality seems meant to convey the message that those who adjust to the *naturally* evolving, "highly developed and product-oriented educational marketplace" will succeed in coming years, while those who resist are dinosaurs who will be left behind.

These sorts of claims represent that arguments against the exploitation of part-time labor are misdirected because focused on ethics and justice rather than the pragmatic, indeed bureaucratic, "realities" of our market-driven world. Using his own estimates to compare the amount of money it costs the university to use adjuncts and graduate assistants to teach writing classes, Murphy concludes that while the university makes money on non-tenure-track labor, they make far less on beginning assistant professors and "might well only break even, or, very likely, actually lose money on the teaching of most senior faculty, particularly those carrying large percentages of graduate courses" (21). Again, this is a rhetoric that seems to make complicity with a bottom-line–focused management prerogative in higher education seem logical, if not progressive, and easily consistent with the social aims of higher education.

Managing Our Disciplinary Identity

No one has any easy answers, but any labor model in our profession should be examined in terms of the way that it positions teaching and literacy. These models tend to define professional compositionists as people who manage teaching labor, rather than teachers themselves, and are couched in a rhetoric that emphasizes efficiency, institutional interests, and managerial prerogatives over local innovation, student interests, and teacher prerogatives. For instance, the term *training* is often used in reference to the various methods departments use—such as required classes, workshops, and mentoring systems—to "prepare" graduate students and adjuncts to teach first-year composition. There are important differences between the "training" and the "education" of new teachers. The term *education* suggests an ongoing process of learning and innovation and at least the possibility of individual growth and development; *teacher education* connotes challenging questions and diverse, perhaps even contradictory, pedagogies. In contrast, "training," a term one encounters regularly in management models and program-administration discussions, suggests the top-down implementation of standard management policies and pedagogies. While teacher education might encourage teaching professionals to develop their own pedagogical approaches, based on conceptions of language and learning that are influenced by their varied ideological orientations and evolve through ongoing inquiry and experience, teacher training describes a dynamic in which pedagogy is efficiently imparted, based on the prerogatives of the trainer/administrator. The term *training* clearly situates the classroom teacher on the bottom rung of the academic ladder. Trained staff who are systematically assessed by their managers for their competence are not colleagues who do research, govern, and contribute to a mutual learning environment. Trainees can, and often are, required to share the pedagogical/ideological orientation of their management, to use a standard syllabus, and to teach required texts. What are the practices and values being disseminated by teachers who are not tenurable, have no active research lives, and may not even make basic decisions concerning the classes they teach? It should be clear that the primary virtues of a trainee, as opposed to a tenure-track faculty member, are not expertise, creativity, and investment, but cheapness and a flexibility that derive from the trainee's institutional vulnerability.

The image of the humanities academic as somehow separate from, and perhaps above, systems of economics and work has always been a bit of a myth, and in an era in which the societal role of higher education is being radically redefined, we certainly cannot afford to cling to that image. I sense that most compositionists are acutely aware of this anyway. After all, a large percentage of the people who do composition work also hold other part-time jobs outside of the university and hardly live the cloistered life of ivory-tower intellectuals. Indeed, because the majority of literacy jobs are typical of so many other low-end jobs created in the new economy—they are unstable, offer little or no hope of advancement, and tend to alienate workers from each other and the hierarchies through which they are managed—much of composition's work force are intimately familiar with contemporary economic realities. The same can be said of many of our students, who very much live in the world of contemporary wage labor. In the large, urban institutions where I have worked as an adjunct, a teaching "assistant,"[1] and finally, as a faculty member, most of my students have also been casualized workers who maintain part- or full-time jobs—as package handlers, waiters, temporary clerical workers and warehouse order pickers, telemarketers, etc.—while taking classes. Moreover, even those tenured or tenure-track compositionists who have more job stability and better working conditions typically spend considerable portions of their careers as administrators trying every semester to fill first-year writing sections with a hodgepodge of lecturers, part-time adjuncts, and graduate teaching "assistants." There was never any golden era for composition. It emerged as a professional discipline during an era of retrenchment, expanding enrollments, and shrinking state appropriations—an era in which universities have become dependent on contingent labor and, increasingly, on the whims of private funding (see Martin; Slaughter and Leslie).

The effective maintenance of a writing program in a typical university requires incredible resourcefulness and a broad range of skills. We should continue to have conversations concerning the many tough, economically based decisions and trade-offs writing program administrators must make. In the present and near-future, cheap, contingent labor is/will be an inevitable element of postsecondary writing instruction—that is an unfortunate fact. However, it is precisely *because* academic work is not separate from national economic and political trends that we have to consider whether our practices as administrators, teachers, and colleagues resist casualization or actually facilitate it. Accounting for our position as workers who are variously situated within large, complex, and economically accountable bureaucracies leaves us with a number of different opportunities concerning the possibilities for the future of our careers, our departments, and our profession. Recognizing that composition work is paid labor, materially situated within bureaucracies, does not mean that professional compositionists must lend legitimacy to a system of labor that further deprofessionalizes teaching. There is a difference between doing what we must because we work under unfortunate circumstances and lending legitimacy to the very assumptions and practices that create those circumstances.

I sometimes hear a troubling inconsistency in conversations among my fellow compositionists. On one hand, we lament the lack of respect our field sometimes continues to suffer among many of our departmental colleagues, yet on the other, we allow, preside over, and now sometimes even justify the terms of a labor dynamic that ghettoizes much of the day-to-day work in our field. To accept as inevitable and necessary the employment of a sub-tier or tiers of staff to teach most writing classes is also to accept as inevitable the secondary status of composition as a field in the humanities.

Who? What? And Where?: Situating Composition

In *Terms of Work for Composition: A Materialist Critique,* Bruce Horner envisions writing classes as sites within which students and teachers examine the historical, social, and institutional foundations of rhetorical conventions and the social material conditions of process. Ultimately, Horner offers a way of seeing and doing work in composition that might more fully account for our *locations*—I use this word in its fullest sense—within institutions:

> If we see the institutional location of the composition course and its inhabitants not as autonomous constraint on actors but as a location reproduced and potentially changed by actors through their practices, then the apparent marginality of that location has potential for both hegemonic and counterhegemonic work. It is not necessary to somehow escape that location, or attempt to liberate students from it, because it is not separate from the "real" world but both constituted by and constitutive of it. (57)

I find Horner's approach to pedagogy very attractive. I wonder, however, how much of the profession is truly prepared to publicly examine the material terms of our work? Are we willing to talk openly with our students about our own hierarchies, our own disparities in salaries, benefits, and institutional power, our unequal access to resources? Are we ourselves prepared to come to a deeper, more-nuanced understanding of how the ongoing imperative to cover large numbers of writing sections cheaply has impacted our thinking concerning literacy and pedagogy?

Deborah Brandt has called for further exploration of the connection between economics and literacy. Brandt is worried that when economic forces are presented in our work at all, "they appear primarily as generalities . . . rarely are they systematically related to the local conditions and embodied moments of literacy that occupy so many of us on a daily basis" (166). Recognizing that literacy situates people economically, Brandt wants us to ask in our research who are the sponsors of literacy within given contexts, and how does that affect the types of literacy that are taught and encouraged? Before we begin to situate our classrooms in the way that Horner advocates, we would be well served to first apply Brandt's question to our own workplace: What impact do the professional status and labor conditions of literacy teachers have on the literacy instruction our students receive? Who sponsors literacy in the university and what are their primary interests, loyalties, and ideological orientations? How is literacy conceived and taught in departments in which the composition manager—whose decision making could be informed at least as much by administrative pragmatism as the current scholarship concerning language and learning—makes the most meaningful curriculum decisions for available courses (syllabus, text, etc.)? When the likely instructor is a flexible laborer with a questionable or tenuous status as a professional, what is the affect on the way that literacy instruction is imagined on campus? When we research a particular aspect of composition or pedagogy, we should situate the teacher within the hierarchy of her institution. It is important to know whether teacher–student conferences are taking place at a private faculty office, a shared desk in a crowded basement, a pair of desks in the hall, or a table at the library. We should note the level of professionalization of the teacher, her access to and familiarity with technology, and the amount of control she has over her curriculum. We should ask whether she participates in professional conversations. Does she have institutional support for research and professional development? Does she get support to attend conferences? What additional demands does she have on her time—another part-time job or jobs? Does she belong to a union? More generally, our research should do a much better job of recognizing the material conditions and economic dynamics within which postsecondary literacy instruction is typically situated.

Managing Our Disciplinary Identity

The discussion of labor in composition touches on two important aspects of our disciplinary identity that are rooted in our ideologically progressive past: our anti-elitism and our identification with the interests of students over the interests of institutions. As a relatively new discipline, the way that modern composition studies is historicized has always been important and often highly contentious business. As Robert J. Connors, one of our most important disciplinary historians, writes, for emerging disciplines "gaining a historical sense means gaining a self" (4). Therefore, understandably, based on their various viewpoints and interests, composition scholars cite different dates, events, and theoretical movements as most important to the formation of modern composition studies prior to the early 1970s: most mention the first conference of College Composition and Communication (1949); the work of Porter Perrin and Albert Kitzhaber in the 1950s; the publication of Richard Braddock, Richard Lloyd-Jones, and Lowell Schoer's *Research in Written Composition* (1963); the Dartmouth seminar of 1966; and Janet Emig's *Composing Processes of Twelfth Graders* (1971) as particularly important elements (Berlin, *Rhetoric and Reality*; Connors; Harris, *Teaching Subject*; North, *Making of Knowledge*; Nystrand, Greene, and Wiemelt). However, while there is some disagreement over the relative importance of specific earlier events and movements, scholars have been nearly unanimous in locating of the emergence of composition as a distinct area of concentration and research during the early 1970s.

The basic story is an important aspect of our shared disciplinary identity. As the story goes, modern composition emerged during the late 1960s and early 1970s, a politically tumultuous period during which colleges and universities were often centers of political activism; open-admissions policies brought about a perceived literacy crisis; the enrollments at public post-secondary institutions ballooned; and first-year composition classes became a major concern for English departments. Early on, we identified with the interests of the nontraditional students who were becoming the new, more diverse, and arguably more truly democratic, face of postsecondary education: nonnative speakers of English, people of color, people from poor or working-class households, and adult students who took classes while working and maintaining families.

As a discipline, we have embraced an often overly romantic view of ourselves that is centered around the teacher in the classroom who spreads democracy and opportunity through literacy education, an image that is vaguely progressive and left of center but without a clearly articulated agenda. In recent years, we have also often managed to avoid, ignore, or render innocuous the progressive politics that have been an important part of our disciplinary heritage and mission. Composition has had a historically problematic relationship with the institutions, and the often literary-studies-focused English departments, within which it has evolved. For instance, Harris has associated the expressivism that informed the pedagogy of many, if not most, composition teachers at least until the late 1970s with a political project that sought to help "the student to assert herself against what was seen as a dehumanizing corporate and university system" (Harris, "Teaching Subject" 27). However, the specific nature and roots of the politics that led to this disposition have not been extensively explored until recently. Our embrace of nontraditional students did not occur in a disciplinary or political vacuum, and the stories of the development of composition studies told by Steve

Parks in *Class Politics: The Movement for the Students' Right to Their Own Language* (2000) and Keith Gilyard in "African American Contributions to Composition Studies" (1999) are very different from our other histories. Parks, for instance, argues that

> more than other disciplines, composition studies owes its current status to the counterhegemonic struggles waged around access to higher education. Without the efforts of the New Left, the Great Society, or Black Power, the reconceptualization of nontraditional students in the academy during the 1960s might not have occurred. Mina Shaughnessy's *Errors and Expectations* (1977) would not have had an existing market to formulate. David Bartholomae's "The Study of Error" (1980) would not have the same bureaucratic and institutional framework through which to be read. (3)

Perhaps because we have focused so intently over the past twenty years on establishing a firm and distinct disciplinary identity and gaining the institutional respect that disciplinary status confers, we have tended to construct disciplinary histories that emphasize our own internal discourses and trends while leaving unexplored greater political factors and disciplinary cross-pollination. Gilyard and Parks help us to better understand the direct relevance of the labor movement, civil rights, and antiwar and anticapitalist movements to our student- and pedagogy-centered orientation. This view of our history supports what I think most compositionists would still like to think about our professional identities—we are primarily politically left-leaning teachers with often ambivalent relationships with the institutions and departments within which we work.

The way that we view our history is important because the management models that seem to be prevailing in composition mark a significant shift in our disciplinary identity—particularly, our focus on progressive, innovative pedagogy, and our identification with the needs of students. Most compositionists continue to profess a primary concern with students and pedagogy; this concern is arguably one of the primary characteristics that separates composition from the rest of English studies. However, I wonder whose interests a model designed to staff tens, at some institutions hundreds, of sections of first-year composition with cheap, semi-permanent, and highly managed labor primarily serves? If the participants in our disciplinary conversations self-identify as managers of labor whose primary interests are training a flexible work force in order to maintain the fiscal health of their institutions, we should recognize that our basic identity as a discipline and profession has shifted radically, and this will have a profound impact on our orientations toward literacy and pedagogy. As the institution's bottom line becomes a paramount concern in our disciplinary conversation, we should expect these efficiency-focused management models to create the same highly standardized, assessment-driven, teacher-proof curriculums that now characterize so much of primary and secondary education. From a management perspective, it will seem much cheaper to plug variously qualified workers into a standardized curriculum designed to produce predictable outcomes than to hire fully credentialed, innovative professionals as teachers. The cost of doing business on the cheap will not show up in departmental budgets, but it will be (and often already is) readily apparent in the writing classroom.

Note

1. In English Studies, the term *assistant* too often refers to people who are teachers who don't assist anyone but are responsible for a considerable portion of a department's composition classes.

13
I Was an Adjunct Administrator

William Vaughn

Think of me as a leading indicator. Sometime during the Mesozoic—perhaps in the Era of New Criticism, or the Age of Appreciation, or as far back as the Philological Period—the field of English hired its first adjunct instructor of composition. Though the fossil record is spotty, we might hypothesize this figure evolved from the earlier species of tutor. Indeed, tutors and adjuncts may, like Neanderthal and Cro-Magnon, have once walked the halls of academe side by side, till, through violence—physical or budgetary—or interbreeding, or terminological natural selection, the adjunct won out, thereupon proliferating to the point where, like the starling, this nonnative species now competes with and threatens other indigenous populations (e.g., professors and graduate students). While I make no claims to have been the *first* adjunct administrator, I suspect that, like the adjunct instructors whose supreme fitness today challenges the whole of the English ecosystem, my own (per)mutation of academic may soon rapidly multiply. Allow me to introduce myself and suggest some lessons that can be drawn from my story.

The first such lesson is that in adjuncting administration, English may be better cultivating its own revolutionary class. The administrative skills needed to reproduce the system of adjunct labor are the same skills required to destroy that labor system. It is one thing to let novice, have-not teachers perform some of the most crucial instruction in the university, but when you further devolve the training and supervision of these teachers onto only slightly more vested senior peers, you are granting this latter group the opportunity to train and supervise in ways that can push labor management to its radical obverse: labor organizing. Every "responsibility" we grant to the relatively disempowered, the more power they can deploy. What may look like administration on the cheap can also serve as economical training in how to collaborate with and radicalize one's peers. Thus, while adjuncted administration is only the latest instance of academic capitalist irresponsibility, it offers a tempting prospect: To learn and practice "responsibility" in ways that can teach us to recapture the administration of the university, whether that translates as unionizing or true faculty governance within existing academic structures.

My own cheap-labor administrative career almost exactly corresponds with my cheap-labor teaching experience (each of which helped underwrite and motivate my organizing career). I became a composition administrator by my second year of grad school at the University of Illinois, in 1992, and served in some administrative capacity for three of the six years I held an assistantship in my department.[1] My first position, which lasted two years, entailed working as a peer adviser to first-year instructors. In addition to providing general support and advice regarding their work, I performed several specific tasks. First, I participated in the week-long orientation that preceded the beginning of the fall semester. My duties typically involved running at least one training session and overseeing my advisees' preparation of their syllabi and initial assignments. Second, I observed and evaluated their teaching. Third, I monitored their marking and grading. Fourth, I coordinated regular group meetings that focused on specific classroom issues. And fifth, I designed and implemented pedagogical workshops for new and veteran instructors alike. My other grad administrative job involved serving as the assistant to the director of professional writing. That position meant supervising orientation; managing the advisers; running our system of client projects (where classes worked on assignments for actual, outside clients in the community); dealing with student complaints; and overseeing other day-to-day affairs of the program.

In any given year, our department might employ ten or more advisers and up to three assistants to the various directors of writing programs. Indeed, in a department that routinely employed close to two hundred grad student and adjunct instructors, it was not uncommon for forty new teachers to be hired in the fall. The responsibility for acculturating these instructors was shared by faculty and grad students, and the former at least nominally oversaw the work of their grad administrative assistants. However, in many respects, the contributions of grad administrators typically outweighed those of the faculty who headed the writing programs. Although the faculty, in most cases, set the tone and established the policies for their programs, much of the day-to-day functioning was directed by grad administrators. To an extent, this reflected the turnover in those faculty positions.[2] In the nine years I worked at Illinois both as a grad employee and adjunct, the three main composition programs—first-year rhetoric, the academic writing program, and professional writing—were directed by nine different individuals, a third of whom were themselves adjuncts. These programs reproduced themselves by way of inertial, self-governing mechanisms aimed at cultivating a resupply of grad administrators from within each system. One recent (adjunct) director of the professional writing program began as my advisee and later served as my assistant when I, as an adjunct, directed the program. We were both deeply influenced by the last faculty professor to run professional writing, but that it has operated successfully for five years without a faculty line devoted to it says something about the program's ingrained structures of self-perpetuation, now entirely coordinated by grad students and adjuncts. The other two writing programs at Illinois do currently have a faculty head, but that in no way diminishes the contributions of the grad administrators who work in these areas. Indeed, the workload of the assistant to the director of first-year rhetoric easily exceeds what I described for my equivalent position in professional writing, and, in general, advisers in rhetoric are busier even than those in my old field. Composition of all kinds at Illinois is now taught almost exclusively by grad students and adjuncts, and it is increasingly administered by them as well.[3]

We might react to this situation in several ways. On the one hand, given the reigning logic of our profession, the above arrangement makes perfect sense. After all, literature specialists are quite happy to unload composition on grad students and adjuncts. Why should not writing pedagogy and administration be dumped on the same group?[4] With regard to the latter duty, it is only appropriate that advice, counsel, and supervision come from colleagues with a background in the same classes staffed by the individuals they are overseeing. If we have been willing to tolerate the wholesale displacement of composition teaching onto unequal partners in the academy, does the same practice with regard to administration risk undermining any sustainable sense of English as a self-governing enterprise? At some point, having outsourced everything but seminars and research, English departments may all recharter themselves in Liberia, the better both to evade taxes and further embrace multiculturalism. English can be remarkably omnivorous in the way it absorbs theories and fields yet bulimic in how it attenuates its own workplace boundaries, expelling here composition, there mentoring and administration. Is running a writing program as glamorous as hosting a conference on cultural studies? Probably not. Is it worth turning over the administration of that program to an adjunct so we can afford to support more research? The decision is rarely so stark, but some version of this dilemma presents itself to any department wishing to reward scholarship while retaining the basic day-to-day services that underwrite research.

So, perhaps the trend toward adjunct administration—if trend it be—does mark the point when our profession is forced to admit it has ceased to function as a self-governing, self-responsible discipline. In which case, what on first blush might appear to be simply the latest phase of a crisis is really a crucial opportunity for addressing it, to reassert governance and reassume responsibility. It should come as no surprise that English departments are common origins for grad employee union efforts. It is not critical theory that motivates the collective action of these employees, for all that such bodies of knowledge may subsequently illuminate the organizing these employees do. We would better understand their efforts as sustained by the very conditions of their work, which produce the critical self-consciousness of abject labor combined with quasi-management skills emerging of necessity in the absence of genuine disciplinary oversight. Degraded work circumstances and displaced mentoring breed organizers better than any seminar ever will.

Indeed, when the grad employee union at Illinois voted to illegally occupy the offices of the school's board of trustees, the English contingent in that occupation consisted largely of current and former grad and adjunct administrators, myself included. (Several others were quite active among those outside the building, providing support.) I participated in that affair even though, as an adjunct, I was no longer formally represented by the union. I did so because I felt responsible toward the people I trained and supervised—because I understood their working conditions and recognized the responsibility we all share in improving them. This understanding and recognition derived from my professional investment, and I would not have had the same sense of investment had I not, almost from the start of graduate school, been asked to assume a role that entailed being responsible for more than just my own career. In a sense, I was an organizer before I realized it. The insights I gained into working conditions and the skills I developed in managing and motivating translated wholesale from administration to organizing. By the same token, our department had been mobilizing for years, not just because the nature of cheap teaching fosters such a desire but because cheap administration further cultivates a larger professional vision among such teachers and refines their ability to plan and execute collective action.

How does it happen that grads and adjuncts take on such roles? In part because of the distaste for administrative work that is ingrained in our profession.[5] One encounters such routine aversion most commonly in the disdain with which we speak of committee work. Arguably the core element of faculty self-governance, it is also among the most-loathed aspects of academic life. In English, the bases of this unpopularity are easy enough to determine: Such work entails bringing together a group of voluble and volatile personalities, trained in the seminar method, to address issues typically less engaging than most seminar topics. It means spending considerable time away from the more pleasant aspects of the profession—reading, teaching, writing—with little compensation for one's efforts, assuming these efforts even achieve an effect. Yet, when members of a department balk at committee work—when they avoid having to talk to one another or even lose the ability to do so altogether—should we be astonished by the ease with which external authorities (campuswide commissions, provosts, state boards) are able to dictate to them? Is it any surprise that the only real, militant resistance to the managed university comes from grad employee and adjunct unions? These groups comprise individuals who *must* talk to one another if they are to solve the structural problems of their exploitation. Organizing is the flexible worker's name for collective self-management.

As academics, our problems with administration—doing it and dealing with it—begin long before we ever step into that first faculty meeting or hear of those initial committee assignments. For when do academics ever practice building consensus or delegating? (I mean real delegating, not the lazy kind that happens every time someone says, "Here, you teach composition.") As graduate students, we learn how to argue, and we cultivate cleverness to impress our professors and intimidate our peers. As teachers, we have the power to assign and enforce the terms of our assignments. Clever banter and the ability to issue directives and set deadlines in no way prepare one to genuinely mobilize people. Indeed, even the movement to unionize grad employees is vulnerable to such academic proclivities. How many meetings did I sit through where we argued endlessly about some iota of strategy, agonized over a definition, or parsed a policy to death? We were only doing what we were trained to do and rewarded for, but often the same tactics that shine in the seminar room frustrate purposeful collaboration. Ultimately, if you do union work long enough, you learn how to work with your peers, precisely because your department/institution/profession has ceded even the pretense of responsible self-government. I will continue to be encouraged about the future of my field so long as more organizers ascend to the professoriate.

Grad students understand the preciousness of faculty jobs, but too often they register that value to justify competitiveness rather than collaboration. The academy's tenure-driven model of success rewards individuals only as individuals, and three decades of siege mentality have done little to change that. We are still all fighting over the same shrinking "prize," teaching our students collaboration in the writing classroom but competing like monopoly capitalists over publication, jobs, and tenure. If we too often thus understand the state of academic labor in terms of social Darwinism, perhaps we can respond as Lamarckians. By understanding organizing as the response invited by decades of failed and displaced administration, we will *become* better administrators through our unionism and transmit these traits to subsequent generations of academics. We need to be helping our students develop collaborative skills that will serve them as organized academic workers, both as representatives of a profession and members of particular departments. They need to learn to defend and improve *jobs in general* even as they aspire for their own job in particular. We must recognize that a profession is more than simply the sum of individual careers. That we too often fail to do so I read as a failure of collective self-administration. Yet, the failure of administration in the managed university is also an invitation to organize another sort of university altogether.

Notes

1. Like most students admitted to my program, I had been offered an assistantship as part of being accepted. Thus, I was teaching undergraduates from the moment I began my studies in English. Small surprise, then, that the following fall, with all of two writing courses under my belt, I commenced mentoring new grad assistants. I like to believe I was selected for this job because my own mentors and supervisors recognized my aptitudes for management and administration. With one-and-a-half semesters of teaching behind me and a stint chairing the textbook review committee underway, I had distinguished myself sufficiently to be entrusted to assist teachers even less polished than I. My own qualifications notwithstanding, however, the need I fulfilled was structural,

and my position would have been staffed by some candidate whose skills somehow set them off from the general applicant pool—which is to say that in choosing mentors for first-time instructors, my department inevitably resorted to the same mode of recruitment it often employed in selecting instructors.

2. I have only anecdotal evidence for supposing this, but my impression is the jobs turned over so often in part because they were not particularly popular assignments.

3. Many English academics freely admit they do not feel equipped to teach first-year composition or to run a program in that or any area of writing. Even composition faculty may balk at the same roles. In replicating literature's tactics of legitimacy, composition has consonantly reproduced its mechanisms of illegitimacy. Literature exalts text and theory over writing, and often, theory over text; composition promotes writing theory at the expense of writing pedagogy. (In the humanities, talking about things is always better than actually doing them, whether the nominal subject be politics or composition.) The real-world consequences of such arrangements are all too apparent. The same era that generates massive amounts of high-quality scholarship also produces scads of lousy jobs. These surpluses are directly related to each other.

4. At Illinois, this trend may be extended within the literature curriculum as well, where the growing population of senior teaching assistants and adjuncts—these latter typically being former TAs—could be deployed as mentors to newer grad student instructors of literature, at least according to one plan proposed by the College of Liberal Arts and Sciences. Many institutions, my current employer included, already use advanced undergraduates as writing tutors and fellows, so one can plot this trend of displacement even further down the food chain, perhaps to a point where no actual teaching takes place any longer, and universities are composed entirely of administrators at one end and students at the other, all professors having either been elevated into the bureaucracy or replaced by grad assistants. I would feel guilty for disseminating such a dystopian blueprint were I not convinced the document has already been vetted and approved by trustees and governing boards of higher education across the land.

5. Administration also gets adjuncted for some of the same reasons composition does: because the typical lit-trained faculty who would rather not teach writing prefer also not to administrate. In saying this, I mean not to ignore the agenda of the managed university. Multiple forces have contributed to the current state of affairs, whereby university work has indeed been corporatized. Businesses as consumers of student-products, students as customers to teacher-clerks, taxpayers as shareholders in educational investments, and administrators as CEOs of university corporations—each of these populations has a part to play in degrading literacy and labor in the academic workplace. I would offer a slight corrective to this familiar narrative, though. I believe those of us in the workplace facilitate our own degradation by shirking responsibility for jobs that are necessary, if relatively unglamorous. The profession's own attitude toward composition helps guarantee that most jobs in that area remain abysmal. I see a similar trend regarding administrative work, and although there may always be certain administrators on whom I might wish unpleasant jobs, it is imperative we cultivate and embrace administrative—that is, *organizing*—skills, if only as a means of protecting our collective interests.

14
Embracing the Logic of the Marketplace: New Rhetorics for the Old Problem of Labor in Composition

Amanda Godley and Jennifer Seibel Trainor

In 1996–1997, we conducted a qualitative study of basic-writing programs on two campuses, both of which are part of a large public research university system. As is typical in universities across the country, basic writing on these campuses serves those students whose literacy skills are deemed in need of remediation before the students can begin their "real" college work. As is typical, these courses are staffed largely by part-time, or underemployed, English teachers. A few years before we undertook our study, writing programs throughout the state were under pressure to get tough on remedial students—expel students who failed to pass through remedial courses in a timely manner and deny admission to students who were unable to meet academic literacy standards when they began university work. At the same time, the programs we studied were experiencing a budget crisis. In response to these pressures, the campuses considered the option of outsourcing their basic-writing courses to local community colleges, where teaching was cheap and where remedial students, it was thought, belonged.

One of the programs, at a campus we call Oakdale, chose this route: Their basic-writing program was outsourced to a local community college in 1994. The community college now hires part-time instructors to staff basic-writing courses taught on the university's campus to university students but at rates much cheaper than those the university pays. The second campus, which we call Bridgewater, charted a different course, one that revamped its writing program so that it was in a position to hire more full-time lecturers to teach writing; it gave full university credit to its students, thus at least partially ending the stigma of remediation.

As researchers committed to changing labor practices in English, we are interested in the relationship between discursive understandings of writing, teaching, students, and labor and the material structures organizing the work of writing teaching in the university, particularly the work of non-tenure-track writing instructors. What particular representations of teachers and students undergird various labor arrangements in writing programs? How might these representations be revised in ways that lead to change?

In this chapter, we revisit the post-outsourcing basic-writing programs at Bridgewater and Oakdale with a focus on another group of instructors—full-time, non-tenure-track faculty. As in our original study, we have given the campuses and all involved pseudonyms following standard ethnographic procedure. As researchers, we interviewed people about their private agendas, motivations, and insights about the configurations of labor in composition on the two campuses. We focus on the discourses used by those involved in defining the terms of work for this group of instructors—administrators, faculty, and lecturers themselves. Although the role of organized labor became increasingly important, particularly at one of the campuses, at the time we conducted the follow-up study, the union had not yet become a significant part of the conversations about lecturers' roles, at least as those conversations were represented in public and institutional documents and by participants in the study.

The number of calls is increasing for the creation of a full-time, non-tenure-track faculty for composition, particularly from those who share what Joseph Harris terms "new materialist" perspectives on labor issues in composition. Unlike earlier writing on labor that focused on the question of composition's status in the university, new materialist scholarship focuses on the conditions and structures that govern the work of teaching: who does what work, for what pay, under what conditions (Harris, "Meet the New Boss"). Underlying this scholarship is a claim that the academy is not, and should not strive to be, separate from the larger material structures that produce it. As Richard E. Miller writes, universities are no longer (or never were) places in which lone scholars are given pure space to produce knowledge and thus reform occurs when academics embrace the bureaucratic and market structures of the university.

Embracing rather than (ineffectually) critiquing the systems that have produced the vexing problem of part-time employment in English is at the heart of some provocative new articulations of what is at stake—and what is possible in terms of change—in the troubled intersections of writing instruction and labor practices. For example, Michael Murphy argues that long-term lecturer positions may offer "some very compelling models for how academia in general might engage the new demands placed upon it in a more highly developed and product-oriented educational marketplace" ("New Faculty" 17). For Murphy, the growing dependence on nontraditional faculty does not have to be seen in doomsday terms: As he writes, teaching provided by the "instructorate" does not necessarily have to be accommodationist, and the academy's potential for doing critical intellectual work does not depend absolutely on the preservation of the traditional professoriate.

In this view, legitimizing the work of composition laborers does not mean extending professional status as compositionists have traditionally argued for. For example, tenure as a route to improved working conditions for writing teachers is viewed as anachronistic—as new materialist arguments imply, it is part of a seductive but ultimately ineffective professionalism privileged in the academy and out of step with the changing nature of university work. Seen in this light, the framing of labor practices as resulting from budgetary constraints conceals a broader change in university culture: It implies that the diminished support for research in particular disciplines, like English, results from lack of demand for our product in the wider marketplace. However, training in advanced literacy *is* in demand. Harris states it bluntly:

> Improving working conditions needs to be posed not simply as a labor issue but also as a means of improving the quality of undergraduate education . . . first-year writing is one of the few things we do that anybody outside of English cares anything about. ("Meet the New Boss" 58–59, 61)

The essence of this claim is that composition can capitalize on the market created by students' desire for, and the public expectation of, advanced literacy training. In turn, composition is positioned to use the institutional and public authority derived from demand for its product to create changes in its staffing practices.

We would like to foreground three premises undergirding these new materialist arguments. One is that the key to improving working conditions for writing teachers is to make more savvy arguments based on student need and market demand and to focus our arguments on the resonate public perception that the teaching of writing is central to the mission of an English faculty. A second, related, premise is that real change can come about when we relinquish the "alluring fantasy" (Harris, "Meet the New Boss") that working conditions can be improved by improving the status of the discipline. Instead, we need to abandon, or at least to subordinate, the struggle for more tenure-line positions and focus instead on the issue of good teaching for fair pay. Finally, both premises lead to arguments for the creation of a different kind of employment: a teaching substructure consisting of professionalized nontenured teachers. This substructure is offered as a model of work in the new university.

In a general sense, we support these ideas: We have argued elsewhere that student need and market demand for literacy skills offer powerful discursive strategies in the fight to improve working conditions in English. We also agree that in order to be savvy rhetoricians of social change (Cushman), it sometimes behooves us to speak the language of the corporate university and to position ourselves discursively in ways that resonate with its logic. Finally, we acknowledge that doing the numbers demonstrates unequivocally that tenure for all composition teachers is a hollow dream, but the logic that these arguments are based on, as their champions readily admit, is a corporate one and it structures the work of composition in ways fundamental to how we talk about labor, literacy, and student need. This logic, as an extension of the managerial project of the expanding corporate economy in the early-twentieth century, "operate[s] as a powerful constraint on the possibilities of argument," as Donna Strickland has recently argued (468). Strickland adds an overlooked dimension to existing histories of composition in the academy (that it was seen originally conceptualized as remedial and that it was feminized). As she shows, it was also corporatized, dealt with by way of a discourse of management and system, a "science of work." Put simply, our choices seem to be to resist or capitulate to market forces, and while Murphy, Miller, Harris, and others are making serious attempts to carve out a middle ground, to suggest a kind of critical pragmatism that might offer us a way to make real albeit limited change, this ground is often crisscrossed with contradictions. Post-outsourcing struggles at Bridgewater and Oakdale serve as a potent example here, raising questions about the efficacy of a rhetoric of student need and a market for advanced literacy to shape arguments about labor and about the slipperiness of apparently straightforward slogans like "good teaching for fair pay."

Student Need Before Working Conditions: A Success?

Originally at Bridgewater, tenured faculty drew on their positions within the university and on a prescient understanding of the rhetorical power of arguments about undergraduate education to resist outsourcing their basic-writing program and to improve working conditions for a number of teachers. In describing the process they went through to accomplish these goals, we would like to highlight three points: The first involves a critical examination of the discourse of student need and market demand for literacy; the second is more complex and involves the ways in which a successful rhetoric of student need often discursively marginalizes teachers, positioning especially part-time teachers as ineffective—unable to meet student need and the third is that embracing a rhetoric of student need that positions need in market terms means complicity in corporate ideologies about students and literacy that, we believe, may not ultimately serve students, writing programs, or teachers.

In 1993, budgetary and ideological pressures were pointing squarely in the direction of outsourcing basic writing at Bridgewater. However, the committee in charge of restructuring the writing program never seriously considered outsourcing, despite its financial appeal as a solution to pressing budgetary problems and despite the administration's attempt to convince the campus and the public that basic-writing students, because they lacked advanced literacy skills, belonged at the community college. The committee's response was material and institutional, as well as rhetorical. For example, the committee members used their position as academic senate members to change the bylaws of the university system. The new basic-writing program proposed by the committee was incompatible with university bylaws concerning credit granted for remedial coursework. Members of the committee had to convince other tenured faculty members on particular academic senate committees that the university system should grant full course credit for courses that were deemed—entirely or in part—remedial. Using their position as composition experts and as senate faculty members, they were able to accomplish this.

The committee was able to improve working conditions in the program by avoiding arguments about labor and focusing instead on student need. This required negating the long-standing belief in composition studies in the value and integrity of the work of writing teachers. As Murphy writes, echoing this belief:

> The work of most of my part-time colleagues is probably better than that done in composition classrooms today by the *average* full-time faculty member teaching writing . . . Most regular part-time faculty I know are not half-prepared and institutionally unsupported itinerants . . . They are committed, expert teachers and curriculum planners whose dedicated hard work is essential to the general intellectual and academic health of their departments and of the universities and colleges in which they work. ("New Faculty" 29–30)

Embracing student need as a platform for reforming labor practices in composition, we want to point out, necessarily requires eliding, questioning, or ignoring Murphy's point of view and arguing instead that part-time employment compromises undergraduate education because it relies on substandard teachers. In this rhetoric, pedagogical value equals market value: You get what you pay for.

At first glance, it appears that by articulating the problem in this way, the compositionists at Bridgewater were not following Alan France, William Lalicker, and Christopher Teutsch's call to use their positions to "extend professional status" to the full- and part-time composition lecturers in the basic-writing program. The rhetorical tack chosen by the committee ultimately positioned issues of labor as ancillary to issues of student need. In order to shore up their argument that the basic-writing program needed to be changed, the committee's report painted a picture of the current basic-writing program and its (part-time) instructorate as *not* in alliance with current theories of composition. For example, rather than arguing that part-time or nontenured instructors are more dedicated to, aware of, and suited to the needs of basic writers than tenured or full-time instructors, the faculty at Bridgewater explicitly argued that the basic-writing students' needs were not being met by such instructors. As we have argued elsewhere, composition has historically attempted to grant disenfranchised teachers respect via a discourse of teacher-heroism that has in turn been used to justify the use of part-time teachers. Although the lecturers teaching in the program at that time felt that the position taken up by the committee reflected their pedagogy and program inaccurately and ungenerously, it ultimately served an important purpose: By contrasting the new writing program and its instructors with the old, the committee could use a discourse of student need coupled with their own position as experts to argue that full-time instructors would better serve students. The committee argued for, and received, funding to create some full-time lecturer positions within the basic-writing program and to increase the contract of these lecturers to 100 percent (80 percent for teaching four courses a year, 20 percent for university service) so that they could take on more administrative and scholarly work within the program and across the university. It should be noted, however, that despite the committee's recommendations, the basic-writing program at Bridgewater still employs a fair amount of part-timers each semester. The funding for all the full-time positions the committee called for has not materialized.

The current position of the full-time lecturers within the Bridgewater basic-writing program offers a portrait of the intellectual instructorate that many are calling for (in his article, Murphy specifically cites our description of the Bridgewater lecturers as a "relatively healthy institutional paradigm"). These lecturers teach two courses a semester (the same course load granted to tenure-track faculty), serve on some university committees, and publish their work. They design new courses, attend professional conferences (for which they receive funding), and are involved in local and national organizations (such as the National Writing Project) and research groups.

However, although they fulfill vital intellectual and bureaucratic roles within the university, the configuration of this bureaucracy ultimately limits the lecturers in important ways. In short, the professionalization of composition lecturers is ultimately at odds with their position in the hierarchy of the university. Lecturers at Bridgewater can and do engage in scholarly work, but because they are not part of the academic senate, they do not hold the power to make decisions or recommendations to the university based on their pedagogical and scholarly knowledge. They can suggest such recommendations to the director of the program who can then relay them to other decision-making bodies, but the university structure does not allow them to call upon their position as experts in composition to make curricular decisions. This can be particularly vexing for the most recently hired lecturers, most of whom hold recent doctoral degrees in composition and are often as well qualified as tenured faculty members to make such decisions. Ultimately, then, the experts on student need are silenced by the university— often unable to use their knowledge to their own or their students' benefit.

Additionally, the terms of the lecturers' contracts require that their formal evaluations are based almost entirely on teaching, not research or service to the university. Thus, even though the tight academic labor market has meant that lecturers in recent years have been hired, in part, on the basis of their research agendas, this research is not seen by the university or the union that represents the lecturers as an integral part of the work they do. Because many of the new lecturers were seeking tenure-track jobs as compositionists when they were hired in Bridgewater's basic-writing program, they often compare their working conditions, salaries, and positions within the university to tenure-track professors and find their own status lacking. Ironically, though the tight job market has allowed the writing program to hire candidates with Ph.D.s, the academic training of these new hires may lead them to seek out better jobs in the near future, leaving the program to fill their positions again and disrupting the continuity that their presence is meant to provide.

Finally, the lecturers' positions are more subject to changes in temporary funding than those of tenured faculty members. The structure of the university requires that lecturer positions (and the basic-writing program) be funded through temporary funds, even when the lectureships are designed to be long-term. Though the Bridgewater campus has continued to fund these positions (and even increased their number slightly per the recommendations of the basic-writing committee), we would argue that their precarious nature undermines the lecturers' position as fully enfranchised workers in composition.

The professionalization of this corps of workers, then, is vexed by contradictions: Lecturers have been hired, in part, based on their scholarly pursuits, and yet, these pursuits are not a significant part of their formal reviews; lecturers are the only instructors—besides graduate students—who teach basic writing, yet they do not have the institutional power or prestige to bring this expertise to bear on institutional or curricular decisions; and lecturers, although granted three-year contracts after six years of service to the university, do not enjoy the same job security that tenured professors do. The corporate logic that organizes the terms of lecturers' work, because it relies on a division of labor that conflates professional and research on the one hand, and subprofessional and teaching on the other, creates layers of contradiction for lecturers at Bridgewater.

Precisely because the members of the committee charged with reforming the basic-writing program were "boss compositionists" (Harris, "Meet the New Boss"), they were able to advocate for changes that drew upon current composition theory, to reposition remedial students—in material as well as discursive ways—and the writing course that served them as integral parts of the university structure and, ultimately, to argue for better labor conditions for composition lecturers. The work of tenured compositionists at Bridgewater, then, gives us a contextualized snapshot of the possibilities for change that arise when tenured faculty use their positions of power within the university to improve the conditions that surround instructors and students. Although this power was used to create a more permanent, less-marginalized instructorate within composition, the limitations imposed by the hierarchical logic of the university ultimately circumscribe the professionalization of this group. Murphy argues that compositionists need to "work within [these] limits to professionalize faculty and instruction as thoroughly as possible" ("New Faculty" 32), but the position of the lecturers at Bridgewater—and even more strongly, those at Oakdale, discussed below—suggest that the limits imposed by this logic and by the corresponding position of composition within academic structures are not so easily circumvented.

Fighting Layoffs at Oakdale

Like Bridgewater, Oakdale is part of a large public research university system, but unlike Bridgewater, a full-time nontenured instructorate serving an upper-division writing program has existed for many years there both before and since Oakdale's basic-writing program was outsourced in 1994. This instructorate has, by all accounts, been a vital part of the university's structure—teaching composition classes, serving on university committees, and making curricular decisions. Recently at Oakdale, members of the administration have called for a substantial reduction in the number of such full-time lecturer positions and for a replacement labor force comprised of one-year lecturers and post-doctorate fellows, more graduate student instructors, and a few tenured compositionists.

The proposed labor changes would add more tiers of composition laborers to an already stratified writing instructorate. The Oakdale campus requires its undergraduates to complete two composition classes in order to graduate; after they pass out of basic writing (through a timed-essay exam or through passing the outsourced basic-writing class), students must complete a first-year composition class and then an upper-division, advanced-writing class. The composition classes at Oakdale, then, are staffed by three kinds of instructors: The basic-writing classes, as mentioned above, are taught by part-timers who are hired through the local community college. The regular first-year composition sections are, for the most part, staffed by graduate students in the department's M.A. and Ph.D. programs. Finally, the upper-division writing course, a required class for all undergraduate students, is staffed by the full-time lecturers, almost all of whom have doctoral degrees and many of whom have come through the English department's own Ph.D. program. These lecturers also mentor graduate students in their first semester of teaching and serve on department and university committees. Like the full-time lecturer positions Murphy calls for and like the lecturers at Bridgewater, these lecturers have seemingly strong job security; they are hired under one-year contracts for the first six years of their employment, and then—per union contract—are given three-year contracts and reviews. Most of the lecturers have been teaching at the university for at least ten, but some up to twenty, years. In all respects, then, these lecturers seem to fulfill the institutional and ethical requirements for good composition instructors that Murphy and Harris call for: They serve the needs of the students and the university by teaching writing and are granted tenure-like (but not tenured) status in return. They have job security and benefits, they serve on committees, and some publish.

However, in the fall of 1999, a new dean of humanities, arts, and cultural studies began to make moves to eliminate these lecturer positions. During the summer of 2000, eight full-time lecturers whose three-year contracts were up for renewal received reduced contracts that, in essence, refashioned them as part-timers, teaching fewer and fewer courses (and receiving fewer benefits) over the next three years. The administration's initial long-term plan was to do away with the full-time lectureships entirely, but when it became clear that this was not logistically feasible given the number of required writing courses, the dean called for the gradual reduction of such lecturers through attrition, the increase of tenured faculty members with expertise in composition, the continued use of one-year lecturers (whose terms would be limited to six years), and the development of post-doctoral positions in English to staff remaining composition classes.

Interestingly, the dean's arguments for the restructuring of the labor of composition at Oakdale also called upon discourses of market forces, student need, and university structure. According to the dean and the chair of the English department, full-time lectureships at Oakdale are funded by monies made available when tenure-track positions are not filled. Conversely, when funds are allocated for long-term, full-time lecturers, they are no longer available to the department for tenure-track hires. In this way, the budgetary structure at Oakdale necessarily requires departments to choose between lecturers and tenure-stream faculty. A long history of hiring lecturers instead of tenure-track faculty to fill university requirements in composition led to what the dean and department chair saw as a critical imbalance between lecturers and tenure-track faculty in the English department and the need for a reduction in the lecturer ranks.

Throughout the debates that took place as these plans were discussed and negotiated, discourses of student need, the role of composition in the current structure of the academy, and fair labor practices were utilized in complex, often contradictory ways. Even the purpose of eliminating the full-time lectureships was hotly debated, with faculty (tenured and nontenured) widely believing that the administration's goal was to reduce spending on the composition program and with administrators consistently asserting that the goal of their plan was to elevate the status and quality of the composition program by hiring tenure-track faculty. Ironically, the Oakdale administration argued for tenured faculty and a research agenda in composition at the very same time that many compositionists were abandoning the widespread battle for tenured writing instructors; and the administration used the argument for tenured compositionists as a justification for the elimination of stable lecturer positions just as more compositionists were embracing the role of nontenured, full-time writing instructors as a realistic and justifiable part of the academic labor force.

When the full-time lecturers' reduced contracts became public knowledge in the fall of 2000, two groups of tenured faculty members spoke out against this decision, one calling upon discourses of student need and the ability of a professionalized instructorate to fulfill it, the other upon discourses of fair labor practices. The tenured faculty within the English department, by all accounts, vocally objected to the idea that current lecturers would not have their contracts continued and couched their objections in terms of fairness. According to the chair of the English department, the faculty was

> of a mind that we couldn't really support the notion of keeping people on and giving them reduced contracts. It's just unfair. And there was a great deal of agreement about that. People kept talking about how these are colleagues, they have invested for years in this university, and that's just not how we should be dealing with them.

Although the discourses of fair labor practices and loyalty—discourses often at odds with corporate rhetoric—ultimately helped ensure that current three-year lecturers would be rehired, it did not address arguments made about student need or the long-term staffing of the composition program. In many ways, the English faculty were not well-positioned institutionally to argue for the full-time lecturer positions on any other grounds: Because none were compositionists themselves or teachers of composition classes, they did not have the same kind of credibility that those in support of lecturers at Bridgewater did. Some more-cynical members of the Oakdale community even suggested that the tenured English faculty's support of the lecturers was simply self-interested: If the lecturer positions were eliminated, tenured faculty would, for the first time in decades, be expected to teach composition courses.

Faculty from outside of the department deployed the logic of the marketplace and connected it effectively to pedagogical and material concerns—serving student need and meeting public demand for increased literacy skills—in their defense of the lecturers' jobs. In part, these faculty members were reacting to a widespread belief that in conjunction with the elimination of the lecturer positions, the upper-division writing requirement was in jeopardy. In a widely circulated letter to an external reviewer of Oakdale's composition program, a professor from the computer science department wrote of his concern that the writing expectations on campus were going "downhill" and would be further compromised by "eroding writing requirements":

> To assume that [lecturers'] long-established excellence could be in any way matched by uninterested ladder faculty or underqualified recent graduates is patently unsound. . . . I believe that the basic problem lies in an unfair and ill-advised competition for scarce resources.

The corporate rhetoric manifest in terms like "scarce resources" was made even more explicit in a letter to the chancellor of the university, in which six Oakdale teaching-award winners also stated their strong objection to the dean's plan to reduce the number of long-term lecturers in composition:

> It is clearly wasteful of experienced classroom resources in a time of documented increasing demand. In addition, if those resources are not maintained and augmented as enrollment growth may dictate, the right of the Senate Faculty to determine degree requirements could also be jeopardized.

The letter goes on to argue that if three-year lectureship positions are discontinued, these positions should be replaced by ladder faculty members, not "a revolving door policy whereby Post-docs assume some teaching duties." By embracing their role in the hierarchy of the university, utilizing corporate and fiscal rhetoric in their descriptions of lecturers' work and advocating for those less enfranchised than them, these tenured faculty members—like those at Bridgewater—were able to use their positions of power (as academic senate members) to change proposed labor practices in the composition program at Oakdale. In a letter to the senate faculty, one composition lecturer noted the widespread belief that the tenure-track faculty members' vocal objection to the reduced contracts influenced the dean's decision to guarantee full-time appointments to current three-year lecturers and added, "We are deeply grateful for it." Other members of the campus community suggested that simply "doing the numbers" convinced the administration that without hiring some lecturers, there would never be enough graduate students, tenured faculty, and post-docs to staff the required composition courses.

As the dean noted in a response to an earlier draft of this chapter, the larger battle over resources and student needs at Oakdale could not be separated from non-English faculty's involvement in this issue:

> The erosion of senate faculty in favor of full-time writing instructors . . . reveals in stark form the increasing marginalization of liberal education, in general, and the humanities, in particular. Pre-professional programs, engineering, and science programs are only too happy to regard the humanities, particularly English, as service departments that should be dedicated to the utilitarian function of improving writing competency and so enhancing marketability of graduates. . . . Those market arguments have had a telling effect on the relative numbers of senate faculty and lecturers at Oakdale in the past decade.

Although non–English-department faculty appeared attentive to student need in their support of the composition lecturers, never mentioned in the public debate was the way in which their departments and students might benefit from retaining the lecturers at the expense of the reputation, budget, and institutional power of the English department.[1] As the dean pointed out, with a ratio of tenure stream faculty to lecturers hovering at 1:1 in the English department, the needs of students across the university—in computer science, biology, or engineering as well as the humanities—may have been served at the expense of the needs of the English department, its national reputation (linked closely to the reputation of tenure-stream faculty members and the placement of graduate students), and its ability to maintain and increase institutional decision-making power and institutional advocacy through academic-senate-committee representation and other forms of representation requiring greater numbers of tenure-stream faculty and a larger program. Although compositionists have long been concerned with the position of composition as a handmaid to English, this concern, as the case of Oakdale strongly suggests, can belie the danger of composition's position as a handmaid of the *university*, particularly when advanced literacy is posited as a commodity and the English department's job to provide it at market rates.

Although the full-time lecturers, like the tenured faculty outside the English department, drew upon the corporate logic already in place and imbued it creatively with an emphasis on good teaching for fair pay, their status within the university reduced their ability to advocate for themselves, much as we saw with Bridgewater. As conversations with the lecturers, the chair of the English department, and the dean revealed, arguments made by the lecturers, even those based in discourses of student need but especially those about working conditions, were viewed with suspicion by the administration. In one interview, the dean explained:

> We had a unit of lecturers who were interested naturally in creating courses so that their positions would continue and so that there would be more. That's laudatory in some ways, but . . . if I can just invent things and I don't have to pay for them, there's no final accountability. And that's what was happening. You had kind of a freelance group out there that wasn't really being supervised by the English department inventing maybe wonderful courses, maybe not. There wasn't any real supervision.

Lecturers, because of their institutional position as workers, not bosses (or, in the dean's words, "supervisors"), were viewed by higher administration as incapable of separating student need from their own job security and working conditions.

Although discourses of student need were employed by both those in favor of and those against reducing the number of full-time lecturers in composition, these notions of student need, and the pedagogical and labor conditions necessary to fulfill them, differed greatly. Some at Oakdale believed that students would best be served by fewer full-time lecturers. Both the chair of the English department and the dean held that new Ph.D.s and graduate students provided equally good, if not better, instruction than seasoned lecturers. The dean argued,

> [Through] my experience looking at evaluations [at other institutions], I've never felt there was any sacrifice. You know how hard it is to keep a freshness of approach. There's always an advantage to everyone to bring in new lifeblood, fresh ideas, ideas about how technology fits into writing. It gives you the best of long-term experience with new blood. I think that's a good thing.

But though she suggested that a mix of short-term and long-term hires would ultimately provide the best instruction and best meet student need, it is unclear who the long-term hires in the Oakdale composition program would be if lecturers and post-docs were limited to three to six years of teaching and if tenure-track composition hires were few.

Similarly, the proposed post-doctoral fellows were seen by some as fulfilling both graduate and undergraduate student needs. Because these fellows would be drawn primarily from Oakdale's own English Ph.D. program, advocates argued that it would serve the needs of English graduate students by providing them with teaching experience, time to publish, and mentoring in these areas. The dean described the proposed post-doc program as

> a support for our students who are qualified. It's what Joe Harris is doing at Duke and it's what the sciences have always had: a period of time when you can consolidate your portfolio, get some extra teaching experience, and you

get a chance to get some articles out. I would like to replace some of the lecturers with post-doc fellows as a part of supporting our whole graduate teaching issue.

In this way, the dean was able to position the issue of student need in ways that served both the economic interests of the university—because post-docs command lower salaries than experienced full-time lecturers—and the needs of graduate students, who may be more competitive on the job market if they teach a variety of challenging courses. This justification was seen by others as privileging graduate student "need" over the need for undergraduates to receive writing instruction from experienced, long-term lecturers. Expressing another view of the hiring practices that best fulfill student need, one English-department faculty member contrasted the proposed hiring practices at Oakdale with the more prevalent use of part-timers elsewhere, saying, "If they [lecturers] go to five- to six-year [limited] appointments and don't go to three-year contracts, that still provides a fair amount of program stability. It's not a freeway-flyer kind of circumstance."

In the aftermath of this debate, full-time writing lectureships at Oakdale—jobs once considered professionalized and stable—began to be eliminated. In our view, this result had much to do with the absence of institutionally recognized compositionists to set the terms of student need, advanced literacy, or good pedagogy. At the same time, the former chair of the English department assembled a task force—made up of people "committed to undergraduate teaching at the university," according to the task-force director—to study the current writing requirements at Oakdale and make recommendations for the future. The task force's recommendations, made public in January of 2001, included increasing the composition requirement to three courses in order to address undergraduate students' need for advanced literacy skills. Although the task force's report noted that there would still be a need for composition lecturers under the proposed plan, both the task force and the administration saw these recommendations as ultimately creating more (English and non-English) tenure-track faculty involvement in composition—a change that both viewed as important to the needs of the university and undergraduate students.[2] The dean explained:

> It's never good at any institution if writing gets detached from the faculty who are responsible for the curriculum, if the faculty doesn't see in some vital way that they need to be involved. . . . That's why administrators when they have a conscience must say no, we must hire people in the tenure-track because those are the people who are ultimately held to account—for the functioning and the health of the university, for the health of the pedagogical and research enterprise of the university. And dedicated and devoted as non-tenure-track lecturers are, they don't have that responsibility. They can walk away at night and any service that they do is compensated. It's a very different mentality.

Those trying to walk the middle ground between fair labor practices and the corporate structure of the academy often articulated the limitations of the lecturers' power within the university and the material conditions and institutional structure of the workplace. The director of the writing task force noted,

> I think we've let composition move into a kind of absentee landlord arrangement where the English department; the academic senate faculty have authority over the program but the responsibility has been delegated . . . And sometimes that provides a kind of resistance to curricular recommendations that may be quite good and thought out.

Similarly, the chair of the English department argued, "We need the intellectual leadership in the writing program that can only be offered by an academic senate person because of the structure of the university." Keenly aware of the power and labor structure of the university, some administrators and faculty members, while in support of maintaining full-time lecturers' jobs, also recognized that undergraduate students' needs might be better served and advocated by tenured faculty in composition. Although few compositionists would argue against the need for more tenured writing experts in any English department today, we must ask: Will the elimination of stable lectureships result in the addition of tenured compositionists?

It remains unlikely that many of the lecturer positions at Oakdale will be replaced with tenure-track faculty. Though the English department recently filled a senior appointment in composition and though the dean has committed to another composition hire next year, the university is facing a hiring freeze, and everyone at Oakdale agrees that the composition program will continue to rely on lecturers, the new post-doc positions, and graduate students. Although the union has filed a grievance against the university on behalf of the lecturers who came up for their sixth-year review and were not granted them, these grievances are in abeyance while the union faces larger labor issues: The lecturers at Oakdale have been working without a contract for two years, and a strike may be imminent.[3] Lecturers whose jobs are in peril have, with the help of union representatives, written letters and met with state elected officials and members of the state's higher education committee. As one lecturer noted, "One feels, however, that there is so much background to explain about lecturers in general and about the particular situation at Oakdale." State representatives—accustomed to receiving one-page, bullet-pointed briefs from lobbyists—live in a material and discursive world far removed from that of academia. Although the union has repeatedly pressed lecturers to talk to their students about the conditions under which they are laboring, many lecturers see this as disruptive to their work as teachers of writing.

These debates about student need and the instructors that best serve them raise the question: How do arguments for the professionalization of lecturers coincide with, and clash with, calls for addressing students' needs? In many ways, the lecturers at Oakdale seemed to be in the process of being de-professionalized because their administrative and curricular decision-making power was taken away and given to tenure-track faculty. Additionally, the lecturers were increasingly seen as replaceable by cheaper and more-flexible kinds of hires—graduate students and post-docs. This points to the difficulty of establishing a second-tier intellectual instructorate even when such an instructorate seems to enjoy tenure-like job security. How long will the seemingly model lectureships at Bridgewater be safe from similar administrative moves? Because lectureships are funded by temporary funds and because they are not accorded the same status and power within the university as tenured faculty, their work and professionalization are limited. Although Murphy notes that "departmental chairs, college deans, and faculty organizations would have to be careful not to let university central administrations use the tiers as managerial devices for, simply enough, demanding yet more work for less pay" (35), the current situation at Oakdale suggests that, given the science of work that structures most universities, it is not clear how such an ethical stance could be maintained.

Notes

1. One possible compromise for this might have been to simply convert the full-time lecturers to tenure-track, senate-faculty status, but this was never suggested by any of the parties involved in the debate.

2. At the time we went to press, no changes reflecting the task force's recommendations had been planned. Many at Oakdale believe that the administration was not willing to pay for the proposed changes in the writing program because they were too expensive.

3. Perhaps not surprisingly, one of the most contested bargaining points in the union's negotiations is not lecturers' pay but their job security.

15

Bureaucratic Essentialism and the Corporatization of Composition

Christopher Carter

Contemporary composition scholars perceive their institutional and social roles in various and competing ways. While some pose as service providers to students and industry, others view themselves as cultural workers who foster critical literacies in both their classrooms and their departments. Some construct the composition classroom as a training ground for real-world writing situations outside the academy, while others see the classroom as itself a very real space where the social tensions that surround and infuse the academy might be discursively negotiated. Still more scholars have contradictory affiliations: They attempt to fill their roles within an administrative hierarchy while encouraging students to become suspicious of hierarchical structures. They attempt to prepare their students for the working world while nevertheless objecting to that world's exploitative practices. Workers in composition often feel that they must temper their idealism in response to the material realities of the academy's increasing corporatization. Richard E. Miller, in *As If Learning Mattered: Reforming Higher Education,* argues that the corporate identity of the university is already entrenched and that compositionists can only serve their students and each other by embracing their essentially bureaucratic roles and working toward incremental gains in their material circumstances. According to Miller, to view oneself as other than bureaucratic amounts to utopianism, which he defines as mere political posturing that can do nothing for compositionists except offer a fantasy of transformation. For him, the conflict over role perception has apparently already been resolved by the university's rigidly compartmentalized structure. To work in such a hierarchical organization is to necessarily be a bureaucrat, and to publicly imagine anything else is to reveal one's ineffectual solipsism.

Yet must the conversations surrounding the academic and social subject positions of compositionists end with mass submission to existing hierarchies? Is the role of the intellectual bureaucrat the most honest and ethical one we can hope to play? According to feminist scholars Amy Goodburn and Carrie Leverenz, composition workers committed to the democratization of the university should oppose the paternalism associated with bureaucratic models of governance. In "Feminist Writing Program Administration: Resisting the Bureaucrat Within," they maintain that though the temptations of stratified administrative authority are subtly pervasive and difficult to resist, teacher-scholars should nevertheless engage in a constant and self-critical endeavor to sustain collaborative decision making. The interactivity and decentered authority that many of us advocate pedagogically, they contend, should also guide our departmental policy negotiations. Following Goodburn and Leverenz, I will argue not only that teacher-scholars should resist urges toward bureaucratic role perception but that the subjectivity named by this "bureaucrat within" is a historical and ideological construct produced by the increasing commercialization of higher education. Rather than merely repressing the authoritarian manager supposedly straining to overtake our consciousness, we should expose the cultural and economic machinery that perpetuates the myth that bureaucratic selfhood is inevitable—that compositionists are essentially bureaucratic.

In *As If Learning Mattered* and "Composing English Studies: Toward a Social History of the Discipline," Miller demonstrates his important concern for factoring student writing and student perspectives into the history of composition in the university. His earnest commitment to the empowerment of student writers represents a consistent theme in his own writing. Miller's embrace of the bureaucratic subject position, then, does not suggest that he consciously views students as units to be molded for the corporate world. He indeed advocates *good* bureaucratic practices that tend toward enhanced material conditions for students and teachers alike. By identifying with and respecting the upper administration of the university, Miller suggests, we can gain the funding and build the environment most amenable to good teacher-student relations and good writing. I am troubled, however, by the potential long-term consequences of a bureaucratic self-identification, even if it can be shown to produce short-term material benefits (and the evidence for managerial improvements in working conditions is slim at best). By answering the call to be good bureaucrats, are we inadvertently stifling the critical and labor-centered approaches necessary to make the university into something other than a highly compartmentalized and managerially dominated institution?

Imagining the university as a space to critique rather than merely practice capitalism requires a deep engagement with the specific structuration of local institutions. Although the bureaucrat values such structural knowledge as a means of increasing institutional efficiency, the same literacy might also be used by scholars and activists in committed opposition to the university's role in perpetuating socioeconomic injustice. The university, for all its progressive pretense, is increasingly visible as a center of inequality and exploitation. As Miller argues, we cannot alter these inequities by standing aloof from corporate academic realities. Yet by constructing such corporatism as natural and inevitable, he stabilizes the very structure he would revise. Ignoring the question of whether academic capitalism is just, he asks instead how composition can best compete in the interdepartmental contest for resources and funding. Failing to acknowledge historical and actual alternatives to capitalist competition, he suggests that we must learn to work within corporate capital's constraints.

As Karen Thompson argues in "Faculty at the Crossroads: Making the Part-Time Problem a Full-Time Focus," Miller's position seems "optimistic" because it "ignores the exploitation of a growing sector of academic employees," it denies "the trend that full-time faculty are on the wane," and it refuses to "acknowledge cost-driven mismanagement of the labor force by our institutions" (188). When Miller asks us to respect the institutional limitations that mediate reform, he implies that the university defines the terms of its own structural revisions and that we had best recognize those terms if we desire any change at all. A more-nuanced and labor-centered analysis of academic restructuring suggests that the "remedy" of intellectual bureaucracy has from the outset been the problem.

The rhetoric of institutional constraint itself constrains our collective ability to imagine the university as something other than a paternalistic congeries of profit-driven small businesses. The language of institutional limits works to ensure that the horizons of corporate possibility are not transgressed. Such limiting rhetoric serves the interests of the university's elite: Their continuing dominance depends upon an academic underclass who knows its boundaries. The good bureaucrat, in appearing to patiently work within those boundaries, sustains as reality political limits that are neither honest nor natural but simply the limit— ideas most useful to hierarchies of decision making and money-gathering. We do nothing to inhibit academic corporatism if we construct ourselves as gentle managers bound by the constraints of an unkind system. This conservatism disguised as progressive bureaucracy carefully protects itself against critique. By articulating and thereby reifying institutional constraints, the bureaucrat creates the illusion that only his selfless negotiations with upper management can possibly lead to material improvements in the institution's working conditions. This story unfolds in a revisionist history carefully sanitized of the enormous and continuing efforts of organized labor. Conspicuously shouldering the burden of incremental change, the canny administrator renders himself humbly heroic. Such heroism, so long as we applaud and imitate it, distracts us from the immediate and pervasive problems of academic capitalism. The bureaucrat asks not whether we can forge a culture of critical social thought but how we can better assimilate to the naturalized corporate culture.

What I call the bureaucratic essentialism endorsed by composition administrators actively works to sustain systems of inequitable labor. Although tenure-track literacy workers might benefit from identifying with upper management, a similar identification by part-time and non-tenure-track instructors makes little sense. Over the past thirty years, good bureaucracy has aggressively institution-alized casualized labor. As defined by the university's administrative elite, the goodness of the good bureaucrat would seem to require servicing the most tu-ition-paying students at the least institutional expense. In composition, the ability of the WPAs to identify with upper management rests in large part on their will-ingness to see composition teaching being done by contingent instructors enjoy-ing low wages, few benefits, and almost no job security. Without these low wages, why would upper university management need to hire composition managers at all? Divorced from any notion of social or economic justice, bureaucratic good-ness equals efficiency and profitability.

Many composition managers, while well-meaning in their efforts to gain fund-ing and resources for their department, covertly reinforce administrative authority. As Gary Rhoades has suggested in *Managed Professionals: Unionized Faculty and Restructuring Academic Labor,* university managers depend on the existence of a large group of part-timers with few institutional rights and limited intellectual liberty in order to consolidate control over curricula and policy. Contingent hiring assures managerial prerogatives while preventing many rank-and-file literacy workers from controlling even minimally the conditions of their pedagogical labor, denying them not only pay but even such perquisites as selecting the course text. Joseph Harris, who endorses bureaucratic incrementalism in "Meet the New Boss, Same as the Old Boss: Class Consciousness in Composition," intends to solve the urgent problems of contingent labor by "pressing for more direct con-trol over staffing and curricula" by professional compositionists (64). Enforcing the voicelessness of contingent workers even as he decries their working condi-tions, Harris imagines that the consolidation of administrative power within composition will serve literacy workers better than their own self-organization. Such an authoritarian consolidation hardly runs counter to the corporate univer-sity's restructuring into competing units of individual managerial responsibility. Although both Miller and Harris ostensibly oppose the notion of the university as an instrument of top-down knowledge transmission, their ready assumption of bureaucratic subject positions actually facilitates pyramidal pedagogy. Good bureaucracy, rather than providing the antidote to patronizing instruction, de-mands it. Because the university's upper administration aims to produce job-ready students—marketable commodities—rather than critical thinkers who might question bureaucratic hierarchies, composition workers should carefully consider whether they wish to reaffirm those hierarchies by adopting management values and practices.

Despite increasing attention to issues of diversity and social justice in writ-ing pedagogy, this discourse has generally glossed over the unjust hiring prac-tices that make writing classes possible. "It appears to be ironic, but true," ob-serve Eileen E. Schell and Patricia Lambert Stock in their introduction to *Moving a Mountain: Transforming the Role of Contingent Faculty in Composition and Higher Education,* that as higher education has become increasingly democratic, admitting and educating millions of minorities, women, older students, low-income persons, the handicapped, and other non-traditional students, academic hiring practices have become increasingly undemocratic. (5)

Schell and Stock point out that composition's reliance on non-tenure-track teaching had steadily worsened in the latter half of the twentieth century, suggesting that the increased social conscience of the discourse had failed to alter departmental labor policies. A sharp distinction seems to exist between pedagogical theory and workplace practice. Although the pedagogies demonstrate an ostensible commitment to cultural equity, the hiring practices show commitment only to exploitative economics.

Increasingly, the function of contingent teachers is to impart to students the requisite skills for negotiating workplace hierarchies. Imagining alternatives to those hierarchies, either within the university or without, is devalued for its apparent utopianism. Confusing cynical realism with materialism, the management sector of composition increasingly adapts curricula to market forces without paying those forces critical attention. Constructing students as mere buyers and potential beneficiaries, the intellectual bureaucrat endorses a university where ideas are not only secondary to money but devoted to it. More and more boldly, administrators construct themselves as servicing paying customers preparing for a life constrained by market logic. Within this context, helping marginalized communities gain access to education is rhetorically imaginable only in terms of reaching previously untapped markets, but there is little rationale for reaching those clients who cannot be made to pay.

Managers who proclaim the ubiquity of corporate hierarchy inadvertently give voice to deep-seated desires. Though they pretend to reluctantly accommodate the realities of corporatization, such realities may be precisely what they want and need to remain in position. The more naturally *present* corporate hierarchy seems, the less effort the managers have to expend to justify the outlandish inequalities pervading that reality. Ironically, when hiring super-exploited teachers to prepare students for business success, the managers position writing faculty as dupes and expendable automatons (in contrast to their own administrative canniness). In employing contingent workers to sell the promise of economic success to students, composition encourages its writing subjects to emulate the bosses of their teachers but not the teachers themselves.

As composition departments encourage students' immersion in capitalist practice, they more openly and egregiously practice capitalist exploitation themselves. This circumstance flows directly out of composition's identification with the values of the corporate university. Having redefined the university's mission in terms of an explicitly endorsed image of corporate excellence, university administrators promote curricula that train students to desire such excellence and to hone their own management skills. The most-excellent students are those who emerge from their coursework as the most-expensive commodities—potential managers. "The valued student," writes Stanley Aronowitz in *The Knowledge Factory: Dismantling the Corporate University and Creating True Higher Education,*

> is the one who earns good grades, which in many cases means only that she tests well and gets good job offers. The doctrine of excellence requires the student to perform according to rules over which she has no control and which proscribe thinking. (159)

For Bill Readings, this ultimately empty doctrine of excellence ruins the university while broadening its cultural allure *(The University in Ruins)*. Promising social ascendancy, yet delivering for only a select few, it exacerbates problems of socioeconomic inequality while claiming to remedy them. The students whom the university does not alienate or marginalize it commodifies. Corporate culture values the student-commodity not for *her/his* capacity to hinder the capitalist machine with critical thought but for *its* capacity to sustain the machine's flow. Skills such as institutional crisis management, money management, and incremental reform within the limits of the profit motive are precisely the skills needed to protect the system of corporate capitalism, and the university is increasingly glad to provide them. Under this system, academic bureaucracy protects academic capital. The dominant Panglossian paradigm, or the notion that the corporate university is at once the *best* and the *only* realizable university, blinds us to its constructedness. Instead of questioning conventional capitalist knowledge, we ourselves promote it.

The seemingly reasonable desire for efficiency accelerates the corporatization of composition and helps to secure teachers' and students' continued assent to the logic of capital. In *One-Dimensional Man: Studies in the Ideology of Advanced Industrial Society,* Herbert Marcuse describes how "pragmatic" capitalist logic is sustained by the seductive notion of progress: "The impact of progress turns Reason into submission to the facts of life, and to the dynamic capability of producing more and bigger facts of the same sort of life" (11). If we submit to the "fact" that university culture "is" business culture—even though that "fact" is constructed and protected by an over-class whose interests it serves—then assuming the role of the bureaucrat can be made to seem reasonable and progressive, insofar as incurring the favor of the university's over-class requires inhabiting its world on its terms. When composition managers submit to corporate facts of life, they are also submitting to the illusion that material progress presupposes corporate complicity. A view of reality that includes the historical struggle of labor unions and social movements—and not just the "facts" of capital accumulation—strongly suggests the opposite of the current pragmatist views. The effort required to construct a more-just workplace need not accord with the agenda of management. Radical change can and probably must be theorized and implemented by academic workers themselves: The full-time, contingent, and student laborers whose social and intellectual futures are interdependent. In my view, the dignity of composition work, and of academic culture more generally, depends on the collective organization and mutual support of labor, not management.

In "Faculty at the Crossroads," Thompson contends that part-timers and full-timers must articulate common desires in order to effectively contest their exploitation in the managed university:

> Once we talk to each other, we might discover that we have common concerns, such as pricing part-time faculty out of the market to save the profession and protecting the future of higher education. (192)

She cites the recent UPS teamsters strike as a telling example of how aggressive organization across lines of job status can enhance the material conditions of workers throughout an institution. United activism occurs when part-timers recognize the extent of their exploitation, and full-timers realize that such exploitation threatens the integrity and security of their own work. Unless workers organize an effort to price out contingent hiring, this hiring practice will continue to flourish as good bureaucratic strategy. Though the bureaucracy counts on job classification as a deterrent to unified resistance, part-time-labor exploitation affects all segments of the workforce. Regardless of their job classification, teachers who effectively advocate social justice and critical thinking will be those who do not ignore corrupt hiring practices on their own campuses. "We should not forget," writes Randy Martin, "that some of the lines between us are drawn in chalk. They have been, and they can be, creatively redrawn" (19). In redrawing those lines and in defending each other's material and intellectual interests as teacher-scholars, we can begin to compose a culture where learning really does matter.

Students who wish to combat their own dehumanization within the managed university might link their struggles to those of their professors. Because the casualization of their teachers' labor threatens to limit the interactivity and critical intensity of their education, students might protect that education by joining the struggle against the bureaucratic deployment of a flexible workforce. Though they serve both as *inputs* and *products* of the fabricated machine of commercial education, they also hold the power to jam its flow. In league with a critical professoriate, students need not settle for, indeed should not have to tolerate, the yoking of their energies to benevolent bureaucracy.

16

Composition and the Future of Contingency: Labor and Identity in Composition

Walter Jacobsohn

It's a directed process, not propaganda. All of this is to say that it is possible to have our educational cake and eat it too. It is possible to do our jobs as others define them: provide *haute couture,* "high literacy," skills, standardized-test-ready cultural literacy. And it is possible to do our jobs as we believe they ought to be done.

—Victor Villanueva Jr., *Bootstraps: From an American Academic of Color*

The university is not a corporate personnel training agency, a research subcontractor, a business, a state agency, a graft machine, or an instrument for oppressing unwelcome facts and opinions. As Jacques Barzun said, "The university is a city, or a city within a city." If our universities fail, our society probably will, too. We want not a University of Utopia, but a university worthier of our lives; not a cocoon of privilege, but a realization of the right relation between democracy and knowledge; not a survival of the master-slave relationship, but the university as the self-governing city, deriving its powers from the consent of the governed.

—Ronnie Dugger, introduction, *Campus, Inc.: Corporate Power in the Ivory Tower*

A relatively new and vital discipline, composition reflects both the structural imperatives of the corporate system and the traditional university hierarchy. This system with its "feudal antecedents," as James Sledd has termed them, is organized in a clear hierarchy: a few theorists isolated on top; on the next tier, a small number of overworked administrators, often untenured; and, finally, a horde of disempowered practitioners.

This labor structure engenders a lack of respect for writing pedagogy and its practitioners from within and without the discipline: Theorists and writing program administrators (WPAs) lack respect for their part-time workers, the workers feel similarly about their masters, and the "hallowed" disciplines refuse to take seriously a discipline with a structure of managed paraprofessionals that very few really understand, partly perhaps because it forecasts the future structure of their own discipline.

It should be no surprise that faced with this insidious hierarchy, the socially progressive intentions of composition theorists often get turned on their heads and become instruments of control over those actually teaching. One brief example is the laudable desire to provide equal opportunity and consistent content to all entering students. In practice, this goal all too frequently becomes the installation of a bureaucratic structure that assigns the same "progressive" multicultural texts across the board for all instructors or imposes the same exit exams for all students. Not only does such an imposed fairness fail but it disempowers both instructors and students: Instructors become low-level wage workers, and students become gulled customers.

All this of course mirrors higher education's seemingly inevitable progress toward an increasingly managed and vulnerable conglomeration of fragmented specializations.

Whose Liberation?

The status and positions of disciplinary insiders and outsiders raise distinct and important questions both about pedagogy and the future of the discipline in its institutional context. To accomplish meaningful change in the quality of higher education and confront the erosion of faculty and student governance, these different voices and experiences must be listened to carefully. No one group owns nor should own the future of higher education.

Whether or not liberatory pedagogy is only for students or for instructors as well—a question fundamental for any disempowered teachers whose only productive pleasure may very well reside in their identification with their students— is more than an academic question. To what degree are instructors and students independent of the system of aspirations and control within which they function? Given their marginalized role in the academy, for contingent instructors to imagine themselves as part of an enlightened academic community is delusional at best. Does this mean that politics now belong in their classrooms in a very different way than for tenured professors? The problem here is not only that they may find it far safer to identify with those who hold power but that even if they do adopt an independent and critical stance, they do not always have the larger experience enjoyed by tenure-stream faculty of the intricacies and interrelatedness of the university's various functions that would make their positions more effective and applicable both for their students and themselves. This lack of power is not only debilitating on a personal and professional level—it also helps to prevent the university from heeding some of the most important voices it needs to confront the future.

The corollary question is whether tenured faculty can identify in good faith with liberatory pedagogy. As members of an institutional bureaucracy, they often fulfill the aims of the university institution and the state as gatekeepers rather than being able to achieve the implicit aims of the theory they espouse. Is it possible for them to have their cake and eat it, too? To what degree does the management-level composition teacher's institutional authority and prestige necessitate a different form of enlightenment? How much genuine choice do we have in our intellectual and pedagogical self-construction?

The discussion of this last question is already well represented by tenured faculty such as Richard E. Miller, who oversees large numbers of contingent faculty at Rutgers University, and his call for the acceptance of the bureaucratic status of higher education faculty so as to better accomplish much needed bureaucratic reform *(As If Learning Mattered)*. Less well-circulated are the positions of adjunct faculty such as Helen O'Grady who is not a member of an enlightened bureaucracy and thus imagines for herself and her peers a very different and more radical program for change.

The starkest differences between them has to do with their very different sense of the real world and their position in it. Miller's "realistic" response to one particular teacher's experience of contingency could well be construed as his response to contingent faculty as a whole:

> Pointing out the manifest injustices of this situation may be personally cathartic; it does not, however, alter the fact that the most pressing problem this teacher confronts is how to construct an inhabitable and hospitable life within these constraining conditions. There are those who would use this situation to raise once more the call to overthrow the system; others would say that the teacher has no choice but to roll over and take it. I would suggest, however, that none of us knows for certain what lies ahead for this teacher, her institution, or the state she works in. We don't know what will happen. All we know for sure is that the future will be like the past in that it will ceaselessly demand of us all that we improvise solutions to problems we never imagined before. ("Arts of Complicity" 27)

Miller goes on to argue that we seriously mistake the sources and breadth of our power. Rather than find agency in a collective movement to change the status of teachers, Miller urges collective identity with the bureaucracy, an answer effectively applicable to only a small and dwindling number of academics. It seems to have escaped him that pointing out injustices could lead to more than just personal catharsis, nor does he interrogate how his position and institutional identity have colored his insights.

O'Grady, on the other hand, though she is constantly improvising to make her own conditions more hospitable, has no sense of her own life, teaching, and intellectual efforts as part of an otherwise enlightened intellectual bureaucracy. She is an outsider who identifies with her students, and this gives her a different kind of insight. She is very aware of how her position informs her insights:

> Critical literacy practices demystify the ideal image of teacherly employment constructed in institutional and radical discourses and serve as a basis for reconfiguring the part-time problem. As we continue to reflect critically on this problem, I hope we can go beyond mere consciousness-raising to dialogue and action. (149–50)

O'Grady is aware that we need to stop thinking that part-time exploitation is either economically necessary or inevitable. She reaffirms her commitment to teaching and improvising a future for herself and her students using Paulo Freire as an inspiration, arguing forcefully that if we fail to "take steps to address the growing use of part-time faculty, we become complicit in failing to deliver educational quality" and furthermore become complicit in "perpetuating an underclass" of contingent teachers (152). O'Grady's marginalization makes Miller's position an attack on the energies she needs to maintain her own resolve. However, the real differences here are structural rather than intellectual, differences in subject positions more than opinions. Miller shows us what it looks like from the inside, O'Grady from the outside. Both these positions are the culmination of the drastically limited subject positions of identity politics that involve identifying with simplistic binary positions: powerful and powerless, victim and victimizer, winners and losers. It would be easy to call O'Grady's position labor and Miller's position management, but this would only emphasize our students' positions as customers, a position debilitating to both them and us. We cannot afford to only identify with the students or the institution. We need O'Grady's critical literacy practices to demystify our practices; we need to be many things, but we always need to be independent critical thinkers. The situation of academia is far too complex for either/or divisions and distinctions (needing at the very least a redefining of what we mean by labor in a postindustrial economy such that among other things, the managers are able to realize that they, too, are labor). For change to occur, we will have to proceed collectively with those who seem to oppose the collective endeavor, the slow change espoused by the relatively comfortable must be married to the fast radical change needed by the most disenfranchised.

Proceeding Collectively—Collaboration?

While the debate over the ownership of liberatory pedagogy helps us to realize some of the divides imposed on our labor and identity, the emerging discourse surrounding new information technology and distance education helps us to see how even the best collective and democratic intentions can end up reproducing exploitative hierarchies and disciplinary power structures. An important consideration to bear in mind with the birth of this new industry is that distance education is especially difficult to control from a labor standpoint because it isolates and alienates its practitioners from each other. Its particular form of transparency, the fact that anybody can review the teachers performance without their knowledge, makes the possibilities of control by outside forces particularly ominous, all the more so when those being evaluated have no real power to begin with. To add to this element of control is the entrepreneurial encouragement inherent to new technology. Anybody with the appropriate technological know-how can set up a distance-education center—it doesn't need a particular space or community that might provide labor and quality standards. This makes for both too much control and not enough. All these factors help to construct knowledge and power as a part of a rigid hierarchy centered elsewhere that creates a chasm between students and instructors that can only be bridged, at the very least, by an enormous amount of work. That the work and the results can be very rewarding has been repeated often—what should not be forgotten is the time and labor involved and who owns that labor. Though technology is expensive now and requires a good deal of expertise that is changing rapidly, and, from a labor standpoint, distance education that is not actually controlled by labor mean that our prospects are further diminished as educators both in terms of our conditions of employment and the kind of space we are able to provide for our students.

The following are questions that concern me as an enthusiastic proponent of the opportunities that technology offers us—they need to concern all of us. Are we going to see distance-education centers sprouting up like mushrooms in virtual space whose only mission is what will sell? Will we merely provide more choice to students at the expense of quality? Because labor does not control disciplines, departments, or universities, what makes us think that we can do better with newer forms of knowledge transmission? As John Dewey bluntly states, "Men hoist the banner of the ideal, and then march in the direction that concrete conditions suggest and reward" (281).

An example of this problem is in the essay, "Distance Education: Political and Professional Agency for Adjunct and Part-Time Faculty and GTAs," a collaboration among graduate students Danielle DeVoss and Dawn Hayden, full professor Cynthia L. Selfe, and full-time non-tenure-track instructor Richard Selfe. The piece challenges traditional claims regarding the liberatory and enlightening role of academics. By trying to reconcile a variety of complex positions, it both purposely and unwittingly demonstrates that the questions raised by distance education make the role, identity, and labor conditions of academics an essential part of any efforts to adapt to the future or reform higher education. By the end of this essay, one realizes how much at cross purposes were the collaborators and how much their different institutional standpoints are reflected in their conflict.

The essay begins with an ambitious collaborative purpose regarding the "institutionalizing" of distance education curricula. Believing that "English studies professionals are in a particularly powerful position" to affect the way distance education is implemented, the authors emphasize the need to "act in concert and with keen attention to the power relations among all stakeholders in these endeavors" (264). The essay also states that distance education serves "as one important site" in which contingent workers take more control "of the decision making and policy making that shapes their professional lives" (263).

With all that is admirable here, the seeds of a dilemma also begin to emerge in the tension we see between teacher anecdotes and the managerial commentary on them. Hayden describes her experiences teaching a distance-education class. Most of the five pages demonstrate how enormously difficult and unsatisfying these experience were. The essay then comments that the anecdote "helps illustrate how problematic and exhilarating these choices can be," even though Hayden has not shown exhilaration except in one comment: "I experienced a range of emotions while teaching that class—usually frustration, but occasionally exhilaration" (263). Although this anecdote allows Hayden to speak in her own voice and so enriches the dialectical opportunities of this essay, one must note that by encapsulating the commentary and then sidestepping the primary content of her narrative, the commentary serves to reaffirm Hayden's subaltern status and to reveal that this essay is not primarily focused on adjunct and graduate student concerns.

The focus of this essay is not the improvement of working conditions for part-timers in technology-rich environments but the need for "English studies professionals" to get involved in technology and distance learning so that they can better control the process and stay in line with the demands of the future from the perspective of fully vested and at least semi-independent "professionals." A good deal is said about how involving adjuncts would make the distance-education experience richer and of better quality, but the details of how it might improve the quality of life or pay of adjuncts are left vague at best. Going through this essay and creatively removing all references to adjuncts and their working conditions leave the argument completely coherent. The reverse is not possible and points to a very different conclusion than the one offered: Namely, that given the actual labor situation and the lack of power of those who are primarily involved in teaching composition, saying yes to technology is more problematic than saying no if the fundamental labor structure is not addressed first. Ultimately, we need to consider the conflicting interests among the stakeholders. All of the authors seem to accept the existing hierarchy and its priorities when they assume that contingent faculty will "learn skills" teaching distance-education classes that will make them more "marketable." From this standpoint, teaching these classes is no longer an aspect of the profession but professional training for a future career. The teaching-with-technology experience becomes the equivalent of being a raw recruit in boot camp with the undergraduate students as objects on the obstacle course. This in effect is no different than treating adjuncts and graduate students as low-level wage workers and students as customers.

What is symptomatic in this essay and many others by management-level compositionists is that the process of changing conditions is intrinsically identified with the administrative bureaucracy of the university. Relatively short shrift is given to the necessity of oppositional structures, unions, and other institutional collectivities, playing a vital role in any enduring solutions. The claim in "Distance Education" is that these problems can be solved internally and collegially, by dialogues among the stakeholders, English studies in particular, by listening to everyone, hearing and questioning; however, relative power within the institution changes all that. A dean may very well believe that by meeting and discussing changes in curriculum with full-time faculty and sending a mailing of these results to hundreds of contingent faculty he has included all the stakeholders. Would a contingent faculty on the end of the mailing list feel the same?

I believe that the kinds of initiatives discussed in "Distance Education" will help produce a genuine commitment to fairness, quality, and responsibility. I also believe that this essay reaffirms how enormously complicated it is to make any changes in the academy, where the need for change becomes an area of further study that pays homage to ideal and unobtainable structures rather than a site for activism and fundamental change. It is not by chance that the term *collegial* has become synonymous not with shared decision making but rather the rubber-stamping of the policies of the real decision makers among the administration and trustees, a fairly typical corporate decision-making structure.

As Sledd has cogently put it in his essay on the Wyoming resolution, "there can be no revolution in the *teaching* of writing until the exploitation of teachers is ended" ("Why" 173). To compromise here is inevitably self-defeating for all academics because the situation of composition faculty is significant for every part of the university. Academics need to think differently about the bonds they have with other teachers and intellectuals regardless of interest, function, status, or institution. The only way to continue to make composition and higher education a vital city with the ideals of inclusiveness, openness to ideas of all kinds, and access to a richer life for our students is to have academics fully realize the need to act collectively, sometimes collegially but above all oppositionally, to change the material conditions of all teachers. Whether we reach out to the wider world or speak only within the institution, we must always bear in mind that we cannot enact this process alone. The exploitation of contingent labor is the most important and far-reaching issue that the university must face. We need to change our practices if we wish to maintain the full involvement of faculty and students in the future of higher education. For this purpose we must make accessible a far broader body of information about the practices of universities and the purpose of higher education than ever before. We have the means.

However, this organized collectivity is not the only place where I would like to begin. Jamaica Kincaid was once asked in an interview how she, as part of an oppressed minority, found a way of navigating the oppressive system. Her response was, "What system?" I want to start here, to nudge these words out of their context, because at that time this question and response seemed both the stupidest and most intelligent thing possible. What was stupid and what was intelligent—which question? How could Kincaid deny that there was an oppressive system, and conversely (of course!), how could her interviewer assume that the system he experienced was the same one for Kincaid? Yet, if we want to be and act freely, we have to make that leap, also suggested by Kincaid's response, that no system is inevitable. To effectively understand and act we must constantly have those questions before us in constant dynamic interplay: System? Whose system? Which system? No system? Their system? My system? Our system? It is in these constant oppositions and challenges to our own positions that we may find the means and courage to act freely and confront both the materiality and repercussions of our own positions.

17
The Lure of "Easy" Psychic Income

Katherine V. Wills

R ecent investigations document composition's reliance on contingent academic labor and the inequalities inherent to that reliance (Schell; Horner;
Crowley). Some compositionists would like to ameliorate labor inequalities by
reducing the high numbers of contingent teachers in the field of composition.
Michael Murphy endorses the addition of non-tenure-track, two-tier lectureships
as a way to stabilize the vagaries of departmental hiring practices ("New Faculty"
35). Although arguments like these have focused on the segment of composition workers who work in composition for the survival income and are not economically solvent, little attention has been paid to the needs and roles of contingent workers who work without economic motivation, instead seeking what
Eileen E. Schell and others have termed *psychic income* (*Gypsy Academics* 16).

According to Schell, *psychic income* entered the nomenclature of composition
when Alice Gillam recounted a story of an adjunct who complained of low pay
and was told by an administrator that she was working for the psychic income
of teaching at a university, not because of pressing financial needs (40). Schell
defines psychic income as the perceived personal, social, and cultural compensation that a job brings to an individual above and beyond wages. Some adjunct
teachers prefer to work for the perceived benefits and status of an academic position, not just for the (pin) money. The notion of psychic income can be a useful
analytical tool in understanding the historical stubbornness of labor problems in
the teaching of writing: why many adjuncts sign on to teach part-time; why most
adjuncts eventually abandon their part-time careers within a few years; and why
many adjuncts eagerly repeat their service year after year despite inequalities deemed
insufferable by other, equally experienced instructors. Psychic income is a powerful lure for workers seeking validation of their intellectual or service contributions. For adjuncts driven by the need of psychic income, fair compensation can
take second place to self-perceptions of an altruistic ethos. Women, especially,
seem to be willing to work to satisfy abstract concepts of duty or service because

part-time teaching falls within a discourse of philanthropy and the respectable, nurturing mother-teacher. The irony is that contingent laborers who set out to work for psychic income often do not receive the compensation they expect.

In order to suggest effective solutions, such as coalition building or unionization, to counter labor inequalities in composition instruction, we must understand why many part-timers continue to teach for substandard wages, under poor working conditions, at the expense of their colleagues' solvency, and perhaps even to the detriment of the teaching of writing. There will be those who take full-time, multi-tier positions or who will acquire advanced degrees in order to become full-time teachers. However, these teachers will not fully overlap with the constituency that takes part-time teaching because they just like to teach. As Sharon Crowley discovered at Wyoming when she suggested that the field would benefit with the elimination of the requirement for first-year composition, contingent labor is not a monolithic group. Steven Biko argues that the oppressor's most powerful weapon is the mind of the oppressed. Adjuncts often internalize their own oppression while working for psychic income literally at the expense of coworkers. Understanding the motivations of everyone who works in the academy can help to ensure sustainable structural and institutional change.

Labor organizers benefit in at least three practical ways by understanding of how psychic income sustains many contingent workers. First, grassroots campus and labor organizers can motivate many contingent workers who have resisted unionization in other localities across the nation. Although it is reassuring to look to the models of Coalition of Contingent Academic Labor and of Rutgers University, many other campuses and their representative contingent workers are not so easily collectivized. Understanding the diverse constituencies of contingent labor helps unionization on a national basis. Second, when organizers understand the cachet of psychic income as a discursive tool among contingent workers, organizers can more effectively connect with a hitherto resistant segment of contingent labor. Resistant workers enter into a dialogue with organizers about the value of mental labor. Third, once organizers have entered into a dialogue with those motivated by psychic income, they can offer alternative historical perspectives to the service-oriented administrative rhetoric.

Coalition builders have ignored workers driven by the ethos of institutional service and mental labor, not subsistence income, focusing instead on the colorful victim stories of the most abjectly affected workers. Collectivization and coalition building require buy-in from as many workers as possible, even when those workers seem, initially, antithetical to the academic labor inequality. In a similar vein, when the Vietnamese of the 1960s sought to collectivize peasant labor, the value of middle-class people's support was initially ignored. In *Fire in the Lake: The Vietnamese and Americans in Vietnam,* Frances Fitzgerald posits that success in creating a broad-based peoples' movement did not occur until organizers educated the better-off middle-class Vietnamese along with the peasants. American campus organizers have relied on transient graduate students and local workers to garner support for collectivization. Little in the literature shows an attempt to see, approach, and re-educate psychic-income workers. It is unclear to what degree this denial is due to resistance of organizers to work with pro-institutional part-timers or just because these part-timers are truly invisible to organizers. Schell notes in *Workplace: A Journal for Academic Labor* that despite efforts to acknowledge and curtail contingent labor, "the part-time and non-tenure-track situation has worsened" ("Toward a New Labor Movement" 7). It is evident that even with activist student support, local worker support, and partial contingent-worker support, the contingent labor movement will need to be bolstered by the commitment of those motivated by psychic income.

My personal experience in part-time teaching has helped me to see the roles part-timers play in perpetuating the problems of contingent labor. This analysis is not meant to blame the victim. Like Schell, I resist the "oft-used tropes of marginalization and victimization" (*Gypsy Academics* 16). Rather, I examine the agency of part-time and non-tenure-track workers and their diverse motives for preferring to teach part-time in the academy. I taught for eight years precisely for a psychic wage, teaching one class per semester in composition because I enjoyed teaching and learning. Most of the part-time coworkers at my campus taught for similar reasons and under similar conditions. I was part of the subset of contingent workers who supported managerial and institutional reliance upon and control over other workers who were economically dependent on their wages. When I began to see that my position as a part-time teacher was detrimental to the earning power of my colleagues, I began to change my perceptions of the value of part-time teaching. I recognized my culpability in sustaining the hollow, if powerful, ethos of the altruistic female teacher in the service of education.

Like many of my fellow contingent workers, I held two common beliefs about working as a part-timer: Part-time teaching at the university is professional, and contingent teaching provides "flexibility" as a benefit. Phillip J. Silvers surveyed fifteen hundred associate faculty at Pima Community College, in Tucson, Arizona, about their reasons for teaching, and he found that many adjuncts believe this as well. When respondents were asked what their primary motivations for teaching at PCC were, they mentioned the following:

- just love to teach—28 percent
- seek flexibility of work—24 percent
- use their expertise—20 percent
- financial—19 percent
- diversion—13 percent (7)

Many respondents initially worked for psychic income in the form of "loving to teach" and sharing their "expertise." However, the turnover in part-timers, especially in composition, requires that we see another dimension. Contingent faculty soon discover that writing instruction in the university is marginalized, and the aura of professional work diminishes. Many more pragmatically discover that writing instruction in the university often is not as flexible for them as it is for administration, as classes are dropped or filled at the last minute for just-in-time staffing. Some find it increasingly difficult to structure even one class around a full-time work schedule or family life. These are a few of the "destructive myths" about contingent labor.

Schell summarizes seven "destructive myths" about adjuncts and why they teach (*Gypsy Academics* 40). I would like to look more closely at three of these items.

1. Contingent instructors are moonlighters who teach for the love of the subject.

The studies of Silvers and others show that many adjuncts do, at least initially, teach for needs other than purely monetary ones. This belief is destructive to the degree that it obfuscates the labor of the workers who work for the money. However, to try to deny that contingent instructors also moonlight for the psychosocial benefits obscures the motivations of workers who work for benefits other than money.

2. Contingent labor is scab labor that threatens policy-making processes.

Scabs are those working in place of striking or locked-out workers. This is not the case with adjunct labor. Yet, teachers who are unreflectively supportive of the policies of the managed university actually do threaten the negotiating power of those who seek better working conditions and fair pay. Pro-institutional adjuncts in the managed university threaten processes that could lead to changes in favor of labor. Using the language of industrial labor, such as *scab,* would more clearly situate the discussion as a *labor* issue.

3. Female adjuncts are depicted as working for pin money and psychic income.

Is it a destructive myth that a segment of contingent female workers work for psychic income? Is it also destructive to ignore the social and economic realities that all contingent workers do not have similar motivations for working? Denying these differences in motivation might actually hinder progress for fair academic employment.

The structures of academic capitalism (Slaughter and Leslie) are driven in part by contingent-laborers' needs for psychic income and encourage what Tiziana Terranova sees as a movement towards the undercompensated labor that is structural to late-capitalist cultural economy (53). Underwaged labor, service work, and adjunct teaching are often driven by an altruistic ethos to serve institutions, especially educational institutions.

In the Silvers survey, 69 percent of the contingent workers were not even aware of the faculty orientation available to "prepare them to teach." Of those who did attend the orientation, 70 percent rated it "acceptable" to "poor." Over 31 percent of the contingent labor force had worked at PCC for less than two years. Of those that taught, almost two-thirds (65 percent) taught only one class per academic year. Over half of the contingent respondents (53 percent) had other full-time jobs. These workers and their conditions, for the most part, do not encourage the disciplinary commitment needed to learn about composition in a critical manner and to teach it effectively. Their conditions are likely to negatively influence student education. When teachers are expendable, students learn that their relations to teachers are not to be valued; we encourage the cynicism of the student eager to get through the hoops of academia and into the "real" world.

I contacted Karen Thompson to better understand the question of psychic income from her perspective as a labor activist. She found the notion of psychic income to be problematic in that it was often used as an excuse by administrators for worker exploitation. For Thompson, the goal of organizing has been "to identify the issues that concern employees, clarify those that have been confused, and get the employees to act in their own interests" (Thompson, Personal interview, 24 Sept. 2002). Thompson shared two anecdotes of part-time lectures. In the first anecdote, a part-time lecturer–full-time lawyer teaches for the psychic perks; he donates his salary back to the university. He did find it discomforting, however, that after many years of lecturing, he never received a pay increase. Though his reason for teaching was for psychic perks, he recognizes the importance of fair treatment. The second anecdote describes what Thompson calls "passing" as a psychic perk. These teachers who like to "pass" as "real" professors and avoid being outed slow down the organizing process. Clearly, contingent workers have multiple and diverse concerns. As organizers enter more discussions with teachers who teach for psychic rewards, more of these teachers may begin to reevaluate their role in labor inequalities. In turn, more psychic workers may join the ranks of labor, not management.

Contingent laborers often set out to work for the perceived professionalism afforded by a part-time teaching position, despite the prevalence of narratives about comp droids, freeway flyers, and gypsy academics, none of which project a professional image. Marjorie Roemer, Lucille M. Schultz, and Russel K. Durst note that

> composition can never have the academic prestige accorded literary studies if it is most identified in people's minds with a course compromised by the staffing patterns that support it, and by the general attitudes on college campuses (or in schools as a whole) that what is elementary is inferior, less challenging, and less worthy of respect. (389)

Mary Pollington compares the material working conditions of part-time English teachers at Brigham Young University and Utah Valley Community College. At both schools, contingent laborers and graduate students taught most classes. Pollington provided the usual list of conditions that affect quality of teaching at both schools: undercompensation, lack of resources, low status, no health insurance, no job security, no guarantee of classes, and no workspace or space for meeting with students. It takes most new instructors only a short while to realize that these are not the conditions of professionals. Stephen J. Leone in another CCCC presentation notes that while high school teachers can be required to take inservice workshops to update their professional knowledge, part-time college instructors receive little or poor training. Leone concludes that many technical teaching problems "have only been compounded by the lack of adequate training we provide our instructors, most of whom are adjuncts," further undermining the myth of professionalism (9). A Southern Association of Colleges and Schools mandated report recognizes that adjunct faculty are not on campus enough to use resources: "It is increasingly difficult and expensive for the University to support the learning resources needs of adjunct faculty who reside away from convenient access to campus-based facilities" (MacFarland 13). Professionalism is increasingly a threadbare mental construct for those toiling in the cellar of the university.

A significant percentage of contingent teachers admit to working for the pleasures of psychic income. As the lure and illusion of psychic income pale for many of these workers, they give up their part-time positions, thereby making space for new and eager contingent workers and graduate students to fill their place, a cohort as-yet unenlightened about the true prospects of their psychic wage. The high rate of turnover among adjuncts encourages undeveloped pedagogy as a consequence of untheorized and unreflective visions of writing practice. Until the public and personal perceptions of part-time teaching in the academic workplace are revised in the light of the false promises of flexible professionalism, labor inequalities will continue to replicate themselves with each generation of academic workers. The consciousness of the workers and the public must both be reshaped. Those in composition and rhetoric who wish to address labor inequalities can do so by approaching those part-time workers who seem the most psychically entrenched in the tenuous reward system of mental labor. Many workers remain willing to discount their mental labor to the extent that they perceive psychic benefits: One task of the organizer will be to diminish the psychic value of mental labor to contingent faculty.

PART FOUR

PEDAGOGY AND POSSIBILITY

18

"Write-to-Earn": College Writing and Management Discourse

Leo Parascondola

> The teacher of English should be equally quick to detect faults and to
> recognize merits of every description . . . The best talent in each school
> . . . cannot be better employed than in teaching the use of the great
> instrument of communication between man and man, between books
> and men, the possession without which learning is mere pedantry, and
> thought an aimless amusement.
>
> —Adams Sherman Hill, "An Answer to
> the Cry for More English" (1879)

This essay attempts an overview of some of the ways in which historically significant management discourses symbiotically intersect with U.S. college
writing instruction, with special attention to the marriage of "write-to-learn"
rhetorics with "write-to-earn" management discourses within higher education.
I associate write-to-learn rhetorics with the more broadly conceived liberal project
of promoting social progress through education: learning at the college level—
through writing. What I call write-to-earn language generally accomplishes utilitarian and instrumentalist views of learning and education, views concurrent with
notions of writing as a neutral medium or technology whose purpose is the transmission of information (Hill's "great instrument of communication"). Not surprisingly, this view of writing as primarily a conduit for facts, and not for the
discovery of knowledge, suited the emerging needs of the corporate economy
under construction in the late-nineteenth century. As many historians of the
university (and of composition) have shown, the corporate need for reliable professional and managerial classes developed simultaneously with the invention of
a modern research university. I will examine these twin developments and show
their relation to composition. I will conclude by examining some consequences
of more-recent practices in the teaching of college writing, practices reflective of

more recent anxieties about the propriety of writing across the curriculum (WAC) and writing-intensive pedagogy.

The prolonged association between education and commercial utility is a matter of wide-ranging historical debate, reflected, for example, in the differences between Francis Bacon and John Henry Cardinal Newman over the concept of utility itself. Spanning a gap of some 250 years, the differences between these philosophers over the nature of higher education offer some useful and revealing insights. Newman's cloistered vision of a liberal university of ideas offers an alternative to Bacon's utilitarian condemnation of "a kind of adoration of the mind . . . by means whereof men have withdrawn themselves too much from the contemplation of nature, and the observations of experience, and have tumbled up and down in their own reason and conceits" (qtd. in Kerr, *Uses* 2).[1] More than two centuries later, Newman responded by suggesting, "Knowledge is capable of being its own end. Such is the constitution of the human mind, that any kind of knowledge, if it really be such, is its own reward" (qtd. in Kerr, *Uses* 2). A contemporary philosopher of education, Clark Kerr, former president and chancellor of the University of California, has published widely in favor of the utilitarian view of education as, if not the best possible option, the dominant historical option. In *Troubled Times for American Higher Education: The 1990s and Beyond* (1994), Kerr emphasizes this point of view:

> The main purposes of higher education have varied greatly from time to time and place to place around the world. Sometimes they have been service to the church, or to the ancient professions, or to an ideology, or to an aristocratic and/ or affluent class, or to the efficiency and power of the nation-state. In modern times . . . the main purpose has come to be: to serve the economy. (51)

As Kerr goes on to point out, serving the economy primarily means providing corporations with a flow of trained workers. For Kerr, these Baconian realities are not only long-historical, remaining true throughout the industrial and technological era, they are practically ahistorical—seemingly essential characteristic of the university in all times and places. That is, the relation of higher education to labor markets is now, *and has always been,* the definitive service of universities and colleges to society:

> Service to the labor market has been from the start an important part of higher education in most of the world and has continued to be so at nearly all times and in nearly all places. . . . There is no Golden Age of pure scholarship alone, and there never was one. (55–56)

The Baconian position seems particularly strong at the present time, when forces from within the business world, public officials, and many others—including students and parents—call for the diversion of university funds into the creation of new scientific and technological knowledge (readily transplanted to business applications promising high profitability). They are, nonetheless, confronted by the humanists espousing a Newtonian liberal vision, often taking the form of nostalgia for nonexistent good old days when intellectual inquiry in U.S. universities was unrestricted by the yoke of utility and promised (if it never quite delivered) a capacious vision of the common good. The humanists want to preserve (or create) a university of ideas that is labor intensive and carries a high overhead.

Within rhetoric and composition, WAC, and writing in the disciplines (WID), the relatively liberal and Newtonian rubric *write-to-learn* has been used both to capture the correlation of the writing process to other cognitive processes and to describe student need. Student need here is usually defined as the strong need of students to display their potential as learners, creators of new knowledge, and chroniclers of their own narratives under hospitable circumstances, suggesting that learning and writing are coterminous and mutually supportive activities. By contrast, what I am calling write-to-earn reflects a different, more Baconian, historical interpretation of those same processes and needs, perhaps more attuned to instrumentalist definitions of writing consistent with the history of U.S. higher education and the burgeoning of professional, technical, managerial, and clerical workers required by the new industrial economy in the late-nineteenth century.

This utilitarian vision of education and writing instruction emphasizes a product-oriented pedagogy sometimes called *general writing-skills instruction* (GWSI), the dominant mode of writing instruction in U.S. universities and colleges since roughly 1875. The most salient tenets of GWSI include teaching the four rhetorical modes (exposition, description, narration, and argument) and an idealized single format (the five-paragraph theme). Within this context, the main purpose of generating writing skill was deemed to be the transmission of information, not the creation or discovery of knowledge (Petraglia). Robert J. Connors has defined this emergent rhetoric as comprising chiefly those types of writing thought to be essential to an enormous and rapidly consolidating national economy: laboratory reports and scientific treatises; assessments of industrial products and processes; reviews and assessments of capital investment; budget reviews; reports to directors and shareholders; a variety of cost efficiency assessments ranging from Taylorite time–labor studies to transportation expenses; business letters; advertising, and more. The list could continue, but I wish to emphasize the wide spectrum of agreement on this point: An impressive array of scholars, from radical anticapitalists such as Scott Nearing, Upton Sinclair, Joel Spring, and Clyde Barrow to procapitalist liberal scholars and public figures such as Clark Kerr and John Kenneth Galbraith, and including conservative historians such as Abraham Flexner, Frederic Rudolph, and Lawrence Veysey, have argued that all concerned assigned the highest national priority to refashioning the U.S. university to make it more responsive to the needs of capital at least in connection with this urgent need to facilitate the transmission of information. This list only skims the surface of scholarship on the subject, but with some variation, its members present a similar scenario for U.S. higher education: The alliance between the university and the corporation was born in the final quarter of the nineteenth century, consolidated by the end of World War I, and renegotiated in the twenty years following World War II, a period that saw the birth of Kerr's "multiversity," a complex edifice reflecting a web of public and private financing, seamlessly uniting scholarship and teaching to the national economy (Kerr, *Uses* 5).

This write-to-earn instrumentalism has never been only the province of students from subordinated classes: It has always been a mainstay of elite instruction as well. For example, Donald Stewart charges Harvard's composition program with:

> (1) reducing writing instruction to a concern for superficial mechanical cor-
> rectness, (2) greatly increasing an unproductive and debilitating fixation on
> grammar instruction, (3) dissociating student writing . . . from any meaningful
> social context, and (4) contributing significantly to the division between com-
> position and literature people in English departments, a division which saw
> writing instruction increasingly become the responsibility of intellectually
> inferior members of English department staffs. (455)

Interestingly, these charges are complicated by John C. Brereton's evaluation that in the period 1880–1910, "The Harvard program marks the only time a major university made such a total commitment to student writing" (11). The creation of the first-year composition course at Harvard after 1874 paradoxically marked the beginning of the end of an era of unprecedented attention to and cultivation of student writing at that university. What had been in the years prior to 1874 a systematic mix of oral and written composition throughout all four years of college in which students did not learn to write in a single course but got instruction at all stages of their academic careers, had by 1900 been reduced to the required first-year course. In *The Origins of Composition Studies in the American College, 1875–1925*, his comprehensive examination of primary documents from that period, Brereton writes of this period before 1900, "For thirty years, the United States' oldest and most prestigious college devoted the majority of its English teaching resources to composition from the first year to senior level. . . . There has never been anything like it" (11).

In *Writing in the Academic Disciplines, 1870–1990*, David Russell traces this reversal, in part, to the effort to remake American higher education along the lines of the German research university with its emphasis on electives and specialization among an elite core of students who were expected to arrive at their institutions with writing skills already polished at the secondary level. Furthermore, Russell's account of the consolidation of writing instruction within newly founded English departments suggests a connection among four concurrent developments in the history of U.S. higher education: the creation of the discipline of English as the study of literature and its criticism; the simultaneous relegation of rhetoric to secondary status; the formation of Connors's instrumentalist "composition-rhetoric"; and the requirement for a transparent notion of writing in service to an expanding industrial economy. Russell traces the trajectory of the new course:

Writing instruction was denied disciplinary status, compartmentalized in English departments, where it competed with the new professional discipline of literary study. In time, freshman English became ubiquitous, nearly always the only institutionwide requirement for writing instruction (or writing) in higher education. And with systematic writing instruction thus marginalized, there arose an implicit assumption that general-composition courses should teach students from any background to write correct and coherent expository prose for any purpose in any social or disciplinary context—and that a student's failure to do so was evidence for more elementary training or *remediation,* as it came to be called. (7–8)

Russell sees common ground among these phenomena in what he describes as "the naïve view of language as transparent recorder of thought or physical reality that grew up with the scientific method in the eighteenth and nineteenth centuries" (10).

This predilection for the German model, many have argued, was typical of educators such as Charles W. Eliot, president of Harvard from 1869–1909, who believed that the nation needed to train a new class of intellectual workers to run a rapidly expanding industrial economy. Russell indicates intellectual and material connections between changes in the status and institutional location of writing instruction and changes in the nature and function of the university (perhaps, echoing Kerr's model of a more contemporary multiversity in service to the economy):

The modern university's compartmentalized, additive organization of knowledge was made possible—or at least made more efficient—by the transparency of rhetoric and the marginalization of writing instruction. The lack of student writing freed the faculty from much paper grading and interaction with students, leaving them more time to pursue those two new ideals which redefined the university in the late nineteenth century: discipline-specific research and utilitarian service. (24)

If *science* and *utilitarian service* were watchwords for an expanding class of professionals and managers, then composition—and its new rhetoric—at Harvard was its beacon.

In *Universities and the Capitalist State: Corporate Liberalism and the Reconstruction of American Higher Education, 1894–1928,* Clyde Barrow provides evidence about the relationship between the rapid growth and consolidation of the U.S. economy in the late-nineteenth century and the educational needs of the emerging professional classes. He demonstrates how these interests were duplicated inside the emerging corporate university through, among other things, the mutual reinforcement of interlocking seats on boards of directors. Examining data from the late-nineteenth and early-twentieth centuries, he argues that "empirical patterns of multiple position-holding among bankers, lawyers, railroad men, engineers, and other heavy industrialists justifies their classification as a single interest group to be designated as corporate finance capital" (40). With class interests such as these dominating the boards of trustees of virtually every major university and college, there was little chance—or opportunity—for contrary interests and voices to be heard. If heard, they were, more often than not, ignored.

As the twentieth century progressed, Barrow claims a "strong empirical presumption" that "governing boards at major private universities came firmly under the direction of corporate officials attached to the dominant financial groups" (42). He goes on to provide similar details for public education. More importantly, however, he is seeking to establish an explanation for, first, the coincidence of interests between the changing class structure and the shifting membership of university governing boards and, second, its effect on curriculum:

> The curriculum was important not so much as a substantive body of knowledge, as for its role in transmitting a coherent corporate identity in which graduates thought of themselves as the heirs of a cultural tradition that defined them as "gentlemen," "college men," members of a "learned profession" or members of an "*educated class.*" Henry Adams . . . concluded that as a consequence of their common education, "lawyers, physicians, professors, merchants, were *classes,* and acted not as individuals, but as though they were clergymen and each profession a church." This view lent some historical plausibility to the ideal of an autonomous corporation of learning, insofar as governing boards shared an identity with the university as the common reference point constituting an *educated class* whose values they generally shared with the academic community. (39) (my emphasis)

As Donna Strickland points out in her important *College English* essay, "Taking Dictation: The Emergence of Writing Programs and the Cultural Contradictions of Composition Teaching," LeBaron Briggs, successor to Adams Sherman Hill as Boylston Professor of Rhetoric at Harvard, hoped as did Hill that their students would develop "the style of a straightforward gentleman" (466). This new class-marked conception of student need establishes a definition marked by the confrontation of incommensurate social identities. By the leadership of the Harvard example, English provided to the university the guarantee that the credentialing process for this class formation would include linguistic conformity.

The years 1874–1900 saw both enormous increases among those attending U.S. universities and colleges and massive social upheavals. While during the period 1850–1880, college enrollments were relatively static, the last quarter-century saw a boom. Between 1890 and 1910 enrollments practically doubled; by 1920, they had doubled again (Brereton 7). Although these increases reflect only a small percentage of the general population, they are significant because they mark the expansion of the professional, technical, and clerical classes. Members of the middle and working classes, admittedly in relatively small numbers, for the first time had access to higher education. The writing practices of elite liberal colleges were rapidly giving way to a corporatized and mechanical vision of writing instruction far more hospitable to the business–education alliance.

Observers as diverse as Albert Kitzhaber and Donald Stewart, Richard Ohmann and Wallace Douglas, Connors, James A. Berlin, Sharon Crowley, Brereton, and Russell have put together a compelling set of claims: Rather than focus on unbridled inquiry and student need as the purpose of writing, instruction concentrated on issues more related to management needs and conformity with the needs of the corporate economy. The cultural logic of university education became the cultural logic of capitalism that, in turn, required a managerial logic, one that could replicate the kinds of vertical organizational models rapidly dominating U.S. business (Yates; Russell).

This new professional, technical, and clerical class provided a new understanding of what writing was good for, what it could achieve in the workplace. The workplace practices of these writers became incorporated in new definitions of writing—the transmission model so dependent on correct usage—because writing was central to concerns about controlling the flow of information while also controlling the workforce. In *Control Through Communication: The Rise of System in American Management* (1989), JoAnne Yates defines systematic management as the key development in the emergence of the modern corporation. She distinguishes systematic management from another development of this period, the more commonly known concept of scientific management, the application of theories developed by Frederick Taylor and his followers. Taylor's concerns were threefold: "time and motion studies of factory work methods, functional foremen, and differential piece rate payments" (10). Systematic management held two central principles: (1) a reliance on systems mandated by top management rather than on individuals and (2) the need for each level of management to monitor and evaluate performance at lower levels (10). The second of these involved a "specific way of gathering, handling, analyzing, and transmitting information" (11).

The second set of principles—monitoring performance (surveillance) and transmitting information (new uses for writing)—demanded the creation of vertical, rather than the more traditional horizontal, forms of communication and control. There must be an unbroken vertical chain of command and communication in order for the huge new corporate enterprises to work smoothly and efficiently. Gone were the days of one-man control and worker input into the production process. JoAnne Yates describes this vertical axis:

> It was not enough to simply systematize existing processes; managers wanted "to rise above the concrete details of the task to think about what is being done." To do so, they needed to establish "a specific way of gathering, handling, analyzing, and transmitting information." Records and reports documented . . . and transmitted this information up to progressively higher levels to provide the basis on which management could analyze what was being done at the lower levels. . . . This function required a change in the kind as well as the amount of internal communication. . . . [R]ecords and reports changed from descriptive to analytic. (13)

This need for newer types of communication and writing in the corporate world coincided exactly with the invention of what Connors has called a "composition-rhetoric," a rhetoric for college writing, in the new modern universities (6). At the office and in the workplace, the need to transmit information and analysis completed the epistemological and political circle. The needs of students increasingly emerged as a reflection of corporate need.

Systematically related to this managerial revolution in the understanding of student need dating back to the inception of composition at Harvard after 1874, we find an increasing reliance on the labor of underpaid and overworked writing instructors. That model became systemic in connection with the managerial vision of writing instruction as a service provided by departments of English to other disciplines. However, breaches have appeared in what has been a virtual wall of uniformity within composition. In a *Profession 99* essay, "'Let's Do the Numbers': Comp Droids and the Prophets of Doom," Richard E. Miller argued that the first-year writing course ought to be taken away from professional compositionists and given to WAC-based graduate assistants and part- and full-time instructors recruited from disciplines other than English in an effort to bolster what he sees as an "ethic of service" that has historically defined the field (103). Miller's emphasis upon the service model of composition work conveniently fits the managerial logic submerged within current disciplinary discourses about the value of writing and the value of faculty work. His suggestions for disciplined-based writing instruction by cohorts of flexible laborers (read: nonunionized graduate students and adjuncts) motivated by a service ethos merely reproduces the century-old logic of a university system in service to capital.

Strickland's valuable contribution is that she offers a two-fold context of class and gender. She examines the material conditions that created "hierarchically arranged writing programs, and second, the attendant cultural values that have made possible the feminization as well as the racialization of composition teaching" (460). The very same class codes calling for gentlemanly conduct at the office and within student essays invoke as well "signifying links between femininity, whiteness, writing, and morality" (460). Her symbol for the cultural work of female subordination and the division of mental from manual labor is the image of a female secretary offered in a 1907 circular from the National Phonograph Company, advertising the Edison Commercial System, a dictation machine.[2] Here is a brief rendering of the ad from Strickland's essay:

> On the left, a suited man reclines in his office chair, one hand leisurely dropped to his side, the other holding a dictating machine's speaking tube. . . . On the right, a demurely dressed woman outfitted with earphones sits up straight at her desk, her hands on the typewriter . . . transcribing the dictated words. The copy, set off in a circle between the two figures, reads: "FROM BRAIN TO TYPE." (457)

Strickland correctly points out that the vast quantities of writing required by the new industrial economy ("voluminous and essential"), organized around the concept of systematic management, necessitated a "division of between conceptual and mechanical labor" (457). Although technologies have changed in the intervening century and the pace of communication accelerated, this arrangement remains virtually intact today. The division of conceptual and mechanical labor is mirrored in a pedagogical division of labor that situates composition at the locus of mechanical correctness and friction-free informational transmission. Furthermore, as Eileen E. Schell points out in her work on the feminization of composition, by 1929 the number of women teaching composition was already high—36 percent in the entire U.S., 42 percent in Midwestern and Western colleges. This was the case despite administrators' insistence in a 1929 survey that "no women" taught in their departments (Schell, *Gypsy Academics* 32).

I would like now to turn to the year 1985 in order to offer an example of the correspondence between more-recent definitions of student need and the needs of capital, one in which write-to-learn has been transformed into write-to-earn. This move is meant in part as an effort to examine problems with Miller's WAC-based solutions to the problems of the first-year writing course and the dependence on part-time, flexible labor. The transformation to write-to-earn has relied upon the conflation of purported humanistic endeavors with more vocational and instrumentalist notions. What I intend to show is that the college writing course is related to the production of credentialed workers, which production, in turn, must fit a corporate model for the production, development, and distribution of industrial products and processes and for the development and circulation of information and services, such that workers and knowledge can be managed in predictable and profitable ways.

In 1985, Anne J. Herrington published articles describing significant differences in two science-based writing courses, laboratory reports and design reports. In laboratory reports, the assumption was that the audience was the professor, to whom the student must demonstrate knowledge of the course material and proficiency in the application of that knowledge in laboratory contexts. In design reports, the assumption was that the audience was an industrial supervisor or "boss" for whom the pertinent gauge of success of any given industrial process or product was "economic feasibility."

Herrington frames her work inside two questions: (1) What function does writing serve in a course in a given academic discipline? and (2) How can teachers create contexts conducive to using writing to achieve their objectives in a given course? These questions, in turn, are placed inside a theoretical assumption: "each classroom represents a community in its own right, situated at once in two larger communities—a school and a disciplinary community" ("Writing" 331, 333). She clarifies the nature of discourse within this community:

> As a community, a classroom is constituted by a group of people who share common understandings of . . . the social aims they are trying to accomplish, roles they assume in specific situations, values, and ways of using language to accomplish their social aims. These common understandings . . . enable

members to communicate with one another and to accomplish their social aims because they can assume they are acting on the same ground rules. When members do not share a common understanding, their aims may not be achieved, they may misinterpret each other, or . . . they may become confused or frustrated in their attempts to communicate. (333–34)

Herrington's choice of chemical-engineering laboratory and chemical-process design courses at this institution hinged on two revelations: These choices allowed her to evaluate near-universal claims for monolithic classroom contexts within WAC literature, and they seemed to represent divergent forums within one academic disciplinary community (335).

She discovered, however, that in chemical-process design reports there was a general assumption about claims and warrants that placed each student-author within a highly contentious application of Aristotle's "greater good." Herrington says that, in design reports, "the following general deliberative warrant was often used: of two things, the one which produces the greater good (in this case, saves money) is the preferred one" (339). It is clear from her discussion that the disciplinary assumption that greater good equates with cost efficiency is not intended as a savings to consumers but as a cost reduction in the design phase of an industrial process and/or product. So, the students' need to prove to the professor that they have mastered the course material, and are, therefore, eligible to engage in any number of disciplinary conversations, appears as the correlative to the students' need to optimize their performance as practicing professionals according to managerial constraints to minimize costs to the company. These definitions of student need coexist and are made to appear unremarkable within a top-down managerial logic of communication for control. Within this model, it appears that a pedagogy built upon critical reflection and inquiry—a search for knowledge (one that is always, however, ideological)—has metamorphosed into a search for knowledge circumscribed by the search for profits.

Another more-recent example of write-to-earn pedagogy deploying a managerial logic was the focus of a series of exchanges on the listserve of the Conference on Basic Writing (cbw-l@tc.umn.edu), a special-interest group of the Conference on College Composition and Communication (CCCC). A member of this e-mail discussion list, Marcia Ribble, published a summary of her pedagogy of a basic-writing course she taught at Michigan State University:

> When I taught bw [basic writing] at Michigan State my students finished the course with a 10 page researched paper in which they had to design a company, develop a diversity plan for the company and follow that plan through implementation. It was tough, but I could promise them that if they could make it through that paper they could probably do any other paper in college til they hit grad school. For the paper they had to research things like what the population projections are for 20 years from now, think about location, available employee groups, groups which are not protected now that might be protected then, etc.

This assignment, fairly complex and sophisticated, asks the basic-writing students to assess the possibilities for starting their own businesses in their local communities, with the above-mentioned multicultural twist accounting for racial or ethnic balance in their local communities.

A concise example of GWSI, write-to-learn, and write-to-earn combined in one, Ribble's pedagogy is very deliberately constructed to unproblematically serve capital ("They had to design a company, develop a diversity plan for the company and follow that plan through implementation") but uses process (and even critical pedagogy) techniques. However, the pedagogy never questions the basic assumptions of capital accumulation. For instance, it attempts multicultural solutions to racism in the workplace, such as developing a "multiracial workforce" without addressing exploitation in the workplace. Questions rapidly come to mind. Does the commonsense specificity of the students' discourse (brought forth by a Freirean generative theme) justify a utilitarian application of what in this instance is a pedagogical triptych of GWSI, write-to-learn, and write-to-earn? Is this unity a misappropriation of critical pedagogy and generative theme? Can capital use generative theme to fortify a pedagogy for its own writing needs? Is critical pedagogy co-opted here?

Whether one's focus is the functionalist, instrumentalist composition-rhetoric produced across the entire nation as other schools attempted to duplicate Harvard's experience or whether one's focus is the amalgamation of the seemingly humanist project of write-to-learn with the managerial logic of write-to-earn, it is clear that managerial discourses are not new to the field. They were present at its birth and now guide the continuing relation of higher education to sustaining labor markets. Prospective professionals and managers of all types and descriptions, including those studying in modern community colleges and comprehensive state universities, need to be trained for a marketplace that depends on writing to survive. Our field, I am arguing, needs to examine more closely the ways that, because it attempts to use education to ameliorate social inequality, actually perpetuates inequality as a result of its conciliatory and harmonious embrace of the assumptions of capital accumulation.

Notes

1. Quotes from Bacon and Newman in Kerr's *The Uses of a University* appear also in the following texts:

Newman, John Henry Cardinal. *The Idea of a University.* New York: Longmans, 1947. 157.

Bacon, Francis. "The Advancement of Learning." *Essays, Advance of Learning, and New Atlantis and Other Places.* New York: Odyssey, 1937. 214.

2. This illustration appears in chapter 2, "Communication Technology and the Growth of Internal Communication," in JoAnne Yates's *Control through Communication: The Rise of System in American Management* (44).

19

The Future of English Departments: Cultural Capital and Professional Writing

Ray Watkins

Professional or business writing courses are in many senses the orphaned cash cows of English departments. "Cash cows," because as a form of vocational education, they attract students at a low labor cost and "orphaned" because these classes are generally understood to be intellectually insubstantial. More than a decade ago Susan Miller famously estimated "that $100 million dollars is spent each year in America on something that we might think of as teaching students to write at the college level" (5). Given the steady rise in enrollment over the last ten years, it seems safe to assume that Miller's estimate remains conservative.[1] Given the ongoing popularity of business and other professional degrees, it also seems safe to assume that a substantial portion of education money is being spent in pursuit of the literate skills needed in professional employment.

In this chapter, I will provide a historical account of the place of business and professional writing in the curriculum of English departments, in hopes of attempting to explain this intellectual neglect of professional writing as pedagogy and as an academic literate practice. At the heart of my explanation lie differing epistemologies of language, each corresponding to the primary forms of cultural capital that have been promulgated by English departments over the course of the last one hundred years.[2] The same economic and social forces that have long shaped the characteristic forms of cultural capital can help to explain our traditional lack of discussion of our own issues as professional workers. Literary studies, despite the common view that places it in firm opposition to business writing (and composition), I will argue, is fully dependent on the ideas and techniques such courses teach.[3]

This essay begins with the contention that the structure of the traditional English department and its increasingly impermeable division into composition and literary studies promotes a misapprehension of the operation of linguistic cultural capital in contemporary U.S. society. This misapprehension affects the professoriate as much as the undergraduate, albeit in different ways. In particular, it inhibits students from understanding how they can best devote their time and energy vis-à-vis the English language. The bifurcation between literature and composition has also helped to reinforce a misguided idea of the efficacy of the writing associated with research.

At the heart of the institutional history of the English department are two very different if not contradictory epistemologies of language, analogous to the two major subject areas of traditional English-language pedagogy. On the one hand, freshman English in particular and composition in general has long been dominated by what James A. Berlin has termed an objectivist epistemology of language.[4] On the other, literary studies have been most decisively shaped by an epistemology rooted in a formalist aesthetic, an epistemology historically associated with, but not reducible to, the so-called New Criticism. Put bluntly, objectivist rhetoric defines language as a transparent medium through which preexisting thought can be expressed. Success is defined in this epistemology in terms of adherence to a predetermined set of linguistic and social norms, the set of more or less consensual agreements often called Standard English. In this ethos or rhetoric, we know the world, quite literally, *through* language; as a result, any perceived failure of written communication is less a matter of a problem with language as such as it is a predicament of human fallibility. To use what many might well see as an outdated terminology, in an objectivist rhetoric, form must necessarily recede in the face of a concern with content. This objectivist rhetoric, of course, is most closely associated with business and professional composition practices.[5]

Put another way, the rhetoric of the formalist aesthetic defines language as an essentially opaque medium in which meaning and thought are created by an act of compositional and interpretive acuity. Success is therefore less a matter of the discovery of the animating thought that preexists writing than a persuasive dynamic, rooted in the contingencies of the social world and the essential ambiguities of language. In this rhetoric, we know the world, quite literally, *as* language; any perceived failure of written communication is less a matter of human fallibility than an inherent, if to some unfortunate, feature of language as such. To return again to what many might see as an outdated terminology, in a formalist aesthetic, content must necessarily recede in light of a consideration of formal properties. A formalist aesthetic, too, is most closely associated with literary study.[6]

I want to emphasize here that in presenting this admittedly crude sketch of these twin epistemologies of language, and their traditional pedagogical and disciplinary associations, I am not seeking to define a metaphysical or existential dilemma (however fascinating we might find the attempt to reach some kind of ideological closure on this set of problems).[7] Instead, I would like to focus on the formative role that these twin epistemologies have had in shaping how linguistic cultural capital has been conceptualized in English departments. The intellectual and institutional relationship between these epistemologies has been, and continues to be, a key force underwriting what I will call here the Modernist English Department (hereafter, the M.E.D.). What interests me in this context is not so much metaphysics as the historical and sociological forms of the twentieth-century English department in the U.S. as a source of linguistic cultural capital.[8] The effects of the twin epistemologies of the M.E.D. have been manifold, of course, but I believe we can sum them up as falling into three main sets of interrelated phenomena. First, in terms of intellectual status and so influence, the literary language/epistemology is *placed over and above* an objectivist language/epistemology; likewise, the literary professor is situated *over and above* the writing instructor in both intellectual status and in material conditions. Within the M.E.D., the literary epistemology and its associated cadres therefore govern *over* the objectivist epistemology and its cadres precisely because the former are intellectually and socially *above* them in the precise sense that the former are more disinterested, that is, less concerned with the mundane and the utilitarian. Although the dominance of men on the tenure track of the literary cadre has eroded in the past fifteen years, the composition labor force is still radically and disproportionately female and dominated numerically by non-tenure-track positions, including graduate students. Second, the M.E.D. has defined the objectivist and literary epistemologies as distinct realms with relatively fixed and persistent borders. Ironically, this has had the effect of mutually delegitimizing *both* objectivist and formalist epistemologies. The well-patrolled frontiers between composition and literature help to create the conditions through which cultural capital is unequally distributed along racial and gender lines. Just as literary language is *said to be* divorced from the language of so-called real life, objectivist language, as the *said to be* nonliterary, can be represented as intellectually unsophisticated.

Third, these intellectual hierarchies and epistemological binaries shape an academic hyper-concern with research as the primary locus of influence and power, at the expense of teaching and, importantly, service and self-governance. Just as literary research/writing has long been seen as the most important intellectual activity in English departments and afforded the highest status, teaching as well as service and self-governance has been seen as mundane and utilitarian, of lesser status, and so of less concern in understanding (and exercising) power and influence. Accordingly, the perquisites of status and institutional power, including tenure, sabbaticals, lower course loads, and smaller class sizes, are distributed to those institutions and individuals within a hierarchy based on research productivity.[9] Composition, it is important to note, is in every way *said to be* secondary to the more important work of literary professors: research comes before service, great works of art, however defined, are more important and intellectually more sophisticated than freshman texts, and so on. This hierarchy works to conceal the research faculty's dependence on the very sorts of language taught to first-year students by adjuncts, graduate students, and women teaching off the tenure track.

I would like to explore a typical example of how the M.E.D. represents cultural capital in the context of business and/or professional writing. For this purpose, I have taken a chart from one of the myriad of Web sites devoted to the professional self-development of business writers, here authored by Tom McKeown (see table). There are a couple of quick points I would like to make about this chart as a model of the continuing relationship between the twin epistemologies of the M.E.D. Business authors, McKeown claims, suffer from a "stubborn reluctance to abandon creative writing in the office" because as students they were taught by literary specialists, who operate by a very different set of epistemological priorities than those he believes ought to dominate the professional environment. McKeown contends that literary English, for example, must always be read more than once to be understood, encourages reflection rather than action, relies on imagery and symbolism rather than charts and numbers, uses a plain over a colorful tone, and so on. In turn, McKeown believes that business English, of course, is more suited to the professional environment precisely because it encourages action rather than reflection, can be read once with full understanding, relies on charts and numbers, and uses a plain tone. What McKeown advocates, of course, is plainly a species of an objectivist epistemology; his "literary English" just as unmistakably a formalist aesthetic. "Business English," McKeown argues, is written and read *as if* language as such were unproblematic; it achieves this transparency through fidelity to grammatical and social norms. "Literary English," on the other hand, is written and read *as if* language were by definition opaque and ambiguous; it must be examined closely in order to be fully understood.

This is a remarkably constricted notion of the literary text. Furthermore, in the contemporary M.E.D., many students would likely be taught by a specialist in rhetoric or composition or by a graduate student in another discipline or by any number of persons with no necessary connection to literary studies. Clearly, McKeown's view is oversimplified at best. Nonetheless, he points to an important reality: Ambitious students emerge from the classrooms of the M.E.D. believing both that an objectivist epistemology is unchallenging intellectually and that the "persistent creativity" more often associated with the formalist aesthetic ought to be their ideal as writers. McKeown rightly contends that the epistemological hierarchy of the M.E.D. potentially leads both to communicative confusion and to a kind of writerly dysfunction.

Ironically, McKeown makes his point largely through hyperbole, a device whose ambiguity is certainly more typical of a formalist than an objectivist epistemology. McKeown's own linguistic strategies suggest that although the use of literary genre may be an ineffective methodology in the workplace, considerations of formal literary devices may not. This is consistent with a very different set of conclusions drawn by Pierre Bourdieu, whose investigation of cultural and literary epistemology provides strong evidence that a formalist aesthetic is an important component in the reproduction and maintenance of status in a capitalist economy and of

---

Differences Between Literary and Business English

Literary Writing	Business Writing
Designed to be read many times	Reveals full meaning on a single reading
Complex expression	Clear expression
Unfamiliar words	Familiar words
Colorful tone	Plain language
Variety expected	Consistency expected
Imagery and symbolism	Numbers and charts
Long, complex sentences	Short, clear sentences
Impossible to read quickly	Can be read quickly
Ambiguity acceptable	Clarity essential

Source: Reprinted by permission of Thomas W. McKeown, *Powerful Business Writing: Say What You Mean, Get What You Want* (Cincinnati: Writers' Digest, 1992).

Notes:

1. Most people have been trained by English teachers of a literary learning: hence the stubborn reluctance to abandon creative writing in the office on the part of some "well-educated" business writers.

2. Even when literary sentences are clear, as in Hemingway's novels, the themes require lengthy reflection.

3. When literary works enforce a specific interpretation, they veer towards propaganda, as in George Orwell's *1984*. True literature has no design on the reader, other than to promote a sense of interconnectedness between individuals of different societies and ages through increased self-understanding, tolerance, and sensitivity to nuance.

---

the capitalist economy itself. Considerations of form, as Bourdieu has shown, serve as markers of a certain distance from necessity, in food and clothing as much as in language. A formalist aesthetic or epistemology is relatively rare and so capable of becoming a marker of status not because it is a more accurate view of language but because the competencies underwriting the deciphering of its codes require a relatively high investment of time and effort.[10]

Although only further research can clarify these issues in the U.S. context, there is nothing to suppose a priori that a certain facility with the formal properties of writing does not function as a form of cultural capital.[11] We cannot deny that McKeown's creative writers might well be put at a distinct disadvantage in the workplace if they spent too much of their time contemplating the aesthetics of form. McKeown may or may not be correct in identifying "literary English" as an investment of cultural capital with a small chance of social or material returns in the professional writing environment, but he is surely mistaken in believing that a persistent formal creativity has no impact on status more broadly defined. Bourdieu's research, however, at the very least, suggests that linguistic cultural capital is much more complex than the structure of the M.E.D. has thus far implied.

To borrow a phrase from Bruno Latour, I would contend that linguistic cultural capital has *never* been modern—that is, that the workings of linguistic cultural capital in a capitalist economy have never been mimetically analogous to the structure of the M.E.D., with its nominally stable epistemological divisions and hierarchies. In this sense, the modernity of the M.E.D. can be seen as less an attempt to reproduce the ways and means of language and knowledge, however critically, and more an attempt to fix the flux of culture.

In the final analysis, I believe, the structure of the M.E.D. represents the historically dominant form of an epistemological compromise with the market economy, a sort of vaccine—if not placebo—against the vicissitudes of linguistic ambiguity, a bit of preventative medicine administered in light of the necessity of communicative and economic efficiency. In effect, the message of the M.E.D. has long been: We will teach you the banalities of a popular, instrumentalist ethos, but only briefly, and only as a kind of remedial preparation for the formalist aesthetic. In return, the subsequent introduction to the vicissitudes and ambiguities of a formalist epistemology were to serve as a kind of warning against a too-certain faith in "objective" representation. In the traditional curricular sequence, students are *first* taught to use language instrumentally to convey knowledge and opinion (freshman composition) and then *second* advised that the representational function of language is highly unreliable (introduction to literature). This curricular binarism leads to the creation of a false division: One of the prescriptive messages that the M.E.D. propagates is that the formalist aesthetic *ought not* to be invested in our working lives, when in reality as we have seen, Bourdieu's work suggests that a persistent formal creativity might well be an important dimension of the ongoing investment of linguistic cultural capital, particularly for the professional cadres.

The other half of the binary is equally false. Despite the hierarchy that places the poem over the undergraduate essay and that says the work of the composition instructor is less rigorous than that of the literary professor, it has simply never been true that the employment of objectivist rhetoric is an uninteresting and insubstantial intellectual challenge. Indeed, much if not all of the disciplinary history of composition studies can be understood as an attempt to demonstrate just how complex and perplexing a task the deployment of an objectivist epistemology can be. Any student in college can tell you that even the most apparently self-evident and rudimentary term of art in objectivist rhetoric—concision, for example, or clarity—can be nearly impossible to pin down as your audience shifts from professor to professor, much less as a student moves among the myriad of so-called discourse communities they face as undergraduate writers. Similarly, any professor can attest to the difficulties of shifting from, say, an audience composed largely of students to one of professors or administrators. Indeed, the codes of the popular instrumental ethos, particularly in a heterogeneous society, have turned out to be just as complicated as that of the formalist aesthetic.

Importantly, too, recent research has persuasively demonstrated that the complexities if not perplexities of the undergraduate—and the professor in her service writing—are precisely the complexities if not perplexities faced by writers "in the wild."[12] Russel K. Durst's book-length study *Collision Course,* for example, can be understood as a valuable investigation into the undergraduate's epistemological problems as they are played out in the composition classrooms of the M.E.D. Recent investigations into professional writing—books such as Jim Henry's *Writing Workplace Cultures,* Rachel Spilka's edited collection *Writing in the Workplace,* and the collection of essays edited by Mary Sue Garay and Stephen A. Bernhart, *Expanding Literacies*—provide moving pictures of the epistemological problematics of workplace writers remarkably analogous to those of the undergraduate. Neither the professional nor the undergraduate, in other words, can in any simple sense apply globally what Jon Hagge has called the "rhetorical commonplaces" of the objectivist epistemology they may or may not have diligently learned in the classroom. Just as a literature professor's notion of concision may well contradict that of a professor of biology, a senior partner at a law firm does not necessarily define written clarity in the same way as an assistant manager of a retail outlet.

The problem with the M.E.D. in short, is not the bifurcation of linguistic epistemology but with our response to it. We need not attempt to resolve a representative dilemma that much evidence indicates is productive in its complexity and its refusal to resolve itself. An English department that recognizes, as Latour suggests, that "We have never been modern" must, in other words, studiously avoid any attempt to subsume objectivist epistemology into formalist epistemology or even to resolve the borders between them. We will do no service to our students if we attempt to persuade them that all language in all situations is ambiguous, or vice versa. As professionals, we, too, have long understood that we cannot afford to write poetry when we need memos; the competencies and conventions that allow us to read and write *as if* language were transparent are as important as those that allow us a careful consideration of the formal properties of language.

Instead, a never-modernist English department must recognize that if students are to exit the university with a full and critical understanding of linguistic cultural capital, they must come away with a more complex understanding of the ongoing investment of these differing epistemologies than the M.E.D. has most often encouraged. In short, as intellectual workers, we must begin to try to understand how these two epistemologies of language are differentially deployed in a capitalist economy. How and why, for example, do writers in our culture shift from an objectivist epistemology to considerations more accurately described as aspects of a formalist aesthetic? Do writers compartmentalize these two views of language, or, as I suspect, are there moments in which the two bleed into each other? When are creative preoccupations with linguistic form economically productive, and why? How do the formal properties of language generate returns on economic capital? More broadly, what happens to our culture if the concerns of a formalist aesthetics of language are made marginal by their conceptual quarantine within universities (when communicative use is *said to be* more important than formal beauty)? Finally, in our relatively affluent society, why are we still teaching students that contemplative concerns must be set aside in the name of economic action?

Clearly, the scope of these issues extends well beyond the effective range of this essay. Nonetheless, I would contend that a never-modernist English department, if it is to attempt to teach students to think critically about language and epistemology, or more accurately, about linguistic competence as cultural capital, must make a concerted attempt to support students' understanding of writing as an intellectual and material process both in relation to historical context and our economic lives in a democratic culture. In practice, this means our pedagogy must include instruction in a kind of epistemological code switching. That is, we should convey to our students an understanding of composition processes in the wild as well as in the classroom, as a complex and shifting movement or set of movements in which choices are made between objectivist and formalist epistemologies of language.[13] Intellectually and practically, we cannot afford to either dismiss an objectivist epistemology as a cop-out to market ideology nor reject a formalist aesthetic as a willful and elitist ignorance of student need. Politically, we need to know much more about professional writing, that is, about service writing, if we are to succeed in defending and in strengthening our institutions.

I would argue, in the end, that ethnographic methodologies—that is, a research model consisting of a combination of textual analysis, interviews, and on-site observations of writers—are ideally suited to the pursuit of these aims. Ethnographic case studies can help socialize the epistemological naturalism of the M.E.D. by asking students to investigate how linguistic cultural capital is strategically invested in the wild. Rather than attempting to prescriptively instruct students about what their linguistic cultural capital ought to be, we could ask them to investigate the use of language in the workplace. To the first and second stages of the inculcation of linguistic capital, we might in this way add a third ethnographic stage, perhaps in the form of an advanced writing course. Similarly, we can reconsider the graduate curriculum's long-standing emphasis on research; clearly, if academic status and influence rest on teaching and service as well as on research writing, the distribution of courses in the Ph.D. program ought to reflect that. Here, too, ethnographic methodologies can help to ensure that future academics have a critical understanding of how English professors are positioned within the circulation of linguistic cultural capital.

Once undergraduates have understood both the popular ethos and the formalist aesthetic in freshman composition and in introductory literature courses, we would ask them to investigate how these forms of cultural capital are invested by writers outside of academic interests, narrowly defined. Graduate education, too, could begin to represent the modes of academic influence as a complex interplay of pedagogy, research, and service. As critical researchers, too, students at both levels could consider the ethical problematics of linguistic epistemology: When is the pressure towards communicative efficiency dehumanizing? At what point might it be necessary to consider form? What is the relationship between status and the employment of the forms of cultural capital represented by each epistemology? In helping our students move toward this more-nuanced view of literacy and of linguistic cultural capital, we can begin to create a repository of skills and knowledge ideally suited to the challenges of our current historical situation.

Notes

1. Despite the nominal crisis in college funding, the university is a vigorous, even thriving institution in the U.S., at least as measured by the size of the undergraduate population. According to the National Center for Education Statistics in *Digest of Education Statistics:*

> Higher education enrollment increased by 13 percent between 1977 and 1987. Between 1987 and 1997, enrollment increased at about the same rate, from 12.8 million to 14.3 million. There was a slight decline in enrollment from 1992 to 1995, but it was overshadowed by large increases in the late 1980s.

2. For the purposes of this essay, I would argue that the modern university has been shaped by three major periods of reform, each contributing to a transformation of U.S. higher education from a system serving an aristocracy to one designed to meet the nominal needs of the professional middle class: first, by the turn of the nineteenth century, the incorporation of graduate schools, on the German model; second, the formation of business and other professional programs by progressives in the second and third decades of the twentieth century; and third, the rapid expansion of educational access following World War II, beginning with the Serviceman's Act of 1942 and continuing through a variety of other affirmative-action programs of the 1960s and 1970s.

3. These problems are extensive, from attacks on tenure to the rising use of part-time instructors to the trend towards electronic forms of correspondence courses. In the National Education Association's *2000 Almanac of Higher Education,* Christine Maitland and Gary Rhoades provide a succinct, if bracing, summary of the state of the profession:

> Managerial restructuring of higher education was part of an assault on public institutions. . . . Privatizing educational services began on the elementary and secondary school levels . . . criticism then turned to public higher education; states reduced financial support, which in turn accelerated privatization. Public colleges and universities sought to reduce costs and generate new revenues by hiring more part-time and contingent faculty at subprofessional wages, investing in instructional technology to reduce faculty labor costs in delivering curriculum, and capitalizing on the intellectual products created by faculty labor. (27)

4. Berlin made this argument in two now-classic books on the history of composition pedagogy, one focusing on the nineteenth century and the other on the twentieth. His explicit advocacy of social-epistemic rhetoric in his later books, particularly, *Rhetorics, Poetics, and Cultures,* implicitly suggests that the objectivist rhetoric is still a common, if no longer so fully dominant, epistemology in language instruction.

5. Each form of cultural capital has its own historically associated pedagogical methodology or methodologies; the formal aesthetic is allied with literary new criticism, as previously noted, as well as with a more traditional belles lettres approach. Again, a for-

malist aesthetic cannot be reduced to these methodologies; for a variety of reasons discussed in this chapter, I would contend that considerations of form play at least some role in any literary pedagogy. Joseph Harris has also provided a useful typology of composition methodologies since 1966, centering on "five key words—growth, voice, process, error, and community—[that] have figured in recent talk about writing and teaching" (*Teaching Subject* ix). One potential avenue of research suggested by this model of differing forms of cultural capital lies in investigating how writers and readers call on either epistemological competency depending on the context, their backgrounds, and so on. In a recent article in the *Business Communication Quarterly,* for example, Srivatsa Seshadri and Larry D. Theye contrast professorial to professional evaluations of writing. "In general," the authors conclude in their abstract, "business professionals judge papers more on substance . . . and less on style . . . than do business faculty" (9).

6. Arguably, *Rhetorics, Poetics, and Cultures* further refines what Berlin terms a social-epistemic epistemology in an attempt to shape a composition pedagogy using, in effect, a formalist aesthetic. Space limitations prevent me from developing a full response to this methodology. I will say, however, that given the distinctly different properties of the objectivist rhetoric, and its subsequent difficulties, I could not recommend eliminating it as a pedagogical subject altogether.

7. Cornel West has termed this willingness to set aside metaphysics in the name of more immediate and pragmatic concerns "the American evasion of philosophy," that phrase being the title of his 1989 book.

8. I am arguing, in effect, that the relationship between composition and literary pedagogy, inside English departments, can be understood as an instance of the ongoing struggle for what Pierre Bourdieu calls a "definition of cultural nobility." This conflict, Bourdieu writes, "has gone on unceasingly, from the seventeenth century to the present day, between groups differing in their ideas of culture and of the legitimate relationship to culture" (*Distinction* 2).

9. It is by now almost a cliché that the young professor, upon arriving at her new tenure-track position, is most often surprised to discover just how much time must be devoted to service. The annual faculty survey conducted by the Higher Education Research Institute indicates that although women have made moderate gains in representation on university faculty, changes in the racial composition are "at a standstill."

10. Individuals who come to the university having already been fully exposed to the formalist aesthetic, Bourdieu argues, have a distinct advantage over those who do not:

> The relative weight of home background and of formal education varies according to the extent to which the different cultural practices are recognized and taught by the educational system, and the influence of social origin is strongest—other things being equal—in "extra-curricular" and avant-garde culture. (*Distinction* 1)

Bourdieu adds:

> The denial of lower, coarse, vulgar, venal, servile—in a word, natural enjoyment, which constitutes the sacred sphere of culture, implies an affirmation of the superiority of those who can be satisfied with the sublimated, refined, disinterested, gratuitous, distinguished pleasures forever closed to the profane. That is why art and cultural consumption are predisposed, consciously and deliberately or not, to fulfill a social function of legitimating social differences. (7)

More emphatically, in an essay published in the *Handbook of Theory and Research for the Sociology of Education,* Bourdieu asserts that the accumulation of cultural capital . . . presupposes a process of embodiment, in-corporation, which, insofar as it implies a labor of inculcation and assimilation, costs time, time which must be invested personally by the investor. Like the acquisition of a muscular physique or a suntan, it cannot be done at second hand (so all effects of delegation are ruled out). (244)

11. "Consumption is, in this case," Bourdieu has written,

a stage in a process of communication, that is, an act of deciphering, decoding, which predisposes practical or explicit mastery of a cipher or code. In a sense, one can say that the capacity to see (voir) is a function of the knowledge (savoir), or concepts, that is, the words, that are available to name visible things, and which are, as it were, programmes for perception. ("Forms of Capital" 2)

12. The phrase is taken from Edwin Hutchins's book, *Cognition in the Wild,* which investigates the intricacies of cognition and culture outside of the laboratory—and the university. My own thoughts on studying writing owe much to Hutchins's methodolog-ical principles.

13. The history of literature includes some famous examples of writers who were exemplary code switchers in this sense. Wallace Stevens, for example, managed to be both a successful insurance executive as well as a poet. Bourdieu's research suggests both that this sort of ability is perhaps less rare than might be imagined and that it could be inves-tigated as both a historical and a contemporary phenomena.

20
The Righting of Writing

Robin Truth Goodman

The first question I ask on the first day of first-year composition class is, Why are we here? The answer is almost always, We are here because this is a required course. To get beyond that, I say, Who is it who is requiring us to be here, why are they requiring it, and in whose interest is composition class required? The answer to this line of inquiry is also remarkably uniform: Composition class is necessary and useful because when we start working, we don't want to make mistakes on office memos—that would be embarrassing!

I once told this to leftist sociologist Stanley Aronowitz who said that if this is what students want, there should be schools where they could learn the grammar and mechanics of business writing in three months, graduate with a certificate, and immediately find a job to apply it. How do students learn to think about writing so instrumentally so that they see writing class as training for service labor and office work, and how can writing class be set up within a different matrix of purposes, intentions, and values?

Expressivism

Much writing about the teaching of writing tends to focus on the value of self-expression for developing the student's sense of personhood, self-respect, and autonomy. The assumptions behind such a methodology are ideological: The deification of self-respect, autonomy, and experience feeds a consumerist logic of free choice and supports a sense that authority can be done away with simply by ignoring it. This dismissal of authority (as though if we do not pay attention to it, it will disappear) sustains and indeed champions the logic of the free market (as well as an individualism servicing the current anti-labor organization of the economy), while making social differences and inequalities into questions of taste and aesthetics rather than power.

Most often, these discussions emphasize self-affirmation, experience, feelings, and the self, most commonly through writing fast and often formlessly in jour-

nals and automatic-writing exercises. Teachers, writes Tom Romano, "know that
. . . [y]oung writers must be cut loose. They must write frequently in high-speed
chases . . . adventures that take various routes" (6). These kinds of perspectives
on the purpose of teaching understand truth and self to be a natural space of
freedom, in their pure forms untouched by authority (but perennially endangered
by it). Within expressivist theories of composition, the idea of the self as a space
of adventure, or high-speed chases, is clearly connected to the consumption of
advertisements and movies promising excitement, emotion, sensation, and
thrills—as well as news articles about the pure-experience adrenaline—rush of
speculation and day-trading, linking stock trading to bungee jumping, skate-
boarding, snowboarding, helicopter skiing, and the like. The early Jean Baudrillard described the sovereign subject of consumption as inhabiting "a marginal
sector of indeterminacy where the Individual, elsewhere constantly constrained
by social rules, might at last—being left to himself in the 'private' sphere—recover a margin of freedom and personal leeway" (81). This consumerist freedom
means the pursuit of happiness outside of any collective constraints, the consumer
therefore appearing as a subject "speaking to oneself" (85).

The natural self on which expressivist theories of composition rely closely con-
forms to current practices of commercialism, particularly those connected with
the rise of neoliberal ideologies. Asserting faith in the unregulated market for its
version of freedom and equality, neoliberalism, as Robert McChesney points out,
is best served "when the population is diverted from information, access, and
public forums necessary for meaningful participation in decision making" (9).
In other words, the encouragement to turn inward also implies encouragement
to turn away and the valuing of pure experience and emotion over social relations. Understanding writing as a personal withdrawal or journey tends to produce subjects disengaged from the struggle for justice. As James A. Berlin argues,
within theories of expressivity,

> political change can only be considered by individuals and in individual terms
> . . . [E]xpressionistic rhetoric is inherently and debilitatingly divisive of po-
> litical protest, suggesting that effective resistance can only be offered by indi-
> viduals, each acting alone. ("Rhetoric and Ideology" 486–87)

Market ideology benefits from this orientation, as it limits the public's will to
involvement, leaving the field of public deliberation open to corporate interests
and other antidemocratic initiatives.

According to expressivist theorists, authority tends to inhibit what Peter Elbow has called the "fluidity" of forces that express the self, its experiences, and
its interests. Elbow would like all ideas to interact and negotiate equally (and have
equal validity) within a fully transparent language community. Elbow argues that
the teaching of writing needs to be founded on the believing game, where students learn to accept each other's ideas without comment, critique, or question.
This he calls "an act of investment" (173) in connection with the postmodern

insight that truths are only relatively relevant and always "flexible" (156), coming together in a marketplace of ideas, within a pre-given set of purely procedural rules or "agreements" (156) and not within an ethical set of standards. This idea that writing is a business transaction performed in full freedom within a certain set of preordained procedures would certainly please *New York Times* foreign correspondent Thomas L. Friedman who has described neoliberal globalization as a "Golden Straitjacket":

> But with the gradual lifting of capital controls in the 1970's, the democratizations of finance, technology and information, the end of the Cold War system and the fall of walls everywhere, there suddenly emerged a vast global plain where investor herds from many different countries could roam freely. (96)

As Zygmunt Bauman indicates, "The deepest meaning conveyed by the idea of globalization is that of the indeterminate, unruly and self-propelled character of world affairs; the absence of a centre, of a controlling desk, of a board of directors, of a managerial office" (*Globalization* 59). Bauman further identifies this radical indeterminacy as a world where "*no one seems now to be in control*" (*Globalization* 58), no body of power to which an appeal can be made for a change responding to nonlocal needs, or rather, concerned with a totality of human interests.

Elbow suggests that this free flow of ideas, opinions, and expressions in the classroom reflects the new global migrant economies, so that unquestioning acceptance of other people's ideas becomes a means for individual writing subjects to override differences, get through "security clearance," and submit to contact with what is alien (186). In fact, as Bauman has pointed out, globalization has led to increased mobility across security borders only at the level of capital: If capital is not satisfied with the local conditions around its operations, it can just leave, while labor (embodied individual subjects) remains confined to specific localities. The movement of persons and their ideas is highly restricted due to finances, legal stipulations, and very active forms of policing. To the extent that Elbow and Friedman acknowledge no structural impediments to the business of exchange suggests the degree to which they themselves identify with capital. Though Elbow has since revised his thesis to include a much less autonomous, more socially nuanced, and socially connected idea of self, he has consistently seen language itself as unleashing subversive and freeing effects, ultimately circumventing a critique focused on the limits imposed by and through language. Despite a substantial bibliography critiquing the views of expressivity developed by Elbow, these free-market values are extremely persistent and continue to be used uncritically in many composition classrooms and much training.

Affirming the equal validity of all opinions serves, as Chandra Talpade Mohanty shows, to conceptualize "race and gender in terms of personal or individual experience" (194). Mohanty warns this privatization of social experience is frequently a way of neglecting the students' own interactions with history and power and undermining the significance of education "as a crucial form of resistance to the colonization of hearts and minds" (191). In order to assume equality and freedom within these frameworks, differences and disagreements as well as structural inequalities need to be ignored or otherwise subordinated to the procedural rules. Furthermore, assuming that all opinions are equally valid fails to recognize the power of the mainstream corporate media to determine truths and set the contours of the speakable, the possible, and the future. Affirming students' beliefs, making them feel good, simply reinforces ideologies based in the inequalities of a class-based society and leaves unconfronted media images that exploit women and people of color and affirm property and ownership as the basis of identity, thereby perpetuating unacknowledged relations of privilege and oppression. Donaldo Macedo and Lilia I. Bartolomé assert that

> mass media educate more people about issues regarding ethnicity and race than all other sources of education available to U.S. citizens. By shunning the mass media, educators are missing the obvious: that is, that more public education is done by the media than by teachers, professors, and anyone else. (2)

The naturalization of the inner core of self means that the teacher does not have to challenge the assumptions that the students adopt from their continual embeddedness in a culture of consolidated corporate media and mass consumption and that "the self" has somehow lain inert and unaltered beneath the artifices imposed by political and commercial authority.

The concept that the natural self is buried underneath layers of civilization that threaten it comes out of the history of depth psychology and psychoanalysis as they developed through the nineteenth-century sciences of empire. These domains advanced a cultural sense that the unconscious is a natural field of primitive play and absolute freedom that can escape from the repressions of authority, paternalistic control, and the imposing, internalized government of the superego, or rather, of conscience. Obviously replete with colonialist configurations of power, such ideas about the self also feed contemporary conceptions of the liberalized global market, where the capitalist self operates in a field of pure freedom, desire, and personal expression devoid of regulations. Donald H. Graves instructs writing teachers:

> A natural environment would mean letting you and the children occupy a room where there was little definition to either territory or process. If I imagine a classroom in which a laissez-faire mood exists, I see the children reading and writing when they want, about what they want, and completing products as they please. A natural environment is an invitation to a jungle-like existence ... [which,] without any structure, allows each child's notion of territory and ownership to compete for center stage. (33)

As in Adam Smith's descriptions of the market as a field for the negotiation of competing, natural self-interests or as in Joseph Conrad's journey to the most primitive center of the self in the jungles of Africa, Graves's classroom is a place where social differences are, on an even playing field, vying for territorial possessions, claiming and mapping the extensions of self. Each social difference starts out equal to every other:

> Some children eat with the family while others pick up food as they wish; some eat fast food while others sit down to a well-prepared meal with carefully defined customs and table manners. Other children are simply hungry or severely undernourished. (33–34)

In other words, Graves relegates socioeconomic class, and even hunger, to an aestheticized, culturalist field of pure expression where inequalities are reduced to matters of style and taste.

Indeed, the expression of difference that occurs with this peeling of the natural self is often defined as a universal natural desire to consume. Nancy Atwell, for example, describes the writing self in the terms of real estate, where the student is to imagine personal expression as a private emotional outlet that happens, for adolescents, in private bedrooms saturated with suburban consumer and media goods:

> My bedroom was my haven. It was where I pretended I was adopted, wrote poetry and kept diaries, taught myself to play the guitar, applied sapphire blue mascara, listened in a trance to the Beatles and Dylan, ate candy, plucked my eyebrows, and lay on my bed fantasizing about boys I'd met and never met. (52)

Besides the absolute assumption of heterosexuality here, Atwell never mentions what kinds of kids have access to such bedrooms and that the sleeping spaces of many young people are not likely to provide such spacious interiors for free thought. In a similar vein, Ken Macrorie has advanced the idea of the "I-Search Paper" to replace the traditional research or term paper. In the "I-Search Paper," the student writes a chronological report of the steps he or she went through to discover a piece of knowledge that he or she had an interest in knowing, a process that, Macrorie states, would unblock "the unconscious flow natural to composition of words into sentences" (29). Macrorie inquires, "What do you need to know about these days? . . . Maybe it's a small thing like deciding what to do with the large amount of money a relative gave you for Christmas or graduation" (66). Macrorie here defines the pursuit of knowledge as similar to reading through a department store catalogue to find the best product for a particular consumer need and naturalizes the subject of composition as the casual recipient of a large amount of money.

Consumption does not exhaust the metaphors that Graves and other education theorists use to talk about the types of freedom that writing offers. Atwell talks about the writing classroom as a system of "management" (104), where each writing topic is the writer's "territory" or personal interest (123), and the day begins when the teacher and the student make a verbal "contract" about what will be accomplished (142). Graves also describes the writing self as a producer. Preparing to write in Graves's classroom involves not just responding to an invitation to return to the pure natural self of the jungle but also performing a set of regimented, "mechanical" tasks (39), such as running messages between classrooms, cleaning the room, dusting, record keeping, escorting visitors, and keeping accounts of milk tickets. These jobs replicate a service-sector organization of labor, where the children learn "skills" to move up on the ladder of value and manage each other within a culture filled with consultants and subservience-training. Graves explains:

> I find that it is best to have the more skilled children handle a new responsibility first, then serve as helpers for other children the succeeding week. . . . When children learn how the entire room works from the vantage point of one job, they . . . learn how to consult with others for help; they especially learn the skill other children possess; and they learn to negotiate and complete their daily tasks. (39)

Learning to write as an expression of freedom means assimilating children into the mechanisms and social relations of corporate labor and particularly the type of labor requiring dull, cookie-cutter, dead-end tasks with little reward in satisfaction, autonomy, or self-expression.

The centering and unquestioning approval of student beliefs, even the apparently uncontroversial focus on self-esteem, helps to turn the classroom into a client-based social unit meant to induce feelings of pleasure, as though school were like the candy store or the mall. Knowledge is emptied of transformative ideas because students need primarily to be entertained. This is the same principle that underlies the current administrative focus on student evaluations as a punitive and draconian measure of teacher worth, where the happiness of the student eclipses other pedagogical concerns and considerations of content. Observes Henry A. Giroux,

> The purpose of teacher authority in this . . . approach is to provide students with forms of therapy that focus largely on uplifting their self-esteem, motivating them, and making them feel good . . . [yet] [e]ducation . . . was never a tool for student motivation . . . on the contrary, the purpose of dialogue was individual and social change. (*Stealing Innocence* 151)

This pleasure-centered client orientation also supports the managerial goal of teachers. Currently, as tenure is attacked and professors work more frequently under contract, student dissatisfaction can lead to a teacher's dismissal, and the teacher's role is therefore increasingly to sell herself to an audience under fear of firing.

Ironically, critical pedagogy has been sometimes understood as the source of this incapacitation of the teacher. For example, Anneliese Kramer-Dahl faults Paulo Freire and Giroux for encouraging teachers to "impose" the voice of the radical intellectual on students:

[W]hat about the analytical method, the "language of critique," which we as critical pedagogy's transformative teachers are supposed to give to our students in order to reveal the ideological distortions in their texts? Is this method of analysis really neutral or is it one "designed to reveal and command assent" to these revelations? If that is so, then, ironically, albeit in the name of empower-ment, the radical teacher may well give them yet another controlling scheme of interpretation, which imposes the "correct" answers on the students. (252)

Rather than impose answers, however, critical pedagogy insists that teachers must continually theorize student experiences, help students to link their experience to broader social and political issues, historicizing and contextualizing cognition, and using writing as a tool for change. This means that teachers use their knowl-edge of the world to oppose power, to make judgments, sometimes causing stu-dents to feel uncomfortable—but the occasional production of discomfort and the imposition of correctness are very different things.

The Demise of the Public

The weakening of teacher authority upheld by expressivist theories of composi-tion stems from the undermining of all things public—including schools—through the transformative trends of capital in an age of globalization: corpora-tization, neoliberalism, and privatization. Critical pedagogy shows how the loss of teacher power—in, for example, present trends of standardization, testing, centralizing of curricula, and competition between schools—is part of a broader scheme that threatens democratic citizenry by shrinking the public spaces in which democratic debate can occur. In radical opposition, critical pedagogy pro-poses reclaiming schools as a space for the analysis of power, not for making it invisible. The reduction of teacher authority is accompanied by a radical increase of authority vested in corporate capital, market logic, and the profit motive.

The ideologies behind writing instruction shore up the political macro-orga-nization of college writing. As Bruce Horner has suggested, we need to examine

how the politics of pedagogy intersect and interact with the politics of the profession, and the material circumstances of teaching, teachers' professional positioning, and larger material circumstances of these, associated with the institutional and historical location of the course, teacher, and students. (*Terms* 76–77)

This means looking at the macro-organization of college composition and aca-demic labor as caught in the same ideological structure as the rhetoric of com-position pedagogy. It can also mean inspecting how these ideologies are ubiqui-tous in determining material inequalities and labor conditions in the social world more generally. Although Horner feels that seeing the ideological as both ubiq-uitous and political undercuts the possibility of privileging any standpoint over another (74), I argue that ideology, even though ubiquitous, is inherently contradictory and that the composition classroom, like other public spheres, is a good place to start the very political action of revealing and unraveling these contra-dictions, indicating how they frame social relations of power, and changing them.

The formal teaching of composition started at Harvard University at the turn of the nineteenth century and was designed to train the elite in humanistic values and language use proper to their position. Composition studies then increased with the 1960s expansion and democratization of the university. Yet, the various efforts to imagine a more democratic pedagogy for composition are being undercut by an economy of severely underpaid adjuncts, part-time administrators, and graduate students who are hired last-minute on a temporary, often non-contract basis, usually without insurance or benefits. As Andrew Ross has observed, this is not because of "the "willingness" of scholars (whether as graduate students or postdoctoral employees) to accept a discounted wage out of "love for their subject" (22). Composition teaching is rarely a matter of voluntary choice: Adjuncts give into the new, corporate organization of labor in the university because they have few alternatives. With the downsizing of universities nationally and even internationally, the possibilities of working in an academic career, working for a democratic future, or even more generally in a non-corporate sector, have been severely curtailed.

The absence of controls for labor fairness in composition teaching discredits claims that freedoms trickle from university capital to university student. Instead what counts as freedom for university managers becomes unfreedom for everyone else, especially labor. Because of the staffing of these classes by parafaculty, the curriculum is often decided and assigned to the teacher by a central department authority, and grading is also often done in committee. Composition teachers are deskilled and expected to perform certain tasks that used to be just a portion of the activities done by the professoriate. In keeping with their reduction in classroom authority, they are also subject to increased surveillance and enjoy fewer protections of academic due process:

> [W]hat remains after the nation State's University of Culture has been replaced by capitalism's University of Excellence is a ghastly institutional shell dominated by the empty rhetoric of the business world, where students are treated as consumers who need to be kept happy by a labor force now subject to endless productivity reviews. (Miller, "Let's" 97–98)

The working reality of composition teachers encourages and enforces submission, consumerist models demanding customer satisfaction, and managerial control. The increasing outsourcing, contracting, and shortchanging of composition labor are not simply a matter of supply and demand in which, as some administrators and high-ranked faculty argue, composition teachers need to justify their existence in terms of the bottom line. Not only is this imperative restricted to adjuncts (i.e., administrators and high-ranked faculty do not need to justify their existence solely in market terms), but it also assumes that educational workers are paid their worth in market terms rather than according to a more-general logic of devaluing the public sphere for the benefit of corporate consolidation and private power.

Composition teaching has colonized English departments and expanded through the university as part of academic capitalism while becoming the target of various conservative critiques of higher education. The large number of students who do not pass composition class or pass without a job-ready literacy has been used by critics to support claims about the unpreparedness of poor and minority students, the deterioration of standards in both higher education and high school, the inefficiencies of tenure, and the so-called dumbing down of students through increased permissiveness, liberal sentimentality, and the move away from canon. Corporate capital is attempting to resolve this contradiction by taking writing out of the university. An initiative to move many writing classes from four-year colleges to two-year junior colleges in New York City's public system includes the expectation that the writing classes will soon come under the direct control of large private corporations, collecting revenue from students as additional tuition and also from English departments themselves, which will be required to use the corporate supplier for outsourcing. This is part of a larger attack on the public sphere where public and educational services are charged to the poor and become products of rising corporate educational interests. The conservative criticism of composition studies and its free-market adherents within participate with governors, state legislators, and corporate "reformers" in sending to public universities, as Stanley Aronowitz has pointed out, "a clear signal . . . that the moment of mass public higher education is over" (*Knowledge Factory* 63). The anti-authoritarian, antifederalist premise that sustains the contradictory combination of certain composition ideologies with conservative criticisms of composition is clearly less "a critique of authority" than a support of neoliberal ideologies that prefer the authority of the market to the authority of a redistributive state maintaining public spaces like education for democratic dialogue and action.

The End of the Political

Why is it that the formulation of an argument causes some students so much trouble and confusion or that some students feel they have nothing to say in a conversation about ideas or in an argumentative essay? I posit here that there is a vital connection between students feeling blocked when it comes to communicating ideas and the configuration of power under neoliberalism, where deliberative power lies in the private, corporate sector rather than in public institutions, so that students do not see the possibilities of making democratic or political interventions. Bauman has argued that the assault on public spaces for public deliberation on public and private concerns has led to the voiding of politics, the inability of citizens to imagine a different world:

> [W]e tend to believe . . . that there is little we can change—singly, severally, or all together—in the way the affairs of the world are running or are being

run; and we believe too that, were we able to make a change, it would be futile, even unreasonable, to put our heads together to think of a different world from the one there is and to flex our muscles to bring it about if we consider it better than the one we are in. (*In Search of Politics* 1)

Certainly, writing assignments about comparative evaluations of different consumer products do not suggest to students that they can challenge the rule of the market. Additionally, when political topics, such as abortion, teenage pregnancy, the death penalty, affirmative action, and drugs, are taken up as isolated capsules where every idea has equal weight in the marketplace of ideas, the dialogue will not show how the possibilities for thinking about these issues are set in place through a system of corporate-managerial ideological production denying freedom of expression to certain points of view that do not conform to market logic.

I proposed to the senior facilitator of a composition curricula I was hired to teach that I would not have a text reader, but instead I would use readings from both the mainstream media and the leftist-progressive press to give students a sense that they did have a stake in politics and that writing could play a role in changing their futures. The facilitator discouraged me, saying that such an approach was difficult to organize, and besides, the mainstream press did not furnish models of writing of the quality the program was seeking for its students. In other words, students were meant to replicate the forms, models, and styles that were preset in standard readers as quality writing.

Nevertheless, I spent the semester talking with students about how *Time* magazine staked its claims to universality in its coverage of the issues, how the articles and the advertising interconnected, how it framed what was important and why, how corporate interests were integrated into the very frames and tones of the stories, how it promoted indifference and a focus on the individual as pure expression in the adventures of consumerism, and how *The Nation* used concrete evidence as opposed to *Time*'s recourses to cuteness and logics of consumption. I pointed out that *Time*'s neglect of evidence provides the basis for the emptying out of political issues. President George W. Bush can thereby declare that the 172 people sentenced to death in Texas during his terms as governor were unquestionably guilty without ever reviewing the cases, or his administration can claim that the terrorist attacks of 11 September 2001 furnished evidence unquestionably requiring a war on Iraq, the evidence suggesting otherwise. Similarly, U.S. Attorney General John Ashcroft can put sixteen hundred people behind bars without showing enough evidence to charge them, instead deploying the rhetorical justification that "we are at war." At the end of the semester, students were asked to write a letter to a politician asking him or her to take a stand on an issue and to furnish the documented reasons that this stand was the appropriate and/or ethical one to take. One student, for example, decided to research the official code of conduct for the New York City police. Unable to find such a document on the Internet or by asking her relatives on the force, she inquired from cops on the beat who told her that they were not certain of the existence of a code of conduct, and if one did exist, they had never seen it. Even more to the point, David Protess, a professor of journalism at Northwestern University, spearheaded student research into Illinois cases in which the defendants had received death sentences. As a result, the students were able to find evidence to overturn eleven death sentences; these results eventually compelled Republican Governor George Ryan to declare a moratorium on executions until a thorough investigation of the state's criminal justice system could be completed, at which point he commuted some of the sentences. Ryan's moratorium, in turn, has inspired and is inspiring other states to do likewise.

Freire makes clear that problem-posing education is not solely about the teacher giving up authority to students, as though the authority of teaching can only be a repressive practice of authoritarianism and so antithetical to freedom of expression. Rather, teaching, for Freire, is about using language to gain a consciousness of the world. In Spanish as in Portuguese, the word *conscientizacao* implies not just knowledge acquisition and a dialectical pursuit of truth but also conscience, or the recognition of ethics. Freire uses this concept to develop an idea of education that is fundamentally directed towards political action and creative transformation. For Freire, says Giroux, "education, in the broad sense, consists of intervening in the world in order to change it" (*Stealing Innocence* 140). Rather than setting up the classroom to replicate and reinforce the logic of corporate-sector service labor and consumerism, teaching needs to lead students to "reject their impotence" by restoring their capacity to act (Freire, *Pedagogy* 59), to improve the world, and to challenge the antidemocratic conquests of corporate neoliberal culture.

Note

I wish to thank Leo Parascondola and Marc Bousquet for their insightful and useful comments on an earlier version of this piece as well as for their information updates. I would also like to thank Mark Goodman for his advice on materials.

21

Knowledge Work, Teaching Work, and Doing Composition

Christopher Ferry

Early in its disciplinary history, composition studies seemed driven by a zeal for institutional reform due, perhaps, to its marginalized position in the academy and to its taking of such figures as Paulo Freire as one of its avatars. Inspired by Freire, Ann E. Berthoff's enjoinders to "look and look again" at our work reminded us that composition was in a state of becoming rather than a state of being. Stephen M. North's valorization of practitioner "lore" and subsequent calls for "teacher research" as a type of knowledge making suggested academic institutions and culture that foregrounded teaching, where teaching informed research rather than the other way round. As the discipline has matured, however, newer voices have emerged to temper the revolutionary zeal. Richard E. Miller, for example, attributes the "perduring appeal" of Freire's rhetoric to the idea that it "covers over our [compositionists'] more primary role as functionaries of the administration's educational arm" ("Arts of Complicity" 18). He wonders further, "If we aren't in the business of liberation, uplift, and movement, however slow, towards a better social world, what is it we're doing in our classrooms" ("Arts of Complicity" 12)? I understand the value of such revisionism, especially in light of the argument I am about to make. I want to caution against a wholesale abandoning of Freirean rhetoric, principles, and pedagogy, however. Freire reminds us of our reformist roots and potential and shows us how, as it gains more disciplinary prestige, composition risks appropriation by preexisting institutional conditions, conditions that recognize and reward certain kinds of work over and above others.

I will begin by trying to account for and perhaps recover Freirean rhetoric and principles in contemporary composition studies, using the idea of the *contact zone* to do so. Next, I will ask if composition gets appropriated at least in part because, during its formation as a discipline, it has resembled too closely previously existing models of academic life. Should compositionists rethink what we do and how we "are" in the academy? Specifically, I will explore the place of work in composition studies so that we may recover the value of being (to paraphrase Joseph Harris) a teaching subject and a teaching discipline. I want to examine how work contributes to what we know about and how we do composition. Further, I want to explore the roles workers play in this knowledge making. Workers in composition inhabit a unique place; they—we—identify our own site-specific problems and must invent solutions on the spot. How do we do this? Does theory inform this work? Or does the work create theory? Finally, I will argue for the equal dignity of knowledge work and teaching work, to show that they are inextricably bound and to tell that each is indispensable to knowing and doing composition.

English Studies, Composition, and the Contact Zone

About seven years ago, the idea of the contact zone seemed poised to become the next big thing in English studies and particularly in composition. Listserve conversations flashed back and forth; entire sessions at the Conference on College Composition and Communication were devoted to exploring the contact zone; no less an eminence than Patricia A. Bizzell proposed reconfiguring English studies according to the parameters of contact zones:

> In short, I am suggesting that we organize English studies not in terms of literary or chronological periods, nor essentialized racial or gender categories, but rather in terms of historically defined contact zones, moments when different groups within . . . society contend for the power to interpret what is going on. (167)

More recently, it seems, interest in contact zones has waned. Maybe the contact zone just wasn't the next big thing we expected or, maybe, after an initial flurry of interest, some surveying and prospecting, so to speak, we moved on, leaving the more intricate work of exploration undone (see North's *The Making of Knowledge in Composition* for more on this tendency in composition research). Still, a return visit to the contact zone may help explain why we in English studies and composition were drawn there in the first place and, as importantly, may yield insights into composition's status within the academic profession. Consider, for example, the situation of the contact zone—that is, how various theorists place it in time and space and how they describe it. For example, Mary Louise Pratt's use of the term *zone,* as well as her definition of contact zones as "social spaces," suggests specific sites bound by time and space (34). Richard Miller adds geological features, "fault lines," along which the zones crack ("Fault Lines" 389–408). What happens when we think of contact zones not as theoretical abstractions but instead as actual places, inhabited by actual people, and what of the arts the inhabitants—students and teachers—use there?

Mary Louise Pratt introduced *contact zone* to English studies' lexicon in 1991. Here is the passage from her *Profession 91* article:

> I propose to say a few more words about this erstwhile unreadable text [Guaman Poma's *New Chronicle and Good Government*], in order to lay out some thoughts about writing and literacy in what I like to call the contact zones. I use this term to refer to social spaces where cultures meet, clash, and grapple with each other, often in contexts of highly asymmetrical relations of power, such as colonialism, slavery, or their aftermaths as they are lived out in many parts of the world today. Eventually I will use the term to reconsider the models of community that many of us rely on in teaching and theorizing and that are under challenge today. (34)

Several years ago, I noted in an e-mail conversation the violence of this language and the potential violence of the space it describes. A few other people disagreed with me, but I pointed out that *clash* and *grapple* do not denote peaceful actions, "highly asymmetrical relations of power" sounds like a phrase copped from Michel Foucault, and few people remember fondly the good old days of slavery and colonialism. What, I wondered further, about Pratt's course "Cultures, Ideas, and Values," in which "[n]o one was excluded, and no one was safe" (39). The response e-mail ran something along the lines of, "Well, if you put it *that* way." But think about it: What a curious and disturbing way to describe our work as teachers of reading and writing and of the primary places, schools and classrooms, where we carry out this work. This phenomenon becomes a bit less mysterious, perhaps, when we realize how many compositionists claim Freire, author of *Pedagogy of the Oppressed*, practically as one of our own. It becomes less mysterious still if we entertain the notion that part of how we in composition studies identify ourselves and our discipline, perhaps a large part, derives from our sense of being besieged.

"Besieged?" you ask. Well, sure. Think of the 1998 article in the *Chronicle of Higher Education*, "Bad Blood in the English Department: The Rift Between Composition and Literature." Allison Schneider notes that, while some influential scholars and professional organizations (namely the MLA) discuss the matter in "fits and starts," the relationship between composition and literature remains "dysfunctional" at best (although I think parasitic might be a more honest term). This story should be familiar to most of us. Worker bees do the heavy-lifting composition work (by which I mean labor) while the (literature scholar) queen bee sits around all day in royal jelly, laying eggs. As I've argued elsewhere ("Theory, Research"), the current professional structure configures teaching work as déclassé. Meanwhile, institutional spoils—prestige, advancement, power, private offices—go to the professional, knowledge-making class. Schneider also interviewed David Bartholomae who avers: "As a professor [of composition], you're not identified with something of great cultural value, like Shakespeare or the English novel, . . . you're identified with the minds and words of eighteen-year-olds" (A15). "But wait a minute," you say. "Hooray for our side! We (and our strife) are featured in the *Chronicle*! We've been noticed!" When you peruse the *Chronicle* each week, before you turn to the job listings, pause over the "New

Scholarly Books" section and check out the composition titles. What? Can't find any? Yes, I say, we are besieged. It's hard to take yourself too seriously as an academic professional when the journalistic voice of academe doesn't consider your scholarship to be, well, scholarship.

Composition, English and the Institution

Perhaps it is easier to understand, then, why so many compositionists choose Freire as an avatar and the contact zone as our realm. What else can we say about the zone, though, especially about how it applies to teaching literacy? I want to call attention to the role played by conquest in determining the shape of contact zones. Pratt explicates Poma's letter as an artifact of the contact zone; yet, Poma composed his letter to King Philip III of Spain after the Spanish conquest of the Inca. Miller also writes about a student essay "Queers, Bums, and Magic" (compare Miller, "Fault Lines") as an artifact; however, the student composed this essay in contexts of constraint: an educational institution and a required composition class. Understanding contact zones within such a domain calls forth significant questions: What are the implications of conquest for shaping the contact zone? Where does conquest place the indigenous culture in relation to the conquerors? Pratt, Miller, and Min-Zhan Lu, for example, locate indigenous cultures on the margins. Freire, however, supplies a more appropriate image in *Cultural Action for Freedom* in which he writes that oppressed and conquered peoples are "buried" beneath or submerged within the oppressor's culture (47–48). Marginalization implies a lateral relationship; the existing culture is pushed to the side, out of the way, as it were, but not necessarily out of sight or earshot. A buried culture, on the other hand, remains out of sight, and its voice must bubble up through the ruin of conquest and structures built by the conquerors.

Here is a useful image that draws on Pratt's own broader scholarly interests. As part of their conquest of the Inca, the Spaniards razed Cuzco, the Inca capitol. They built their basilica on the site of the Temple of the Sun; the altar stood (and stands today) on the spot formerly occupied by the sun shrine. The Spaniards let stand the foundations of the Inca temple; the Inca Temple of the Sun literally supports the Roman Catholic church building. While many descendants of the Inca profess Roman Catholicism today, the ancient Inca religion punctuates their new faith (Freire writes of a Bolivian superstition of hail stones as the souls of unbaptized children, a legend that cultural anthropologists have traced directly to Inca belief [*Education* 104]).

Just so, composition (the course) supports full-time-equivalent–poor literature programs, largely by exploiting the labor of graduate students and part-time faculty. According to Robert Scholes, moreover, there's "little incentive" to improve this situation (despite, I must add, composition's growth as a discipline):

> The more economically you can teach those writing courses—which is to say, the more students you can cram into them and the worse you can pay the

teachers—the better off the literature faculty is. There's a real conflict of interest. (qtd. in Schneider A14)

Is it any wonder that within the institution composition continues to be buried as a service course with all the nasty connotations of that word (see Crowley, *Composition in the University*) but none of the positive ones (see Harris, "Meet the New Boss")? Composition-the-course, upon which compositionists base their claims to disciplinary status, continues to be taught by those with little or no institutional and professional status: adjuncts, part-timers, apprentice graduate assistant teachers (many of whom do not study composition and who may resent teaching it), or (junior) literature faculty who have "done an exam area" in composition and who, while not necessarily disdaining composition, have little incentive to continue their professional development in the area. The irony, though, is this: As it has gained some status and recognition, composition-the-profession has embraced this view of teaching work and of composition-the-course and in so doing has abandoned its reformist roots. Composition certainly enjoys a higher profile (if not increased respectability) within academic institutions. Nevertheless, we still find ourselves clashing and grappling not only with our colleagues in English studies but with a class culture of professional academics that threatens, I think, to claim us. Perhaps we are paying the price of professionalization, as Bruce Horner argues:

> Enacted within the discourse of professionalism, and in response to the ongoing, and longstanding, marginalization of composition teachers and students within English specifically and academic institutions generally, this desire [to make the work of composition legitimate] has come to be expressed in terms of making Composition a professional academic discipline. . . . One result is that theory and practice, scholarship and teaching have been set in opposition. ("Traditions" 375)

Has extant academic culture co-opted composition, sundering it from its roots, pitting our reformist, teaching-work origins against the more glamorous prospect of entrenched knowledge work? Or, in a more sinister turn of events, have we in composition simply chosen to fit in?

Institutional Development and Teaching-Work

Laurence R. Vesey traces the development of higher education in the United States in his *Emergence of the American University*. Before the Civil War, colleges prepared young men for careers in law or the ministry; after the war, however, newly emergent universities, based largely on a model imported from Germany, focused on scientific research. Further, just as colleges gave way to universities, so also did the teaching work and workers of the old institutions give way to a new knowledge-making, research-conducting faculty. Vesey describes this change on the part of the faculty as an "emotional absorption" of the "'spirit of inquiry'":

One had to believe that the unknown was worthier of attention than the known, perhaps even that once an area became a part of the widely agreed upon body of knowledge research in it would lack a certain glamour. More fundamentally, the researcher had to believe that he was making contact with "reality" itself—in other words, that gold as well as dross existed in the universe and that his special training made him capable of knowing the difference. . . . Research thus demanded a close respect for the unique, nugget-like fact—especially when such a fact violated a previous theory. (135–36)

Thus appears what we today know as disciplinary knowledge, "sheltered," as Vesey says, in "specialized departments of knowledge." Moreover, as knowledge making becomes the primary work of university faculty, teaching diminishes drastically in importance: "The most pronounced effect of the increasing emphasis upon specialized research was a tendency among scientifically minded professors to ignore the undergraduate college and to place a low value upon their function as teachers" (Vesey 143–44).

More recently, Jerry Herron describes the divide between knowledge work and teaching work as the difference between "being a professional" and "having a job" (56). University faculty, he argues, have never worked in the received sense of the word: "Fundamental to the discourse of academic professionals is the distinction between real work and our work, between the real world and our world" (47). When academics *do* discuss work, moreover, they/we usually mean writing, our knowledge making:

[T]he distinction between "work" and all the other things that go on in academic institutions might best be summarized as one between scholarship, which is real, and teaching, which is not. When academics talk about work, then, what they refer to invariably is writing, and especially writing intended for publication, either in articles (preferably articles accepted by "refereed" journals) or books (preferably ones published by a "good" publisher, which is to say, one as little "commercial" as possible). (47–48)

In other words, academic professionals (including English professionals), as constituted by current institutional norms, must preserve the class system so as not to reveal the nature of their own work, which is not teaching but instead knowledge making. Work may be what other people do, but a backlash inheres in this position: Academic professionals isolate themselves not just within specialized departments of knowledge but from the world and from their own institutions as sites in need, perhaps, of reform:

By maintaining our . . . "ideological" position as regards the otherness of work and the ironic value of canonical "culture," we remain absent from the site of social transformation and withhold from it whatever critical intelligence we have at our disposal. (Herron 62)

Within this overarching academic class structure, Herron notes the "nonprofessional taint" clinging to composition (55). This situation may help explain why compositionists say so little in professional forums about teaching work, the labor of being with students and for students as Freire would have it, or of reading student papers and thinking of things to write in response. Such topics are "unprofessional," according to Herron, precisely because writing instruction is part of the academic "working class"; moreover, institutional, disciplinary, and professional prestige hinge on keeping composition working class: "The important fact about writing, then, is that it is working class; and the important thing for the other members of the profession is that it should remain so. Otherwise, their own supervisory security might be in jeopardy" (56).

In 1988, Herron gave supervisory roles vis-à-vis composition over to traditional literary professionals; while composition studies was growing, perhaps even burgeoning, it was still firmly ensconced within (buried beneath?) literary studies. Certainly, some fourteen years later, composition has come more into its own (My informal observations at the 2000 and 2001 MLA conventions suggest that graduate students with degrees in rhetoric and composition typically scored double-digit interviews, far more than the three or so my classmates and I celebrated in 1990.) Although these may indeed be halcyon days for composition-the-profession, what about composition-the-job, tied as it is to composition-the-course with which we warrant our professional claims? Within English departments and institutions of higher education, I am convinced, composition continues to be regarded as working class. According to a *Chronicle* report on the use of graduate student and part-time workers, only in English departments at baccalaureate institutions does more than 50 percent of full-time tenure-track faculty teach undergraduate courses. At doctoral institutions, by comparison, only 30.5 percent of undergraduate courses are taught by such faculty (Cox A14). A far bleaker problem, though, is that, within composition studies itself, composition-the-course carries on as labor, distinct from professional work. As Horner argues:

> The discourse of professionalism limits how we think of the work of Composition, defining legitimate work as the acquisition, production, and distribution of print codified knowledge about writing: the production and reception of (scholarly) texts. In this discourse, the work associated with such activities as teaching is deemed "labor," the implementation of the work of professional knowledge. (375)

During 2000's round of MLA interviews for jobs at my institution, with its four-and-four course load, more than one otherwise-eager candidate was heard to wonder when she or he would find time to do her or his "own work," what with all that teaching. Vested institutional interests prevail, it seems, as does the hegemony of the academic professional class. I have to wonder, though, with only so many WPA, writing center director, and WAC coordinator positions to go around, but plenty of composition sections to teach, what do new compositionists expect to do? Indeed, what has composition-the-profession lead them to expect?

Harris has argued that circumstances of professional life directly benefit the English establishment ("Meet the New Boss"). I believe they benefit the emergent composition establishment as well. Tenured (composition) faculty has a steady stream of graduate students to take its courses but does not itself have to teach first-year writing. These "boss compositionists," as James Sledd first dubbed them, in turn model a professional existence—one free of such uncouth practices as teaching first-year writing—that helps keep composition in its place. Although Harris is on the right track, I think, I add this central fact about teaching work: We read student texts, not "great" texts. We do not write groundbreaking analyses or exegeses but rather responses to these modest efforts. This is what disturbs us most, that compositionists might not be, as Kurt Spellmeyer says, "knowledge-workers" ("After Theory" 901), trading in big ideas but instead teamsters, performing the heavy lifting necessary to keep the university going.

Woe is I?

Perhaps the foregoing reads as yet another sob story emanating from "Comp Hell," the territory so vividly described in James Hynes's sidesplitting *The Lecturer's Tale*. I am a tenured associate professor and director of writing at my institution. I am a boss compositionist. I teach lots of first-year writing, every semester. By schooling and by disposition, I am steeped in composition's reformist ethic. I believe that I cannot incite the revolution in composition class and that I am not always in the uplift business. What I can do, though, is recognize and name my complicity—and my profession's complicity—in maintaining an institutional culture that assigns little value, and even less dignity, to teaching work. Institutions will not simply grant us value and dignity—no matter how exactly we duplicate their structures. Instead, we must claim these qualities for ourselves and in so doing reform the institutions. We might begin in our own graduate programs. Instead of replicating themselves in students, boss compositionists should transcend their boss-ness and collaborate with students to create cohorts of tenure-track professionals who understand composition-the-profession as indistinguishable from composition-the-course. Our profession, composition, must not set knowledge work in opposition to teaching work; rather, the work of composition and compositionists must be to oppose the institution in seeking to reform it.

22

Composition, Culture Studies, and Critical Pedagogy in the Managed University

Donald Lazere

I would like to pursue a few issues raised in the roundtable on "Composition, Cultural Studies, and Academic Labor" in the issue of the journal *Workplace: A Journal for Academic Labor*[1] that accompanies this collection (Carter). I am particularly interested in following up on Eileen E. Schell's astute comment:

> I think the critique of Cultural Studies and the critique of particular strains of political pedagogies is related to a perpetual anxiety in composition studies about what pedagogical traditions and knowledge we produce in the field versus the knowledges we import/borrow from other fields: a sort of playing out of "local knowledge" versus "imported knowledge." (Carter)

My own down-and-dirty definition of cultural studies is "critical study of the significant intersections between politics and every realm of culture." How, then, do the teaching of composition and the study of literacy lend themselves to cultural studies and critical pedagogy within the managed university and within what context of disciplinary knowledge? I have addressed this question at length in several articles and in the collection I edited, *American Media and Mass Culture: Left Perspectives* (1987), particularly the section titled "Media, Literacy, and Political Socialization," which draws from the disciplines of developmental psychology, sociolinguistics and political socialization, general semantics, communications, and orality/literacy studies in surveying the destructive cognitive effects of mass politics and culture that literacy instruction needs to counteract. So I will just develop some key points from those works here.

I think lefties get into trouble with colleagues and the public when they fail to define the appropriate time, place, and manner for introducing political issues in college writing instruction, so that they appear to be just replacing such instruction with political indoctrination. To begin with, I believe that the most appropriate such site is in advanced composition courses, in the disciplinary context of instruction in academic discourse, critical thinking, semantics, argumentative rhetoric, the research paper, and evaluation of sources. Of course, many colleagues have integrated politics and critical pedagogy legitimately within the aims of first-year and even basic writing courses; I have not taught much at that level lately, though, and I do know politicizing courses there is a much-harder sell to colleagues and the public than at the advanced level. It is, of course, one of the scandals in the politics of literacy instruction and of English departments that not many colleges have a fully funded and developmentally staged sequence of writing courses spanning two or three years, which would mitigate much of the wrangling over political pedagogy.

I suppose the distinctive, and controversial, aspect of my approach has been the case it makes that more-or-less conventional academic modes and course structures are not only compatible with but can be highly effective for critical pedagogy. A paradox of the managed university is that it has continued to allow for sites of opposition, within the traditions of the liberal arts, despite its overall structure of domination. Thus, there is ample, mainstream, professional warrant for addressing political issues in writing courses. For example, in 1975, the NCTE passed the following:

> Resolved, that the National Council of Teachers of English support the efforts of English and related subjects to train students in a new literacy encompassing not only the decoding of print but the critical reading, listening, viewing, and thinking skills necessary to enable students to cope with the sophisticated persuasion techniques found in political statements, advertising, entertainment, and news. (Dieterich ix)

Likewise, the Rockefeller Foundation's Commission on the Humanities in 1980 emphasized

> the humanities lead beyond "functional" literacy and basic skills to critical judgment and discrimination, enabling citizens to view political issues from an informed perspective. . . . The humanities bring to life the ideal of cultural pluralism by expanding the number of perspectives from which questions of value may be viewed, by enlarging young people's social and historical consciousness, and by activating an imaginative critical spirit. (qtd. in Commission 30)

> The entire secondary school curriculum should emphasize the close relationship between writing and critical thinking. . . . English courses need to emphasize the connections between expression, logic, and the critical use of textual and historical evidence. (qtd. in Commission 44)

A list entitled "Basic Critical Thinking Skills" in the California State Department of Education's Model Curriculum for Grades 8–12 in 1984 included the following abilities:

Recognize bias, emotional factors, propaganda, and semantic slanting. The ability to identify partialities and prejudices in written and graphic materials. Includes the ability to determine credibility of sources (gauge reliability, expertise, and objectivity).

Recognize different value orientations and different ideologies.

These various sources suggest ways in which a critical approach to politics can and should be incorporated into advanced college writing classes, through a rhetorical-semantic framework within which students (and citizens in general) can learn to understand and participate in political controversies, guided but not indoctrinated by teachers or scholars. This framework applies Gerald Graff's notion of "teaching the conflicts" to the analysis of contemporary American political rhetoric. For example, my "Teaching the Political Conflicts: A Rhetorical Schema" outlines units of study in a second-term argumentative and research writing course applying various critical thinking skills to understanding:

1. the semantic ambiguity, complexity, and subjectivity in public usage of political terms like left-wing, right-wing, liberal, conservative, radical, moderate, capitalism, communism, socialism, marxism *and* fascism, social class, and labor *and management*

2. broad and specific ideological differences between the political left and right, along with the wide range of positions *within* both

3. the psychological factors that frequently bias political sources *and ourselves* as readers and writers, teachers and students, such as ethnocentrism, authoritarianism, rationalization, compartmentalization, defense mechanisms, stereotyping, and prejudice

4. sources and modes of propaganda and politically partisan, biased, or deceptive rhetoric in sources and cultural texts (mainly political discourse, mass news, and entertainment media), particularly in the form of special interests, conflicts of interest, and special pleading

5. means of locating and evaluating conflicting sources on political issues and of incorporating comparative critical analysis of them in papers

This pedagogical framework necessitates self-critically problematizing one's own subject position as a teacher, researcher, or writer, in relation to the positions of one's students and of sources they (and we) research and write about. In this way, the teacher-scholar is free to present her own perspective but it is not privileged or forced on students as uncontested, monologic truth—simply as one subjective viewpoint to be understood by students and tested dialogically against opposing ones. The teacher's responsibility in grading students then becomes not whether they have agreed with her views but simply how clear an understanding of the opposing views and arguments at issue they have expressed in discussion and writing.

In my particular coursework and scholarship, the introduction of definitions of *socialism, social class,* and *labor* and *management* as terms in political semantics enables me to present sources and arguments in support of my own partiality to democratic socialism, the working class, and organized labor, while making it clear that this is precisely a partisan viewpoint and assigning students to find the best conservative sources they can attempting to refute these arguments. In this context, it seems to me coy for teachers or scholars to pretend to be neutral analysts of the rhetoric of labor-management conflicts, because we are partisans as laborers in relation to university administrators and trustees as managers. Indeed, I think honesty demands that we inform students about the conflicts we are engaged in concerning collective bargaining, education funding, and working conditions as well as our solidarity with nonacademic campus employees, because these issues impinge directly on the quality of their education. This is all the more true for faculty adjuncts and graduate teaching assistants, whose own condition as exploited employees and increasingly as members of incipient unions is knowledge that students should be made aware of toward their understanding of the politics of education. This is not to say that we should turn the classroom into a soapbox on these issues or that they should exclude broader subject matter but only that these issues and our subject position in them can form a valid part of a broad understanding of the rhetoric of labor, management, and social class.

The pedagogical model I have set forth has evolved strictly from my own years of teaching experience, and I have presented it as just one possible example of a cultural studies–critical pedagogy approach to composition, open to disagreements, revisions, or alternatives. The many recent, excellent community-based service learning and literacy projects at their best have bridged the gap between local, adult cultures and academic discourse, presenting a whole different perspective on developmental issues based on a predominantly eighteen- to twenty-year-old student body. Although I admire these projects greatly, I have not had the chance to participate in them and would welcome suggestions from teachers who have about integrating their approach with mine.

Previous articles developing my teaching-the-political-conflicts approach have, surprisingly, provoked only one instance of criticism from the quarter where it would most be expected, the political right, in a couple of swipes by Lynne Cheney (see my response in "Ground Rules for Polemicists: The Case of Lynne Cheney's Truths"). Far more virulence has come from postmodernist, multiculturalist "progressives" within composition studies, for example, Kurt Spellmeyer in a hostile review in the October 1996 *CCC* of editors Karen Fitts and Alan France's *Left Margins: Cultural Studies and Composition Pedagogy* and in particular my chapter, "Teaching the Conflicts about Wealth and Poverty." Other examples are a subsequent exchange with France and me in the May 1997 *CCC* and an exchange by Aaron Schutz and Anne Ruggles Gere with me in *College English,* January, 1999, about their article "Service Learning and English Studies: Rethinking 'Public' Service." These critics object to my affirmation of politically progressive aspects in academic discourse and to my support of that affirmation in the disciplines of developmental psychology, sociolinguistics and political socialization, general semantics, communications and orality/literacy studies. They and similarly dogmatic champions of pluralism and diversity insist on models of composition restricted to personal writing, local communities and cultures, identity politics, alternate literacies, and "little narratives." They position these models unproductively in opposition to academic discourse, instead of seeking to integrate the two; they also tend to oppose cultural studies, critical pedagogy, or any notion of a developmental sequence of writing instruction toward a more cosmopolitan perspective on the rhetoric of national and international politics and economics, which I submit that all citizens need for self-defense in the age of the global economy and managed university.

In a manner that is often aggressively anti-intellectual, such critics simplistically associate these concerns with outmoded "grand narratives" and all the allegedly oppressive, elitist aspects of academic discourse. Listening to them, one would think professors have gained nothing in all our years of education and scholarship worth conveying to students. In attempting to avoid coercing students into academic discourse and culture, they commit their own form of coercion, as they patronizingly deny students access to the cosmopolitan discourse and culture they themselves take for granted.

Thus, Spellmeyer scoffed at my account of many of the agricultural-management majors and other students I taught in the upscale rural setting of California Polytechnic State University, San Luis Obispo, as provincially conservative, authoritarian, and prejudiced, and he ridiculed my project of introducing them to more cosmopolitan political views. He defended such students' "freedom in a composition course to think and write about their lives without coercion and disparagement." The difficult issue here that Spellmeyer and other celebrants of postmodernist pluralism have evaded is the limits of an expressivist, therapeutic concept of composition courses in regard to students whose writing is militantly prejudiced. Local cultures and "little narratives" are as often reactionary as they are progressive, while academic culture is for many students the gateway to progressive political consciousness, as it was for me, coming from a conservative, provincial background.

Of course, I agree with most other compositionists today that we should respect students' diverse home cultures and personal experiences (though not to the point of indulging closed-mindedness and bigotry) and that we should seek every way of enabling them to connect their local cultures and voices with the culture of academic discourse (which, to be sure, is subject to its own ethnocentric prejudices). "Diverseologues" like Spellmeyer, Schutz and Gere, however, have exacerbated polarization between the two rather than seeking ways to overcome it. They believe that they are the true political progressives, but their indiscriminate celebration of diversity is profoundly conservative in reproducing the atomizing effects of capitalist economy, culture, and education. As the power structure of the national and global economy, with mass media and the managed university among its key agents, becomes ever more monolithically concentrated, diverseologues only contribute to the dispersal of progressive social constituencies that need more than ever to be uniting in an opposition movement, of the kind that cultural studies and critical pedagogy aim to advance.

I must note that a successful approach to teaching in the mode I have outlined here largely depends on several favorable conditions for instructors. This kind of pedagogy can best be undertaken by teachers with the security and continuity of employment—in a tenure track and preferably tenured position—that enable them to take experimental risks and to refine their material year after year. Moreover, the whole package of disciplinary background knowledge that I have recommended requires years of study, in graduate school, in faculty research projects, in the amount of leisure time usually available only to full-time university faculties. Of course, the patterns of orthodox graduate education and research in the prestigious realms of the English profession are usually diametrically opposed to this kind of study, with admirable exceptions in some graduate cultural studies or rhetoric programs and schools of education.

All of this is to say that my approach to teaching is pretty forbidding for contingent faculty members, without security of employment, adequate graduate study, research support for teaching advanced composition, or the option to teach the same course, with their own choice of textbooks and syllabus, term after term. Here is yet another way in which educational conventions impede critical political consciousness, in the placement of the burden of teaching composition on those at the bottom of the academic ladder, without sufficient preparation, support, time, and security. It is all reminiscent of a suggestion J. Mitchell Morse made long ago in *The Irrelevant English Teacher* that first-year writing should be taught by the most-senior faculty, drawing on their long years of study, refinement, and pedagogical authority, while graduate seminars should be taught by new Ph.D.s, fresh on the latest developments in their field but relatively inexperienced in teaching. Thus, the English profession inadvertently reproduces the upside-down priorities not only of the managed university but of global and American capitalism.

Note

1. The journal *Workplace: A Journal for Academic Labor* can be found at <http://www.workplace-gsc.com>.

Afterword: Educating for Literacy, Working for Dignity

Gary Rhoades

Although I hardly need say this to teacher-scholars of composition, rhetoric matters, for readers and for writers. In writing my essay, I tried to pay close attention to my own rhetorical choices and devices; however, I began several steps behind, having been trained in the often obtuse language of sociologese. I study unions (faculty, staff, and graduate employees) and the restructuring of the professions in higher education. From this vantage point, I offer not an authoritative review of the state-of-the-art in composition but rather an amicus commentary on the paths that might emerge from the struggles that surround and are embedded in this field of academic work. My aim is to stimulate, enrich, and perhaps frame multiple possibilities for collective action.

The diction and ethos of my title are the consequence of conscious choices. The first phrase, "educating for literacy," intentionally foregrounds the educational objectives of literacy work, which the contributors to the volume make clear are the subject of much dispute. In my view, any collective action of personnel in this area should center in their identity the distinctive educational activity in which they are engaged. Composition personnel are educators. Yet, they are also workers, and the phrase "working for dignity" focuses on the overriding objective of gaining dignity for those sub, para, part-time, contingent, and nonfaculty (the reader can pick the descriptor(s) of choice) educators who teach the overwhelming proportion of composition classes. I offer alternatives to "wanna-bes" intentionally call attention to multiple possibilities, avoiding the urge to define the future in terms of a single narrative. I also aim to undermine the wanna-be aspirations that underlie some paths being pursued by compositionists, whether they involve seeking status within the profession relative to English literature or within institutions increasingly oriented to the revenue generation and production flexibilities of academic capitalism and managed professionals. Finally, I employ the terminology of acting *collectively* to speak to the unionization that many of the volume's contributors see as the answer and to suggest that unionization should be seen as a beginning (and a means to an end), not as an ending (and as an end in itself).

Educating for Literacy

I came to my reading of the debates about literacy as an outsider to composition but an insider to academe. I was and am relatively illiterate, functionally, in composition, at first not understanding terminology such as *abolitionists* and acronyms such as *fyc,* first-year composition. Yet, in another sense, the disputes were not only intellectually recognizable, they were emotionally familiar, resonating with similar(ly) heated, ongoing discussions in the fields of my graduate training (sociology) and professorial work (education). Politically, and aesthetically, I am familiar with this discourse. Perhaps not coincidentally, my fields, like composition, are positioned far from the top of academic and institutional hierarchies. Indeed, therein lies a source for common cause, though constructing any coalition seems highly unlikely in the current context. An internal war of attrition wears us down and distracts us from key focal points of activity within and beyond the academy; the binary foundation of competing camps undercuts our ability to work cooperatively and collectively on key linchpins for change.

Ray Watkins, Christopher Carter, and other contributors clearly set out the competing positions of compositionists on literacy. On the one hand, there are those for whom educating for literacy refers to a functional literacy driven by employer demands external to the academy. This instrumentalist approach to literacy emphasizes objectivist rhetoric taught in utilitarian courses focused on business and professional writing. In the eyes of most contributors to this volume, such a model means that composition educators become "service providers to students and industry . . . construct[ing] the composition classroom as a training ground for real-world writing situations outside the academy" (Carter). On the other hand, there are those for whom educating for literacy refers to a critical literacy driven by academic demands within the academy, within the humanities and social sciences, within English, and within the field of composition. This approach to literacy emphasizes the "rhetoric of the formalist aesthetic" (Watkins), which privileges literary over objectivist language. Such a model makes composition educators "cultural workers who foster critical literacies . . . see[ing] the classroom as itself a very real space where the social tensions that surround and infuse the academy might be discursively negotiated" (Carter). Although it is more than simply an ancillary part of this latter position, feminist compositionists promote critical literacy that questions established (patriarchal) power structures.

Yet, the debate is replete with binaries that on closer inspection break down. Are functional and critical literacy mutually exclusive (and within the functional conception are there differences between traditional views of a literate population and modern views of literate employees)? Can they be mutually supportive? Would it not be desirable to embed critical literacy in efforts to make students more functionally literate? Even the most mundane of formal communications,

the memo, can be strengthened by literary language. Do we not want techni-
cally capable critical rhetoricians whose formalist aesthetic rhetoric is leavened
by some measure of mechanical clarity?

Similarly, how can we classify literacy education as being oriented either to
the utilitarian and instrumental ends of external, private-sector employers (business and professional communication) *or* to the (non-utilitarian and academic
communication?) ends defined internally by academe? Are there not profound
differences in the rhetorical contexts of various businesses and professions external
to academe, as there are profound rhetorical variations within the academy? Are
there no similarities between the rhetorical rules of engagement among mana-
gerial/professional employees in the private sector and those that hold within the
academy? After all, are not our academic hierarchies related to external social
hierarchies, such that we perpetuate them with language codes and hierarchies?
Are not our academic settings also places of professional and bureaucratic employment in which certain functional rhetorical rules prevail? Moreover, what
of public sector employment (in government and not-for-profit settings), which
accounts for a substantial proportion of employment? Does it fit within the (private) employer-versus-academe binary? Does it require a set of rhetorical rules
all its own? Are there not variations by sector and level of public employment?
Does the public-private dichotomy stand firm as differences between the two
sectors are increasingly being blurred and as hybrid forms of organization combining the two emerge?

My intent in suggesting that these binaries collapse under their own weight
is not simply to undermine existing structures of thought and action; rather, I
hope to facilitate the construction of alternatives that enable and involve collective action across and beyond the boundaries of current lines of struggle.

Some of the contributors to this volume seek to move beyond the current
binaries in the composition wars.

Steve Parks's essay offers an example of moving explicitly, systematically, and
aggressively beyond the academy in breaking down dichotomies in composition.
Indeed, the essay is in its own form a nicely interwoven articulation of multiple
literacies and rhetorics. It is at one and the same time a clearly presented, concrete set of proposals for revising four components of a traditional writing program (grounded partly in current practice) and a schematic narrative of a dream,
supported in closing by a poet (Yeats), with the words, "In dreams begin responsibilities." Parks's aim, like so many promoters of critical literacy, is to connect
students and faculty more directly and consistently with a larger struggle for
economic justice. In teaching students and in faculty-development workshops,
then, Parks speaks to the possibilities of literacy attained through collective writing
that creates connections with other laborers and employees.

I would encourage compositionists to go even further; in addition to a modernist, industrial-era focus on labor, educating for literacy should encompass a
postmodern, postindustrial focus on leisure and consumption. Functional literacy

can be not only for managers but for consumers. Intertwining functional and critical literacies can translate into consumer advocacy, learned and effected through various rhetorical forms. One could further broaden the focus to reach beyond labor and consumer advocacy, and back in time, to connect literacy to the formation and effective operation of a citizenry and a democracy. Again, educating for literacy towards these ends would involve intertwining functional and critical literacies. Preparing people for (pro)active citizenship would mean providing them with not only the minimal, mechanical means for reading and writing but also a measure of the formal aesthetic, which is functional in its capacity to be understood by and to mobilize the masses and the government. At the same time, in conceiving of new models of educating for literacy, compositionists should attend to recent developments in the tools of their trade, which promise to impact the form as well as the function of literacy work. I do not believe that new informational and instructional technologies will make paper and pen(cil) obsolete or that face-to-face classrooms and live campuses are a phenomenon of the soon-to-be-past. That would be foolish. However, it would be equally foolish to ignore the way these new instruments of communicating are impacting forms and functions of literacy. One need only watch a teenager instant messaging, consider the thousands of e-mails we compose and read each week, scroll through the official communications that are increasingly on-line, read an on-line journal, or view a Web page to realize that the processes and products of writing are changing, with profound implication for composition educators.

It should not be hard to see how instructional technologies could be used to mechanize the process of educating for literacy. Professionals and administrators who promote the use of instructional technologies decenter the active, discretion-exercising professional, the instructor, with a fascinating rhetorical twist. They have framed the "problem" in education in the following binaries: the (subtext, failed) model of the past is professor centered and passive, involving passive (subtext, ineffective) education through lecturing; the (subtext, innovative) model of the future is learner centered and active, involving interactive (subtext, effective) education through the use of high tech, instructional technology, and software. The mechanical instructor is privileged as active and innovative over the human instructor, who is cast as passive and inflexible. Technology has come to be conflated with innovation, which has come to be conflated with effective instruction.

One example of such conceptions is evident in William H. Thelin and Leann Bertoncini's essay, "When Critical Pedagogy Becomes Bad Teaching: Blunders in Adjunct Review." Although they do not address technology, the application should be clear: The preferred approach to teaching was to follow pre-prepared exercises and assignments that are said to be student-centered and collaborative, although no student has really had input into them. The text that was to be used "was set up in worksheet fashion, complete with . . . fill-in-the-blank–type questions . . . Every single class plan and every last assignment had been constructed for us." All that need to be added to their tale would be assignments that could be graded by machine, and software packages that could "interactively" run students through their exercises.

Robin Truth Goodman, in her essay in this volume, also taps into the significance of the customer-centered view of education. Connecting the process to trends of globalization, corporatization, and neoliberalism, she points to the outcomes of many theories of writing and education:

> The centering and unquestioning approval of student beliefs, even the apparently uncontroversial focus on self-esteem, helps to turn the classroom into a client-based social unit meant to induce unrestricted feelings of pleasure, as though school were like the candy store or the mall.

At the same time, academic institutions are by and large not good at trying to be capitalists, and we should pass up no opportunity to emphasize that point in ways that also emphasize the serious shortcomings of private-sector practices and industries (e.g., the savings and loans). It is also important to pose desirable alternatives.

Working for Dignity: Beyond the Horizons of Wanna-bes

As with the literacy debates, the composition work debates seem dichotomous but are interrelated. On the one hand, many compositionists are seeking legitimacy within the academic profession and within the field of English in particular. On the other hand, many others are seeking legitimacy within an increasingly corporatized university. In my view, either road leads ultimately to the frustration that awaits all wanna-bes—neither camp is ever likely to be fully accepted by the groups from which they seek acceptance.

I say this not with the disdain of an elitist, or of someone who has made it but with the empathy of a fellow traveler. I am familiar with this terrain, for the field in which I work is riven by similar sets of competing aims. I have played in this academic game and have employed what Amanda Godley and Jennifer Seibel Trainor call a "critical pragmatist" approach, using the language of the corporate university to more favorably position the units in which I work. In the short term, and in particular situations, such a strategy can be effective; indeed, I would argue for the desirability of polyvalent possibilities and multiple strategies that are sensitive to different contextual realities, which vary by time and place (by field and institution and by institutional type). I would also argue that we need to move beyond the horizons of wanna-bes, for I have witnessed first hand, and in the scholarship I have pursued, the outcomes of internecine battles about what road to take. My conclusion is that these internal disputes are the wrong battles to be fighting with the wrong opponents at the wrong time. They distract us from the key issues.

Consider the ongoing debate prompted by Sharon Crowley's argument that fyc should be abolished. The tenor and content of much of the abolitionist discussion speaks to an internal focus of a particular, and particularly narrow, expression of academic life. For all the attention this debate has attracted and all the emotion it has generated, I believe that fyc is not the central issue. Indeed, I would go further. The rhetoric of "abolish (or publish) or perish"[1] requires a reality check. First, apart from the issue of whether assistant professors actually perish, academically or otherwise, if they do not gain tenure (many move on to academic careers in other institutions), most faculty in the U.S. do not work in a publish-or-perish setting; we read so much about the matter because it is the minority who live with the pressure to publish who do most of the writing about this and other issues. I appreciated and enjoyed Bill Hendricks's comments in this volume:

> Equally strange, to me, is Crowley's contention that faculty who spend too much time teaching comp reduce their chances of getting tenure. In my department at California University, for instance, where there are currently seventeen tenure-track, four full-time adjunct, and one part-time adjunct faculty, all twenty-two English Department members regularly teach our required composition courses, and sixteen of the seventeen tenure-track faculty are tenured. To move beyond my own workplace, what of all of the full-time permanent faculty that, Crowley acknowledges, are teaching composition at community colleges, liberal arts colleges, and nonresearch universities?

The abolish-comp-or-never-gain-professional-recognition rhetoric does not even resonate within the academy at large, let alone in the broader society. It is a false universal and a faulty foundation upon which to build a strong position for compositionists.

A second reality check is that politically, efforts to increase professional status by jettisoning a field's least prestigious parts have a long history of failure. I work in a field (education) that has tried, in many research universities, to gain prestige by dropping the burdensome, "low-prestige" work of teacher education. I feel safe in asserting that such Ed schools have not gained substantial status as a result. I am not claiming that fyc is an unimportant issue, but if the hope is to gain professional prestige for compositionists by abolishing fyc, we are headed down the wrong road. William Vaughan's imagery on this point is telling: "English can be remarkably omnivorous in the way it absorbs theories and fields yet bulimic in how it attenuates its own workplace boundaries, expelling here composition, there mentoring and administration."

It is not only lower-status fields that find themselves in increasingly problematic positions, as Richard Ohmann so nicely points out in his essay: "Are there any strong professions these days, as medicine and law were strong a few decades ago? . . . I . . . believe there is a good case that the forces of agile capitalism are undermining most or all of the professions." Thus, as I noted in *Managed Professionals,* the commodification of medical services by HMOs, with its impact on physicians' professional autonomy, suggests one possible future for academe. In this context, does it make sense to strive for what we believe the strong professions or fields in academe have? As much as I believe in the value of Ray Watkins's service expertise, is it really the road to respect? I think not. Seeking status within the academy is a fool's paradise. It is even more of a fool's paradise to seek status within a low-status field (English) that has declining status within the academy. (I should know about low status, positioned as I am in an Ed school.)

The status anxiety that surrounds such efforts to gain professional legitimacy tend to isolate and individualize faculty, undermining our ability to think internally about forming common cause with various other fields and subfields that address similar issues of educating for literacy and working for dignity. Rather than jettisoning less-prestigious parts of English or composition, faculty in these fields should be forming coalitions with faculty in other academic fields to work collectively within the institution.

The professional-respect project also distracts us from key issues outside the academy that affect our lives within the academy. It insulates us, focusing us on enhancing our prestige within an occupation and institutional setting that are already privileged in relative terms. There are substantial literacy problems and workplace issues outside of the academy to which we must become connected in our educational work. Why? Because the collective political position of white-collar employees in the not-for-profit sector is contingent on broad public support for the work they do, whether they are nurses, schoolteachers, social workers, or academics. In our conceptions of educating for literacy and working for dignity, we need to connect with public schools, families, and communities beyond the academy. We must foreground our educational role not to enhance our professional prestige internally but to clarify for publics externally the role that we play in enhancing public and private lives. From such a standpoint, it would be unwise to abandon a commitment to teaching "basic" literacy (for that is what abolishing fyc sounds like); instead, we would foreground the ways that compositionists are working to enhance the multiple literacies that are central to our society, rhetorically expanding social understandings of literacy. There lies a foundation for politically strengthening our goal of working for dignity, of negotiating better conditions of employment.

Contributors to this volume identify a second strategy of compositionists working for dignity. Although it can be cast as an alternative to the professional-status project, it is actually related to it; and although it can be characterized as one approach, it actually encompasses distinctive political positions. The project seeks legitimacy in employing institutions that are increasingly capitalist in nature. For some, this objective is pursued on the basis of a genuine (conservative) commitment to managerial goals of providing basic literacy services. For others, so-called critical pragmatists, the objective may be pursued as a realistic, reformist approach to improving composition's state and status. As in many political struggles, those on the left (many of this volume's contributors) are more disdainful of "(neo-)liberals" than they are of the managerialists, invoking their own capitalist rhetoric in critiquing "boss compositionists." Either wanna-be position (of capitalist or worker) is as self-destructive as that of the professional wannabee.

And I use the term *wanna-be* intentionally, to undermine these positions, as well as, more importantly, to undermine the notion that universities and colleges have been fully corporatized and are successful capitalist enterprises.

Crowley nicely articulates the pragmatist position:

> Money, or better, profit, is now the bottom line. When was the last time you argued for any change at your campus(es) by claiming that your proposal would improve the quality of instruction? Those arguments just don't work any more—they're not even heard. (Carter)

Similarly, Michael Murphy suggests that compositionists need to "find ways to negotiate the university as a corporation, as a profit center . . . by making [improvements in instruction] sound like smart business moves" (Baker). The two wanna-be paths of good professional and economically strategic professional are linked.

Whatever the extent to which Crowley is right about arguments based on quality or other noneconomic criteria currently not being heard in the academy, I believe that we cannot stop voicing them. More than that, we cannot cede the (public) ground of the academy to capitalist rhetoric and logic. We need to continue to conserve and expand the spaces in which arguments grounded in public interest and professional expertise are articulated and advanced. If we strategically adopt the rhetoric and logic of academic capitalists and eschew other rhetorics and logics from our repertoires, then the battle has been lost, with little resistance. We also need to challenge the rhetoric about corporatization in academe, not by repeating it in the aggrieved tones of those who have been overrun by the infidels but by questioning and hoisting it by its own petard, with our own ironic and probing forms of discourse. Contrary to what Crowley and so many others are now saying, colleges and universities are neither entirely about nor particularly good at profit, though some folks and forces may wish they were. Most entrepreneurial efforts run either in the red or on the backs of publicly subsidized monies.

In a thoughtful, nuanced treatment of strategies in composition, Godley and Trainor clarify the problems of embracing the market's logic and language. Acknowledging that it seems to make sense for compositionists to improve working conditions by making "more-savvy arguments based on student need and market demand," thereby "position[ing] ourselves discursively in ways that resonate with its [the corporate university's] logic," they also caution that working within this logic can be problematic and self-defeating. The institutional cases they walk us through reveal a corporate logic that positions labor as ancillary to student need. In short, the pragmatists' strategy can backfire, decentering and leading to the deskilling and/or outsourcing of instructional work, to the detriment of student need.

The pitfalls of taking on the corporatist rhetoric suggest the need for, in Michael Murphy's words, "guerilla rhetoricians." We need to move beyond not only dichotomies and wanna-bes but also beyond the repeated invocations against corporatization of the academy, even when those are part of declarations against such privatization. In repeatedly naming the extent of the problem, we inflate and enhance its reality and power beyond its current proportions, overlooking the problems, contradictions, false starts, false economies, bad investments, and failures that have accompanied corporatization. We need instead to not only deconstruct and disrupt but also to sabotage and derail the course of academic capitalism, and the career tracks of its wanna-bes, whether they be would-be CEOs or petite-bourgeois professors.

Yet, the guerilla metaphor is inadequate to the task. For what is also required is more open and constructive alternatives to current images and certainties about higher education's, and composition's, future. That leads me to the issue of collective action.

Collectively Acting as a Beginning, Not an End

Many of the contributors to this volume pose unionization as an alternative and an answer to the current challenges faced by compositionists in particular and by faculty in general. A much-smaller number speak to the challenges of unionizing and to charting and undertaking particular future courses of action collectively. Unionization can seem to be the happy resolution and ending, overlooking the challenges surrounding organizing, bargaining, and grievance. I do not want to substitute Thomas Hardy for Jane Austen and say that efforts to organize the academy are as doomed as Jude's efforts to enter Christminster, undermined by the social structures of the day, but the move to organize collectively is the contested beginning of an exploration, and a means to an end, not an ending, or an end in itself.

To reach the full potential of academic unionism, compositionists must first work with other faculty across boundaries of discipline, full or part-time status, and institutional type. That means, as Hendricks says, getting over a sense of being "specially victimized": "I think that advancing labor justice for composition teachers will probably require letting go of some of our *professional* grievances as composition teachers." Thus, although Eric Marshall asserts, "More perhaps than any other academic discipline, composition remains a primary site of managerial opportunism and labor exploitation," he, like Hendricks, also sees the need to get beyond internal divisions:

> At the end of the day, we are one faculty. . . . Unions must organize and mobilize faculty and staff, full- and part-time, to begin to change public attitudes towards higher education, convincing people, for instance, of the fundamental need to subsidize public higher education.

I think it is no coincidence that such views are articulated by two authors with direct experience of collective bargaining.

The internal professional boundaries and divisions that we construct and defend can be major obstacles to collective action. We can redraw these chalklines because unlike professionals in the private sector, some of the tools of the academic workplace are ours—the language, rhetoric, and reason of higher education. I understand the import of the material and of power (see *Managed Professionals*). It is not just a war of words; but words help frame and mobilize and garner external support. Words can help undermine the corporate push in higher education, and they can be a part of the struggle to promote alternatives, a rhetoric of possibilities.

In mobilizing collectively, and gaining public support, it is important not to utilize one-way analogies or to pursue one- or two-dimensional unionization. Both strategies can feed into as much as challenge corporatization. In regard to the first point, Eileen E. Schell and Jamie Owen Daniel point out that we must not lay claim to the status of proletarianized workers, comparing adjuncts to migrants. These one-way analogies (few migrant workers refer to themselves as adjunct teachers) will not serve us well externally, nor do they position us well internally.

We need a rhetoric that undermines, not by simply labeling the phenomena of corporatization but by rhetorically undercutting corporate legitimacy through highlighting its material shortcomings and failures. In a neoliberal, hypercapitalist society, privatization or corporatization is seen as unproblematic. Using such language does little to question the substantive success of the phenomenon, and it does not call up short the academic managers who would like to be like captains of industry. Our rhetoric must point out the inadequacy of these academic would-be capitalists, these capitalist wanna-bes, these for the most part sandbox capitalists, these low-grade or snake (oil) capitalists, these status-seeking capitalists, these guaranteed-income managerial capitalists who take no risks, these socialists—for themselves parading in capitalist attire. I could go on, with pleasure, but the above captures the basic sentiment. To get beyond the corporate university, one has to rhetorically emphasize not only the aspirations of academic capitalists but also the extent to which the aspirations have fallen significantly short of realization. The more we seek to become like capitalist enterprises, the more we move away from our strengths and expose our endemic weaknesses, becoming a hybrid form combining the worst attributes of its dual sources. As Katherine V. Will shows, this is neither good business nor good education.

Yet, we also need a rhetoric of possibilities that builds and offers up feasible and attractive alternatives. In Schell's words, those need to be "rhetorics that enable coalition building," "rhetorics of common cause, not . . . of entitlement." She cites my work along these lines, in which calling for a post-modern approach to agency and action and infusing the private sphere with public forms of economic, political, and normative control. But what exactly does this all mean in practice in regard to unions?

Without seeking to offer one clear vision, let me try to clarify a more postmodern combination of multiple identities and paths of work and struggle for those who are educating in literacy. First, I would echo Hendricks about collective action: "Organized labor includes more than unions." For those involved in educating for literacy that can mean forming common cause with other educators, who may or may not be unionized, in foregrounding educational issues and matters from the perspective of professionals in education. Whether or not one is in a bargaining unit, there are various significant issues and decisions surrounding the organization and delivery of education over which managers are laying greater claim, in the name of short-term production "efficiencies," at the expense of clients and professionals. Academics need to reassert and extend their involvement in regard to the scope and configuration of curricula in the colleges and universities in which they work, not simply as specialists and advocates of particular fields but as educators with a central role in defining curricula. Similarly, academics need to increasingly take on and advance positions in regard to choices about the delivery of education, whether that means negotiating class size or devoting greater attention to the educational considerations surrounding the selection and use of various instructional technologies. The more that the above sorts of decisions move beyond the purview of academics, the less voice and choice faculty will have in classrooms and the less that classrooms will have to do with educating for any field of study or expertise.

In the context of faculty unions, such matters are related to what is increasingly seen as central to the future of white-collar unions in the public sector, a focus on matters of quality and accountability. Thus, advocates of so-called new unionism encourage greater attention to quality in the performance and evaluation of professionals. I see this as ceding too much to managers, as if professional issues are separate from managerial ones; they are not. My suggestions go beyond an individualistic conception of new unionism, focusing on higher-level organizational decisions about education that affect quality and should be addressed by faculty as collectives.

Whatever their professional purview, in the end, academics work in organizations that are managed by others. In colleges and universities, as in other organizations, employees' basic conditions of work are substantially worsening, and employers are systematically gaining greater flexibility in personnel and organizational decisions. Academics must recognize that they are employees and on this basis align with others within and beyond the academy. Such alignment should foreground shared bread-and-butter issues around which all employees can unite. For example, an overriding issue for graduate employees who are unionizing or unionized is the provision of basic health-care insurance. Faculty already have insurance but have also already witnessed substantial erosion of such benefits in ways that have reduced their overall salary and benefits. Here is a coalition-building issue that can link educators to larger communities and networks—for all employees are working to maintain dignity in a so-called postmodern world in which there is an increasing emphasis on consumption, not production, and thus on consumers, not producers or employees. The growth sector of the workforce is service providers, and we are providers of educational services. There is potential, then, for academics to work collectively and rhetorically to impress upon policy makers that most of us are not only consumers but also employees and that there is a link between improving basic working conditions and improving the quality of service provided.

In the context of faculty unions, the role of faculty as employees should clarify the continued significance of aggressively pursuing a so-called old unionism. Such a strategy involves ongoing consideration of basic bread-and-butter issues such as salaries and perquisites, as well as basic protections to ensure due process and job security. It reminds us that the contest, in Hendricks's words, is not between "composition teachers on one side, hierarchy and hierarchs on the other" but rather is between, as it has long been, capital and labor. In this context, it should be clear that employers seek to make all work analogous to that most-flexible and postmodern form of labor, the part-time employee. Thus, rather than blaming tenured faculty for hierarchy and arguing that tenure should be abolished, we should expand job security and economic justice provisions to all employees so that they, too, effectively enjoy the benefits of tenure.

To those who argue that such a self-interested stance is not in the interests of consumers or the general public, we must rhetorically ask, why not, in a society that now seems to privilege the self-interested stance of the private sector over the public. More than that, we should recognize, that in a service-sector domi-nated economy, there is a growing frustration with the quality of service provided in the private sector (if you are calling about . . . , push "1"). That general un-happiness is particularly evident in an arena once characterized by professional control that has come to be increasingly corporatized—health services. Were any consumers happy to learn that physicians' pay in HMOs is linked to incentives such as the number of patients they see, the amount of drugs they prescribe, and the limits they impose on hospital stays? Is there any real support for organizing the work of medical professionals according to the private-sector practice of payment by commission?

What am I getting at? There may be, in various realms, as much support for "publicizing" employment practices (not just in the sense of making them pub-lic but in making more like public-sector practices) as there is for privatizing them. We must increasingly engage in creative, constructive rhetorical efforts that high-light the value of public-sector practices (e.g., there is really no analogous word to *privatizing,* so perhaps we need to create a new version of *publicizing* in which the *c* is pronounced as a *k*).

If we associate short-term, narrow, economic efficiency with privatization, what sorts of benefits might we associate and rhetorically emphasize with publicization? One value is that various practices are open to review and consideration by the public, in the interests of the consumers, the employees, and/or society at large. Thus, for instance, we already have a language and rhetoric of (and a legal struc-ture for supporting) whistle-blowing that clearly questions the value of business and bureaucratic hierarchies in favor of publicizing knowledge and decision mak-ing. We need to not only actively defend such structures within the academy, with the attendant value of academic freedom, but also to emphasize the need to export such public-sector values into private-sector settings. Should engineers in manufacturing concerns be fired for blowing the whistle on unsafe design shortcuts and bypasses? Should physicians in HMOs be disciplined for calling into question and challenging management (in companies and hospitals) about the provision of care? Reemphasizing the importance of (re)publicizing professional employment (in the public and private sectors) is to stress the significance of professionally defined rules of practice relative to practices encouraged by revenue-seeking organizations when it comes to consumer and public benefit.

Another value that we associate with public-sector entities is democratization through the advancement and protection of civil rights. Democracy is contingent on the space to publicly explore and debate and pursue a wide range of ideas and issues. Colleges and universities constitute a central institutional site for such activity. For that reason they must be expanded, not downsized or right-sized or prioritized in a close to the market, supply-side sense. They are fundamentally political and cultural/ideological institutions, as the conservative right rightly understands, not only economic ones. Our rhetoric should foreground that.

Moreover, for there to be increased democratization, colleges and universities must pursue a project of increasing access to higher education, which requires rebuilding and reemphasizing the broad public commitment to expanding educational opportunity in higher education. As Aronowitz emphasizes:

> In the United States, after a generation during which the state afforded nearly every high school graduate the opportunity to attend college, the higher learning is once more treated as a privilege. At the same time, educators and public officials remind us that it is no longer merely a stepping stone to the middle class but has become a necessity in our knowledge-based economy. If this is so, a fundamental political question remains: How can we generalize tuition-free higher education and make it a major priority of public expenditures. (*Knowledge Factory* 170–71)

What has all this to do with compositionists? In my view, a lot. The above issues are of central significance for composition educators, and those who are educating for literacy and working for dignity have particularly significant roles to play in efforts such as those suggested above. Compositionists are involved in work that is central to the basic functions of a democratic, capitalist society and are in a position in their daily work as individual professionals, as well as in their collective activity as organized employees, to engage in various forms of advocacy to publicize and democratize organizations, social relations, and education. Herein lies a third-dimensional unionism, focused not only on new unionism issues of professional purview and quality or on old-unionism, basic bread-and-butter as well as job-security issues but also on matters of the broader public interest. I think what is called for in higher education is a public-professional, public-interest–oriented unionism. It will be a challenge to organize academics accordingly. Any such paths of action will be hotly contested, within the profession and the union as well as outside them. The multiple possibilities, and priorities among them, are only beginning to be defined. I believe that those involved in composition education, from graduate employees to contingent faculty, to tenure-track faculty, can play a lead role rhetorically and materially in shaping future forms of professional work, union activity, and higher education provision.

Note

1. The phrase "abolish or perish" is a reference to the Tony Baker roundtable with Sharon Crowley.

WORKS CITED

CONTRIBUTORS

INDEX

WORKS CITED

Abram, Michael E. "Graduate Student Assistants and Collective Bargaining: What Model?" *PMLA* 115 (2000): 1188–91.

Alberti, John. "Returning to Class: Creating Opportunities for Multicultural Reform at Majority Second-Tier Schools." *College English* 63 (2001): 561–84.

"Almanac, 2000–2001." *CHE* 47.1 1 Sept. 2000.

American Council of Trustees and Alumni. *Defending Civilization.* 2001. Sept. 2002 <http://www.goacta.org>.

Anson, Chris, and Richard Jewell. "Shadows of the Mountain." Schell and Stock 47–75.

Applebee, Arthur. *Tradition and Reform in the Teaching of English: A History.* Urbana, IL: NCTE, 1974.

Aronowitz, Stanley. *The Knowledge Factory: Dismantling the Corporate University and Creating True Higher Education.* Boston: Beacon, 2000.

———. "The New Corporate University: Higher Education Becomes Higher Training." *Dollars and Sense* (March/April 1998): 32–35.

Atwell, Nancy. *In the Middle: New Understanding about Writing, Reading, and Learning.* Portsmouth, NH: Boynton/Cook, 1998.

Baker, Tony, moderator. "Abolish or Perish? Managed Labor in Composition: A Round-table Discussion with Sharon Crowley." *Workplace: A Journal for Academic Labor* 4.1. June 2001. <http://www.workplace-gsc.com>.

Baringer, Sandra. "Kudos to the A2K Coalition: Over 40,000 Petition Signatures Gathered, and a Nationwide A2K II on the Horizon." *California Part-Time Faculty Association Pro-News* 3.1 (2000): 1+.

Barrow, Clyde. "The New Economy and Restructuring of Higher Education." *Thought and Action* (Spring 1996): 37–52.

———. *Universities and the Capitalist State: Corporate Liberalism and the Reconstruction of American Higher Education, 1894–1928.* Madison: U of Wisconsin P, 1990.

Bartholomae, David. "Composition, 1900–2000." *PMLA* 115.7 (2000): 1950–54.

Baudrillard, Jean. *The Consumer Society: Myths and Structures.* London: Sage, 1998.

Bauman, Zygmunt. *Globalization: The Human Consequences.* New York: Columbia UP, 1998.

———. *In Search of Politics.* Stanford: Stanford UP, 1999.

Berlin, James A. "Rhetoric and Ideology in the Writing Class." *College English* 50.5 (1988): 477–94.

———. *Rhetoric and Reality: Writing Instruction in American Colleges, 1900–1985.* Carbondale: Southern Illinois UP, 1987.

————. *Rhetorics, Poetics and Cultures: Refiguring College English Studies.* Urbana, IL: NCTE, 1996.

————. *Writing Instruction in Nineteenth-Century American Colleges.* Carbondale: Southern Illinois UP, 1984.

Berthoff, Ann E. *The Making of Meaning.* Portsmouth, NH: Boynton, 1981.

Bérubé, Michael. *The Employment of English: Theory, Jobs, and the Future of Literary Studies.* New York: New York UP, 1998.

————. *Public Access: Literary Theory and American Cultural Politics.* London: Verso, 1994.

Bizzell, Patricia A. "Opinion: 'Contact Zones' and English Studies." *College English* 56 (1994): 163–69.

Bizzell, Patricia A., and Bruce Herzberg, eds. *Negotiating Difference: Cultural Case Studies for Composition.* Boston: Bedford, 1996.

Boston Coalition on Contingent Academic Labor. "Adjuncts Unite! Newsletter." Flier. Coalition on Contingent Academic Labor conference, San Jose, CA, 12 Jan. 2001. 2 pp.

————. "A Ten-Point Program." Campus Equity Week Resource Room. 12 Mar. 2001 <http://www.cewaction.org/resources/cocal10.html>.

Bourdieu, Pierre. *Distinction, A Social Critique of the Judgment of Taste.* Cambridge, MA: Harvard UP, 1984.

————. "The Forms of Capital." *Handbook of Theory and Research for the Sociology of Education.* New York: Greenwood, 1986. 241–58.

Bousquet, Marc. "The Waste Product of Graduate Education: Toward a Dictatorship of the Flexible." *Social Text* 70 (Spring 2002): 81–104.

Bové, Paul. *In the Wake of Theory.* Hanover, NH: Wesleyan UP, 1992.

————. *Intellectuals in Power: A Genealogy of Critical Humanism.* New York: Columbia UP, 1986.

Brandt, Deborah. "Sponsors of Literacy." *CCC* 49 (1998): 165–85.

Brantlinger, Patrick. *Crusoe's Footprints: Cultural Studies in Britain and America.* New York: Routledge, 1990.

Brasket, Deborah. "Welcome to CPFA PRO-NEWS!" *California Part-time Faculty Association Pro-News* 3.1 (2000): 1.

Brereton, John C., ed. *The Origins of Composition Studies in the American College: 1875–1925: A Documentary History.* Pittsburgh: U of Pittsburgh P, 1995.

Brodsky, David. "Democratic vs. Corporate Governance." *Workplace: A Journal for Academic Labor* 4.2. 2002. <http://www.louisville.edu/journal/workplace/brodsky.html>.

Brown, Johanna Atwood. "The Peer Who Isn't A Peer: Authority and the Graduate Student Administrator." George 120–126.

Bullock, Richard, and John Trimbur, eds. *The Politics of Writing Instruction: Postsecondary.* Portsmouth, NH: Boynton/Cook, 1991.

Bush, George H. W. "Message to the Congress Transmitting Proposed Legislation on Education Excellence." 5 Apr. 1989. 16 Apr. 2003 <http://bushlibrary.tamu.edu/papers/1989/89040501.html>.

California. State Board of Education. *Model Curriculum Standards, Grades Eight Through Twelve.* Sacramento: State of California, 1984.

Campbell, John. *Dry Rot in the Ivory Tower.* Lanham, MD: UP of America, 2000.

Carlin, James F. "An Address to the Greater Boston Chamber of Commerce, Nov. 4, 1997." *MTA Today* 28 Nov. 1997: 9.

Carroll, Jill. "How to Be One of the Gang When You're Not." (column). *CHE* 18 Jan. 2002. 18 Jan. 2002 <http://chronicle.com/jobs/2002/01/2002011801c.htm>.

Carter, Christopher, moderator. "A Roundtable with Cary Nelson: Composition, Cultural Studies, and Academic Labor." *Workplace: A Journal for Academic Labor* 4.1. 2001. <http://www.workplace-gsc.com>.

"Casual Nation." A Report by the Coalition of Graduate Student Employee Unions. December 2000. Coalition of Graduate Student Employee Unions. Jan. 2001 <http://www.cgeu.org>.

CCCC Committee on Part-Time/Adjunct Issues. "Report on the Coalition on the Academic Workforce/CCCC Survey of Faculty in Freestanding Writing Programs for Fall 1999." *CCC* 53 (2001): 336–48.

CCCC Executive Committee. "Statement of Principles and Standards for the Postsecondary Teaching of Writing." *CCC* 40 (1989): 329–36.

Cohen, David. "The Worldwide Rise of Private Colleges." *CHE* 9 March 2001: A47–49.

Commission on the Humanities. *The Humanities in American Life: Report of the Commission on the Humanities.* Berkeley: U of California P, 1980.

Connors, Robert J. *Composition-Rhetoric: Backgrounds, Theory, and Pedagogy.* Pittsburgh: U of Pittsburgh P, 1997.

Council of Writing Program Administrators. "Evaluating the Intellectual Work of Writing Administration." 28 July 2002. 14 Mar. 2003 <http://www.cas.ilstu.edu/English/Hesse/intellec.htm>.

Cox, Ana Marie. "Study Shows Colleges' Dependence on Their Part-Time Instructors." *CHE* 1 Dec. 2000: A12–A14.

Crowley, Sharon. *Composition in the University: Historical and Polemical Essays.* Pittsburgh: U of Pittsburgh P, 1998.

———. *The Methodical Memory: Invention in Current-Traditional Rhetoric.* Carbondale: Southern Illinois UP, 1990.

———. "A Personal Essay on Freshman English." *Pre/Text* 12 (1991): 156–76.

"CUNY Adjuncts Unite! Now Is the Time to Testify at a Public Hearing on Adjunct Issues." E-mail flier. 1 Feb. 2001.

Cushman, Ellen. "The Rhetorician as an Agent of Social Change." *CCC* 47 (1996): 7–29.

Daniel, Jamie Owen. "Making Better Connections: Some Thoughts on Rhetoric and Solidarity as We Struggle for Academic Unionization." *Workplace: A Journal for Academic Labor* 3.1. May 2000. <http//www.louisville.edu/journal/workplace/issue5/owendaniel.htm>.

Daniell, Beth. "Narratives of Literacy: Connecting Composition to Culture." *CCC* 50 (1999): 393–410.

Daniels, Rich. "Last Tuesday in Seattle." *Workplace: A Journal for Academic Labor* 3.1. May 2000. <http://www.louisville.edu/journal/workplace/issue5/daniels.htm>.

Department of Labor Women's Bureau. "Flexible Workstyles: A Look at Contingent Labor." Conference summary, Washington, DC. 1988.

DeVoss, Danielle, Dawn Hayden, Cynthia Selfe, and Richard Selfe Jr. "Distance Education: Political and Professional Agency for Adjunct and Part-Time Faculty, and GTAs." Schell and Stock 261–86.

Dewey, John. *The Quest for Certainty: A Study of the Relation of Knowledge and Action.* New York: Minton, 1929.

Dietrich, Daniel. "Resolutions." NCTE Resolution (1975). *Teaching about Doublespeak.* Ed. Dieterich. Urbana: NCTE, 1976. ix–x.

Donnolly, John. "Panel of Scientists to Tackle Terrorism." *Boston Globe* 13 Oct. 2001: A1.

Downing, David B. "Beyond Disciplinary English: Integrating Reading and Writing by Reforming Academic Labor." *Beyond English, Inc.: Curricular Reform in a Global Economy.* Ed. Downing, Claude Mark Hurlbert, and Paula A. Mathieu. Portsmouth, NH: Boynton/Cook, 2002. 23–38.

———. *Changing Classroom Practices: Resources for Literary and Cultural Studies.* Urbana: NCTE, 1994.

———. "The 'Mop-up' Work of Theory Anthologies: Theorizing the Discipline and the Disciplining of Theory." *Symploke* 8.1–2 (2000): 96–116.

Dugger, Ronnie. Introduction. *Campus, Inc.: Corporate Power in the Ivory Tower.* Ed. Geoffrey D. White and Flannery C. Hauck. Amherst: Prometheus, 2000.

Durst, Russel K. *Collision Course.* Urbana: NCTE, 1999.

Ehrenreich, Barbara. *Fear of Falling: The Inner Life of the Middle Class.* New York: Pantheon, 1989.

Elbow, Peter. *Writing Without Teachers.* London: Oxford UP, 1973.

"Faculty Survey." Education Research Institute, Cooperative Institutional Research Program. 2000.

Faigley, Lester A. "A Letter to CCCC Members." March 1996.

Ferry, Christopher. "Theory, Research, Practice, Work." *Under Construction: Working at the Intersections of Composition Theory, Research, and Practice.* Ed. Christine Farris and Chris Anson. Logan: Utah State UP, 1998. 11–18.

"Final Report of the MLA Committee on Professional Employment." *PMLA* 113 (1998): 1154–87.

Fitts, Karen, and Alan France, eds. *Left Margins: Cultural Studies and Composition Pedagogy.* Albany: SUNY P, 1995.

Fitzgerald, Frances. *Fire in the Lake: The Vietnamese and the Americans in Vietnam.* New York: Little, 2002.

Foucault, Michel. *Discipline and Punish.* London: Lane, 1977.

France, Alan, William Lalicker, and Christopher Teutsch. "Response to 'Traditions and Professionalization: Reconceiving Work in Composition.'" *CCC* 52 (2000): 273–75.

Frank, Thomas. "The God that Sucked." *The Baffler* 14 (2002). <http://www.thebaffler.com/gts.html>.

Freire, Paulo. "Cultural Action for Freedom." *The Politics of Education.* Trans. Donaldo Macedo. New York: Bergin, 1985. 43–65.

———. *Education for Critical Consciousness.* New York: Seabury, 1973.

———. *Pedagogy of the Oppressed.* 1970. 20th ed. Trans. Myra Bergman Ramos. New York: Continuum, 1993.

Friedman, Thomas L. *The Lexus and the Olive Tree.* New York: Farrar, 1999.

Gappa, Judith M. *Part-Time Faculty: Higher Education at a Crossroads.* ASHE–ERIC Higher Education Report No. 3. Washington, DC: Assoc. for the Study of Higher Educ., 1984.

Garay, Mary Sue, and Stephen A. Bernhart. *Expanding Literacies.* Albany: SUNY P, 1998.

George, Diana, ed. *Kitchen Cooks, Plate Twirlers and Troubadours: Writing Program Administrators Tell Their Stories.* Portsmouth, NH: Boynton/Cook, 1999.

Gerber, John C. "CCCC Facts." *CCC* 7 (1956): 117–20.

Gillespie, Kim. "Composition and Literature: How Ideology Naturalizes Inequity in English Departments." *The Writing Instructor* (Spring/Summer 1988): 105–14.

Gilyard, Keith. "African American Contributions to Composition Studies." *CCC* 50 (1999): 626–44.

Giroux, Henry A. *Stealing Innocence: Youth, Corporate Power, and the Politics of Culture.* New York: St. Martin's, 2000.

———. "Writing and Critical Thinking in the Social Sciences." *Teaching as Intellectuals: Toward a Critical Pedagogy of Learning.* Westport, CT: Bergin, 1988. 54–73.

Gleason, Barbara. "Evaluating Writing Programs in Real Time." *CCC* 51 (2000): 560–88.

Goggin, Maureen Daly. "The Disciplinary Instability of Composition." *Reconceiving Writing, Rethinking Writing Instruction.* Ed. Joseph Petraglia. Mahwah, NJ: Erlbaum, 1995. 27–48.

———. "The Tangled Roots of Literature, Speech Communication, Linguistics, Rhetoric/Composition, and Creative Writing: A Selected Bibliography on the History of English Studies." *RSQ* 29.3 (1999): 63–89.

Goggin, Maureen Daly, and Susan Kay Miller. "What Is *New* about the 'New Abolitionists': Continuities and Discontinuities in the Great Debate." *Composition Studies* 28.2 (2000): 85–112.

Goodburn, Amy, and Carrie Leverenz. "Feminist Writing Program Administration: Resisting the Bureaucrat Within." *Feminism and Composition Studies: In Other Words.* Ed. Susan C. Jarratt and Lynn Worsham. New York: MLA, 1998. 276–90.

Goodman, John F. "Reflections of a Battle." *Steelabor* 65.5 (November/December 2000): 2–3.

Graff, Gerald. *Beyond the Culture Wars: How Teaching the Conflicts Can Revitalize American Education.* New York: Norton, 1993.

———. "Hidden Intellectualism." *Pedagogy* 1.1 (2001): 21–36.

———. "Is There a Conversation in This Curriculum? Or, Coherence Without Disciplinarity." Raymond 11–28.

———. *Professing Literature: An Institutional History.* Chicago: U of Chicago P, 1987.

Graham, Margaret Baker, Elizabeth Birmingham, and Mark Zachry. "A New Way of Doing Business: Articulating the Economics of Composition." *JAC* 19 (1999): 679–97.

Gramsci, Antonio. *Selections from the Prison Notebooks.* Ed. and trans. Quintin Hoare and Geoffrey Nowell Smith. New York: International, 1971.

Graves, Donald H. *Build a Literate Classroom.* Portsmouth, NH: Heinemann, 1991.

Green, Daniel. "Abandoning the Ruins." *College English* 63 (2001): 273–87.

Griffin, Susan. "Speaking from the Middle." *Forum* A4–A5. *CCC* 50 (1998): A4–5.

Grimm, Nancy Conroy. "'The Way the Rich People Does It': Reflections on Writing Center Administration and the Search for Status." George 14–25.

Guillory, John. *Cultural Capital: The Problem of Literary Canon Formation.* Chicago: U of Chicago P, 1993.

Gullette, Margaret Morganroth. "The American Dream as a Life Narrative." *Profession 2001* (2001): 99–108.

Gunner, Jeanne. "Among the Composition People: The WPA as English Department Agent." *JAC* 18.1 (1998): 153–65.

———. "The Fate of the Wyoming Resolution: A Professional Seduction." *Writing Ourselves into the Story: Unheard Voices from Composition Studies.* Ed. Sheryl Fontaine and Susan Hunter. Carbondale: Southern Illinois UP, 1993. 107–22.

Hagge, John. "The Spurious Paternity of Business Communication." *Journal of Business Communication* 26.1 (1989): 33–35.

Halimi, Serge. "How Neo-Liberalism Took Over the World." 19 Jan. 2002. *Portside* <www.portside@yahoogroups.com>. Rpt. of *Le Monde diplomatique* 19 Jan. 2002.

Harney, Stefano, and Frederick Moten. "Doing Academic Work." Martin 154–80.

Harris, Joseph. "Meet the New Boss, Same as the Old Boss: Class Consciousness in Composition." *CCC* 52 (2000): 43–68.

———. *A Teaching Subject: Composition since 1966.* Upper Saddle River, NJ: Prentice, 1997.

Harvey, David. *The Condition of Postmodernity.* Oxford, UK: Blackwell, 1990.

———. *Spaces of Hope.* Berkeley: U of California P, 2000.

Hawhee, Debra. "Composition History and the *Harbrace College Handbook.*" *CCC* 50 (1999): 504–23.

Helmers, Marguerite. *Writing Students: Composition Testimonials and Representations of Students.* Albany, NY: SUNY P, 1994.

Henry, Jim. *Writing Workplace Cultures: An Archeology of Workplace Cultures.* Carbondale: Southern Illinois UP, 2000.

Herrington, Anne J. "Classrooms as Forums for Reasoning and Writing." *CCC* 36 (1985): 404–13.

———. "Writing in Academic Settings: A Study of the Contexts for Writing in Two College Chemical Engineering Courses." *Research in the Teaching of English* 19 (1985): 331–59.

Herron, Jerry. *Universities and the Myth of Cultural Decline.* Detroit: Wayne State UP, 1988.

Hesse, Doug. "The WPA as Father, Husband, Ex." George 44–55.

Hill, Adams Sherman. "An Answer to the Cry for More English." Brereton 45–56.

Hoare, Quintin, and Geoffrey Nowell Smith, trans. and eds. Preface. *Selections from the Prison Notebooks.* By Antonio Gramsci. New York: International, 1971. ix–xv.

Holbrook, Sue Ellen. "Women's Work: The Feminizing of Composition." *Rhetoric Review* 9 (1991): 201–29.

Horner, Bruce. *Terms of Work for Composition: A Materialist Critique.* Albany: SUNY P, 2000.

———. "Traditions and Professionalization: Reconceiving Work on Composition." *CCC* 51 (2000): 366–98.

Hoskin, Keith W. "Education and the Genesis of Disciplinarity: The Unexpected Reversal." Messer-Davidow, Shumway, and Sylvan 271–304.

Houghton Mifflin. "So Much to Teach, So Little Time." *Adjuncts.com*, Houghton Mifflin's College Division. 5 Aug. 2002 <http://www.college.hmco.com/adjuncts>.

Hurlbert, C. Mark, and Michael Blitz, eds. *Composition and Resistance.* Portsmouth: Boynton/Cook, 1991.

Hutchins, Edwin. *Cognition in the Wild.* Cambridge, MA: MIT P, 1996.

Hynes, James. *The Lecturer's Tale.* New York: Picador, 2001.

Jameson, Fredric. "Culture and Finance Capital." *The Cultural Turn.* London: Verso, 1998.

———. *The Political Unconscious: Narrative as a Socially Symbolic Act.* Ithaca: Cornell UP, 1981.

Jay, Paul. "Beyond Discipline? Globalization and the Future of English." *PMLA* 116.1 (2001): 32–47.

Kavanagh, Patrick. "Creating a More Perfect Union: Cultivating Academic Citizenship in the Face of Higher Education Restructuring." *Forum* 3.1 (1999): A8–13. Insert in *CCC* 51.1 (1999): A8–13.

Kelley, Robin D. G. "The Proletariat Goes to College." *Will Teach For Food: Academic Labor in Crisis.* Ed. Cary Nelson. Minneapolis: U of Minnesota P, 1997. 145–52.

Kernan, Alvin, ed. *What's Happened to the Humanities.* Princeton: Princeton UP, 1997.

Kerr, Clark. *Troubled Times for American Higher Education: The 1990s and Beyond.* Albany: SUNY P, 1994.

———. *The Uses of the University.* 4th ed. Cambridge, MA: Harvard UP, 1995.

Knoblauch, C. H., and Lil Brannon. *Rhetorical Traditions and the Teaching of Writing.* Upper Montclair: Boynton/Cook, 1984.

Kolodny, Annette. *Failing the Future: A Dean Looks at Higher Education in the Twenty-first Century.* Durham, NC: Duke UP, 1998.

Kramer-Dahl, Anneliese. "Reconsidering the Notions of Voice and Experience in Critical Pedagogy." *Feminisms and Pedagogies of Everyday Life.* Ed. Carmen Luke. Albany: SUNY P, 1996. 242–62.

Lafer, Gordon. "Graduate Student Unions Fight the Corporate University." *Dissent* Fall 2001. 5 Aug. 2002 <http://www.dissentmagazine.org/menutest/sitewide/pamphlet.htm>.

LaFranchi, Howard. "Free Market Vs. Free Education." *Christian Science Monitor* 15 Sept. 1999: 6. 15 Mar. 2003 <http://www.csmonitor.com/cgi_bin/wit_article.pl?script/1999/09/15/p651.txt>.

Larson, Magali Sarfarti. *The Rise of Professionalism: A Sociological Analysis.* Berkeley: U of California P, 1977.

Latour, Bruno. *We Have Never Been Modern.* Trans. Catherine Porter. Cambridge, MA: Harvard UP, 1993.

Lauter, Paul. "American Studies, American Politics and the Reinvention of Class." *From Walden Pond to Jurassic Park.* Durham: Duke UP, 2001: 34–63.

———. *Canons and Contexts.* New York: Oxford UP, 1991.

———. "Retrenchment—What the Managers Are Doing." *Radical Teacher* 1 (Dec. 1975): 27–35. Rpt. revised in Lauter, *Canons and Contexts* 175–97.

———. "A Scandalous Misuse of Faculty: 'Adjuncts.'" *Universitas* 2 (Dec. 1978). Rpt. revised in *CHE* 14 May 1979: 72; and in Lauter, *Canons and Contexts* 198–209.

Lazere, Donald. *American Media and Mass Culture: Left Perspectives.* Berkeley: U of California P, 1987.

———. "Ground Rules for Polemicists: The Case of Lynne Cheney's Truths." *College English* 59 (1997): 661–85.

———. "Teaching the Political Conflicts: A Rhetorical Schema." *CCC* 43 (1992): 194–213.

Leatherman, Courtney. "AAUP Reaches Out and Takes Sides." *CHE* 23 Jun. 2000: A16+.

———. "Do Accreditors Look the Other Way When Colleges Rely on Part-timers?" *CHE* 7 Nov. 1997: A12.

———. "NLRB Lets Stand a Decision Allowing Professors at a Private College to Unionize." *CHE* 7 Jul. 2000: A14.

———. "NLRB Rules TAs at Private Universities Have the Right to Unionize." *CHE* 10 Nov. 2000: A14.

———. "Part-Time Faculty Members Try to Organize Nationally." *CHE* 26 Jan. 2001: A12–A13.

———. "Tenured Professors Show Willingness to Walk Out over Use of Lecturers." *CHE* 22 Sept. 2000: A16–17.

———. "Union Organizers Propose Code of University Conduct." *CHE* 1 Dec. 2000: A16.

———. "Use of Non-Tenure-Track Faculty Members is a Long-Term Trend, Study Finds." *CHE* 5 Apr. 1999.

Leitch, Vincent B. *American Literary Criticism from the Thirties to the Eighties.* New York: Columbia UP, 1988.

Leone, Stephen J. "The Reality of Computers at the Community College Level." Paper presented at Forty-Eighth CCCC Convention. Phoenix, Arizona. 14 Mar. 1997.

Levidow, Les. "Marketizing Higher Education: Neoliberal Strategies and Counter-Strategies." *Cultural Logic* 4.1 (2001). <http://eserver.org/clogic/4-1/4-1.html>.

Lewin, Tamar. "Corporate Culture and Big Pay Come to Nonprofit Testing Service." *New York Times* 14 Dec. 2002, natl. ed.: 1+.

———. "Survey Shows 27 Presidents of Colleges Top $500,000." *New York Times* 17 Nov. 2002, natl. ed.: 24.

Lewis, Lionel S. *When Power Corrupts.* New Brunswick, CT: Transaction, 2000.

Lovett, Clara. "The Dumbing Down of College Presidents." *CHE* 5 April 2002: B20.

Lu, Min-Zhan. "Professing Multiculturalism: The Politics of Style in the Contact Zone." *CCC* 45 (1994): 305–21.

Lucas, Christopher J. *American Higher Education: A History.* New York: St. Martin's, 1994.

Macedo, Donaldo, and Lilia I. Bartolomé. *Dancing with Bigotry: Beyond the Politics of Tolerance.* New York: St. Martin's, 1999.

MacFarland, Thomas W. "Changes in Nova Southwestern University's Full-Time and Part-Time Faculty: Fall-Term 1995 to Fall Term 1998." Report of Nova Southeastern University Office of Research and Planning. Oct. 1999.

Macrorie, Ken. *The I-Search Paper: Revised Edition of Searching Writing.* Portsmouth, NH: Heinemann, 1988.

Mailloux, Steven. "Disciplinary Identities: On the Rhetorical Paths Between English and Communication Studies." *RSQ* 30.2 (2000): 5–29.

Maitland, Christine, and Gary Rhoades. "Innovative Approaches to Bargaining." *2000 Almanac of Higher Education.* NEA. 2001. 27–41. <http://www.nea.org/he/healma2k>.

Marcuse, Herbert. *One-Dimensional Man: Studies in the Ideology of Advanced Industrial Society.* 1964. Boston: Beacon, 1991.

Marshall, T. H. "Citizenship and Social Class." *Class, Citizenship, and Social Development: Essays by T. H. Marshall.* Garden City, NY: Doubleday, 1964.

Martin, Randy, ed. *Chalk Lines: The Politics of Work in the Managed University.* Durham, NC: Duke UP, 1998.

———. "Education as National Pedagogy." *Chalk Lines: The Politics of Work in the Managed University.* Ed. Martin. Durham, NC: Duke UP, 1998. 1–29.

Marx, Karl. *Capital: A Critique of Political Economy.* Vol. 1. Trans. Ben Fowkes. Introduction by Ernest Mandel. New York: Penguin, 1996.

McChesney, Robert. Introduction. *Profit over People: Neoliberalism and Global Order.* By Noam Chomsky. New York: Seven Stories, 1999. 7–16.

McKeown, Thomas W. *Powerful Business Writing: Say What You Mean, Get What You Want.* Cincinnati, OH: Writer's Digest, 1992.

McQuade, Donald. Preface. *The Harper American Literature.* 2nd compact ed. New York: Harper, 1996.

Menand, Louis. "The Demise of Disciplinary Authority." Kernan 201–19.

———, ed. *The Future of Academic Freedom.* Chicago: U of Chicago P, 1996.

Messer-Davidow, Ellen, David R. Shumway, and David J. Sylvan, eds. *Knowledges: Historical and Critical Studies in Disciplinarity.* Charlottesville: UP of Virginia, 1993.

Meyer, Russell J., and Sheryl A. Mylan. *Voices and Visions: An Integrated Approach to Reading and Writing.* New York: St. Martin's, 1995.

Micciche, Laura. "More than a Feeling: Disappointment and WPA Work." *College English* 64 (2002): 432–58.

Michael, John. *Anxious Intellects: Academic Professionals, Public Intellectuals, and Enlightenment Values.* Durham, NC: Duke UP, 2000.

Miller, Richard E. "The Arts of Complicity: Pragmatism and the Culture of Schooling." *College English* 61 (1998): 10–28.

———. *As If Learning Mattered: Reforming Higher Education.* Ithaca: Cornell UP, 1998.

———. "Composing English Studies: Toward a Social History of the Discipline." *CCC* 45 (1994): 164–79.

———. "Fault Lines in the Contact Zone." *College English* 56 (1994): 389–408.

———. "'Let's Do the Numbers': Comp Droids and the Prophets of Doom." *Profession* 99 (1999): 96–105.

Miller, Susan. *Textual Carnivals: The Politics of Composition.* Carbondale: Southern Illinois UP, 1991.

Mishel, Lawrence, Jared Bernstein, and John Schmitt. "Measuring Prosperity When Better Isn't Good Enough." *EPI Journal* (Fall 2000): 12 pp. 15 Mar. 2003 <http://www.epinet.org/journal/2000Fall/swa.html>.

"MLA Moves to Encourage the Use of Full-Time Faculty Members." *CHE* 12 Jan. 2001: A12.

"MLA Survey of Staffing in English and Foreign Language Departments, Fall 1999." MLA. New York: MLA, 1999.

Mohanty, Chandra Talpade. "On Race and Voice: Challenges for Liberal Education in the 1990s." *Cultural Critique* 14 (Winter 1990): 179–206.

Morse, J. Mitchell. *The Irrelevant English Teacher.* Philadelphia: Temple UP, 1972.

Moser, Rich. E-mail to Eileen E. Schell. 2 March 2001.

Mountford, Roxanne. "From Labor to Middle Management: Graduate Students in Writing Program Administration." *Rhetoric Review* 21 (2002): 41–53.

Murphy, Michael. "Adjuncts Should Not Just Be Visitors in the Academic Promised Land." *CHE* 29 Mar. 2002. B14–15.

———. "New Faculty for a New University: Toward a Full-Time Teaching-Intensive Faculty Track in Composition." *CCC* 52 (2000): 14–42.

Murray, Donald M. *Learning By Teaching: Selected Articles on Writing and Teaching.* Montclair, NJ: Boynton/Cook, 1982.

Nast, Thomas. "The American Twins." Cartoon. *Harper's Weekly* 7 Feb. 1874: 136.

National Center for Education Statistics. U.S. Dept. of Educ. *1993 National Study of the Post-Secondary Faculty* (NSOPF-93). <http://nces.ed.gov>.

———. *Digest of Education Statistics, 2000.* NCES 2001-034. <http://nces.ed.gov/pubs2001/digest/>.

———. *New Entrants to the Full-Time Faculty of Higher Education Institutions,* NCES 98-252. By Martin J. Finkelstein, Robert Seal, and Jack Schuster. Washington, DC: 1998. <http://nces.ed.gov>.

NCTE Resolution (1975). *Teaching about Doublespeak.* Ed. Daniel Dieterich. Urbana: NCTE, 1976. ix–x.

NEA. "Full-Time Non-Tenure-Track Faculty." *Update* 2.5 (1996). Redaction of NSOPF-93. 1–4.

Nelson, Cary. "Between Crisis and Opportunity: Introducing the Future of the Academic Workplace." *Will Teach for Food: Academic Labor in Crisis.* Ed. Nelson. Minneapolis: U of Minnesota P, 1997. 3–31.

Nelson, Cary, and Stephen Watt. *Academic Keywords: A Devil's Dictionary for Higher Education.* New York: Routledge, 1999.

Newfield, Christopher. "Recapturing Academic Business." Martin 69–102.

North, Stephen M. *The Making of Knowledge in Composition*. Portsmouth, NH: Boynton, 1987.

———. "On the Business of English Studies." *The Relevance of English*. Ed. Robert P. Yagelski and Scott A. Leonard. Urbana, IL: NCTE, 2001.

———. *Refiguring the Ph.D. in English Studies*. Urbana, IL: NCTE, 2000.

Nystrand, Martin, Stuart Greene, and Jeffrey Wiemelt. "Where Did Composition Studies Come From? An Intellectual History." *Written Communication* 10 (1993): 267–333.

O'Grady, Helen. "Trafficking in Freeway Flyers: (Re)Viewing Literacy, Working Conditions, and Quality Instruction." Schell and Stock 132–55.

Ohmann, Richard. *English in America: A Radical View of the Profession*. Hanover, NH: Wesleyan UP, 1976. Rpt. Middletown: Wesleyan UP, 1996.

———. "Historical Reflections on Accountability." *Radical Teacher* 57 (Fall 1999): 2–7.

———. "Thick Citizenship and Textual Relations." *Citizenship Studies* 3.2 (1999): 221–35.

Parascondola, Leo. "NYU Teaching Assistants Win Major Gains." E-mail posting. 4 Feb. 2002. *Workplace: A Journal for Academic Labor.* 5 Aug. 2002 http://www.louisville.edu/journal/workplace/issue5/nyutawin.html>.

Parks, Steve. *Class Politics: The Movement for the Students' Right to Their Own Language*. Urbana, IL: NCTE, 2000.

Payne, William M., ed. *English in American Universities*. Boston: Heath, 1895.

Peirce, Neal. "Facing America's Vast Income Gap." *Baltimore Sun* 6 Sept. 2001, final ed.: 15A. <http://www.sunspot.net/search/bal-archive-1990.htmlstory>.

Pennsylvania. State System of Higher Education and the Association of Pennsylvania State College and University Faculties. *Agreement Between Association of Pennsylvania State College and University Faculties and State System of Higher Education, July 1, 1999 to June 30, 2002*. Harrisburg: Commonwealth of Pennsylvania, November 1999.

Petraglia, Joseph. "Introduction: General Writing Skills Instruction and Its Discontents." *Reconceiving Writing, Rethinking Writing Instruction*. Ed. Petraglia. Mahwah, NJ: Erlbaum, 1995. xi–xvii.

Phillips, Peter. "A Win for Higher Education in California." Press release. Sonoma State University, California Faculty Association. 28 Mar. 2002. 5 Aug. 2002 <http://www.projectcensored.org>.

Pollington, Mary. "A Tale of Two Campuses: The Part-Time English Teacher at Brigham Young University and Utah Valley Community College." Paper presented at CCCC Convention, Cincinnati, Ohio. Mar. 1992.

Porter, James, Patricia A. Sullivan, et al. "Institutional Critique: A Rhetorical Methodology for Change." *CCC* 51 (2000): 610–41.

Pratt, Linda Ray. "Disposable Faculty: Part-Time Exploitation as Management Strategy." *Will Teach for Food: Academic Labor in Crisis*. Ed. Cary Nelson. Minneapolis: U of Minnesota P, 1997. 264–77.

Pratt, Mary Louise. "Arts of the Contact Zone." *Profession 91* (1991): 33–40.

PSC/CUNY FY 2002 Budget Programmatic Priorities for the City University of New York. New York: Professional, 2001.

Raymond, James C. *English as a Discipline, or Is There a Plot in This Play?* Tuscaloosa: U of Alabama P, 1996.

Readings, Bill. *The University in Ruins*. Harvard UP, 1996.

Reiman, Jeffrey. . . . *And the Poor Get Prison: Economic Bias in American Criminal Justice*. Boston: Allyn, 1996.

"Report of the ADE Ad Hoc Committee on Staffing: Executive Summary." Association of Departments of English. Spring 1999. 12 Mar. 2001 <http://www.ade.org/reports/index.htm>.

Rhoades, Gary. *Managed Professionals: Unionized Faculty and Restructuring Academic Labor.* Albany: SUNY P, 1998.

———. "Medieval or Modern Status in the Postindustrial University: Beyond Binaries for Graduate Students." *Workplace: A Journal for Academic Labor* 2.2. Nov. 1999. <http://www.louisville.edu/journal/workplace/issue4/rhoades.html>.

Rhoades, Gary, and Sheila Slaughter. "Academic Capitalism, Managed Professionals, and Supply-Side Higher Education." *Social Text* 15.2 (1997): 9–38. Rpt. in Martin, *Chalk Lines* 33–68.

Rhodes, Keith. "Marketing Composition for the Twenty-first Century." *Writing Program Administration* 23.3 (2000): 51–69.

Ribble, Marcia. "Basic Writing Texts." Listserve of the CCCC Conference on Basic Writing 25 Jan. 2001. <cbw-l@tc.umn.edu>.

Robertson, Linda, Sharon Crowley, and Frank Lentricchia. "Opinion: The Wyoming Conference Resolution: Opposing Unfair Salaries and Working Conditions for Postsecondary Teachers of Writing." *College English* 49 (1989): 274–80.

Rodby, Judith, and Tom Fox. "Basic Work and Material Acts: The Ironies, Discrepancies, and Disjunctions of Basic Writing and Mainstreaming." *Journal of Basic Writing* 19.1 (2000): 84–99.

Roemer, Marjorie, Lucille M. Schultz, and Russel K. Durst. "Reframing the Great Debate on First-Year Writing." *CCC* 50 (1999): 377–92.

Romano, Tom. *Clearing the Way: Working With Teenage Writers.* Portsmouth, NH: Heinemann, 1987.

Rose, Mike. *Possible Lives: The Promise of Public Education in America.* New York: Penguin, 1995.

Rose, Shirley K., and Irwin Weiser, eds. *The Writing Program Administrator as Researcher: Inquiry in Action and Reflection.* Portsmouth, NH: Boynton/Cook, 1999.

Rosman, David. E-mail to Eileen E. Schell. 9 Sept. 2001.

Ross, Andrew. "The Mental Labor Problem." *Social Text* 63 (Summer 2000): 1–31.

Russell, David. *Writing in the Academic Disciplines, 1870–1990: A Curricular History.* Carbondale: Southern Illinois UP, 1991.

Saltman, Kenneth J. *Collateral Damage.* New York: Rowman, 2000.

Schell, Eileen E. *Gypsy Academics and Mother-Teachers: Gender, Contingent Labor, and Writing Instruction.* Portsmouth, NH: Boynton/Cook, 1998.

———. "Toward a New Labor Movement in Higher Education: Contingent Labor and Organizing for Change." *Workplace: A Journal for Academic Labor* 4.1. June 2001. 26 Sept. 2002. <http://www.louisville.edu/journal/workplace/issue7/schell.html>.

———. "What's the Bottom Line?: Literacy and Quality Education in the Twenty-first Century." Schell and Stock 324–40.

Schell, Eileen E., and Patricia Lambert Stock. "Introduction: Working Contingent Faculty in[to] Higher Education." Schell and Stock 1–44.

———, eds. *Moving a Mountain: Transforming the Role of Contingent Faculty in Composition Studies and Higher Education.* Urbana, IL: NCTE, 2001.

———. "Working Contingent Faculty into Higher Education." Schell and Stock 185–95.

Schneider, Allison. "Bad Blood in the English Department: The Rift Between Composition and Literature." *CHE* 13 Feb. 1998: A13.

Scholes, Robert. *The Rise and Fall of English.* New Haven: Yale UP, 1998.

Schrag, Peter. "Defining Adequacy Up." *Nation* 12 Mar. 2001. 18+.

Schuster, Charles I. "The Politics of Promotion." Bullock and Trimbur 85–95.

Scott, Tony. "Interview with Karen Thompson." *Workplace: A Journal for Academic Labor* 2.2. Nov. 1999. <http://www.workplace-gsc.com>.

Sennett, Richard. *The Corrosion of Character: The Personal Consequences of Work in the New Capitalism.* New York: Norton, 1998.

Seshadri, Srivatsa, and Larry D. Theye. "Professionals and Professors: Substance or Style?" *Business Communication Quarterly* 63.3 (Sept. 2000): 9–23.

Shea, Rachel Hartigan. "The New Insecurity." *U.S. News and World Report* 25 Mar. 2002. 40.

Shor, Ira. *When Students Have Power: Negotiating Authority in a Critical Pedagogy.* Chicago: Chicago UP, 1996.

Shumway, David. *Creating American Civilization: A Genealogy of American Literature as an Academic Discipline.* Minneapolis: U of Minnesota P, 1994.

Silvers, Phillip J. "Utilization of Associate Faculty at Pima Community College: A Report on Surveys of College Associate Faculty and Department Heads." Office of Research and Planning. Tucson, AZ: Pima Community College, 1990. 1–32.

Simon, William E. *A Time for Truth.* New York: Reader's Digest, 1978.

Singleton, Donna. "The Names We Resist: Revising Institutional Perceptions of the Nontenured." Hurlbert and Blitz 32–41.

Slaughter, Sheila, and Larry L. Leslie. *Academic Capitalism: Politics, Policies, and the Entrepreneurial University.* Baltimore: Johns Hopkins UP: 1999.

Sledd, James. *Eloquent Dissent: The Writings of James Sledd.* Ed. Richard D. Freed. Boston: Boynton/Cook, 1996.

——. "Return to Service." *Composition Studies* 28 (Fall 2000): 11–32.

——. "Why the Wyoming Resolution Had to Be Emasculated: A History and a Quixoticism." *JAC* 11.2 (1991): 269–81.

Slevin, James. "Depoliticizing and Politicizing Composition Studies." Bullock and Trimbur 1–22.

Smallwood, Scott. "Success and New Hurdles for T.A. Unions." *CHE* 6 July 2001: A10–12.

Soley, Lawrence C. *Leasing the Ivory Tower: The Corporate Takeover of Academia.* Boston: South End, 1995.

Sosnoski, James J. *Modern Skeletons in Postmodern Closets: A Cultural Studies Alternative.* Charlottesville: U of Virginia P, 1995.

——. *Token Professionals and Master Critics: A Critique of Orthodoxy in Literary Studies.* Buffalo: SUNY P, 1994.

Spellmeyer, Kurt. "After Theory: From Textuality to Attunement with the World." *College English* 58 (1996): 893–913.

——. "Marginal Prospects." *Writing Program Administration* 21.2–3 (1998): 162–82.

——. "Out of the Fashion Industry: From Cultural Studies to the Anthropology of Knowledge." (review essay) *CCC* 47 (1996): 424–36.

Spilka, Rachel, ed. *Writing in the Workplace: New Research Perspectives.* Carbondale: Southern Illinois UP, 1998.

"Statement from the Conference on the Growing Use of Part-Time and Adjunct Faculty." *ADE Bulletin* 119 (Spring 1998): 19–26.

Stephens, Joe. "Hard Money, Strong Arms And 'Matrix': How Enron Dealt with Congress, Bureaucracy." *Washington Post* 10 Feb. 2002.

Stewart, Donald. "Harvard's Influence on English Studies: Perceptions from Three Universities in the Early-Twentieth Century." *CCC* 43 (1992): 455–71.

Stimpson, Catharine R. "A Dean's Skepticism about a Graduate Student Union." *CHE* 5 May 2000: B7–8.

———. "Feminist Criticism." *Redrawing the Boundaries: The Transformation of English and American Literary Studies.* Ed. Stephen Greenblatt and Giles Gunn. New York: MLA, 1992. 251–70.

Storer, Chris. E-mail to Eileen E. Schell. 2 Mar. 2001.

Strickland, Donna. "Taking Dictation: The Emergence of Writing Programs and the Cultural Contradictions of Composition Teaching." *College English* 63 (2001): 457–79.

Sullivan, Francis J., Arabella Lyon, Dennis Lebofsky, Susan Wells, and Eli Goldblatt. "Student Needs and Strong Composition: The Dialectics of Writing Program Reform." *CCC* 48 (1997): 372–91.

"Summary of Data from Surveys by the Coalition on the Academic Workforce: A Cross-disciplinary Study on the Use and Treatment of Part-time Adjunct Faculty." Nov. 2000. Amer. Hist. Assoc. <http://www.theaha.org/caw/cawreport.htm>.

Tassoni, John Paul, and William H. Thelin, eds. *Blundering for a Change: Errors and Expectations in Critical Pedagogy.* Portsmouth, NH: Boynton-Cook, 2000.

Terranova, Tiziana. "Producing Culture for the Digital Economy." *Social Text* 18.2 (2000): 33–58.

Thompson, Karen. "Faculty at the Crossroads: Making the Part-time Problem a Full-Time Focus." Schell and Stock 185–95.

———. Personal interviews by e-mail exchange with Kathleen V. Wills. 19 Sept. 2002 and 24 Sept. 2002.

———. "The Ultimate Working Condition: Knowing Whether You Have a Job." *Forum* (Winter 1998): A19–24. *CCC* 49 (1998): A19–24.

Tirelli, Vincent. "Adjuncts and More Adjuncts: Labor Segmentation and the Transformation of Higher Education." Martin 181–201.

Toulmin, Stephen. *Human Understanding: The Collective Use and Evolution of Concepts.* Princeton: Princeton UP, 1972.

Trainor, Jennifer Seibel, and Amanda Godley. "After Wyoming: Labor Practices in Two University Writing Programs." *CCC* 50 (1998): 153–81.

Trimbur, John. "Writing Instruction and the Politics of Professionalization." *Composition in the Twenty-First Century: Crisis and Change.* Ed. Lynn Z. Bloom, Donald A. Daiker, and Edward M. White. Carbondale: Southern Illinois UP, 1996. 133–45.

Trudgill, Peter. *Sociolinguistics: An introduction to Language and Society.* New York: Penguin, 1983.

van der Werf, Martin, and Goldie Blumenstyk. "A Fertile Place to Breed Businesses: Campus-based Incubators Try to Help Entrepreneurs Bring Brainstorms to Market." *CHE* 2 Mar. 2001: A28–29.

"The Vanishing Professor." 2000. American Federation of Teachers. Jan. 2001. <http://www.aft.org/higher_ed/reports/professor/index.html>.

Vergnani, Linda. "In South Africa, Bond University Faces Government Hostility." *CHE* 9 March 2001. A51.

Veysey, Laurence R. *The Emergence of the American University.* Chicago: U of Chicago P, 1965.

Villanueva, Victor, Jr. *Bootstraps: From an American Academic of Color.* Urbana, IL: NCTE, 1993.

Virno, Paolo. "The Ambivalence of Disenchantment." *Radical Thought in Italy: A Potential Politics.* Ed. Michael Hardt and Virno. Minneapolis: U of Minnesota P, 1996. 13–36.

Ward, Irene, and William J. Carpenter, eds. *The Allyn & Bacon Sourcebook for Writing Program Administrators.* New York: Longman, 2001.

Watkins, Evan. "The Educational Politics of Human Resources: Humanities Teachers as Resource Managers." *Minnesota Review* 45–46 (1996): 147–66.

———. *Work Time: English Departments and the Circulation of Cultural Value.* Stanford: Stanford UP, 1989.

West, Cornell. *The American Evasion of Philosophy: A Genealogy of Pragmatism.* Madison: U of Wisconsin P, 1989.

"Who Is Teaching in U.S. College Classrooms?" Nov. 2000. Coalition on the Academic Workforce. Jan. 2001 <http://www.theaha.org/caw/pressrelease.htm>.

Worsham, Lynn. "Writing Against Writing: The Predicament of *Ecriture Féminine* in Composition Studies." *Contending with Words: Composition and Rhetoric in a Postmodern Age.* Ed. Patricia Harkin and John Schilb. New York: MLA, 1991. 82–104.

Yates, JoAnne. *Control Through Communication: The Rise of System in American Management.* Baltimore: Johns Hopkins UP, 1989.

Yates, Michael. "Lambs to the Slaughter." *Workplace: A Journal for Academic Labor* 1.2 Dec. 1998. 14 pars. 15 Mar. 2003 <http://www.workplace-gsc.com/workplace2/yates.html>.

Zaidi, Ali Shehzad. "At Adelphi: The Lengthening View." 1998. <http://venus.soci.niu.edu/archives/TOMPAINE/aug98/0197.html> or <http://nyfma.tao.ca/archive/1998/nyfma00381.html>.

Zweig, Michael. *The Working Class Majority: America's Best Kept Secret.* Ithaca, NY: ILR–Cornell UP, 2000.

CONTRIBUTORS

Leann Bertoncini is an adjunct instructor at the College of Mount Saint Joseph, teaching composition and speech. A former editor of the *New Growth Arts Review,* she is interested in fiction writing and using pop culture in her speech classes. She presents her theories and research regularly at the Teaching Academic Survival Skills national conference.

Marc Bousquet is an associate professor of English at the University of Louisville where he teaches politics and literature, critical theory, and new-media studies. He is a member of the board of Teachers for a Democratic Culture and the founding editor of *Workplace: A Journal for Academic Labor* (http://www.workplace-gsc.com). He is the author of articles appearing in *JAC, Social Text, EBR, College English,* and elsewhere and the editor (with Katherine Wills) of the forthcoming collection *The Informatics of Resistance: The Electronic Mediation of Social Change* (available at http://www.alt-x.com).

Christopher Carter is a graduate fellow in rhetoric and composition at the University of Louisville. He is currently the coeditor and Web designer of *Workplace: A Journal for Academic Labor.*

David B. Downing is a professor of English at Indiana University of Pennsylvania where for the past fourteen years he has been teaching critical theory, cultural studies, and institutional critique in the doctoral program and literary theory, composition, and American literature in the undergraduate program. Most recently, he coedited with Claude Mark Hurlbert and Paula Mathieu the collection of essays *Beyond English, Inc.: Curricular Reform in a Global Economy* (2002). For nearly twenty years, he has been editor of the journal *Works and Days.* A 2003 issue is titled "Information University: The Rise of the Education Management Organization" and features the work of Marc Bousquet and a range of other teachers, scholars, and graduate students.

Christopher Ferry is an associate professor of English and the director of writing at Clarion University. He teaches composition and rhetorical and literary theories as well as courses in pedagogy.

Amanda Godley is an assistant professor in the Department of Instruction and Learning at the University of Pittsburgh. Her recent publications include

"After Wyoming: Labor Practices in Two University Writing Programs" (*CCC* 1998, with Jennifer Seibel Trainor). Another work with the working title "Negotiating Gender Through Academic Literacy Practices" is to appear in *What They Don't Learn in School.*

Robin Truth Goodman is an assistant professor of English at Florida State University. She has worked as an adjunct of English and Women's Studies in and around the New York metropolitan area. Her books include *Strange Love: Or How We Learn to Stop Worrying and Love the Market* (cowritten with Kenneth J. Saltman, 2002) and *Infertilities: Exploring Fictions of Barren Bodies* (2001). Goodman is presently working on a book on feminism, education, and postcolonial literature with the working title "World, Class, Women: Global Literature, Feminism, and the Politics of Education" (forthcoming, 2003).

Bill Hendricks teaches English at California University of Pennsylvania. He represents his union in the legislative assembly of the Association of Pennsylvania State College and University Faculties and in the Monongahela Valley Central Labor Council. His primary research interest is academic labor.

Walter Jacobsohn is in his third year away from academia and is working on his own writing: stories, poetry, and especially drama. He was a non-tenure-track writing instructor at Seton Hall University and worked for seven years at Long Island University–Brooklyn, where he was an active participant in the union. He has also worked at Middlesex County College in New Jersey and the Queens College Workers Extension Campus at City University of New York. While at LIU–Brooklyn, he coedited the English department literary journal, *Downtown Brooklyn: A Journal of Writing* (1996, 1997). Jacobsohn has published several essays on issues in academic labor, the most recent of which is "The Real Scandal in Higher Education" (*Moving a Mountain: Transforming the Role of Contingent Faculty in Composition Studies and Higher Education,* 2001).

Ruth Kiefson teaches at Roxbury Community College in the Boston area and is secretary of the Roxbury Community College chapter of the Massachusetts Community College Council Professional Association.

Paul Lauter is Allan K. and Gwendolyn Miles Smith Professor of Literature at Trinity College in Hartford. He is the general editor of the *Heath Anthology of American Literature* and of the American literature volumes in the New Riverside series. For many years, he was active in the faculty-staff union of the State University of New York as well as in other activist organizations like Radical Teacher and Resist. His most recent book is *From Walden Pond to Jurassic Park.*

Donald Lazere is a professor emeritus of English at Cal Poly State University and a member of the national steering committee of Teachers for a Democratic Culture. He is the editor of *American Media and Mass Culture: Left Perspectives.* He has organized several MLA and CCCC panels and published many articles and reviews on the politics of culture and literacy in *College English, New Literary History, College Composition and Communication, Profession* (MLA annual), and *Radical Teacher* and in general-circulation journals including *Tikkun,*

In These Times, the *New York Times,* the *Los Angeles Times,* the *San Francisco Chronicle,* the *Baltimore Sun,* and *Newsday.*

Eric Marshall was a City University of New York adjunct lecturer from 1991 to 2002. He has authored a number of articles on academic labor, and he co-founded CUNY Adjuncts Unite, the CUNY Graduate Center Adjunct Project, the International Coalition of Contingent Academic Labor (COCAL), and the Campus Working Group of the North American Alliance for Fair Employment (NAFFE). He is a past vice-president for part-time instructional staff of the Professional Staff Congress and the CUNY faculty union, and he worked as an organizer for the American Federation of Teachers. Currently, he works for the New York State United Teachers.

Randy Martin is a professor of art and public policy and the associate dean of faculty and interdisciplinary programs at the Tisch School of the Arts, New York University. He is the coeditor of *Social Text,* the editor of *Chalk Lines: The Politics of Work in the Managed University* (2000) and the author of the *Financialization of Daily Life* (2002) and *On Your Marx: Relinking Socialism and the Left* (2001), as well as three other books: *Critical Moves: Dance Studies in Theory and Politics* (1998), *Socialist Ensembles: Theater and State in Cuba and Nicaragua* (1994), and *Performance as Political Act: The Embodied Self* (1990).

Richard Ohmann is a professor emeritus of English at Wesleyan University. He is the author of many books, most prominent among them *English in America: A Radical View of the Profession* (republished in 1996 on its twentieth anniversary), *Politics of Letters, Selling Culture: Magazines, Markets, and Class at the Turn of the Century,* and the forthcoming *Politics of Knowledge.* He is a former editor of *College English* and a contributor to and editor of *Radical Teacher.* He is also a founding member of the Radical Caucus of MLA and continues to serve on its steering committee.

Leo Parascondola is the coordinator of Bridge to College, a college preparatory program for adult learners at CUNY on the Concourse, Bronx, New York. He is also a doctoral candidate in English at the CUNY Graduate Center, where he is completing a dissertation in rhetoric and composition under the direction of George Otte. He serves on the steering committees of the MLA Graduate Student Caucus and Radical Caucus and is also a member of the MLA Delegate Assembly (2000–2003) and a founding member of the working-class studies special-interest group of the CCCC. In addition, he is a frequent contributor to *Workplace: A Journal for Academic Labor.*

Steve Parks is an associate professor of English at Temple University, where he directs New City Writing (www.newcitywriting.org) and Teachers for a Democratic Culture (www.tdc2001.org). As director of New City Writing, Parks has developed a community-based press, a network of community–university–public school writing centers, and a community arts literacy network. Through Teachers for a Democratic Culture, he was also a founder of the Progressive SIG–Caucus coalition, an organization of progressive composition-rhetoric organizations.

Much of the theory behind this organization work is detailed in his *Class Politics: The Movement for the Students' Right to Their Own Language*. Along with Lori Shorr, he is currently working on a book-length project about the everyday practice of cultural studies, which links their activist work to recent theoretical debates.

Gary Rhoades is a professor of higher education and the director of the Center for the Study of Higher Education at the University of Arizona. His *Managed Professionals: Unionized Faculty and Restructuring Academic Labor* was published in 1998.

Eileen E. Schell is an associate professor of writing and rhetoric and the director of the composition and cultural rhetoric doctoral program at Syracuse University. She is the author of two books on the politics of contingent labor in composition studies: *Gypsy Academics and Mother-Teachers: Gender, Contingent Labor, and Writing Instruction* (1998) and a coedited collection (with Patricia Lambert Stock) entitled *Moving a Mountain: Transforming the Role of Contingent Faculty in Composition Studies and Higher Education* (2001), which won the CCCC Best Book Award of 2003. She is a member of the CCCC's Committee on Contingent, Adjunct, and Part-Time Faculty (CAP).

Tony Scott is an assistant professor of English at the University of North Carolina at Charlotte. He is an associate editor of *Workplace: The Journal for Academic Labor* and a member of the CCCC's committee to improve the working conditions of part-time/adjunct faculty.

Donna Strickland is an assistant professor of English at Southern Illinois University Carbondale. While a graduate student at the University of Wisconsin–Milwaukee, she served as both an assistant writing program administrator and a union steward for the Milwaukee Graduate Assistants' Association. Her work has appeared most recently in *College English, Composition Studies,* and *JAC*.

William H. Thelin is an associate professor of English at the University of Akron. He has spent most of his professional life studying the impact of political agendas on the teaching of writing. He coedited (with John Tassoni) *Blundering for a Change: Errors & Expectations in Critical Pedagogy* (2000).

Jennifer Seibel Trainor is an assistant professor of English at the University of Pittsburgh where she directs the Western Pennsylvania Writing Project and teaches courses in composition, literacy, and education. Her publications include "After Wyoming: Labor Practices in Two University Writing Programs" (*CCC* 1998, with Amanda Godley), "Being Material Enough: New Directions for Reforming English" (*College English,* 2001) and "Critical Pedagogy's 'Other': Constructions of Whiteness in Education for Social Change (*CCC* 2002). She is a winner of NCTE's Promising Researcher Award and is currently working on a qualitative study of multicultural literacy education.

William Vaughn directs the program in first-year composition at Central Missouri State University. A founding member of the Graduate Employees' Organization, IFT-AFT–AFL-CIO, at the University of Illinois, he has written widely on academic labor issues and early American literature.

Ray Watkins is an assistant professor of English at Eastern Illinois University, where he teaches freshman writing, advanced composition, and professional writing courses (www.academic-worksite.com). He is a departmental representative for the University Professors of Illinois, local 4100, a member of the Workplace Editorial Collective, and a member of the board of Teachers for a Democratic Culture.

Katherine V. Wills is completing a dissertation in rhetoric and composition at the University of Louisville. She has taught as an adjunct instructor for eight years. She is the breaking-news editor of *Workplace: A Journal for Academic Labor.*

INDEX